"The libertarian quest for 'land. finds 'land that is used by all,' and the ugly conflation of the two sends the champions of personal liberty in search of guns, indentured servants, and death squads."
—Cory Doctorow

"They don't like hobbles and they can't stand fences, and so today's libertarian frontiersmen are looking for land, lots of land, perhaps in New Zealand. Or maybe they'll jet to Mars, build cities in the thick of Honduras or string barges together and create a floating republic, anything to avoid regulations, laws, and oversights. Ray Craib's brilliant *Adventure Capitalism* is a fascinating story of some spectacular fiascos, but it also makes a more profound point: there does exist a class of super-billionaires so rich they'd rather leave the world in ruins than admit humans are social beings and our survival requires recognition that we need each other."
—Greg Grandin

"Of the many fine histories of the rise of neoliberalism and class war from above, this is the most remarkable—an astonishing story of the global misadventures of Michael Oliver and other modern freebooters as they seek to establish their own Fantasy Islands from the Caribbean to the South Seas. The book tracks a half-century of disaffected capitalists seeking exit from civilized society, from Old Money in revolt against the 1960s to Silicon Valley's Seasteading Institute. Along the way, it makes the malignant ideas of today's libertarians manifest in a way that no exegesis of von Hayek or Ayn Rand can do, unpacking a gruesome geography of land grabs, mercenary uprisings and secessionist plots where the dreams of billionaire investors become the nightmares of postcolonial people and places. If you don't care for libertarian ideas before you read this book, you will surely despise them by the end, while gaining a better grasp of the fundamental misanthropy that animates the right wing of the capitalist class."
—Richard Walker, author of *Pictures of a Gone City: Tech and the Dark Side of Prosperity in the San Francisco Bay Area*

Adventure Capitalism

Editor: Sasha Lilley

Spectre is a series of penetrating and indispensable works of, and about, radical political economy. Spectre lays bare the dark underbelly of politics and economics, publishing outstanding and contrarian perspectives on the maelstrom of capital—and emancipatory alternatives—in crisis. The companion Spectre Classics imprint unearths essential works of radical history, political economy, theory and practice, to illuminate the present with brilliant, yet unjustly neglected, ideas from the past.

Spectre

Greg Albo, Sam Gindin, and Leo Panitch, *In and Out of Crisis: The Global Financial Meltdown and Left Alternatives*

David McNally, *Global Slump: The Economics and Politics of Crisis and Resistance*

Sasha Lilley, *Capital and Its Discontents: Conversations with Radical Thinkers in a Time of Tumult*

Sasha Lilley, David McNally, Eddie Yuen, and James Davis, *Catastrophism: The Apocalyptic Politics of Collapse and Rebirth*

Peter Linebaugh, *Stop, Thief! The Commons, Enclosures, and Resistance*

Peter Linebaugh, *The Incomplete, True, Authentic, and Wonderful History of May Day*

Richard A. Walker, *Pictures of a Gone City: Tech and the Dark Side of Prosperity in the San Francisco Bay Area*

Silvia Federici, *Patriarchy of the Wage: Notes on Marx, Gender, and Feminism*

Raymond B. Craib, *Adventure Capitalism: A History of Libertarian Exit, from the Era of Decolonization to the Digital Age*

Spectre Classics

E.P. Thompson, *William Morris: Romantic to Revolutionary*

Victor Serge, *Men in Prison*

Victor Serge, *Birth of Our Power*

Karl Marx, *Critique of the Gotha Program*

Adventure Capitalism

A History of Libertarian Exit, from the Era of Decolonization to the Digital Age

Raymond B. Craib

SPECTRE

PM

Contents

List of figures

"This was a business in which truth and delusion appeared equally doubtful."

—Joan Didion, *The Last Thing He Wanted*

Introduction

ONCE UPON A TIME, A WEALTHY MAN SET OUT TO ESTABLISH HIS OWN COUNTRY. HE found a shallow reef over which the waters of a vast ocean had lapped since time immemorial. He hired a company to dredge the ocean floor and deposit the sand on the reef. An island would be born, upon which the man had a concrete platform built, a flag planted, and the birth of the Republic of Minerva declared. The monarch of a nearby island kingdom was not impressed. He opened the doors of his kingdom's one jail and assembled an army of prisoners. The monarch, his convicts, and a four-piece brass band boarded the royal yacht and descended upon the reef, where they promptly removed the flag, destroyed the platform, and deposed, in absentia, the man who would be king. And Minerva returned to the ocean.

The story of Michael Oliver, his short-lived 1972 Republic of Minerva, and the response of the King of Tonga is not the stuff of fairy tales (although it does have a certain Grimm quality: in the process of deposing Oliver, one prisoner allegedly murdered another, creating the strange circumstance in which a state's murder rate exceeded the size of its population).[1] Nor is it an uncommon story, an isolated event ripe for consumption as a chronicle of crazy, rich Caucasians. In the US, particularly after the Great Depression and then World War II, with the dramatic geopolitical changes wrought by decolonization and the Cold War, battles were waged over the meaning of ideals such as democracy and freedom, often pitting those who believed in individual liberty and social equality against those who prioritized the former over the latter.[2] In the midst of such struggles, individuals concerned with protecting their wealth, their safety, and their freedom from what they perceived to be a growing government and a threatening rabble, sought to exit the nation-states to which they belonged and to establish their own independent, sovereign,

---

1   George Pendle, "New Foundlands," *Cabinet* 18 (Summer 2005): 65–68.
2   See Greg Grandin, *The Last Colonial Massacre: Latin America in the Cold War* (Chicago: University of Chicago Press, 2004), which tracks this struggle across the century in Guatemala.

and private countries on ocean and island spaces. Oliver's Minerva, as well as his subsequent efforts in the Caribbean and the Pacific, was embedded in this world, a broader world of libertarian exit. Such libertarian exit projects—how and why they came about, in what forms and to what ends, and their ongoing legacies manifest in current initiatives such as seasteading and free private cities—are the subject of this book.

It is worth saying at the outset that none of Michael Oliver's projects came to fruition. In retrospect they can appear as quixotic undertakings, idealistic and half-baked schemes drawn up in the sitting room of his home in Carson City, Nevada. Even America's libertarian godfather, Murray Rothbard, saw such plans as little more than a self-indulgent series of "cockamamie stunts." He suggested that exit strategists would do better to "come back to the real world and fight for liberty at home."[3] Maybe he was right. After all, Oliver's efforts all came to naught. So what are we left with? Narrating a brief history of failure? A tale of a man tilting at windmills? Words congealing to reveal a panorama of dreamy aberration? Perhaps. Then again, perhaps not. Exit projects, even if they did not come to fruition, have causes, effects, and meanings worth recuperating and examining. For one thing, Oliver was not alone. He was the most visible figure in a broader exit collective that included an array of wealthy investors driven by both ideological and economic motives. The 1960s and 1970s saw a surge in projects designed to allow individuals to exit the nation-state, for a range of reasons, and so much so that one Los Angeles-based libertarian drew up a typology of forms of exit, encompassing a range of possibilities from limited withdrawal, to urban retreat, to sea-mobile nomad. In recent years, these projects have become part of exit lore as Silicon Valley techno-utopians devise their own escape pathways, whether it be seasteading, private start-up cities, or space colonization. Dismissing such projects and their predecessors as "cockamamie stunts" offers little in the way of explanation and understanding and, as a result, forecloses the possibility of serious analysis and engaged critique.

Nor were exit projects somehow fringe or marginal undertakings, regardless of the "peripheral" locales in which they unfolded. Exit strategists, precisely because they are looking to establish a new territorial entity on a planet with limited territorial opportunity, have had to range geographically, legally, and politically far and wide in order to try to bring their plans to fruition. By necessity, they paint on a broad canvas. As a result, the aspirations

---

3   Rothbard, "From the Old Curmudgeon: My New Year's Wish for the Movement," in Murray Rothbard, *The Complete Libertarian Forum, 1969–1984* (Auburn, AL: Ludwig von Mises Institute, 2012), 1238. Originally published in *Libertarian Forum* 8, no. 12 (December 1975).

and activities of Michael Oliver intersect with the history of twentieth-century capitalism, broader processes of decolonization, the reconfiguration of the British empire, the 1960s counterrevolution, the growth of American libertarianism, the formation of offshore economies, and the possibilities of digital escape. In equal measure tragic and comic, predictable and yet awash in eddies of the unexpected, his is a story that crosses paths with a host of twentieth century figures and figurations: Fidel Castro and the Koch brothers, American segregationists and Melanesian socialists, Honolulu-based real estate speculators and British Special Branch spies, soldiers of fortune and English lords, finance gurus and Oceanian master navigators, and CIA operatives and CBS news executives. Oliver's history, in other words, is a history of our time. Given the new iterations of exit now being promoted and pursued, it may also be a history of our future.

Libertarian Americana

Private attempts to create a new country are not new. There are a range of examples to which one could point: the exploits of filibusterer William Walker and his mid-nineteenth-century invasion of Nicaragua; Josiah Harding's aspirations, which inspired Rudyard Kipling, to be a king in central Asia; James Brooke's reinvention of himself as the Rajah of Sarawak in Borneo; or Orélie-Antoine de Tounens's mid-nineteenth-century declarations that he had established a constitutional monarchy, with himself as king, in the Patagonia.[4] Empire by private contract was a quotidian aspiration in the nineteenth century. As historian Steven Press has demonstrated, private contract and adventurist schemes characterized the colonization of many parts of Africa.[5] Or take the case of Edward Gibbon Wakefield's business venture of the 1820s and 1830s. His New Zealand Company sought to colonize the southwestern Pacific Islands bearing the company's name, populate them with wealthy investors, and have them worked by a migrant labor force that had no

4   On William Walker, see Michel Gobat, *Empire by Invitation: William Walker and Manifest Destiny in Central America* (Cambridge, MA: Harvard University Press, 2018); on Harding, see Rudyard Kipling, "The Man Who Would Be King," in Kipling, *The Man Who Would Be King: Selected Stories* (London: Penguin, 2011) and Ben Macintyre, *Josiah the Great: The True Story of the Man Who Would Be King* (New York: HarperCollins, 2004); on Brooke, see Nigel Barley, *White Rajah: A Biography of Sir James Brooke* (Boston: Little Brown, 2002); on Tounens, see Bruce Chatwin, *In Patagonia* (London: Penguin Classics, 2003 [1977]), 16–21.
5   Steven Press, *Rogue Empires: Contracts and Conmen in Europe's Scramble for Africa* (Cambridge, MA: Harvard University Press, 2017); Charles Maier, *Once within Borders: Territories of Power, Wealth and Belonging since 1500* (Cambridge, MA: Harvard University Press, 2016), esp. 218–21.

hope of settling there themselves.[6] In the process, indigenous Māori would find themselves dispossessed of their lands. Simultaneous with Wakefield's efforts were those of Scottish adventurer Gregor MacGregor, the so-called Cacique of Poyais, who in the 1820s claimed to have been granted millions of acres of land by the king of the Miskito nation in what is now Honduras. MacGregor, taking strategic advantage of the opportunities unleashed by the North and South American wars of independence and the subsequent processes of decolonization, called the territory Poyais and crafted a crest for official documents, a manifesto regarding desirable immigrants, land-share documents, and a map of the region granted to him by the king. Hundreds of settlers bought into the scheme, but upon arrival on the Caribbean shores they found no bank, infrastructure, or opera house, as promised, but instead a tangle of jungle, uncertainty, and despair.[7]

Echoes of such projects can be heard in the pitches of the libertarian exit strategists of the twentieth and twenty-first centuries, reworked in the context of a Cold War and a decolonizing world and updated with a particularly US libertarian inflection. US libertarianism is an ideology best described as devoutly capitalist and agnostically antistatist (unlike in most of the world, in which "libertarian" is synonymous with "anarchist," a political ideology and practice opposed to both the state and capitalism). It is a broad tradition that traverses a spectrum from neoliberal to anarcho-capitalist. Foundational neoliberal and libertarian theorists—Friedrich Hayek, Ayn Rand, Murray Rothbard, and Milton Friedman—had sharp disagreements and some, such as Rand, refused the designation "libertarian" entirely. Even so, they share

---

6 On Wakefield, see Onur Ulas Ince, *Colonial Capitalism and the Dilemmas of Liberalism* (New York: Oxford University Press, 2018); Matthew Birchall, "History, Sovereignty, Capital: Company Colonization in South Australia and New Zealand," *Journal of Global History* (2020) and, for a brief informative summary, Mark O'Connell, *Notes from an Apocalypse: A Personal Journey to the End of the World and Back* (New York: Doubleday, 2020), 89–90.

7 MacGregor has traditionally been understood as little more than a con artist, an accusation that dogged him even in the early years of his projects. Recent revisionist work has sought to situate MacGregor more concretely in his context in order to understand how issues such as debt, decolonization, and imperialism shaped the range of possibilities for various actors in the 1820s Caribbean and South America. See, for example, Damian Clavel, "What's in a Fraud? The Many Worlds of Gregor MacGregor, 1817–1824," *Enterprise & Society* (2020): 1–40; and Matthew Brown, "Inca, Sailor, Soldier, King: Gregor MacGregor and the Early Nineteenth-Century Caribbean," *Bulletin of Latin American Research* 24: 1 (2005), 44–70. Brown situates MacGregor in a wider transimperial Caribbean, a world reconstructed with originality and insight in Ernesto Bassi, *An Aqueous Territory: Sailor Geographies and New Granada's Transimperial Greater Caribbean World* (Durham, NC: Duke University Press, 2017). See also Vanessa Mongey, *Rogue Revolutionaries: The Fight for Legitimacy in the Greater Caribbean* (Philadelphia: University of Pennsylvania Press, 2020).

in common certain features that I explore in greater detail throughout the book and that I subsume under the category of libertarian: a disdain for the welfare and regulatory state (not the state per se); a radical commitment to free enterprise; a fetishization of the rugged individualist and unencumbered entrepreneur; a fear of the masses; a worldview that conflates communism, socialism and fascism; and an ontology that equates individual private property rights with freedom.[8] This hypercapitalist orientation sets the exiters I discuss apart from other kinds of exit societies that one might conjure from the historical record: maroon communities forged by runaway slaves; acephalous highland communities composed of peoples fleeing state conscription and enslavement; semisedentary peoples who sought to remain one step ahead of encroaching states and settlers; some of the "rogue revolutionaries" who roamed the late-eighteenth and early-nineteenth century Atlantic and Caribbean seeking to create multinational and multiethnic countries of their own; or autonomous territories such as those founded by the Zapatistas in Chiapas, Mexico.[9] All of these might be considered experiments in territorial

---

8   I discuss libertarian politics in relation to my protagonists further in the first chapter, but it is worth briefly noting here that this is a "big tent" definition of libertarianism. It is a definition that may not satisfy purists, but it is one that allows me to highlight the fact that the lines between, say, neoliberal and libertarian or social conservative and libertarian are neither static nor easily drawn. Libertarianism proved a popular and powerful current in political culture and the neoliberal revolution that began to take shape in the 1960s, one that resonated simultaneously with social conservatives' embrace of property rights freedom and transnational liberals' embrace of a borderless world of free trade. In *The Libertarian Reader*, David Boaz, the cofounder of the libertarian Cato Institute, accentuates precisely this: a number of thinkers are situated on a spectrum that could be termed libertarian who did not necessarily appropriate the term for themselves, even if it was available. Boaz, *The Libertarian Reader: Classic & Contemporary Writings from Lao-Tzu to Milton Friedman* (New York: Simon & Schuster, 2015). That Lao-Tzu has been included in collections of both anarcho-capitalists and anarcho-communists, as in Peter Marshall's *Demanding the Impossible: A History of Anarchism* (Oakland: PM Press, 2010), is indicative of a wider conflation, at times confusion, of libertarian and anarchist politics which I explore further in chapter two.

9   See James C. Scott, *The Art of Not Being Governed: An Anarchist History of Upland Southeast Asia* (New Haven, CT: Yale University Press, 2010); Pierre Clastres, *Society against the State: Essays in Political Anthropology*, trans. Robert Hurley (New York: Zone Books, 1989); Peter Linebaugh and Marcus Rediker, *The Many-Headed Hydra: Sailors, Slaves, Commoners, and the Hidden History of the Revolutionary Atlantic* (Boston: Beacon, 2013); Mongey, *Rogue Revolutionaries*; Andrej Grubačić and Denis O'Hearn, *Living at the Edges of Capitalism: Adventures in Exile and Mutual Aid* (Berkeley: University of California Press, 2016); Raúl Zibechi, *Territories in Resistance: A Cartography of Latin American Social Movements*, trans. by Raymor Ryan (Oakland: AK Press, 2012); Max Rameau, *Take Back the Land: Land, Gentrification and the Umoja Village Shantytown* (Oakland: AK Press, 2012 [2008]); and Rhiannon Firth, "Utopianism and Intentional Communities," in Carl Levy and Matthew S. Adams, eds., *The Palgrave Handbook of Anarchism* (London: Palgrave Macmillan, 2019), 491–510. Belgian geographer and communard Elisée Reclus argued against the creation of privileged exit communities, or what he called "Icaries on the outskirts of the bourgeois

exit but they share little in common, ideologically and structurally, with those of Michael Oliver, of seasteaders, and of the advocates of free private cities. Form should not be privileged over content. Any analysis of exit needs to understand what it is people are striving to leave but also what they are striving to build. A maroon community of former slaves who escaped plantation exploitation bore little in common with, say, an ecovillage built around the logics of green capitalism. Exile communities that grew from collective efforts to mitigate capitalist exploitation and labor subjugation and that grew organically from the ground up are not comparable to escape plans that privilege property acquisition and individual sovereignty and tend to be preplanned and engineered from above. It is as hard to imagine prominent exit advocate and Silicon Valley iconoclast Peter Thiel (a financial backer of seasteading, which I examine in chapter five) living in Zapatista Liberated Territory in Chiapas as it is to imagine Zapatista organizer and theoretician Subcomandante Marcos luxuriating on a private seastead off the coast of Tahiti. They bear distinct, and largely incommensurable, understandings of what constitutes freedom and of what constitutes oppression.

Libertarian exit projects are outgrowths of a long, ongoing process of the remaking of global capitalism and the nation-state. Although at one level libertarian exit constitutes a self-conscious ideological challenge to the current form of nation-state territorial sovereignty and market regulation, at another level exit is not a challenge to the idea of the state itself. The form of global capitalism that has generated exit initiatives is one born of an inextricable relationship between states and markets, such that the radical embrace of the latter necessarily entails accommodating oneself to the former. Leo Panitch and Sam Gindin, among many others, have argued persuasively that "the role of states in maintaining property rights, overseeing contracts, stabilizing currencies, reproducing class relations, and containing crises has always been central to the operation of capitalism."[10] Libertarians are no less dependent on such statist good will than are the multinational corporations who absorb much of our attention. This should not be understood as hypocrisy per se—we all live within structures not of our own making, and the subjects of this book readily admitted to some role for the state—but recognizing the inextricable

---

world." "In our plan for existence and struggle," he wrote, "it isn't a little coterie of companions that interests us. It's the whole world." Quoted in Kristin Ross, *Communal Luxury: The Political Imaginary of the Paris Commune* (London: Verso, 2015), 119.

10   Quoted from Leo Panitch and Sam Gindin, *The Making of Global Capitalism: The Political Economy of American Empire* (London: Verso, 2013), 1. See also Ellen Meiksins Wood, *The Origin of Capitalism: A Longer View* (London: Verso Press, 2002). For a classic statement, see Mikhail Bakunin, "Property Could Arise Only in the State," in G.P. Maximoff, *The Political Philosophy of Bakunin* (New York: Free Press, 1953).

relationship between capitalism and the state will go some way to helping to understand the selectivity of libertarian ideology and the nature of exit projects.

Duty-free living

The operating premise for Michael Oliver was to carry out what he called a "moral experiment" by designing a new country run through contractual, capitalist relations that, in theory, would provide the maximum possibility of individual freedom. To be sure, these were also enterprises with a profit motive. The benefits of tax havens and offshore financial centers, for example, figured directly in the libertarian exit calculus.[11] More contemporary exit projects such as seasteading and private cities at times are promoted as moral experiments committed to human freedom but they too are entrepreneurial in that a cornerstone of their foundation is to make money. Exiters of course might not see any contradiction between the moral and the entrepreneurial. At some level, for exit libertarians the profit motive *is* the moral experiment; the individual at play in the market is the sine qua non of freedom. Exit is thus not solely a means by which libertarians can implement their ideas; it is a fundamental part of the idea itself—a right to opt out of and opt into societies with the ease of a wealthy consumer. The commitment to a "moral experiment" helps explain why such projects are repeatedly pursued with such vigor despite the costs and the headaches involved. After all, if the idea was to avoid paying taxes or to make more money, most of the individuals involved in such schemes had the necessary resources to employ a team of tax consultants and attorneys and numerous offshore financial centers and tax havens beckoned. There was little need to design elaborate escape plans. Similarly, circumventing the regulatory state could be achieved without undertaking radical territorializing projects. The last half century of antigovernment, antitax, and anticommunist rhetoric among US conservatives and libertarians has been matched in practice by forms of social and territorial secession such

11   Anthony van Fossen, *Tax Havens and Sovereignty in the Pacific Islands* (St. Lucia, Queensland: University of Queensland Press, 2012); van Fossen, "Secessionist Tax Haven Movements in the Pacific Islands," *Canadian Review of Studies in Nationalism* 28 (2001): 77–92. More broadly see Ronen Palan, *The Offshore World: Sovereign Markets, Virtual Places, and Nomad Millionaires* (Ithaca: Cornell University Press, 2006); Nicholas Shaxson, *Treasure Islands: Uncovering the Damage of Offshore Banking and Tax Havens* (London: Palgrave-Macmillan, 2011); Vanessa Ogle, "Archipelago Capitalism: Tax Havens, Offshore Money, and the State, 1950s–1970s," *American Historical Review* 122, no. 5 (December 2017): 1431–58; and Ogle, "'Funk Money': The End of Empires, The Expansion of Tax Havens, and Decolonization as an Economic and Financial Event," *Past & Present* 249, no. 1 (November 2020): 213–49. For discussion of the distinction between a tax haven and an offshore financial center, see van Fossen, "Secessionist Tax Haven Movements," 90.

as gated communities, common interest developments, privatized education systems, illegal but ongoing racial covenants and redlining, tax loopholes, and (more recently) the buying and selling of national citizenship, among others.[12]

If exit was a moral experiment, it was also a means of self-protection. In the 1960s and the 1970s Oliver and others did not see forms of social secession as a strong enough bulwark against their fears nor as adequate means to undertake their experiments. As I show in chapter one, Oliver, a Lithuanian Jew who was the only member of his family to survive the Holocaust, worried that his adopted country in the 1960s teetered on the brink of totalitarianism. He thus saw exit as the most viable way to survive and thrive, and he spent much of the decade of the 1970s traversing the globe in the hopes of establishing a new country. The more recent exit strategists, many of whom align with the start-up ethos of Silicon Valley, share some things in common with Oliver, not least of all an adoration of Ayn Rand. But there are some differences. For one, they hew more closely than Oliver to the Nietzschean aspects of Rand. What I mean by this is that their projects are not driven by a fear of the masses and totalitarianism—they seem indifferent to the general public and express disdain for democratic politics—but by an urge, a will, to bend reality to their design. They seek not to escape the state but to recast it in their own image. A libertarian new country would not only create territorialized governance structures that, at least in theory, would make the market sovereign and emancipate the individual from the overbearing constraints of bureaucratic regulation; it would also, if successful, provide a competitive alternative to existing states, forcing them to change in order to keep their populace, largely by loosening their regulatory apparati. In other words, it would bring governmental and legal systems into the market.

By championing exit over voice (voting, organizing, unionizing, demonstrating, insurgency, or a myriad other forms of asserting political subjectivity), to use the vocabulary Albert Hirschman developed in his seminal *Exit, Voice, and Loyalty*, exit libertarians offer a particularly constrained version of freedom, one acquired not through collective struggle and social solidarity but through territorial and individual secession.[13] Freedom, a collective social

12   For an excellent study of the selling and buying of citizenship that provides insight into a kind of parallel universe to the one I examine, see Atossa Araxia Abrahamian, *The Cosmopolites: The Coming of the Global Citizen* (New York: Columbia Global Reports, 2015). The most well-known citizenship purchase of recent vintage is Peter Thiel's acquisition of New Zealand citizenship.

13   Hirschman, *Exit, Voice, and Loyalty: Responses to Decline in Firms, Organizations and States* (Cambridge, MA: Harvard University Press, 1970). For a thoughtful engagement with Hirschman's work in relation to exile—rather than exit—see Grubačić and O'Hearn, *Living at the Edges of Capitalism*.

condition, instead becomes a private place.[14] This is why, at least in theory, exit goes beyond expatriation because ideally it would allow one to leave one's country and become a member of an alternative, even if state-like, territorial entity governed solely by private contract. But that requires a space upon which to forge such a polity. And thus libertarian exit has proven untenably ambitious, in part because there is no blank slate out there upon which to build such a form and in part because we inhabit a social world that cannot be circumvented by mere spatial separation. Thus, the grand ambition of exit often comes to resemble, in practice and despite its best efforts, the mundane reality of expatriation. The marketed product is less new-country utopia than time-share sovereignty; more J.W. Marriott than Thomas More. It is revealing that exiters traditionally have expressed little desire to give up their respective citizenship documents and assume a posture of principled statelessness, even if they willingly experimented in places with very real stateless populations (the New Hebrides, for example, as I discuss in chapter four). Although built on the idea of escaping oppression and totalitarianism (however those might be defined), exit was always premised on maintaining the ability to return at will. In a form of having one's cake and eating it too, libertarian exiters sought to wed, on the one hand, emancipation from traditional state regulation, taxation, and governance with, on the other hand, the benefits of citizenship and an international system of sovereign protections, the two conjoined in a territorial configuration within which one can live protected yet, so to speak, duty-free.

Speculative nonfictions
Ideals do not gently become reality. Oliver did not merely theorize exit. He attempted it and, in the process, saw his aspirations confront the brute reality of ... well, reality. In examining his projects and their afterlives I have sought to reconstruct a social history of libertarian practice to complement the growing body of intellectual history on neoliberal and libertarian thought.[15] At

---

14 I have been inspired here by Rosalind Williams's discussion of Jules Verne in *The Triumph of Human Empire: Verne, Morris and Stevenson at the End of the World* (Chicago: University of Chicago Press, 2013), esp. 118 but, more generally, Part 1.

15 The literature is substantial. For excellent starting points, see Quinn Slobodian, *Globalists: The End of Empire and the Birth of Neoliberalism* (Cambridge, MA: Harvard University Press, 2018); Grégoire Chamayou, *La Société Ingouvernable: Une Généalogie du Libéralisme Autoritaire* (Paris: La Fabrique Editions, 2018); Dominic Losordo, *Liberalism: A Counter History* (London: Verso, 2011); Daniel Stedman Jones, *Masters of the Universe: Hayek, Friedman, and the Birth of Neoliberal Politics* (Princeton, NJ: Princeton University Press, 2014); Philip Mirowski and Dieter Plehwe, eds., *The Road to Mont Pelerin: The Making of the Neoliberal Thought Collective* (Cambridge, MA: Harvard University Press, 2015); Kim Phillips-Fein, *Invisible Hands: The Businessmen's Crusade against the New Deal* (New York: W.W. Norton, 2010); Wendy Brown, *Undoing the Demos: Neoliberalism's Stealth*

the same time I have sought to emphasize how these projects, as well as the recent iterations of seasteading and free private cities, impacted the peoples living in the places where exiters intended to impose their designs. It is a basic point but one worth emphasizing because it would be all too easy to narrate these stories as satire, to see in them little more than fodder for a parody of millionaires gone wild. Such an approach does little to deepen our understanding of libertarian exiters' motivations and their projects' effects. It also a reproduces a certain lazy orientalism, ignoring as it does the histories of the places in which they sought to establish themselves. The fact that libertarian escapists found little success in the Caribbean and the Pacific resulted from many factors, including the larger structural and geopolitical dynamics within which they operated as well as their own ignorance and arrogance regarding the places in which they landed. But it also resulted from the complexities they encountered on the ground. Resistance came from people who had had enough and were not ready to trade one colonial master for another; who were not ignorant of the potential consequences of libertarian escape projects; who had their own understandings of property, territory, the ocean, and the land that did not dovetail with that of these new arrivals; or who were willing to struggle with limited resources to see their own understanding of freedom—not perfect or ideal but not the market-driven idea of freedom libertarians were selling—prevail. If many resisted, others accommodated. Some residents and leaders supported exit projects, seeing in them opportunities to use foreign investors and speculators to their own ends, whether it be to steer their own political destinies, to stave off more radical change, to make money, or because of shared ideological perspectives. Exit projects were rarely, if ever, simply imposed from outside and onto a uniformly intransigent population.

Thus, while this is a history of libertarian exit through the lens of its advocates, I am attentive to the history of the social, political, cultural, and economic worlds within which they insinuated themselves: places such as Tonga, the Bahamas, Vanuatu, and more recently Tahiti and Honduras. It is not coincidental that Oliver and his backers, searching for spaces upon which to implement their plans, looked to areas of the globe undergoing, in some form, decolonization. Indeed, Oliver was explicit: it was in such locales that exit plans were most likely to succeed given the political uncertainties and opportunities provided by the demise of colonial rule. In a troubling inversion of the idea of self-determination, wealthy libertarians pursued personal freedom on

Revolution (Boston: Zone Books, 2016); Jennifer Burns, *Goddess of the Market: Ayn Rand and the American Right* (New York: Oxford University Press, 2009), and for an insider perspective, Brian Doherty, *Radicals for Capitalism: A Freewheeling History of the Modern American Libertarian Movement* (New York: Public Affairs, 2007).

the lands and waters of colonized peoples struggling to be structurally free of foreign rule. Such activities and histories should serve also as a reminder that seemingly "peripheral" and, in this instance, archipelagic spaces deserve to be recentered in the history of global capitalism, decolonization, and the making of the modern world.

A brief road map is in order. The opening chapter revisits the 1960s as a decade in which libertarian thought and practice exploded and, at the same time, dovetailed in important ways with growing social conservativism. I situate Oliver's 1968 exit plan *A New Constitution for a New Country* in the political and social context of rising fears of social unrest as well as demographic, ecological and economic crises. The next three chapters examine Oliver's projects, which spanned the decade of the 1970s, in close detail. I begin in chapter two with the Republic of Minerva project and examine why Oliver and his backers turned to oceans and islands as sites for constructing a libertarian refuge. I explain why the project foundered and explore the history of the reefs themselves in relation to the jurisdictional claims of Tonga and a broader Native Pacific world of mobility, history, and use. Chapter three follows Oliver's efforts—along with a small cabal of soldiers of fortune (many ex-CIA) such as Mitchell Livingston WerBell—to colonize rather than build an island, in this case Abaco in the Bahamas. I explore how these efforts became wrapped in a noir underworld of arms smuggling, mercenary activity, anti-communism, and white supremacy as the Bahamas sought its independence. Chapter four turns to Oliver's last concerted effort at exit on the island of Santo in the New Hebrides where a secessionist rebellion complicated the process of decolonization and the creation of the independent state of Vanuatu. Unlike the previous two projects, this one resulted in violence and an uprising that led to deaths and the displacement of hundreds of ni-Vanuatu (Native Vanuatu), a sobering reminder of the real-life consequences of libertarian adventurism.

Chapters five and six take up more recent iterations of exit as manifested in two cases: first, that of San Francisco's Seasteading Institute which seeks to build private, sovereign platforms on the high seas (chapter five) and, second, those of Silicon Valley techno-libertarians and former officials in the administration of Ronald Reagan to create charter or "free private cities" in Honduras on territory ceded to investors and overseen by international arbitration boards (chapter six). There are others of course, most notably the off-planet aspirations of Elon Musk, Jeff Bezos, and Richard Branson. But here I limit myself to the earthbound efforts. These iterations are not direct descendants of Oliver's labors. They espouse a certain social progressive outlook (polyamory, drug legalization, and the like) and are strongly influenced by the techno-utopian world of Silicon Valley, neither of which figured in the designs of Oliver. And as noted earlier, they appear less driven by existential fears of mass politics and totalitarianism than by a Promethean elitism and a disdain for democratic politics. Even so, they share much in common with Oliver's aspirations, particularly in their desire to retrofit territoriality, governance, and sovereignty along libertarian lines. And in the end, all these projects are, in some sense, forms of speculative nonfiction—places where imaginative and investment futures converge.

PART I
Any Distant Archipelago
(1960s–1980s)

CHAPTER ONE

Libertarian Exit

Fear and Loathing USA

1968: A YEAR WHEN "THE LIBERTARIAN POSITION TOOK OFF LIKE A JET," RECALLED Robert Lefevre, founder of the Freedom College whose attendees in the mid-1960s included brothers Charles and David Koch. A year of embold-ened embrace of capitalism and free-market fundamentalism, of aspirations to defeat the New Deal and compete with the New Left, and of university campuses producing a generation of newly minted MBAs. A year in which the promise of communes was offset by the tragedy of the commons, as biologist Garrett Hardin termed it in his seminal *Science* essay; in which young leftists read Herbert Marcuse and young libertarians read Ayn Rand and an MIT graduate founded the libertarian magazine *Reason* and a *Playboy* column-ist reminded readers that Ayn Rand had a nineteenth-century forerunner in Lysander Spooner, whose libertarian tract *No Treason: The Constitution of No Authority* "may be the most subversive document ever penned in this nation." A year that welcomed the dawning not of the age of Aquarius but that of Atlantis, the favored reference point for libertarians' utopian aspirations. And the year in which one of those libertarians, forty-year-old Michael Oliver, published his exit manifesto entitled *A New Constitution for a New Country*. The first edition appeared in February. It sold so well that a second edition appeared three months later, in May 1968.[1]

---

1   Interview with Lefevre in Duff Whitman Griffith, "Before the Deluge: An Oral History Examination of Pre-Watergate Conservative Thought in Orange County, California," (Unpublished MA thesis, California State University at Fullerton, 1976), p. 13f, included interview dated September 28, 1972, with Robert Lefevre. On the Koch brothers and The Freedom College, see Brian Doherty, *Radicals for Capitalism: A Freewheeling History of the Modern American Libertarian Movement* (New York: Public Affairs, 2007), 407. On the "new generation of MBAs," see Leo Panitch and Sam Gindin, *The Making of Global Capitalism: The Political Economy of Empire* (New York: Verso, 2013), 121. On the 1960s as a conservative youth decade, see Rick Perlstein, *Before the Storm: Barry Goldwater and the Unmaking of the American Consensus* (New York: Nation Books, 2009 [2001]). For the quote by Spooner, "Playboy after hours," *Playboy* (April 1968), 23. The quoted passage became a standard in libertarian magazines, beginning with Thomas Jacobsen, "American Liberation Front," *Innovator*, Autumn 1968, 7–6.

A declaration of purpose

Michael Oliver was born Moses Olitzky in Kaunas, Lithuania in 1928. At the time, Kaunas was a cosmopolitan city. A former resident and acquaintance of Olitzky's described it thus: "Nearly a third of its one hundred thousand residents were Jewish. For decades it had been a favored asylum for all sorts of political refugees. It was a bit like some small Eastern European version of Beirut or Casablanca, with its Nordic gentiles, its Poles and Russians, its Germans and Jews, in a place forever on the border of the next war."[2]

War arrived in 1940, first with a brief Soviet incursion and then, in the spring of 1941, with a German occupation. German troops and Lithuanian patrols rounded up the city's Jews and transported them to the Seventh Fort, hastily converted by the Nazi command into a concentration camp, where they murdered the men and raped and murdered the women. Between eight and twelve thousand Jews died.[3] Olitzky, along with most of the city's surviving Jews as well as many who had fled to Kaunas from neighboring Poland after the German invasion, was forcibly moved into a ghetto on the outskirts of the city. In the summer of 1944, the Nazi command relocated many of the ghetto's surviving inhabitants, including Olitzky, to the Stutthof concentration camp near Danzig (Gdansk, Poland). From Stutthof, he and other prisoners were moved in railway cattle cars across Poland to Lager 10, a newly constructed camp outside of Dachau. Liberated by US troops while on a forced march from Dachau in the spring of 1945, Olitzky then spent two years in a displaced persons camp before emigrating to the United States in 1947. His parents and four siblings all had been murdered.[4]

Once in the US, Olitzky changed his name to Michael Oliver, became a naturalized American, joined the Air Force for a five-year stint, and worked for companies on radar and satellite tracking systems. By the 1960s he had married, started a family, and set roots down in Carson City, Nevada. He owned and operated a land development company as well as the Nevada Coin Exchange, specializing in the sale of gold and silver coins which he advertised

---

2   Solly Ganor, *Light One Candle: A Survivor's Tale from Lithuania to Jerusalem* (New York: Kodansha International, 1995), 23.

3   Ibid., 78–79.

4   He is documented as having arrived at Stutthof on July 19, 1944. See "Olitzky, Moses. Konzentrationslager. Stutthof (Art der Haft 1, Gef. Nr. 49767)," Arolsen Archives (ITS) Collection, United States Holocaust Memorial Museum. Details on life in the ghetto and the move to Stutthof, and subsequently Dachau, can be found in the work of Olitzky's contemporary and friend Solly Ganor (born Solly Genkind). Ganor, *Light One Candle*, chaps. 14, 15, and 22. Olitzky recounts briefly his history in Mike Oliver, "An Open Letter to George Soros," accessed January 15, 2019, https://www.energytruth.com/Manhattan2.pdf.

as security investments in the pages of the *Wall Street Journal*, *Barron's*, and the libertarian magazine *Innovator*. Over the course of the decade Oliver became a millionaire and began to translate his wealth into a hedge against what he feared was a growth in totalitarianism in the US. This hedge was to be a new country, founded on laissez-faire principles and the initial structure of which he outlined in his 1968 constitution.[5]

Oliver crafted his constitution for an imagined libertarian territory freed from bureaucratic constraints and the regulatory apparatus of the welfare state. But, most importantly, he envisioned his territory as freed from the persistent threat of the masses and mob rule. The book contained a declaration of purpose, a plan of action, and a constitution with eleven articles. Oliver designed the constitution as an improved version of the United States Constitution—improved in that it would "spell out the details whereby government can, at the same time, properly protect persons from force and fraud and also be prevented from exceeding this only legitimate function."

> Is it not time for developing a Constitution which is to conform completely to the premise that man has full rights to his life and property and must not infringe upon the same rights of others? Is it too difficult to show *in detail*, rather than by general statements, how a nation can be established, maintained, and defended if founded on such a basis? Have plans been made to provide a means for honorable persons to escape the increasing horror of civil strife and coming economic collapse? These timely questions are being asked today by many worthwhile persons who desire to survive the onslaught of totalitarianism.[6]

---

5   Oliver, *A New Constitution for a New Country* (Reno, NV: Fine Arts Press, 1968), passim. The most thorough and serious history of Oliver's projects can be found in Anthony van Fossen, "Secessionist Tax Haven Movements in the Pacific Islands," *Canadian Review in Studies in Nationalism* 28 (2001): 77–92; and van Fossen, *Tax Havens and Sovereignty in the Pacific Islands* (St. Lucia, Queensland: University of Queensland Press, 2012), chap. 3, both of which provide brief but careful and accurate overviews of the three projects (Minerva, Abaco, and the New Hebrides) that I discuss in more detail throughout the book. Additional details on Oliver's life appear in Nancy Faber and Ross H. Munro, "Spears and a Nevada Businessman Help a South Pacific Island Proclaim Itself a New Country," *People* 14, no. 3, July 21, 1980; FBI Letter Head Memorandum (LHM), Las Vegas, Nevada, September 11, 1974, "M. Oliver Newsletter," accessed June 8, 2016, https://www.maryferrell.org/showDoc.html?docId=112625#relPageId=2&tab=page; Robert L. Meiers, review of *A New Constitution for a New Country*, *Capitalist Country Newsletter* 1, no. 2 (August 1968): 1; *Capitalist Country Newsletter* 1, no. 4 (October 1968): 2; *An Investment in the Vemarana Federation*, mimeograph (Santo, New Hebrides: Vemarana Federation, 1980); and "Designing a Free Country: An Interview with Michael Oliver," *Reason* (December 1, 1972).

6   Oliver, foreword to *A New Constitution*. Emphasis in the original.

The book's opening "Declaration of Purpose" left little to the imagination: "Let the establishment of 'social meddlers' reap its own harvest; let the innocent person, who tried in vain to stop the onslaught of totalitarianism, escape the horror."[7] Given the horror Oliver had himself experienced as a young Jewish man, and the horrific violence visited upon his family, it is no surprise that he watched intently for signs of encroaching totalitarianism. His own experience had taught him to be aware of the suddenness with which the world can turn and of the pervasive undercurrents of violence that coursed through the social world. But what remains to be explained is why he sought refuge in American libertarianism, particularly given that some of its proponents espoused a social conservatism rife with its own racial and exclusionary undertones.

Libertarians rising

The libertarian energies of 1968 did not arise spontaneously. Advocates of free markets and free enterprise had been organizing intensely over previous decades to turn aspects of the postwar developmental state toward private gain. The Mont Pelerin Society (MPS), the American Enterprise Institute (AEI), the Foundation for Economic Education (FEE) and the Institute for Economic Affairs (IEA), founded as think tanks to fight the New Deal, promoted positive images of large corporations and sought to make free-market ideologies palatable to a broader public. The IEA had been founded by former British fighter pilot and chicken farmer Antony Fisher who found inspiration in the *Reader's Digest* condensed version of Friedrich Hayek's seminal work *The Road to Serfdom* which had conveniently deleted Hayek's "support for a minimum standard of living for the poor, environmental and workplace safety regulations, and price controls to prevent monopolies from taking undue profits."[8] Leonard Read had been promoting and disseminating Hayek's work through the FEE as part of his "freedom philosophy."[9] In the 1960s Charles and David Koch, Robert Mellon Scaife, and future Supreme Court Justice Lewis Powell, among others, began to strategize around how to challenge what they perceived to be a state intent on expanding further and further into

---

7   Ibid., n.p.
8   Jane Mayer, *Dark Money: The Hidden History of the Billionaires Behind the Rise of the Radical Right* (New York: Doubleday, 2016), 45, who draws from Angus Burgin, *The Great Persuasion: Reinventing Free Markets since the Great Depression* (Cambridge, MA: Harvard University Press, 2012); on Fisher, see Mayer, *Dark Money*, 79–80 and Doherty, *Radicals for Capitalism*, 477–80.
9   On Read, see Lawrence Glickman, *Free Enterprise: An American History* (New Haven, CT: Yale University Press, 2020), chap. 6.

corporate life and profits.[10] Armed with substantial wealth, the Koch brothers and Scaife, as well as conservative allies such as Coors Brewing Company scion Joseph Coors, pumped additional sums of money into militantly conservative institutions and think tanks in order to wage a battle of ideas and launch public relations campaigns in favor of a concept long out of favor: the free market.[11] This entailed not only championing a self-regulating and theoretically isolated market but also critiquing the regulatory and welfare state as inefficient and a problem rather than solution to pressing social and economic issues.

Political culture too was shifting. Arizona Senator Barry Goldwater's *Conscience of a Conservative* (1960) had drawn readers' attentions to the ideas of free-market economists Hayek and Ludwig von Mises, and, by the time he ran as the Republican candidate for the presidency in 1964, he had been organizing for close to a decade to challenge the modern Republicanism characteristic of the Eisenhower administration.[12] Goldwater's 1964 campaign energized manufacturers and entrepreneurs and inadvertently introduced Ronald Reagan to a ready public; Milton Friedman did a stint as Goldwater's economic advisor before moving on to publish a regular column in *Newsweek* magazine starting in 1966.[13] A younger generation tuned in: William F. Buckley's Young Americans for Freedom, an organization he created at Yale University in 1960 to give voice to conservative students' concerns, grew rapidly to the degree that by the end of the decade it had divided into "trad" (traditionalist conservatives) and "rad" (libertarian) wings.[14]

On the west coast libertarian ideas found fertile soil. Northern California's counterculture and tech culture expressed strong libertarian tendencies. The cofounder of *Wired* magazine, Louis Rossetto, moved from Nixon supporter in 1968 to "libertarian anarchist" by 1971, immersing himself in the writings of individualist thinkers such as Benjamin Tucker, Lysander Spooner, and Ayn Rand and copublishing "The New Right Credo—Libertarianism."[15] Stewart Brand published his *Whole Earth Catalog*, designed for an audience scholar

---

10   Mayer, *Dark Money*, chap. 2.

11   Ibid., 79; Daniel Stedman Jones, *Masters of the Universe: Hayek, Friedman, and the Birth of Neoliberal Politics* (Princeton, NJ: Princeton University Press, 2012), 4–7 and Glickman, *Free Enterprise*.

12   Kim Phillips-Fein, *Invisible Hands: The Businessmen's Crusade against the New Deal* (New York: W.W. Norton, 2010), 127 for "modern Republicanism"; Lisa Duggan, *Mean Girl: Ayn Rand and the Culture of Greed* (Berkeley: University of California Press, 2019), 69, on Goldwater's book.

13   Doherty, *Radicals for Capitalism*, 308; on Goldwater and Reagan's emergence in his shadow see Phillips-Fein, *Invisible Hands*, 146–47.

14   Doherty, *Radicals for Capitalism*, 353.

15   Fred Turner, *From Counterculture to Cyberculture: Stewart Brand, the Whole Earth Network, and the Rise of Digital Utopianism* (Chicago: University of Chicago Press, 2008), 209–10.

Fred Turner has called the New Communalists: members of the counterculture who "turned away from political action and toward technology and the
transformation of consciousness as the primary sources of social change."[16]
New Communalists drew from cybernetics and the counterculture to argue
that communities were coherent systems in which "everything was connected,
connected by feedback, kept in balance, in touch with the environment, even
with the animals and plants and rocks, in unity, as one single whole, one planet,
shrunk into a village by communication technology."[17] If, for some, postwar
cybernetics and information technology generated deep suspicion and critique,
captured with particular force in Herbert Marcuse's *One-Dimensional Man* (1964)
and the Frankfurt School's distrust of media and consumer capitalism more
generally, for the New Communalists this synergy between communalism and
cybernetics seemed potentially liberating.[18] Marshall McLuhan's optimistic
theorizations regarding technology and community resonated widely, spur-
ring further interest in an electronic world within which one could create the
possibilities for horizontal rather than hierarchical control and communities in
which the decentralization of authority would be the norm.[19] John Kenneth
Galbraith's *The New Industrial State* (1968) suggested, albeit from a slightly
different perspective, that an emerging corporate "technostructure" created
workplaces that diffused power and flattened the distinctions between labor
and management.[20]

Patterns of exploitation remained. The Californian Ideology, with its
blend of libertarian, countercultural, and techno-utopian currents, championed a capitalist operating system, rooted in classical liberal ideals such
as laissez-faire, rugged individualism, and self-governing and self-regulating

---

16   Turner, *From Counterculture to Cyberculture*, 4. See also Richard Walker, *Pictures of a Gone
      City: Tech and the Dark Side of Prosperity in the San Francisco Bay Area* (Oakland: PM Press,
      2018), chap. 10, especially for a stronger emphasis on political economy, and Richard
      Barbrook and Andy Cameron, "The Californian Ideology," in Peter Ludlow, ed., *Crypto
      Anarchy, Cyberstates, and Pirate Utopias* (Cambridge, MA: MIT Press, 2001), 363–87.
17   Thomas Rid, *Rise of the Machines: A Cybernetic History* (New York: W.W. Norton, 2016),
      157. One can hear the echoes of laissez-faire in the understanding of cybernetics as a
      self-regulating system with an internal logic that will always "strive 'toward homeostatic
      optima.'" *Rise of the Machines*, 177.
18   Marcuse, *One-Dimensional Man: Studies in the Ideology of Advanced Industrial Society*, 2nd
      ed. (Boston: Beacon Press, 1991 [1964]); see also Erich Fromm, *Escape from Freedom*, 2nd
      ed. (New York: Holt, 1969 [1941]), especially the foreword.
19   Rid, *Rise of the Machines*, 173; see also Barbrook and Cameron, "The Californian Ideology."
20   See Ralph Miliband, "Professor Galbraith and American Capitalism," and the discus-
      sion in Greg Albo, "Capitalism, Technology, Labor: An Introduction." Greg Albo, Leo
      Panitch, and Alan Zuege, eds., *Capitalism, Technology, Labor: Socialist Register Reader*, vol.
      2 (Chicago: Haymarket Books, 2020), 6–12 (and for discussion of Galbraith and Miliband's
      critique, 8–9). Miliband's critique was originally published in the *Socialist Register* in 1968.

ecologies and economies. If "The Man" was the enemy, his avatar was not the capitalist but the bureaucrat, not the economic system but the State. And while libertarian counterculture valorized individual emancipation, in its practice it often generated new situations of authoritarian control in which white and male ("The Man") power structures prevailed, a reality that still characterizes the tech world of Silicon Valley to this day.[21]

Libertarianism found its most passionate expression, perhaps, in California's "Gold Coast" of Southern California, as local-born author Kim Stanley Robinson called it in one of his early novels.[22] By the 1960s Orange County in particular had become a conservative stronghold and an expanding epicenter of libertarianism.[23] Here, and in neighboring Los Angeles and Santa Monica, libertarian ideas circulated through a substantial growth in conservative-leaning bookstores and within a rapidly growing zine culture sporting titles such as *Bullsheet*, *Invictus*, *Libertarian American*, and *Living Free*, some of which bled in to parts of the New Left.[24] One of the most important of the Los Angeles zines, *Innovator*, had close to one thousand subscribers, nearly a quarter of whom were based in Orange County and Santa Monica.[25] Little more than agricultural fields and cow towns in the 1930s, with a population of about one hundred thousand, Orange County neared a million inhabitants by 1960, transformed by the arrival of transplants from Midwestern states such as Iowa and Minnesota, by GIs who had experienced the West Coast sunshine during the war years and returned after their service, and by the growth of the military-industrial and aerospace complexes.[26] Surveyors subdivided vast expanses of the county's land while the government subsidized postwar homeownership: an Orange County boom ensued. One of the obvious ironies of the story is that libertarianism took root in a place transformed by

21 Karrie Jacobs, "Utopia Redux," in Ludlow, ed., *Crypto Anarchy*, 349–52; Barbrook and Cameron, "The Californian Ideology"; Turner, *From Counterculture to Cyberculture*, 208 and 255–61; and *All Watched Over by Machines of Loving Grace*, Episode 2: "The Use and Abuse of Vegetational Concepts," dir. by Adam Curtis (May 2011, BBC Two).

22 Kim Stanley Robinson, *Three Californias: The Wild Shore, The Gold Coast, and Pacific Edge* (New York: Tor Books, 2020). *The Gold Coast* was originally published in 1995.

23 Lisa McGirr, *Suburban Warriors: The Origins of the New American Right* (Princeton, NJ: Princeton University Press, 2001); Michelle Nickerson, *Mothers of Conservatism: Women and the Postwar Right* (Princeton, NJ: Princeton University Press, 2012); Perlstein, *Before the Storm*, chap. 7.

24 For an excellent discussion and mapping of the bookstores, see Nickerson, *Mothers of Conservatism*, chap. 5; on zine culture see Doherty, *Radicals for Capitalism*, 374–75.

25 *Innovator*, Autumn 1968, 7–21. The editors included a note that "no special promotion has been conducted in S.C. [Southern California] under present management. Several libertarian periodicals originating elsewhere have reported similarly high proportion [*sic*] of subscribers in S.C."

26 Perlstein, *Before the Storm*, chap. 7.

government subsidies and what is arguably the most socialist institution in the US—the military. A number of libertarians who participated in Oliver's projects were retired military personnel, including Orange County veteran Morris Davis, an aviation and electrical engineer who would be appointed (not elected) the first and only president of the Republic of Minerva. Davis lived in Anaheim, and his neighbors were by and large active or retired military officers whom he characterized as "conservatives" but also included members of the ultraconservative John Birch Society. Davis had been raised as an FDR Democrat and then voted for Eisenhower, but, after his daughter introduced him to the writings of Ayn Rand, he embraced libertarianism.[27] Davis and Oliver soon began collaborating.

Trinities

"The real cure for this country is for the productive people to leave, and let the moochers tax each other."[28] The phrase, although penned by Michael Oliver, could have been lifted directly from a speech by John Galt, the capitalist hero of one of Oliver's favorite books, Rand's *Atlas Shrugged* (1957). For his new constitution, Oliver looked not to legal scholars or comparative political models for inspiration. Rather, he looked to a novelist and an economist. "Those who read and studied the novels and philosophy of Ayn Rand," Oliver wrote, "and the economic treatises of [Ludwig] von Mises and other free enterprise advocates will agree that man may yet find his way to freedom." Mises was a passing note. It was Rand—an anomaly as a woman in the male-dominated worlds of political economy and libertarianism—who served as Oliver's philosophical guide. "The promise of the free enterprise advocate," he wrote, in a Randian turn of phrase, "is and must be that pursuance of one's rational self-interest is a *totally* moral goal."[29]

Free enterprise was not a self-explanatory term nor was it one on which even its own advocates could necessarily agree.[30] Rand argued as strenuously with fellow capitalist travelers as she did with mainstream and leftist critics. Libertarians, like any other ideological collective, were a motley bunch, and they charted a variety of paths to emancipation. Positions ranged from those who hewed closely to classical liberalism, with certain twentieth-century modifications, to others who embraced social conservatism to still others

27 Interview with Morris Davis, in Griffith, "Before the Deluge," Davis interview, 2–3.
28 *Capitalist Country Newsletter* 2, no. 1 (February 1969): 2. The language is commonplace at the time with repeated invocations of the "undeserving poor" and "cultures of dependency." See Stedman Jones, *Masters of the Universe*, 64.
29 Oliver, *A New Constitution*, 20 and 23. Emphasis in the original.
30 For a careful study that historicizes the phrase, see Glickman, *Free Enterprise*.

who advocated radical structural change. If one were to offer up a libertarian triumvirate for the era, it would be Friedrich Hayek, Murray Rothbard, and Ayn Rand. The body of literature that has been produced on and about just these three authors alone is substantial, and an in-depth examination of their works is beyond the scope of this study. However, a brief sketch of the general parameters of their thought will be useful in understanding why Oliver and others gravitated toward Rand when envisioning a possible future.

At one end of the libertarian spectrum can be found Murray Rothbard, often considered a founding figure of anarcho-capitalism.[31] He had no truck with any form of state accommodation and argued that even national defense and the protection of private property rights should be services provided through agencies competing with one another in an unregulated market.[32] For Rothbard, the accommodation of some state functions was a Faustian bargain with the regulatory devil that could only end in a kind of state metastization. With rigid consistency, Rothbard had an absolute intolerance of any state form and insisted on a world governed solely through private contract and agreement between individuals. He was opposed not only to regulating and taxing bureaucracies but also opposed repressive ones, such as the police and the military, traditionally construed as necessary to the protection of property. Thus Rothbard's occasionally strange bedfellows appear not so strange: his disdain for the growing Cold War state apparatus of the 1960s and his opposition to the Vietnam War found him allied with intellectuals and protestors of the New Left against social conservatives and those libertarians willing to

---

31 Numerous debates exist regarding whether or not anarcho-capitalism is really a thing. My own position here is that we would do better to think through the range of thought that could be captured under the general term "libertarian"—which at least in its US variety is sharply distinct from anarchism—than to draw on a neologism which puts two antithetical terms (anarchism and capitalism) together. At the minimum our terms need to respect what has long been the classical anarchist position—adamantly in favor of collective self-government and just as adamantly against both the state and capitalism as structures that inhibit collective self-government and equality. For a study that takes a broad approach to libertarianism, see David Boaz, *The Libertarian Reader: Classic & Contemporary Writings from Lao-Tzu to Milton Friedman* (New York: Simon & Schuster, 2015 [1997]) and, for anarchism, Peter Marshall, *Demanding the Impossible: A History of Anarchism* (Oakland: PM Press, 2010). For a work that concretely roots anarchism in its industrial capitalist and socialist roots, see Lucien van der Walt and Michael Schmidt, *Black Flame: The Revolutionary Class Politics of Anarchism and Syndicalism* (Oakland: AK Press, 2009). For collected essays that expand the history of anarchism beyond Europe, see Barry Maxwell and Raymond Craib, eds., *No Gods, No Masters, No Peripheries: Global Anarchisms* (Oakland: PM Press, 2015) and Steven Hirsch and Lucien van der Walt, eds., *Anarchism and Syndicalism in the Colonial and Postcolonial World: The Praxis of National Liberation, Internationalism, and Social Revolution* (Leiden, NL: Brill, 2010).

32 Rothbard, *For a New Liberty* (New York: Macmillan, 1973), 18. See also Doherty, *Radicals for Capitalism*, esp. 265–70.

tolerate a state in the name of anticommunism. "The Right-wing masses," he wrote, "care little and know nothing about liberty or economics; they are 'for' Christ and the Constitution, and they are against foreigners, Communists, atheists, and Jews."[33]

Although the alliance soon soured, and Rothbard would become an outspoken supporter of police repression and ally himself with the paleo-conservatism of Pat Buchanan in the 1980s, it was enough to further alienate many of his market-libertarian brethren, as was his apparent advocacy of revolutionary violence. In a 1969 talk to a gathering at the Great Shanghai Restaurant in upstate New York, an event organized by exit advocate Werner Stiefel, Rothbard was described as "brilliant, witty, charming, erudite—and frightening" for advocating "revolution and 'all other necessary means' to overthrow the present 'government-industry' power structure."[34] Rothbard unsettled attendees with his claims that he discerned "libertarian aspects in the Russian and Chinese revolutions" and, in a clear reference to the New Left, that he supported cooperating with 'wrong' philosophies because they are moving in the 'right' direction."[35] Rothbard's positions, which at points seemed much too sanguine about the dangers of the mob, disturbed many. Among them was Michael Oliver, who likely had Rothbard in mind when he wrote the following:

> In 1966 I began to see that the United States could be taken over by elements similar to the Nazi Storm Troopers. When I see that someone starts throwing bombs, shooting from roof tops, starting fires, and block-ing streets, I see Storm Trooper tactics. If we permit this to continue, these elements who scream for "freedom" to do this violence will take over the United States and install a fascist regime. Although this is being done in the name of "liberalism" and "freedom now," I'm not concerned here with semantics but only with actual facts. Let me say here that *those libertarians who give aid and comfort to such elements are helping destroy the*

---

33   Quoted in Doherty, *Radicals for Capitalism*, 259.

34   Warner Stevens, "Rothbard Draws a Big Crowd," *Atlantis News* 2, no. 3 (February 7, 1969): 1.

35   Ibid., 2. Not all were opposed, of course. One of Rothbard's supporters, mimicking the language of French anarchist Pierre-Joseph Proudhon, asked: "Do you seriously object to depriving people of the right to be fleeced, exploited, monopolized, inspected, directed, regulated, numbered, rated, stamped, authorized, prevented, indoctrinated, spied on, seized, censured, fined, imprisoned, shot, enslaved, outraged, and dishonored? Does the fact that many people are content to live this way make government inviolable?" And, in a clear reference to the strategic stakes—between exit or revolution—asked, "Must we in the name of justice be forced to desert our homeland simply because the majority is docile and we are not?" *Atlantis News* 2, no. 5 (March 7, 1969): 1.

United States only to have it replaced with a regime which is unimaginably worse. Such "libertarians" are part of the problem rather than the solution.[36]

Unsurprisingly, then, Oliver hewed philosophically and politically closer to a vein of libertarian thought that sought to find an equilibrium point between maximum individual freedom (what he would have called choice) and minimal government (what he would have called necessity). He might logically have found such a position in Hayek's seminal works. Hayek, after all, deeply opposed state participation in economic life and he made little distinction between fascism and socialism, seeing in both a deadly dependence on a central state and, as he titled his most well-known text, a "road to serfdom."[37] Hayek and his students, such as Milton Friedman, did not take the position Rothbard took, nor did they want to resurrect nineteenth century classical liberalism. Rather, they sought to remake liberalism for the postwar world: a new, or neo-, liberalism.[38] The point for Hayek and his intellectual comrades was twofold: first, unlike Rothbard who argued that any state apparatus is inherently totalitarian, Hayek argued that the origins of totalitarianism could be found in the "continental liberalism"—or totalitarian democracy—espoused by Voltaire, Rousseau, and Condorcet rather than in the "authentic liberalism"—or liberal democracy—that he linked back to Adam Smith and Edmund Burke.[39] The second, and closely linked, point was that this authentic liberalism did not mean that the market should have increased freedom from state sovereignty but rather that markets, not states, should be sovereign.[40] This does not mean states cease to exist. They continue to exist but only in order to ensure the sovereignty of economic exchange and to secure the status of authentic liberalism.[41]

---

36   "Designing a Free Country: An Interview with Michael Oliver," *Reason* (December 1, 1972). My emphasis.

37   Hayek, *The Road to Serfdom* (Chicago: University of Chicago Press, 1944).

38   Quinn Slobodian, *Globalists: The End of Empire and the Birth of Neoliberalism* (Cambridge, MA: Harvard University Press, 2018); Gregoire Chamayou, *La société ingouvernable: Une généalogie du libéralisme autoritaire* (Paris: La Fabrique, 2018).

39   Chamayou, *La société ingouvernable*, 225–33.

40   I am indebted here to Fred Block's superb introduction to Karl Polanyi, *The Great Transformation: The Political and Economic Origins of Our Time* (Boston: Beacon Press, 2001, 2nd ed. [1944]). See also Mark Fisher, *Capitalist Realism: Is There No Alternative?* (Winchester, UK: Zero Books, 2010) and James Davis, "At War with the Future: Catastrophism and the Right," in Sasha Lilley, David McNally, Eddie Yuen, and James Davis, *Catastrophism: The Apocalyptic Politics of Collapse and Rebirth* (Oakland: PM Press, 2012), 77–107, esp. 90–91.

41   Block, introduction to Polanyi, *The Great Transformation*; Mark Fisher, "How to Kill a Zombie: Strategising the End of Neoliberalism," in Fisher, *K-Punk: The Collected and Unpublished Writings of Mark Fisher* (London: Repeater Books, 2018), 539–44; David Harvey, *A Brief History of Neoliberalism* (New York: Oxford, 2005).

Such an approach is at times termed "minarchist" in that its supporters advocate for a minimalist state to undertake very limited functions, such as the protection of property rights, providing for the national defense, and protecting property holders from direct violence, fraud, and theft. But the term is something of a misnomer if we understand it to mean a smaller state. In order to protect private property, the state has expanded the scope of its activities and created an array of new institutions. Minarchism thus refers less to the size of the state per se—it may take a sizeable military and police force to successfully fulfill its functions of defending private property—than to the limited range of its activities.[42] When Milton Friedman argued that government should be limited to protecting "freedom both from enemies outside our gates and from our fellow-citizens," he emphasized that freedom meant "to *preserve* law and order, to *enforce* private contracts, to *foster* competitive markets."[43] To preserve, to enforce, and to foster: that is not a small-state manifesto. Indeed, both Hayek and Friedman believed that the collective benefit that would come from private competition would only occur with strong state involvement. (It is worth recalling that the privatization of Chile's economic and social life, inspired by the teachings of Hayek and guided by the visible hand of Friedman and his Chicago Boys, took place under a massive, repressive military apparatus which came to power through an antidemocratic and illegal coup d'état.)[44] There is of course little new in such an assertion. From its very origins capitalism was a state-led, centrally planned project: the coercion of the market resulted from coercion by the state.[45] Capitalism was no product of immaculate conception.

---

42   For a useful collection of essays arguing minarchist and individual anarchist positions, see Roderick T. Long and Tibor R. Machan, eds., *Anarchism/Minarchism: Is a Government Part of a Free Country?* (Aldershot: Ashgate, 2008).

43   Friedman, *Capitalism and Freedom* (Chicago: University of Chicago Press, 2002 [1962]), 2. My emphasis.

44   Hayek himself repeatedly voiced his support for Pinochet's dictatorship, suggesting that a "liberal" dictatorship was preferable to a "democratic government lacking in liberalism." For a trenchant overview, see Greg Grandin, *Empire's Workshop: Latin America, the United States, and the Rise of the New Imperialism* (New York: Metropolitan Books, 2006), esp. chap. 5. For an evaluation based on a close reading of Hayek's own words, see Andrew Farrant, Edward McPhail, and Sebastian Berger, "Preventing the "Abuses" of Democracy: Hayek, the "Military Usurper" and Transitional Dictatorship in Chile?" *American Journal of Economics and Sociology* 71, no. 3 (July 2012): 513–38. For a libertarian critique of Hayek's ideas of a liberal autocrat, see Jesse Walker, "The Mad Dream of a Libertarian Dictatorship," *Reason*, July 12, 2017. For an excellent series of essays on Hayek, the Chicago Boys, and Pinochet, see Corey Robin, "When Hayek Met Pinochet," https://coreyrobin.com/2012/07/18/when-hayek-met-pinochet/.

45   Ellen Meiksins Wood, *The Origin of Capitalism: A Longer View* (London: Verso Press, 2002), 62; Polanyi, *The Great Transformation*, 250.

These minimalist positions dovetailed well with the perspectives of Ayn Rand. Rand's story is well known.[46] Born Alissa Zinovievna Rosenbaum in Russia in 1905 to a prosperous Jewish family, Rand left in 1926 for the US, where she lived first in Los Angeles and then eventually New York City. Based on her family's experiences in the wake of the Russian Revolution—revolutionaries expropriated her father's pharmacy and subdivided the family's home in order to house more people—as well as her time in Southern California, a growing hotbed of libertarian and individualist self-fashioning as well as the center of aspiring screenplay writers, Rand created a specific set of ideas of what constituted a free society and set them forth in a collection of novels and essays that garnered her substantial attention. Through Rand's work ran two parallel threads of concern: that communism be challenged and defeated at every turn and that the state be empowered only to safeguard certain individual rights, in the form of national defense, a police force, and a judiciary. Rand agreed with economist Mises, an admirer of her writings who held that the state's only legitimate function was as a defender of private rights and a producer of security.[47] Police, a judiciary, and a military served to ensure the rights of property owners and thus such institutions could not be left to the vagaries of the market. In what would become a holy trinity, the state's functions congealed around protecting property owners from direct violence, theft and fraud and ensuring the workings of an ostensibly free market. Individual sovereignty—a foundational cornerstone of the libertarian edifice—would be achieved through market sovereignty, protected by a nightwatchman state.

All of this would seem to suggest that Rand would find common cause with Hayek. Yet she had little patience for him. Why? For one, Hayek hedged his neoliberal bets. He may have worried of the dangers of democracy and railed against centralized planning, but he also blurred the line between what he considered acceptable and unacceptable planning. Attentive to the excesses and consequences of laissez-faire, he supported certain state interventions such as health care, unemployment insurance, public assistance to families, and minimum wages as a form of insurance against revolution.[48] For Rand,

46 For works on Rand, with varying degrees of critique, see Duggan, *Mean Girl*; Jennifer Burns, *Goddess of the Market: Ayn Rand and the American Right* (New York: Oxford University Press); and Corey Robin, *The Reactionary Mind: Conservatism from Edmund Burke to Sarah Palin* (New York: Oxford University Press, 2011), chap. 3.

47 Slobodian, *Globalists*, 33. For Oliver, "the only true and proper function of government is to protect its citizens from force and fraud." This according to a draft of Oliver's constitution for Abaco. See Andrew St. George, "The Amazing New-Country Caper," *Esquire* (February 1975), 153.

48 Burns, *Goddess of the Market*, 104; see also Melinda Cooper, "Neoliberalism's Family Values: Welfare, Human Capital, and Kinship," in Dieter Plehwe, Quinn Slobodian,

Hayek's willingness to even discuss the possibility of state intervention with regard to wages and social security—even if as a means to combat the appeal of communism or the possibility of revolution—was a betrayal of the individual and a first step in an inevitable slide into communism. Hayek is "pure poison," Rand wrote, acidly observing that "the man is an ass, with no conception of a free society at all."[49] Nor did she have any love for Rothbard's variety of libertarianism, a label which she refused and a philosophy which appeared to her as a naive and dangerous gamble that could open the door to mob rule of the kind her family experienced under the Bolsheviks and a communist takeover. At least some form of a state was needed. Without it, she asked, who would protect private property rights? Who would jail the communists? Freedom was not a free-for-all.

Rand found a wide audience as readers drew life lessons from her works of fiction, copies of which by the early 1960s had sold in the hundreds of thousands. Mike Wallace interviewed her in 1959; Johnny Carson had her on his late-night show three times in 1967 alone; and Alvin Toffler interviewed her in 1968 for *Playboy*.[50] Despite her disdain for Rothbard, and despite her rejection of the term, Rand made libertarianism morally palatable and narratively compelling to her readers, even if critics routinely panned her books. Her scathing critiques of collectivism and the Soviet Union found a ready audience in Cold War America, particularly among businessmen and capitalists who felt maligned and unappreciated. Her thousand-page tome *Atlas Shrugged* revived capitalists as admirable captains of industry responsible for the wealth and pleasure of contemporary life enjoyed by the common man. In Rand's hands, capitalists appeared as hunky entrepreneurs rather than dour company men, with sex lives that would rival those of the most ardent free love advocates, although the bedroom was not immune to the boardroom ideals of selfishness and competition she valorized and, despite her dictums against force and violence, Rand wrote disturbingly ambiguous scenes of rape and violent sexual conquest. The crux of her work constituted a verbal frontal assault on the New Deal and the welfare state. In *Atlas Shrugged* she painted an apocalyptic landscape of a US overrun by collectivists and freeloaders, in which mediocrity reigns supreme and the capitalist captains of industry are seen as the enemy. In response, and inspired by the shadowy figure of John Galt,

---

and Philip Mirowski, eds., *Nine Lives of Neoliberalism* (London: Verso, 2020), 105; Nancy MacLean, *Democracy in Chains: The Deep History of the Radical Right's Stealth Plan for America* (New York: Penguin, 2018), 40.

49   Burns, *Goddess of the Market*, 104.

50   Duggan, *Mean Girl*, 7–8, 69; Alvin Toffler, "Playboy Interview: Ayn Rand," *Playboy* (March 1964), 35–43.

entrepreneurs and capitalists go on strike. In an act which captivated readers such as Michael Oliver and inspired repeated real-life simulacra, the captains of industry withdraw from society to a capitalist retreat where they await the collapse of the society around them, on the ashes of which they plan to build a society based exclusively on self-interest and free enterprise. They exit to Galt's Gulch, an Atlantis hidden away in a valley high in the Rocky Mountains.

Fear and loathing I: The masses

Rand's doctrines were Oliver's doctrines. He feared the seemingly anarchistic tendencies of Rothbard, and he feared the ostensibly socialistic encroachments in Hayek. Both seemed portents of what he feared most: populist totalitarianism. The Nazis had murdered his parents and three of his siblings; the Bolsheviks—"my term for communists and Leftist terrorists," he later wrote— had killed his older sister.[51] Exemplified by Hitler and Stalin, fascism and communism were murderous ideologies (despite the fact that communism won the war against fascism).[52] They were, as Hayek, Rand, Hannah Arendt, and an array of liberal intellectuals and commentators agreed, manifestations of totalitarianism.

The liberal consensus of the 1950s and 1960s held that the success of American politics derived from an absence (real or perceived) of the grand ideologies believed to lead to totalitarian politics. Life in a free society meant, to some degree, living with uncertainty and anxiety. Totalitarian man, wrote Arthur Schlesinger, reiterating what sociologist Erich Fromm had articulated in 1941, is "man without anxiety."[53] Absolutism, unyielding certainty, were suspect. Yet Oliver's and Rand's positions were nothing if not absolute. They were, at some level, forms of political agoraphobia, the palliative for which could be found in the reductionist individualism and closed coherence of Objectivism and an idealized free market. The possibilities that the laws of

---

51   The phrase appears in an e-mail he sent to fellow Nevadan and right-wing assembly-person Sharron Angle. Angle, *Right Angle: One Woman's Journey to Reclaim the Constitution* (Bloomington, IN: AuthorHouse, 2011), 194. And thus his assertion: "But whereas I find a great number of things terribly wrong with our government, still I do not wish to see its destruction, for it will only be replaced by a dictatorship of incomprehensible evil." Oliver, *Capitalist Country Newsletter* 1, no. 5 (November 1968): 2.

52   The statistics are telling: Soviet forces were responsible for 93 percent of German military casualties during the nearly three-year period from June 22, 1941 (when Germany invaded Russia), to June 6, 1944 (D-Day). Louis Menand, *The Free World: Art and Thought in the Cold War* (New York: Farrar, Straus & Giroux, 2021), 3, citing David Reynolds, *From World War to Cold War: Churchill, Roosevelt, and the International History of the 1940s* (Oxford: Oxford University Press, 2006).

53   David Cochran, *American Noir: Underground Writers and Filmmakers of the Postwar Era* (Washington, DC: Smithsonian Institution, 2000), 7; Fromm, *Escape from Freedom*, x.

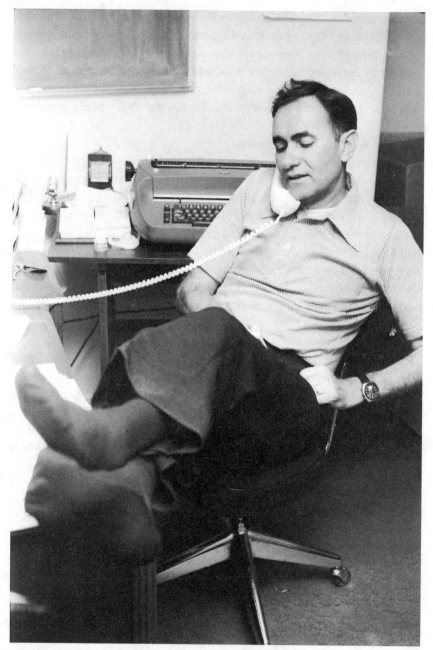

Fig. 1.1: Michael Oliver. Pictures of Oliver are rare. This one comes from a series of images taken by Andrew St. George when he met with Oliver in June 1974, in Carson City, NV.

Courtesy of Andrew Szentgyorgyi.

the market—rather than, say, the laws of nature or the laws of history—could be totalitarian remained unacknowledged. Thus, in his flight from anxiety Oliver escaped into a form of political absolutism that could have its own totalizing tendencies. And while he might find comfort in the writings of Hayek, Mises, or Rose Wilder Lane (who equated social security with National Socialism), no writer offered a more simple, direct, and unyielding absolutism than Rand.[54] Fellow traveler Murray Rothbard suggested as much. He discerned in Rand's Objectivist philosophy cause for concern. Her obsession with rationality, for example, appeared to be an irrational assault on human freedom and individuality. Objectivism left little room for whimsy, passion, jealousy, agonism ... in a word, humanness. But most troubling of all, in the cult of personality that surrounded Rand, Rothbard saw a "perfect engine for complete totalitarianism."[55]

But for many readers, Rand was liberating. Her work resonated with libertarians not only because it celebrated individual prowess and creativity but also because of its willingness to articulate a structural solution for dealing with the masses, prone to shirking their work and susceptible to charismatic demagogues. Rand's appeal derived also from the melodramatic simplicity she distilled out of a complex political world: the heroic creator versus the lazy and inferior masses who pose a danger to capitalism and freedom. For Rand, the masses or the mob were the broad swathe of humanity understood to be intellectually inferior and a social impediment to the creativity and entrepreneurialism of the producers. As a young woman planning her first novel Rand had drawn from the real-life trial of child murderer William Hickman for inspiration, appreciating "his immense explicit egotism—*a thing the mob never forgives*; and his *cleverness*, which *makes the mob feel that a superior mind can exist entirely outside its established morals*."[56] She could have been quoting Max Stirner or Friedrich Nietzsche, whose *Thus Spake Zarathustra* was her first English-language literary purchase.[57] Rand's heroic capitalists—invariably male, handsome, tall and white—were veritable Nietzschean supermen, their

---

54 Robert Lefevre, an important figure in the libertarian movement in Orange County, CA, of the 1960s and 1970s, identified Wilder Lane's book as the beginning of his conversion to libertarianism. See Griffith, interview of Lefevre in "Before the Deluge," interview transcript p. 3. On Wilder Lane's equating of social security with National Socialism, see Grandin, *The End of the Myth: From the Frontier to the Border Wall in the Mind of America* (New York: Metropolitan Books, 2019), 189.

55 The quoted passage is from Doherty, *Radicals for Capitalism*, 261. For a more detailed discussion of Rothbard's fraught interactions with, and concerns about, Rand, see Burns, *Goddess of the Market*, 144–45 and 151–53.

56 Cited from Duggan, *Mean Girl*, 2–3 (my emphases except "cleverness"); see also Robin, *The Reactionary Mind*, 91.

57 Robin, *The Reactionary Mind*, 90.

endowments unquestionable and their authority (like Rand's) absolute. The masses, in exchange, constituted little more than a collective inhibition on creative genius and leaches on entrepreneurial greatness. They were worthy only of disdain.

For Oliver the mob was something more: an unruly and frightening mass out of which populist violence threatened to emerge at any moment. His language could mirror Rand's when he railed, for example, against "social meddlers" who opposed the free enterprise system or when he criticized how the government robbed society's producers by creating vast welfare programs or pursued inflationary policies and deficit spending or favored labor over capital and taxed corporations at too high a rate.[58] But it was the masses—as a mob—and their susceptibility to demagoguery that concerned him more than their impeding of entrepreneurial activity and the capitalist accumulation of wealth. Oliver viewed the 1960s rebellions, protests, and demonstrations as akin to existential threats. While he logically could have feared the populist, often apocalyptic and violent, politics of the right—the John Birchers and the Minutemen, the Ku Klux Klan and the Christian anticommunist crusaders—it was the populations acting in the name of "liberalism" and "freedom now" whom he accused of employing "Storm Trooper tactics."[59]

Escape from freedom

Oliver's conclusions resulted from a skewed reading of the social and political context out of which protests for historical, racial, and gender justice arose. Urban insurgencies, protests, political organizing from below, and social movements of the era were nothing if not expressions of a deep desire to finally see the promise of freedom and equality expanded to those who had historically been denied both. As philosopher John Rawls argued in his 1971 book *A Theory of Justice*, understood at the time as "the major philosophical treatise of the decade," justice at a basic level meant equality.[60] Protests and mobilizations were also efforts to rewrite the histories and stories that for too long had justified exclusion and inequality, including many that provided a basis for

---

58 Oliver *A New Constitution*, 11–15
59 For a brief and illuminating discussion of the apocalyptic anti-Communists of the 1960s, see Perlstein, *Before the Storm*, chap. 8. For a fictional version—although one suspects less fictional than it might appear—see James Ellroy's *Underworld U.S.A. Trilogy*: vol. 1, *American Tabloid* and *The Cold Six Thousand* and vol. 2, *Blood's a Rover* (New York: Everyman's Library Contemporary Classics, 2019).
60 Rawls, *A Theory of Justice* (Cambridge, MA: The Belknap Press, 1971). For the quotation, see Samuel Huntington, "The United States," in Michael Crozier, Samuel Huntington, and Jojo Watanuki, *The Crisis of Democracy: Report on the Governability of Democracies to the Trilateral Commission* (New York: Columbia University Press, 1975), 62.

libertarian arguments. Social movement protests of the period, for example, challenged the narrative that touted immigrant pluck and the pioneer spirit as the bases for the country's wealth, pointing instead to how such wealth—the property largely of white Americans—had been built on theft, fraud and violent expropriation. The US was, as Chicano historian Rodolfo Acuña would put it, an "occupied America," a term with which activists and intellectuals of the American Indian Movement would have agreed.

Critics drew inspiration from Karl Marx's discussion of primitive accumulation in which he had argued that individual private property resulted from acts of "conquest, enslavement, robbery, murder" that were then subsequently legitimated with laws of enclosure, titles of ownership, and stories of a "diligent, intelligent and ... frugal elite."[61] Libertarian thinkers such as philosopher Robert Nozick and economist Murray Rothbard countered by attempting to fit the square peg of contemporary private property rights into the round hole of primitive accumulation and dispossession.[62] Nozick, in contrast to others, admitted that reparations or some other form of compensation was due to those who had been made worse off as a result of unjust acquisition. Even so, for many the irony was palpable: existing private property rights so zealously guarded by libertarian advocates resulted from the very acts of direct violence, fraud, and theft that they themselves opposed. As political theorist Robert Nichols has argued recently (by cheekily inverting the famous pronouncement of anarchist philosopher Pierre-Joseph Proudhon), theft is property.[63]

---

61   Marx, *Capital: A Critique of Political Economy*, vol. 1 (New York: Penguin Books, 1990 [1867]), 873–74.

62   Nozick, *Anarchy, State, and Utopia* (New York: Basic Books, 1974); Rothbard, *For a New Liberty*. This history of blood and fire may be in part the reason why libertarians often emphasize created rather than acquired resources in their arguments, thereby circumventing the question of "aggression" and the "wresting" of preexisting goods. Laura S. Underkuffler, *The Idea of Property* (New York: Oxford University Press, 2003), 120 (esp. n63). My efforts to understand Nozick, Rawls, and Rothbard have been aided by Underkuffler's text as well as A. John Simmons, "Historical Rights and Fair Shares," *Law and Philosophy* 14, no. 2 (May 1995): 149–84; Xioaping Wei, "From Principle to Context: Marx versus Nozick and Rawls on Distributive Justice," *Rethinking Marxism* 20, no. 3 (July 2008). For excellent intellectual histories of how thinkers sought to reconcile illiberal actions with liberal aspirations, see Onur Ulas Ince, *Colonial Capitalism and the Dilemmas of Liberalism* (New York: Oxford University Press, 2018) and Emilia Viotti da Costa, *The Brazilian Empire: Myths and Histories,* revised edition (Durham, NC: University of North Carolina Press, 2000), esp. chap. 3.

63   Robert Nichols, *Theft Is Property: Dispossession and Critical Theory* (Durham, NC: Duke University Press, 2020); Proudhon, *What Is Property? Or an Inquiry into the Principle of Right and of Government* (1840). Nichols' point is fundamental: property—a historically

As well as land grabbing through colonial expansion, the wealth of the nation derived from another form of theft: more than two centuries of enslaved labor.[64] Violence and fraud against a significant portion of the country's population did not end with the abolition of slavery. It persisted in forms of redlining and housing covenants, voter suppression and intimidation, racial gerrymandering, new forms of forced labor, radical inequities in the application of the law and sentencing, and police violence and racist terrorism, even as free enterprise advocates and libertarians posited themselves as enslaved victims of the welfare state.[65]

Similarly, rarely did the daily labor within or beyond the household performed by the spouses of the major free-market activists and thinkers (all male with the exception of Rand) figure into the considerations of what made their own projects and wealth possible. Rarely did their vision of freedom include gender emancipation—freedom from dependency on the male head of household, freedom from the expectations of unwaged work in the nuclear family, and freedom from the gendered constraints imposed by a model of the market that made men, but not women, theoretically equal partners in contractual exchange. They opposed the "nanny state"—itself a highly

---

produced category and relation—becomes ontologically prior to history. Useful here is Marx's note on property and capital in his appendix to vol. 1 of *Capital*:

Although the formation of capital and the capitalist mode of production are essentially founded not merely on the abolition of feudal production but also on the *expropriation of the* peasantry, craftsmen and in general of the mode of production based on the *private ownership by the immediate producer of his conditions production*; although, once capitalist production has been introduced, it continues to develop at the same rate as that private property and the mode of production based on it is destroyed, so that those immediate producers are expropriated in the name of the *concentration of capital* (centralization); although the subsequent systematic repetition of the process of *expropriation* in the 'clearing of estates' is in part the act of violence that *inaugurates* the capitalist mode of production—although all this is the case, both the *theory of capitalist production* (political economy, philosophy of law, etc.) and the capitalist himself in *his own mind* is pleased to confuse his mode of property and appropriation, which is based on the expropriation of the immediate producer in its origins, and on the acquisition of the labour of others in its further progress, with its opposite: with a mode of production that presupposes that the *immediate producer privately owns his own conditions of production*.

Marx, *Capital*, 1083 (emphases in the original).

64   Historian David Blight has found that "in 1860, slaves as an asset were worth more than all of America's manufacturing, all of the railroads, all of the productive capacity of the United States put together." The quote from Blight is taken from Coates, "The Case for Reparations." On capitalism and slavery see Eric Williams, *Capitalism and Slavery* (Durham: University of North Carolina Press, 1994 [1944]) and, more recently, Edward Baptist, *The Half Has Never Been Told: Slavery and the Making of American Capitalism* (New York: Basic Books, 2014).

65   See Glickman, *Free Enterprise*, 200–209.

gendered phrase—but not the dramatically gendered economic inequalities that ensured male domination of both the (private) household and the (public) commonwealth.[66] Indeed, for all of the attention given to the individual, it was the heteronormative family that provided a kind of social predictability and stability with well-defined gender roles, work routines, internal hierarchy, and a gendered division of labor, to the degree that Hayek and Friedman had their gender troubles in articulating whether the ontological site of freedom was the individual or the family.[67] Political theorist Wendy Brown has noted that in the work of such economists families are not an aggregate of "generic individuals" but a social configuration that begins with the assumption of a male head of household who interacts as an individual with the market. In the meantime, the labor of the female partner is unwaged labor, yet another form of primitive accumulation.[68] The heteronormative family became a kind of mini state in which women were denied property in themselves, unfree, bound both by material constraints and by what Betty Friedan called in 1963 "the feminine mystique."[69]

Demands for racial, class, and gender justice confronted substantial resistance. Conservative defenders of traditional gender roles responded harshly to Friedan's work and the subsequent founding of the National Organization of Women (NOW). Supporters of Goldwater linked motherhood with morality, the family with tradition, as they sought to undermine Lyndon Johnson and promote a law-and-order program to combat a perceived national decay.[70] Johnson's signature on the 1968 Omnibus Crime Bill and Safe Streets Act did little to assuage concerns. Oliver accused the government of fomenting "internal hate and violence" with unfulfilled promises to certain groups, repeating long-standing conservative complaints about government "favoritism to noisy minorities," as former Republican vice-presidential nominee John Bricker put it.[71] Even worse, claimed Oliver, US administrations now tolerated "elements who ... openly counsel the burning of cities, murder, and other violence." He lashed out at how social meddlers displayed a "'soul brother' forgiveness ...

66 See Stephanie Coontz, *The Way We Never Were: American Families and the Nostalgia Trap*, 2nd ed. (New York: Basic Books, 2016), chap. 6, esp. 160–61.

67 Brown, *Undoing the Demos*, 100; Melinda Cooper, "Neoliberalism's Family Values: Welfare, Human Capital, and Kinship," in Dieter Plehwe, Quinn Slobodian, and Philip Mirowski, eds., *Nine Lives of Neoliberalism* (London: Verso, 2020), 95–119.

68 Brown, *Undoing the Demos*, 100–107; Silvia Federici, *Caliban and the Witch: Women, the Body and Primitive Accumulation* (Brooklyn: Autonomedia, 2004).

69 Coontz, *The Way We Never Were*, 50; Friedan, *The Feminine Mystique* (New York: W.W. Norton, 1963). See also Federici, *Caliban and the Witch*, esp. 61–132.

70 Nickerson, *Mothers of Conservatism*, 162–63.

71 Oliver, *A New Constitution*, 18; for the Bricker quote, see Glickman, *Free Enterprise*, 202.

toward today's destroyers" and thereby ensured the streets would be "filled with fire and blood to an extent which may make the Detroit riots pale by comparison."[72]

> Even at this very moment, plans are being made, men are being trained, and weapons are being stockpiled to utterly burn to the ground most of the major American cities.... Leaders of the revolutionary groups have been given their orders. Some have already made the required tour to obtain first-hand instructions from headquarters of those foreign countries, which specialize in fomenting revolution and which have vowed to destroy the United States. The pattern is familiar ... first mob protests; then, riots; finally, full scale revolution.[73]

This litany of concerns went beyond grievances with Keynesian economics, big government and the threat of communism to instead intersect with a gamut of conservative and reactionary social views about movements demanding racial, gender, and class justice.[74] Oliver's fear of, and focus on, riots and revolutions elided the long history of violence, counterrevolution, and radically unequal social conditions that generated such insurgencies in the first place. His rhetoric drew from an additional strand of libertarianism, one that not only embraced the language of small government and expanding private enterprise but also a racialized and exclusionary program for the protection of individual private property rights in the context of opposition to the civil rights movement. Efforts to address the continuing structural and institutional, as well as personal, violence experienced by African Americans, such as the 1964 Civil Rights Act, led opponents to embrace what historian Nancy MacLean has termed "property supremacy," in which they voiced their opposition to racial equality in the language of the defense of property and effectively, as Martin Luther King observed, valued "property above people."[75] Goldwater's opposition to the Civil Rights Act—centered on his belief that it would "destroy the American way of life, free enterprise, property rights, [and] individual freedom"—captured such libertarian conservatism well.[76] Thus his 1964 bid for the presidency sought, among other things, to end Social Security, to overturn

---

72 Oliver, *A New Constitution*, 18
73 Ibid., 16. For a history of the era, see Perlstein, *Before the Storm*.
74 Stedman Jones, *Masters of the Universe*, 15, and, more broadly, Nancy MacLean, *Democracy in Chains*.
75 For the MacLean phrase and a succinct discussion, see Duggan, *Mean Girl*, 82; King is quoted in Robin D.G. Kelly, "What Kind of Society Values Property over Black Lives?" *New York Times*, June 18, 2020. See also Kevin Kruse, *White Flight: Atlanta and the Making of Modern Conservatism* (Princeton, NJ: Princeton University Press, 2005).
76 Quoted in Glickman, *Free Enterprise*, 201.

the Civil Rights Act through arguments based on property rights and state rights, and to cut back on public education.[77] He lost the election, but the following that coalesced around his movement expanded over the course of the decade, championing a libertarian conservatism.

Goldwater's defeat seemed to confirm for some observers that the system itself was immune to dramatic change. While some preached that a counter-revolution takes time, others pondered if reform, let alone a counterrevolution, was even possible.[78] Michael Oliver was one such skeptic. Mirroring the language of economist James Buchanan, who argued that "no existing political constitution contains sufficient constraints or limits," Oliver suggested that the US constitution had numerous totalitarian clauses, and thus oppression was built into the very foundation of the US government.[79] "The U.S. was never a truly free country," wrote Oliver. "The principles upon which it was founded were never fully sound, for a consistent philosophy upon which to base a free country did not exist in 1776."[80]

The social mobilizations that worried Oliver and the Civil Rights Act which angered conservatives sought to fulfill the promise of freedom and equality that subjugated populations had been denied. Their opponents appropriated the language of "freedom" as a means to segregationist ends: "freedom of association" and "freedom of choice" in cities such as Atlanta, historian Kevin Kruse argues, functioned as new vocabularies of discrimination.[81] With an emphasis on choice, association, and, above all, property, opponents of civil rights amped up their libertarian lexicon, loosening the language of freedom from its traditional moorings, of the oppressed emancipating themselves from those with privileges to defend and hierarchies to maintain, and attaching it to its inverse: a defense of hierarchy and privilege.[82] Those who espoused freedom most loudly expressed limited sympathy for those who had historically been denied it.

In the context of large-scale structural inequality, growing class conflict, and institutional and racialized violence, libertarian exit looked like a new variation on an old theme: white flight. In much the same way that French intellectuals such as Roland Barthes and Michel Foucault pronounced "the death of man" in the 1960s at the very moment "that colonized peoples

---

77   MacLean, *Democracy in Chains*, xxvi.

78   On Buckley and counterrevolution, see ibid., 88.

79   For the Buchanan quote, ibid., xxviii.

80   *The M. Oliver Newsletter*, April 1969, 2.

81   Kruse, *White Flight*, esp. chaps 6 and 9. Kruse quotes Ralph McGill, the editor of the *Atlanta Constitution*: "You may be assured, sir, that the freedom of choice plan is, in fact, neither freedom nor a choice. It is discrimination." Kruse, *White Flight*, 238.

82   Fromm, *Escape from Freedom*, 1; see also Robin, *The Reactionary Mind*.

demand[ed] and appropriate[ed] to themselves the status of men," so did exit strategists pronounce the need to abandon the broader polity—and eventually the republic—at the same time that historically marginalized and oppressed peoples appeared finally, after generations of struggle and exclusion, to have arrived.[83]

Fear and loathing II: Ecology, economy, and crisis

Oliver was not alone. Many of his compatriots shared his concerns, and his book sold well. Published in February of 1968 in arrangement with a press based in Reno, Oliver's manifesto for a new country sold so quickly that a second printing came out in May of that same year. He inserted an updated order form doubling the price (see fig. 1.2). Sales still grew. By the early 1970s, names on a mailing list inquiring about his Minerva project (the subject of the next chapter) totaled fifteen thousand.[84] Fears of collectivism, totalitarianism, and civil strife dovetailed with an array of broader cultural conversations about impending planetary crises, including overpopulation and overconsumption, threats of nuclear annihilation, ecological devastation, and monetary collapse. The impressions and fears these generated fed into a growing movement to envision new ways of living on (or, eventually, off) the planet, some of which resonated with libertarians even if promulgated by authors with different ideological proclivities.[85]

In the late 1960s prognosticators had the Malthusian blues. The decade began with the threat of nuclear bombs, with the struggle over Berlin followed shortly thereafter by the Cuban Missile Crisis. By the end of the decade a

---

83 The quoted passage and discussion of Barthes and Foucault is from Kristin Ross, *Fast Cars, Clean Bodies: Decolonization and the Reordering of French Culture* (Cambridge, MA: MIT Press, 1996), 163. The point is more than just comparative. Foucault in particular would take a neoliberal turn in the late 1970s as he sought out a "Left alternative" to socialism, bureaucracy and revolution. See Mitchell Dean and Daniel Zamora, *The Last Man Takes LSD: Foucault and the End of Revolution* (London: Verso, 2021).

84 Griffith, "Before the Deluge," interview transcript with Morris Davis, 7 (Griffith mistakenly writes one hundred and fifty thousand in his introduction to the interview transcript. See Griffith, "Before the Deluge," 48.)

85 On such new anxieties see the second foreword written for the 1965 edition of Fromm's *Escape from Freedom*. On the implications of catastrophic thinking and anxieties, see Sasha Lilley, "The Apocalyptic Politics of Collapse and Rebirth," in Sasha Lilley, David McNally, Eddie Yuen, and James Davis, *Catastrophism: The Apocalyptic Politics of Collapse and Rebirth* (Oakland: PM Press, 2012), 1–14. For excellent intellectual and cultural histories, see W. Patrick McCray, *The Visioneers: How a Group of Elite Scientists Pursued Space Colonies, Nanotechnologies, and a Limitless Future* (Princeton, NJ: Princeton University Press, 2012); Daniel Deudney, *Dark Skies: Space Expansion, Planetary Geopolitics, and the Ends of Humanity* (New York: Oxford University Press, 2020), esp. chap. 6; and Fabian Locher, "Neo-Malthusianism, Environmentalism, World Fisheries Crisis, and the Global Commons, 1950s–1970s," *Historical Journal* 63, no. 1 (2020): 187–207.

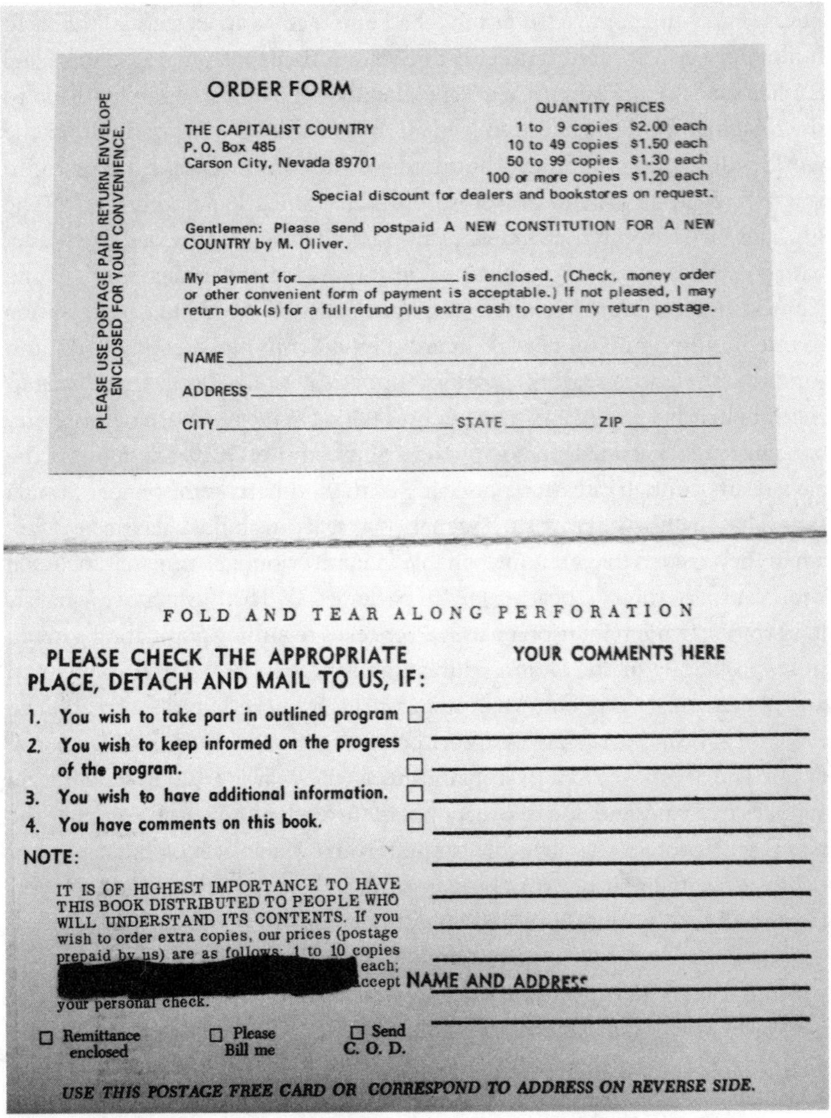

ORDER FORM

PLEASE USE POSTAGE PAID RETURN ENVELOPE
ENCLOSED FOR YOUR CONVENIENCE.

QUANTITY PRICES

THE CAPITALIST COUNTRY
P. O. Box 485
Carson City, Nevada 89701

1 to 9 copies $2.00 each
10 to 49 copies $1.50 each
50 to 99 copies $1.30 each
100 or more copies $1.20 each

Special discount for dealers and bookstores on request.

Gentlemen: Please send postpaid A NEW CONSTITUTION FOR A NEW COUNTRY by M. Oliver.

My payment for_____ is enclosed. (Check, money order or other convenient form of payment is acceptable.) If not pleased, I may return book(s) for a full refund plus extra cash to cover my return postage.

NAME_____

ADDRESS_____

CITY_____ STATE_____ ZIP_____

FOLD AND TEAR ALONG PERFORATION

PLEASE CHECK THE APPROPRIATE PLACE, DETACH AND MAIL TO US, IF:

YOUR COMMENTS HERE

1. You wish to take part in outlined program ☐
2. You wish to keep informed on the progress of the program. ☐
3. You wish to have additional information. ☐
4. You have comments on this book. ☐

NOTE:

IT IS OF HIGHEST IMPORTANCE TO HAVE THIS BOOK DISTRIBUTED TO PEOPLE WHO WILL UNDERSTAND ITS CONTENTS. If you wish to order extra copies, our prices (postage prepaid by us) are as follows: 1 to 10 copies _____ each; _____ accept **NAME AND ADDRESS** your personal check.

☐ Remittance enclosed   ☐ Please Bill me   ☐ Send C. O. D.

USE THIS POSTAGE FREE CARD OR CORRESPOND TO ADDRESS ON REVERSE SIDE.

Fig. 1.2: A new order: Oliver updated the order form in the second printing of his book to capitalize on the success, doubling the price. The old order form (bottom) remained in the book while a new form (top) was printed and glued onto the opposing page.

Oliver, *A New Constitution for a New Country*, 2nd ed. (Reno: Fine Arts Press, 1968). Author's copy.

new bomb—the population bomb—had emerged as an existential threat to humanity, one captured with effect in yet another 1968 phenomenon: Paul Ehrlich and Anne Ehrlich's *The Population Bomb*. The prologue left little to the imagination: "The battle to feed all of humanity is over. In the 1970s the world will undergo famines—hundreds of millions of people are going to starve to death in spite of any crash programs embarked upon now."[86] The Ehrlichs, in an inspired moment of narrative panache, provided the reader with possible scenarios if population control was not undertaken soon. In one, Chinese nuclear bombs land on the West Coast of the US in 1972 resulting in one hundred million deaths. In another, a Communist-controlled Latin America (the entire region!) sparks geopolitical intrigue that then leads to thermonuclear war, fifteen "monster fires raging in the northern hemisphere," and, in an unacknowledged nod to Nevil Shute's novel *On the Beach* (1957), the slow death through radiation poisoning of the southern hemisphere's population. That the Ehrlichs saw such scenarios as real possibilities seemed evident when they argued that an unreasonable scenario would be one that included "monster space ships ... bearing CARE packages."[87] The Ehrlichs were hardly lone voices. Lyndon Johnson included concerns regarding population growth in his 1965 State of the Union address, and the *New York Times* raised it in a 1968 editorial.[88] Pop culture, not surprisingly, picked up the thread. The 1973 film *Soylent Green*, starring Charlton Heston as New York City Detective Frank Thorn, imagined a dystopian future (the year is 2022) in which food supplies had vanished due to overpopulation. Soylent Industries supplies the planet with protein pills allegedly created from ocean plankton but, as Thorn discovers, actually made from human corpses. The film was based on Harry Harrison's 1966 book titled *Make Room! Make Room!*[89]

Inextricable from concerns with overpopulation were those of over-consumption. Indeed, the Ehrlichs' own work had been prompted, in part, by concerns regarding the rise of industrial fishing and the potential deple-tion of ocean stocks due to population increases. Other writers and thinkers

86   Paul Ehrlich and Anne Ehrlich, *The Population Bomb* (New York: Ballantine Books, 1968), prologue.

87   Ibid., 72–80. Nor, evidently, would they accept an idea as outrageous as a more equitable distribution of existing staples or wealth. Demographic anxieties merged with paranoia about "communist" redistribution.

88   Thomas Robertson, *The Malthusian Moment: Global Population Growth and the Birth of American Environmentalism* (New Brunswick, NJ: Rutgers University Press, 2012), 1.

89   Locher, "Neo-Malthusianism," 207; see also Iain McIntyre, "Eco-Death: Catastrophe and Survival in 1960s and 1970s Science Fiction," in Andrew Nette and Iain McIntyre, eds., *Dangerous Visions and New Worlds: Radical Science Fiction, 1950–1985* (Oakland: PM Press, 2021), 98–100.

shared such concerns. The very same year that the Ehrlichs published their book, Garrett Hardin published "The Tragedy of the Commons," an essay that painted an ominous portrait of overexploitation of the world's resources and catapulted the author to fame despite (or perhaps because of) its misinformed ideas about the historical commons. Hardin's essay, published in *Science*, worried about the overuse of commonly held resources in a world of population growth. He propagated a vision of the commons as an unmanaged space upon which a veritable free-for-all regarding resources ensued. In Hardin's rendering, those who held resources in common did not operate with myriad rules, obligations, responsibilities and expectations. Such mythmaking drew from a long tradition of spurious claims about "primitive" agriculture—such as slash-and-burn—and its alleged connections to famine, environmental devastation, and civilizational collapse.[90] Hardin's "glum thesis" came in for substantial critique, not least by British social historian E.P. Thompson, who, with deadpan precision, observed that Hardin presumed that "commoners have no common sense."[91] But perhaps that was the point. Hardin's ideas resonated with the libertarian moment and the age of Rand with its assumptions about commons and commoners and its valorizations of rational choice, utility maximizing individuals, and private property rights in the midst of a global war against a vague but omnipresent communist menace.[92] It also coincided with a broader pessimism—seen in films such as *The Planet of the*

---

90   The best-known recent example of the "ecocide" argument is Jared Diamond, *Collapse: How Societies Choose to Fail or Succeed* (New York: Penguin, 2005). For a robust refutation, see Patricia McAnany and Norman Yoffee, eds., *Questioning Collapse: Human Resilience, Ecological Vulnerability, and the Aftermath of Empire* (New York: Cambridge University Press, 2010). For an essay that shows how ideas about conservation and ecological management could be used in counterinsurgency campaigns and justifications, see Anthony Andersson, "Green Guerrillas and Counterinsurgent Environmentalists in the Petén, Guatemala," *Global Environment: A Journal of Transdisciplinary History* 14, no. 1 (2021): 15–57.

91   E.P. Thompson, "Custom, Law, and Common Right," in Thompson, *Customs in Common: Studies in Traditional Popular Culture* (New York: New Press, 1993), 107. See also Elinor Ostrom, *Governing the Commons: The Evolution of Institutions for Collective Action* (New York: Cambridge University Press, 1990); Carol Rose, "The Comedy of the Commons: Custom, Commerce and Inherently Public Property," in Rose, *Property and Persuasion: Essays on the History, Theory and Rhetoric of Ownership* (London: Routledge, 1995); and Lewis Hyde, *Common as Air: Revolution, Art and Ownership* (New York: Farrar, Straus & Giroux, 2010). A contemporary counter to the Ehrlich and Hardin perspective is Murray Bookchin, *Post-Scarcity Anarchism* (Berkeley, CA: Ramparts Press, 1971).

92   For valuable contrasting perspectives, researched and written in the 1970s, that take up these points see James C. Scott, *The Moral Economy of the Peasant: Rebellion and Subsistence in Southeast Asia* (New Haven, CT: Yale University Press, 1976) and Samuel Popkin, *The Rational Peasant: The Political Economy of Rural Society in Vietnam* (Berkeley: University of California Press, 1979). For an excellent discussion of how Malthusian explanations contain a "common-sense" defense of capitalism, see Eddie Yuen, "The Politics of

Apes (1968) and read in speculative fiction such as Frank Herbert's *Dune* (1965)—regarding the future of the planet, as well as serious efforts at "futurology" to foresee the fate of the planet, such as those offered up by the Club of Rome (founded in 1968).[93] In 1972 the Club of Rome commissioned and published a seminal report entitled *The Limits to Growth* and that same year the United Nations held an international conference on population, followed soon after by international conferences on the environment and food, in the midst of a growing and widespread famine in parts of the globe.

The trinity of overpopulation, overconsumption, and anticommunism merged in the language of carrying capacity. Along with the concept of a "closed ecological system," carrying capacity had been articulated originally by the military in relation to submarine environments and soon expanded to deal with questions of space travel and space colonization, the latter questions first outlined with scientific complexity by Russian inventor Konstantin Tsiolkovsky.[94] Many of the questions related to planetary crisis initially had been asked and investigated by the Office of Naval Research, NASA, and the Atomic Energy Commission. In the wake of Kennedy's 1961 announcement regarding space exploration, federal agencies financed a series of meetings at Princeton University with the participation of the Ecological Society of America. Central issues addressed included how to manage sewage, water, and air in a self-contained and closed ecosystem; how to, in other words, produce what Eugene Odum, one of the lead ecologists at the Princeton conferences, called a "steady state." It did not take long for such ecological perspectives to complete the circuit and be applied to earth itself. The planet was its own ecosystem with its own "carrying capacity"—an ecological cabin, essentially—as Buckminster Fuller, an innovative designer and cartographer, highlighted with the title of his 1969 book, *Operating Manual for Spaceship Earth*.[95]

Subsequent discussions of "carrying capacity" led some, such as Hardin, to espouse what he would call "lifeboat ethics" and argue that not everyone is entitled to an equal share of the planet's resources. Rather, rich nations

Failure Have Failed: The Environmental Movement and Catastrophism," in Lilley et al., *Catastrophism*, 15–43, esp. 29–30.

93 On *Dune*, see Daniel Immerwahr, "Heresies of Dune," *LA Review of Books*, November 19, 2020; on the Club of Rome in the context of astrofuturism, see De Witt Douglas Kilgore, *Astrofuturism: Science, Race, and Visions of Utopia in Space* (Philadelphia: University of Pennsylvania Press, 2003), 154–55.

94 The following is indebted to Peder Anker, "The Ecological Colonization of Space," *Environmental History* 10, no. 2 (April 2005): 239–68; see also Deudney, *Dark Skies*, chaps. 6 and 7 and, for the discussion of Tsiolkovsky, 183.

95 Anker, "The Ecological Colonization of Space," 241–43; Fuller, *Operating Manual for Spaceship Earth* (Carbondale: Southern Illinois University Press, 1969). For a succinct overview of Fuller's work, see Deudney, *Dark Skies*, 192–95.

(the lifeboats) were under siege from poor migrants and refugees (attempting to climb into the lifeboats) and thus some kind of imagined captain needed to make the "harsh" but necessary decisions to deny them entry and, at the same time, ensure rich nations access to the planet's food resources. Hardin portrayed himself as a renegade voice willing to speak the hard-nosed, practical truths that others, particularly the liberal intelligentsia, were too afraid to admit. His calculus, he argued, admitted no "bigotry or chauvinism."[96] Hardin's questionable truths provided further ammunition for nativist and racist discourses that mobilized the language of overbreeding, genetics, and "lebensraum" to defend white, colonial settler property rights. Later in life Hardin would ally himself with anti-immigrant and nativist organizations such as FAIR, as would Anne Ehrlich, coauthor of *The Population Bomb*.

Along with fears of ecological and demographic crisis came fears of monetary collapse. Here too libertarians staked a claim, populating the ranks of the so-called goldbugs. Goldbugs put their faith in metals, and particularly gold, because they feared government intervention in the economy would result in monetary disaster. Central planning was the cause of economic turmoil rather than the solution and paper money generated by the government was its vector. "Paper," Ayn Rand assured the readers of *Atlas Shrugged*, "is a check drawn by legal looters upon an account which is not theirs."[97] Libertarian goldbugs thus turned to hard money—gold.[98] They confronted a small problem however: Franklin D. Roosevelt's 1933 executive order had banned private ownership of gold in order to prevent a run on banks during the Depression.[99] The order required American citizens holding gold to turn it over to the government in exchange for US dollars. The gold collected, housed in Fort Knox, created the largest gold reserve in the world. In 1944, as war persisted in Europe and East Asia, representatives of governments from around the globe met to determine how to restructure and regulate the international monetary system. The aim in part was to mitigate the possibility of subsequent financial crises, of the kind that facilitated the rise of fascism, through regulation of markets and international finance. The agreements, known familiarly as Bretton Woods after the location in New Hampshire

---

96   Garrett Hardin, "Lifeboat Ethics: The Case against Helping the Poor," *Psychology Today* 8 (September 1974): 38–43.

97   Cited from Finn Brunton, *Digital Cash: The Unknown History of the Anarchists, Utopians, and Technologists Who Create Cryptocurrency* (Princeton, NJ: Princeton University Press, 2019), 179.

98   Doherty, *Radicals for Capitalism*, 472–73. On money, metals, and digitalia more broadly, see Brunton, *Digital Cash*.

99   Steve Mariotti, "When Owning Gold Was Illegal in America: And Why It Could Be Again," *Huffington Post* (June 27, 2016).

where delegates met, established the International Monetary Fund, and set controls on speculation and currency values. The agreements determined that gold would serve as the basis for international transactions, despite the efforts of economist John Maynard Keynes, one of the key architects of the postwar world financial order, who had proposed the creation of a new currency (*bancor*) for such transactions. The adoption of gold instead meant that, because the US at the time—due to its relative stability and safety during the war years—held most of the world's gold, countries effectively pegged their currencies to the US dollar. Each dollar was valued at "one thirty-fifth of an ounce of gold."[100] An ounce of gold thus maintained a stable value during the 1940s, 1950s, and 1960s, hovering always around US$35 an ounce, the base value that had been established by the US Treasury under Roosevelt. This began to change in the 1960s. The dollar became increasingly overvalued, and gold supplies in the US depleted as foreign governments redeemed their dollars for gold at the denominated one thirty-fifth of an ounce. As early as 1960 gold sold for $40 an ounce on the London market.[101]

Over the course of the 1960s various US libertarian prognosticators predicted economic crisis and sought, as their foreign counterparts were permitted to do, to convert their dollars into gold. A National Committee to Legalize Gold formed and forged relationships with a number of members of Congress while goldbugs gave lectures to sell-out crowds at Carnegie Hall and audiences of the *Phil Donohue Show*.[102] Popular culture too accentuated the power and value of gold. For Rand's capitalist creators, bars of gold were measures of "objective value."[103] Ian Fleming's *Goldfinger*, originally published in 1959 and with the film version starring Sean Connery released in 1964, had James Bond battle Auric (a gold-derived name) Goldfinger, a man obsessed with the metal and intent on controlling the global gold market by irradiating US gold reserves in Fort Knox.[104] Bond's superior M tasks him with stopping Goldfinger due to gold's importance for British national economic security.[105]

The value of gold increased slightly in 1968 and then began to soar in value, particularly in 1971 when President Richard Nixon abandoned the gold standard, effectively delinking the US dollar from the value of any underlying

---

100   David McNally, *Monsters of the Market: Zombies, Vampires, and Global Capitalism* (Chicago: Haymarket Books, 2011), 158.
101   Leo Panitch and Sam Gindin, *The Making of Global Capitalism: The Political Economy of American Empire* (New York: Verso, 2013), 122–23.
102   Doherty, *Radicals for Capitalism*, 474.
103   Rand, *Atlas Shrugged*, as quoted in Brunton, *Digital Cash*, 180.
104   Fleming's *Goldfinger* (1959) initially bore the title *The Richest Man in the World*.
105   See the discussion in Lisa Funnell and Klaus Dodds, *Geographies, Genders and Geopolitics of James Bond* (London: Palgrave MacMillan, 2017), 139–41.

commodity and allowing it to float freely vis-à-vis other currencies. Purchase and ownership of gold was made legal again in 1974 and an ounce of gold was worth US$183, more than five times its value only seven years prior.[106]

By then, the goldbugs who had stayed the course were rich, including Michael Oliver. He ran a coin business, buying and selling gold and silver coins exempt from the ownership prohibitions, which he advertised with doom-laden portents of a monetary apocalypse.[107] "Have you made your security investment against the coming monetary collapse?" headlined one of his advertisements.[108] Gold, it would seem, truly was a "talisman of fear," as the head of the Bank of England's research department told Fleming's Bond. "Fear, Mr. Bond, takes gold out of circulation and hoards it against the evil day."[109]

A suitable place
One could prepare for that evil day by attending libertarian investment specialist Harry Browne's "How to Survive a Monetary Crisis" seminar. Browne, author of *How You Can Profit from the Coming Devaluation* (1970) and *How I Found Freedom in an Unfree World: A Handbook of Personal Liberty* (1973), distributed to attendees a "Retreater's Bibliography" especially prepared by Atlantis Enterprises Ltd.[110] Prepping for exit meant hoarding gold and buying land, to the degree that mainstream media outlets such as the *Washington Post* reported on "talk of buying gold coins and keeping them in the office safe, of owning a piece of land to retreat to when the trouble starts."[111] Libertarian magazines such as *Innovator*, in which Browne and Oliver both advertised their services, informed worried readers of various escape routes. Contributor Tom Marshall, for example, offered a detailed analysis of forms of exit on offer. Marshall had moved to Southern California in 1963 and, with fellow young libertarians based in Santa Monica and Los Angeles, founded Preform, an organization dedicated to creating a new country run entirely on the principles of laissez-faire capitalism. Although Preform never moved beyond the

106 David McNally, *Monsters of the Market*, 156–59. Values of gold in this paragraph come from Only Gold, accessed April 6, 2017, http://onlygold.com/Info/Historical-Gold-Prices.asp; and The Balance, accessed May 21, 2019, https://www.thebalance.com/gold-price-history-3305646.
107 Individuals were allowed to possess up to $100 worth of gold, and various exceptions were made for rare coins, jewelry, and industrial holdings.
108 *Innovator*, Autumn 1968, 7–4.
109 Ian Fleming, *Goldfinger* (London: Penguin, 2008 [1959]), 75–76.
110 *Innovator*, Autumn 1968, 7–18; Browne, *How I Found Freedom in an Unfree World: A Handbook of Personal Liberty* (n.p., 1973); Doherty, *Radicals for Capitalism*, 473. Browne ran as a candidate for the US presidency on the Libertarian ticket in 1996.
111 Quoted in Andrew St. George, "The Amazing New Country Caper," *Esquire*, February 1975, 60.

planning stages, the members laid out their ideas—including the designing of a voluntary constitutional government named the Association of Free Isles and the formation of a group of Isle Development Corporations in place of local governments to provide some services—in a newsletter and inspired future exiters.[112] Preform also published *Innovator* and began incorporating personal pages in which readers advertised for fellow retreaters, advocated for exit projects, and critiqued others. Marshall, writing under the penname El-Ray, provided a primer to readers on the differences between "retreat" and "self-liberation." A retreater, Marshall wrote, could tolerate the status quo but wanted "survival insurance in case politico-economic conditions worsen[ed]. He acts in response to depredations of State."[113] A self-liberator, in contrast, minimized his "vulnerability to the State so that he need not greatly concern himself with the details of its crimes."[114] Marshall went so far as to categorize and "price" various retreat and exit strategies, from "clandestine urban" and "underground shelter" (forms of retreat) to "sea-mobile nomadic" (a form of self-liberation).[115]

Michael Oliver had little desire to establish a fortified capitalist community in the Rocky Mountains—even if Ayn Rand had envisioned such a space—or pursue a life of urban clandestineness off the grid. Nor was he interested in being a sea nomad. Marshall's retreaters and self-liberators were too timid for Oliver's liking. He wanted to build a self-governing, private territory in which the very promises of libertarian theory could be fulfilled. For this he required a locale not already under the sovereign control of another state or that a state would be willing to sell him for his purposes. In the high era of decolonization—between 1945 and 1960 alone the number of nation-states represented in the United Nations doubled, in large part due to decolonization in Asia, and grew further with decolonization in Africa, the Caribbean and the Pacific over the course of the 1960s—Oliver seemed assured that he could find a government with which to negotiate.[116]

---

112 John Snare, "The Nation Builders' Struggle," *Reason* 4, no. 8 (December 1972): 29–35..

113 El Ray, "Self-Liberation Ways: A Compilation and Evaluation," *Innovator*, Spring 1969, 7–44.

114 Ibid.

115 Ibid. A well-known "sea-mobile nomad" of the era was another Southern Californian libertarian, L. Ron Hubbard of Scientology fame, who spent much of his existence between 1967 and 1975 at sea on one of his four ships.

116 On the pace of decolonization see Jan Jansen and Jürgen Osterhammel, *Decolonization: A Short History*, trans. Jeremiah Riemer (Princeton, NJ: Princeton University Press, 2019), 10–12 and Raymond Craib, "Cartography and Decolonization," in James Akerman, ed., *Decolonizing the Map: Cartography from Colony to Nation* (Chicago: University of Chicago Press, 2017), 11–71

A surprising number of nearly uninhabited, yet quite suitable places for establishing a new country still exist. [...] Many such places are scarcely developed colonies whose governmental or other activities are of little or no concern at all to their "mother" countries. There will be little problem in purchasing the land, or in having the opportunity to conduct affairs on a free enterprise basis from the very beginning. Though the "mother" country may show unwelcomed interest when the new country prospers, time for imposing its edicts will by then have passed. The land will be bought from a colony whose "mother" country is not powerful; yet even the larger colonial powers are diminishing control and interference over lands outside their boundaries, thereby providing a wider choice of locations for the new country.[117]

An optimistic evaluation, as Oliver would repeatedly learn in the coming decade. Between 1968 and 1971 alone, Oliver made exploratory visits to the Bahamas, the Turks and Caicos, Curaçao, Surinam, New Caledonia, French Guiana, Honduras, and the New Hebrides to gather information on climate, taxation, and land quality and to explore the possibilities of building a libertarian country.[118] Such visits revealed the difficulties confronting any would-be world builder looking to land on distant shores. Purchasing land was no problem. But purchasing sovereignty was. And thus his first real effort unfolded on a space long seen as open and as a place of refuge: the ocean.

117   Oliver, *A New Constitution*.
118   Oliver, *Capitalist Country Newsletter* 1, no. 2 (September 1968): 3; Oliver, *The M. Oliver Newsletter* (December 1969/January 1970), 1; *The M. Oliver Newsletter* (April 1970), 1; John Snare, "The Nation Builders' Struggle."

CHAPTER TWO

The Lure of Atlantis

Ocean, Empire, and the Minerva Reefs

VICTOR SERGE, A DISSIDENT REVOLUTIONARY AND FUGITIVE PURSUED BY JOSEF Stalin's agents throughout the 1930s and 1940s, reflected on his continual flight for safety: "For as long as humans have been persecuting and killing one another, hunted men have sought salvation on the seas ... and it is surely fugitives, rather than conquerors, who led the way to new worlds."[1] Yet Serge did not find refuge on the seas. He found it, like comrades Leon Trotsky and Simón Radowitzky, in Mexico. Disillusioned, hounded, perpetually on the run, barely one step ahead of his assassination, Serge had by then reached a pessimistic conclusion: "There are no more islands to discover. . . . The urban labyrinth is a safer bet than any distant archipelago."[2]

By the time Serge died in Mexico, in 1947, it may have been the case that there were no more islands to discover but some humans still sought salvation and new worlds on the sea. The difference is that what were once places of refuge for the hunted, the persecuted, and the subordinated had now become places of exit and investment for the propertied. Michael Oliver's fear of the masses and of social unrest was all too real. He was a haunted man. But, wealthy and well-established in Carson City, he was hardly a hunted man. By 1971, he had spent the better part of three years investigating possible sites for a new country, a place to which he and like-minded allies could escape. From the New Hebrides to Honduras, Costa Rica and Surinam, Oliver and his backers found they could buy land but not independence.[3] Oliver learned a hard fact: few were the spaces available upon which to build a new world. He would need to be more creative and daring in thinking of locations. With

---

1   Serge, *Unforgiving Years*, trans. Richard Greeman (New York: New York Review Books, 2008), 92. Serge completed the book in 1946, a year before his death.

2   Ibid.

3   On the effort in July 1970 to create a libertarian state in New Hebrides, see Anthony van Fossen, *Tax Havens and Sovereignty in the Pacific Islands* (St. Lucia, Queensland: University of Queensland Press, 2012), 110. See also Roy Bongartz, "How to Launch a Country," *Saturday Review of the Society* 1, no. 2 (February 17, 1973): 10. On Oliver's efforts from 1975 to 1980 to create a libertarian enclave in the New Hebrides, see chapter four.

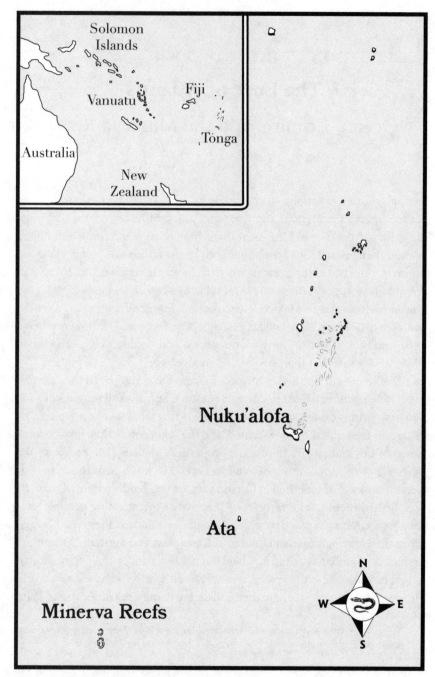

Fig. 2.1. Map of Tonga, with shading to denote reefs.
Map by John Wyatt Greenlee.

substantial backing from a group of investors, Oliver founded his Ocean Life Research Foundation. The Republic of Minerva was underway. A distant archipelago beckoned.

Exit geographies

That oceans and islands have figured prominently in exit efforts should come as no surprise. Both have long constituted spaces upon which to situate arguments and plot fantasies about the market, exchange, politics, and society. It was under the ocean (not upon it) that Captain Nemo, antihero of Jules Verne's *Twenty Thousand Leagues under the Sea*, sought to escape the tyranny of nation-states. On the ocean, as much as under it, proved similarly appealing. In one of his less well-known works, *The Self-Propelled Island*, Verne narrated the geography of the island Pacific by using as his primary narrative device a large, artificial floating island inhabited solely by bickering billionaires, a prescient vision of twenty-first-century seasteading.[4] The high seas were and are still frequently invoked, even if mistakenly, as spaces of nonsovereignty and lawlessness, the last great frontier for those seeking freedom from the state, whether it be for purposes of profit-making through illegal fishing and exploitation of labor or in order to experiment with new forms of political and social life.[5]

But it is "remote" and small islands that, more than any other spatial form, have constituted the locus for imaginative experiments in political, legal, and social engineering, from Francis Bacon's *New Atlantis* and Thomas More's *Utopia* to H.G. Wells's *The Island of Dr. Moreau* and William Golding's *Lord of the Flies*. For one thing, such islands seem to be clearly defined, circumscribed territorial entities and thus "natural geographic model[s] for the classic

4   Verne, *The Self-Propelled Island*, trans. Marie-Thérèse Noiset (Lincoln: University of Nebraska Press, 2015 [1895]).
5   William Langewiesche, *The Outlaw Sea: A World of Freedom, Chaos, and Crime* (North Point Press, 2005); Ian Urbina, *The Outlaw Ocean: Journeys Across the Last Untamed Frontier* (New York: Knopf, 2019). More broadly see Philip Steinberg, *The Social Construction of the Ocean* (Cambridge: Cambridge University Press, 2001); Helen Rozwadowski, *Fathoming the Ocean: The Discovery and Exploration of the Deep Sea* (Cambridge, MA: Belknap Press, 2005); Liam Campling and Alejandro Colás, *Capitalism and the Sea: The Maritime Factor in the Making of the Modern World* (London: Verso, 2021); Peter Linebaugh and Marcus Rediker, *The Many-Headed Hydra: Sailors, Slaves, Commoners and the Hidden History of the Revolutionary Atlantic* (Boston: Beacon Press, 2000); Epeli Hau'ofa, *We Are the Ocean: Selected Writings* (Honolulu: University of Hawai'i Press); Lauren Benton, *The Search for Sovereignty: Law and Geography in European Empires, 1400–1900* (Cambridge: Cambridge University Press, 2010); and Philip E. Steinberg, Elizabeth Nyman, and Mauro J. Caraccioli, "Atlas Swam: Freedom, Capital, and Floating Sovereignties in the Seasteading Vision," *Antipode* 44, no. 4 (September 2012): 1532–50.

territorial conception of a state."⁶ In addition, islands have the advantage of evoking laboratory-like conditions under which great natural, political and social experiments can unfold without the noise of contingency or the burden of history or the taint of politics. Given that one of classical liberalism's founding myths grew out of the fertile soil of a distant archipelago, it is not surprising how much islands figure in libertarian exit fantasies.⁷ Alexander Selkirk's seven-year struggle as a castaway isolated on Juan Fernández off the coast of Chile served as the historical basis for Daniel Defoe's *Robinson Crusoe*, a novel which had the effect of turning remote islands into an overdetermined geographic form upon which to stage the performance of individualism.⁸ The island became, in effect, an ideal libertarian political ecology: a space upon which the drama of individualism, of man alone, could be staged.

In this sense islands are not distant outposts, temporally and spatially removed from the centers of modernity and power, but perhaps precisely the opposite: spaces of hyperpresent experimentation and upon which the most enduring myth of modern times—that the sovereign individual and competition are the foundations of social relations—has been naturalized.⁹

---

6   Sina Najafi and Christina Duffy Burnett, "Islands and the Law: An Interview with Christina Duffy Burnett," *Cabinet* 38 (Summer 2010): 60–66.

7   On Crusoe, see especially James Dunkerley, *Crusoe and His Consequences* (New York: OR Books, 2019); Stephen Hymer, "Robinson Crusoe and the Secret of Primitive Accumulation," *Monthly Review Press* 63, no. 4 (September 2011); Martin Green, *Dreams of Adventure, Deeds of Empire* (New York: Basic Books, 1979); and Campling and Colás, *Capitalism and the Sea*, chap. 6; and, particularly insightful in how she links Crusoe to Jules Verne and science fiction, Lydia H. Liu, "Robinson Crusoe's Earthenware Pot," *Critical Inquiry* 25, no. 4 (Summer 1999), 728–57.

8   Inspired by Defoe and Adam Smith, Reverend Joseph Townsend, in his 1786 *Dissertation on the Poor Laws*, used those very same islands to turn social form into natural law, arguing that the islands were a laboratory in which one could see at work the natural operations of power. From Aristotle to Hobbes to Smith, human community meant some form of law and government but, for Townsend, as Karl Polanyi argues, "on the island of Juan Fernandez there was neither government nor law; and yet there was balance between goats and dogs." Polanyi continues:

>   No government was needed to maintain this balance; it was restored by the pangs of hunger on the one hand, the scarcity of food on the other. Hobbes had argued the need for a despot because men were like beasts; Townsend insisted that they *were* actually beasts and that, precisely for that reason, only a minimum of government was required. From this novel point of view, a free society could be regarded as consisting of two races: property-owners and laborers. The number of the latter was limited by the amount of food; and *as long as property was safe*, hunger would drive them to work. No magistrate was necessary, for hunger was a better disciplinarian than the magistrate.

Polanyi, *The Great Transformation: The Political and Economic Origins of Our Time* (Boston: Beacon Press, 2001 [1944]), 119–20.

9   Daniel Immerwahr has suggested that until the mid-twentieth century fictional islands were "godforsaken outskirts of civilization." Immerwahr, *How to Hide an Empire: A*

The marketplace, a very real and delimited space, slowly became an abstract category ("the market") and then finally a naturalized principle ("human nature") which then was used to explain the social processes out of which it had itself emerged, and perhaps nowhere was "the market" more frequently and literally naturalized than on islands.[10] It is telling that the geographic counterpoint to the temperate island of fierce competition was the vast Siberian tundra of cooperation, where Russian anarchist Peter Kropotkin observed that, *pace* Darwin, species survival depended on cooperation and mutual aid.[11]

Islands and ocean spaces have been attractive not only because they are conceived of as laboratory spaces but also because they are very often sites of nonsovereign and ambiguous political forms.[12] As legal historian Christina Duffy Burnett has argued, with specific attention to US empire and the insular

---

History of the Greater United States (New York: Farrar, Straus & Giroux, 2019), 340. An alternative reading would suggest they were the beating heart of the hyperpresent and the loci for experiments in imagining the future. I use "hyperpresent" here because, while islands may not have been godforsaken and marginal sites, neither were the experiments undertaken on them necessarily that innovative. Many of the experiments more closely resemble the realist dystopias of J.G. Ballard (especially in his novels *Cocaine Nights* and *Super-Cannes*). On islands as laboratories see Elizabeth DeLoughrey, *Routes and Roots: Navigating Caribbean and Pacific Island Literatures* (Honolulu: University of Hawai'i Press, 2007), 8–15; Ernesto Bassi, "Small Islands in a Geopolitically Unstable Caribbean World," *Oxford Research Encyclopedia: Latin American History* (March 2019); Steinberg et al., "Atlas Swam"; on islands as a narrative genre, see Ralph Crane and Lisa Fletcher, *Island Genres, Genre Islands: Conceptualisation and Representation in Popular Fiction* (London: Rowman & Littlefield, 2017) and, with specific reference to Robinson Crusoe-style narratives located in the Pacific, Ian Kinane, *Theorising Literary Islands: The Island Trope in Contemporary Robinsonade Narratives* (London: Rowman & Littlefield, 2017).

10 Jean-Cristophe Agnew, *Worlds Apart: The Market and the Theater in Anglo-American Thought* (Cambridge: Cambridge University Press, 1988), esp. introduction and chapter one; Peter James Hudson, "On the History and Historiography of Banking in the Caribbean," *Small Axe* 18, no. 1 (March 2014): 22–37. Defoe, as Raymond Williams observes, "for all his close and specialised observation of what was happening in the fields and markets [of England and Wales], did not, in his novels, consider their underlying social reality" but instead composed fictional worlds of "isolated individuals" in isolated places to simplify apprehension of the workings of improvement and market. Williams, *The Country and the City* (Oxford: Oxford University Press, 1973 [1975]), 62.

11 Peter Kropotkin, *Mutual Aid: A Factor in Evolution* (Mineola, NY: Dover Books, 2006 [1902]). For an excellent intellectual history of why and how Kropotkin's and Darwin's ideas took root in different geographic contexts, see Daniel Todes, *Darwin without Malthus: The Struggle for Existence in Russian Evolutionary Thought* (New York: Oxford University Press, 1989).

12 See Yarimar Bonilla, *Non-Sovereign Futures: French Caribbean Politics in the Wake of Disenchantment* (Chicago: University of Chicago Press, 2015); Tracey Banivanua Mar, *Decolonisation and the Pacific: Indigenous Globalisation and the Ends of Empire* (Cambridge: Cambridge University Press, 2016), 39–41; Stewart Firth, "Sovereignty and Independence in the Contemporary Pacific," *The Contemporary Pacific* 1, no. 1/2 (Spring/Fall 1989): 75–96; Daniel Immerwahr, *How to Hide an Empire: A History of the Greater United States* (New York: Farrar, Straus & Giroux, 2019).

cases resulting from the Spanish-Cuban-American War of 1898, "Islands serve as the site for legal experimentation and for some questionable legal innovations."[13] Of equal significance, in the post–World War II world many island territories were often the last to decolonize. Much of the Pacific remained under colonial control into the 1970s and a significant portion still exists somewhere between dependence and independence. Such political opacity and geopolitical vulnerability made them attractive locations for those looking to get some territorial purchase on their libertarian dreams.

The lure of Atlantis

Settling on the ocean is a difficult business. Take the case of Leicester Hemingway. In 1964, Hemingway parked an eight-by-thirty-foot bamboo raft, anchored to an old Ford engine block buried in the sand, eight miles off of the coast of Bluefields, Jamaica.[14] Because the raft sat anchored beyond the three-mile coastal limit and a hundred-fathom curve, Hemingway, with a bottle of Seagram's 7 in hand, could proclaim the birth of the independent Republic of New Atlantis on July 4, 1964.[15] The date of independence was purposeful: Hemingway had little desire to escape the US or renounce his citizenship. Indeed, having encouraged birds to defecate on one end of the raft, he ceded that portion of it to the US under the criteria established in the 1856 Guano Islands Act, which allowed US citizens, on behalf of the US, to claim possession of unoccupied islands, rocks, or keys that contained guano.[16] The other half of the raft he intended as his own private country.

Hemingway was nothing if not earnest. His experiment may have attracted bemused attention, but he took it quite seriously. Over the course of two years he drafted a constitution (modeled closely on that of the United

13 Duffy Burnett as quoted in Najafi and Burnett, "Islands and the Law." See also Christina Duffy Burnett, "The Edges of Empire and the Limits of Sovereignty: American Guano Islands," *American Quarterly* 57, no. 3 (September 2005); Duffy Burnett and Burke Marshall, eds., *Foreign in a Domestic Sense: Puerto Rico, American Expansion, and the Constitution* (Durham, NC: Duke University Press, 2001); and Immerwahr, *How to Hide an Empire*.

14 The details of the venture can be found in the Leicester Hemingway New Atlantis collection [hereafter LHNA], Harry Ransom Humanities Center, University of Texas at Austin. For a brief overview, see Andy Warner and Sofia Louise Dam, *This Land Is My Land: A Graphic History of Big Dreams, Micronations, and Other Self-Made States* (Chronicle Books, 2019), 48–51.

15 Don Bevona, "Rise of a New Republic: New Atlantis Hq. for Research," *New York Herald Tribune* (September 13, 1964), in folder 1.1, LHNA. For the bottle of Seagram's 7, see "World's smallest, newest country," *Printers' Ink* (September 25, 1964), 50, in folder 1.1, LHNA.

16 Bevona, "Rise of a New Republic." On the Guano Islands Act of 1856 see Duffy Burnett, "The Edges of Empire and the Limits of Sovereignty," and Najafi and Burnett, "Islands and the Law."

States), created an array of postage stamps, developed a currency (the Scruple, valued at fifty cents US but also imbued with "moral worth"), declared Lady Bird Johnson a member of his "Order of the Golden Sands," and raised his two young daughters on the platform with his wife, along with a public relations specialist and his assistant.[17] The experiment ended when a hurricane destroyed the raft in 1966, much to the chagrin of Hemingway, who only months earlier had lamented "the possibility of ending as a flounder rather than a founder."[18] He remained thus forever in the shadow of his older brother, Ernest.

A few years after New Atlantis sank, a new Atlantis arose, this one the brainchild of pharmaceutical engineer Werner Stiefel. Writing under the pseudonym Warner K. Stevens, Stiefel released a short book in 1968 entitled *The Story of Operation Atlantis*. The book, described by one of Stiefel's former acolytes as "John Galt's speech in *Atlas Shrugged* after a good editor got hold of it and deleted the preachy mumbo-jumbo," narrated the author's ongoing efforts to found a country beyond the bounds of existing nation-states.[19] Forty-seven at the time, Stiefel shared much in common with Michael Oliver: he and his family had suffered Nazi persecution and been forced to flee Germany; he feared a "worldwide drift toward statism"; he found inspiration in Ayn Rand; and he sought to exit the nation-state.[20] And like Oliver, Stiefel did not oppose government per se but rather feared the power of the bureaucratic and regulatory state and the democratic masses upon whom it relied for support.[21] "I witnessed within my lifetime the complete demonetization of our currency, the growth of rampant government intervention in our once free economy, the monstrous sequelae of the antitrust movement, the birth of social security and the welfare state, the massive conscription of our young men to fight in the far corners of the globe for ill-defined reasons, the cancerous growth of

---

17   Bevona, "Rise of a New Republic." For the currency, folder 1.3, LHNA; for the flag, folder 1.4, LHNA; and for the constitution, folder 1.5, LHNA.

18   Hemingway to Lady Mary [Hirth], undated, ca. 1966, folder 1.2, LHNA. Hirth was a librarian in the University of Texas system who put together an exhibit of the New Atlantis project with the New Atlantis flag, stamps, photographs, and currency on display. Her labor is the reason the New Atlantis materials are now archived at the Harry Ransom Humanities Center at the University of Texas in Austin.

19   Halliday, "Operation Atlantis and the Radical Libertarian Alliance: Observations of a Fly on the Wall," *Formulations* 30 (Summer 2002), 24–31, 36.

20   Warren K. Stevens, *The Story of Operation Atlantis* (Saugerties, NY: Atlantis Publishing Co., 1968), 1. Stevens was a pen-name used by Stiefel. See also Halliday, "Operation Atlantis." For a good introduction to Stiefel's project see Isabelle Simpson, "Operation Atlantis: A Case Study in Libertarian Island Micronationality," *Shima: The International Journal of Research into Island Cultures* 10, no. 2 (2016): 18–35.

21   Stevens, *The Story*, 2. "We will have 'government' in Atlantis," he wrote. "The explanation is that we use the word in the sense of a 'spokesman for those who voluntarily and individually consent to be spoken for.'"

the coercive labor movement, the emergence of the Big Brother consumer protection movement," or, in short, what he summarized as the "abandonment of the very heritage of freedom that caused America to become great."[22]

What was to be done? According to Stiefel, neither democratic practice nor emigration provided much of a solution. Exit was the only option, but the question still remained: where?

> A South Sea island? A remote vastness in the Canadian north? A life of a rootless nomad, self-sufficient and aloof? This alternative is both admirable and ideologically pure. For the flint-hearted few, withdrawal is without doubt a satisfying and rationally consistent solution. The American pioneers did it, and built the world's greatest nation in the process. Today, however, no unclaimed territory is left and there is no hope of avoiding the heavy hand of the state over the long pull. Let a remote withdrawal community ever begin to thrive and we can count on Attila's agents appearing on dogsled, Form 1040 in one hand and a tommy-gun in the other.[23]

Stiefel's solution? "The only free places left on the earth are the high seas."[24] Enter Operation Atlantis. It had three stages. The first involved Stiefel's purchase of the Sawyerkill Motel, off of Interstate 87 in the upstate New York town of Saugerties, where libertarians could gather and forge a community. Stiefel advertised for "immigrants" to his libertarian motel colony although one could easily have mistaken them for renters: they paid Stiefel $90 per month for a room, in which Stiefel installed a small refrigerator and electric range, and in exchange received fresh sheets and towels each week.[25] On Sundays the motel hosted Freedom Forums where nearby libertarians, as well as recently arrived "immigrants," gathered and discussed various topics related to libertarianism. Libertarians of various perspectives on the east coast—such as the Maryland contingent of the Society for Rational Individualism—would come some distance in order to attend the forums which occasionally included such high-profile figures as anarcho-capitalist Murray Rothbard or MIT physics student Erwin Strauss, who would go on to write the exit bible *How to Start Your Own Country*.[26]

---

22 Ibid., 3.
23 Ibid., 8.
24 Ibid., 8.
25 Halliday, "Operation Atlantis."
26 Strauss, *How to Start Your Own Country* (Boulder, CO: Paladin Press, 1999 [1984]). Strauss's book provides an encyclopedic, broad but thin, overview of various micronation and exit projects.

The second stage of the Atlantis project involved the acquisition of an ocean vessel that would function as an independent nation in international waters until (stage three) the construction of an artificial island could be completed. Each of these stages was designed to make a profit for the initial investors and to be self-supporting. By establishing Atlantis as a proprietary community inhabited only by individuals who voluntarily agreed to the terms of their lease contracts, Stiefel endowed it with a limited government that did not violate nonaggression principles, thereby making Atlantis acceptable to both limited-government libertarians and anarcho-libertarians.[27]

Atlantis did not happen. After two years spent building a ship inside of a twenty-three-foot-high geodesic dome—inspired by architect and engineer Buckminster Fuller, who himself was attempting to build a floating city in Tokyo Bay—the Atlanteans prepared to set off down the Hudson River for the Bahamas in 1971. Upon launching, the ship capsized and caught fire. After righting and repairing the vessel, they set off again and made it to the Bahamas, at which point a hurricane sank the ill-fated ship.

Dreams must perish

Whether Stiefel's Atlantis had any chance of success even if the vessel had survived is uncertain. When he designed his Atlantis project, he sought to ensure that the artificial island passed muster with the US government, wanting it constructed "as close to the shores of the U.S. as international law will permit and Uncle Sam will tolerate."[28] But Uncle Sam proved intolerant. Stiefel and other libertarian exiters turned to the high seas just as the seas and the seabeds became new areas of high priority among states as places for exploration and colonization in the wake of World War II and as battlegrounds in the Cold War. The US government, for example, dedicated significant amounts of federal monies to marine science research centers such as Scripps and Woods Hole; oceanography and marine engineering boomed; and the US military devoted increasing attention to deep ocean colonization.[29] In 1964 the navy launched its Sealab program, designed to explore the depths to which "aquanauts" could go and how in such conditions they might live.[30]

27   See Halliday, "Operation Atlantis."
28   Ibid.
29   Locher, "Neo-Malthusianism," 195.
30   Mindy Weisberger, "U.S. Navy's 'Aquanauts' Tested the Boundaries of Deep Diving. It Ended in Tragedy," *Live Science* (February 12, 2019); Rachel Squire, "Seabeds. Sub-marine Territory: Living and Working on the Seafloor During the Sealab II Experiment," in Kimberley Peters, Philip Steinberg, and Elaine Stratford, eds., *Territory Beyond Terra* (London: Rowman & Littlefield, 2018), 221–36.

Fantasies of a new Atlantis sprouting on the seabed proliferated. Along with Sealab a host of underwater habitats appeared, some fostered by governments, others the result of collaborations with well-known figures such as Jacques Cousteau and marine biologist Sylvia Earle.[31] Futurist Alvin Toffler, in his 1970 bestseller *Future Shock*, forecast the coming of a "new Atlantis" and an approaching life aquatic. "The opening of the sea may also bring with it a new frontier spirit," wrote Toffler, "a way of life that offers adventure, danger, quick riches or fame to the initial explorers. Later, as man begins to colonize the continental shelves, and perhaps even the deeper reaches, the pioneers may well be followed by settlers who build artificial cities beneath the waves—work cities, science cities, medical cities, and play cities, complete with hospitals, hotels and homes."[32]

Less hyperbolic in its oratory and more sober in its conclusions was the 1969 report assembled by the Stratton Commission, which included a range of experts and heads of industries, from professors of oceanography and law to the director of Standard Oil, the undersecretary of the navy, and North Carolina's commissioner of fisheries. Their report, *Our Nation and the Sea*, set out a range of suggestions for a "national ocean program" that would address how the US would use the resources of the sea in the future, particularly given concerns regarding population pressures and a potential dearth of foodstuffs. While the committee recommended procedures for exploitation of ocean resources—and even, presciently, foresaw the possibilities of privately operated "seasteads" in coastal waters—they also recommended proceeding with caution: while they recognized the economic possibilities, they also expressed concern over possible negative consequences. "Today," they wrote, "man's damage to the environment too often is ignored because of immediate economic advantage. To maximize the present economy at the expense of the future is to perpetuate the pattern of previous generations, whose sins against the planet we have inherited."[33] The report concluded by recommending the creation of a National Oceanic and Atmospheric Agency, a request which the administration of US President Richard Nixon fulfilled in 1970.[34]

31   See Chris Michael, "What Lies Beneath: Our Love Affair with Living Underwater," *Guardian*, June 8, 2020.

32   Alvin Toffler, *Future Shock* (New York: Random House, 1970), 169.

33   The Commission on Marine Science, Engineering and Resources, *Our Nation and the Sea: A Plan for National Action* (Washington, DC: US Government Printing Office, 1969), 1; for seasteads, see ibid., 72.

34   The Commission on Marine Science, *Our Nation and the Sea*, 230–50; Locher, "Neo-Malthusianism," 195–96. On the laws of the sea, see United States Department of State, Bureau of Intelligence and Research, Office of the Geographer, "National Claims to Maritime Jurisdiction," Limits in the Seas, no. 36, 5th Revision (Washington, DC,

Simultaneous with the Stratton Commission, maritime expert Elisabeth Mann Borgese, working with the Club of Rome and arguing against the exclusionary Malthusianism that characterized Garrett Hardin's "Tragedy of the Commons," began drafting principles outlining the need to understand the ocean as part of a common heritage of mankind, a space of interdependence, and a resource that belonged equally to all sovereign entities, rich and poor alike.[35]

But what all this interest meant was increased attention—unwanted attention—to surreptitious efforts to colonize or otherwise claim ocean spaces. As government interest grew, legal uncertainties proliferated regarding the status of seamounts and reefs, the continental shelf, and the questions of national jurisdiction over resources based on distance from shore or depth to the seabed. A year after the release of *Our Nation and the Sea*, a district court issued a verdict in a complicated case regarding private seasteads that had been winding its way through the courts for five years. The case, which began in 1965, involved Louis M. Ray, president of Acme General Contractors, Inc., who had sought to dredge the area around the Long and Triumph reefs, east of Homestead, Florida, in order to build a twenty-acre resort. His efforts foundered when US courts and the US Army Corps of Engineers found his proposal in violation of the Outer Continental Shelf Lands Act.[36] The OCSLA resulted from efforts by governments to assert rights beyond the traditional three-nautical-mile limit, arguing that states had a right to protect natural, even if oceanic, resources. In 1945, for example, US President Harry S. Truman, in response to concerns over oil shortages during the war, issued an executive order asserting the rights of the US government to the mineral resources of the continental shelf of the contiguous US.[37] Based on criteria that established the continental shelf as "the natural zone that gently sloped off the shore of continents up to a depth of 100 fathoms, or 600 feet," in one move Truman had expanded the

---

1985). Between 1970 and 1985, some twenty-seven million square nautical miles came under coastal state jurisdiction. See Frederick Fales Monroe, "Coastal State Control and Global Ocean Harvest," unpublished PhD dissertation, School of International Service, American University, 1990, 138.

35 For a retrospective overview, see Elisabeth Mann Borgese, *The Oceanic Circle: Governing the Seas as a Global Resource* (Tokyo: United Nations University Press, 1998). For a valuable discussion, see R.S. Deese, *Climate Change and the Future of Democracy* (Cham, Switzerland: Springer, 2019), esp. chap. 4.

36 On Louis Ray's project, see Samuel Pyeatt Menefee, "Republics of the Reefs: Nation-Building on the Continental Shelf and in the World's Oceans," *California Western International Law Journal* 25 (1994): 81–111, esp. 85–95.

37 See Dan Margolies, "Jurisdiction in Offshore Submerged Lands and the Significance of the Truman Proclamation in Postwar U.S. Foreign Policy," *Diplomatic History* 44, no. 3 (June 2020): 447–65; and Megan Black, *The Global Interior: Mineral Frontiers and American Power* (Cambridge, MA: Harvard University Press, 2018), 148.

country's territorial sovereignty by some 760,000 square miles, an expansion rivaled only by the Louisiana Purchase more than a century prior.[38] Then in 1953 the US Congress dramatically modified what counted as the continental shelf, shifting the criteria from depth to distance such that three miles from the shoreline would come under coastal state jurisdiction and three to ten miles became the purview of the federal government.[39]

For Ray and his Acme corporation these questions regarding where jurisdiction ended proved paramount. The issue was complicated further by the fact that the US Department of the Interior, the US Department of State, the Florida state government, and the US Army Corps of Engineers offered varying opinions on the status of the reefs and jurisdiction.[40] The laws regarding submerged lands and the continental shelf provided avenues for governments to assert sovereignty over areas that fell beyond the coastal zone of political jurisdiction based on at least two criteria: the right of the secretary of the army to prevent the building of "artificial islands and fixed structures" that could obstruct navigation and the right of the federal government to assert jurisdiction over the seabed and subsoil of its continental shelf in order to protect natural resources for possible exploration and exploitation.[41] This was the position ultimately taken by the US government. In 1970, a district court verdict found on behalf of the government's position and condemned Acme's plans. The court concluded its verdict with a revealing flourish: "The dreams of the separate groups for a new nation must perish, like the lost continent 'Atlantis,' beneath the waves and waters of the sea which constantly submerge the reefs."[42]

Be that as it may, Michael Oliver was just getting started. The ocean was vast.

Revelation

In August 1971, Oliver began the arduous process of building an island in the southwest Pacific. That month several of the project's backers arrived at the Minerva Reefs. A small crew erected two mounds on the reefs, made from coral wrapped in chicken wire and encased in concrete, upon which they then constructed vertical markers, rising to a height of some twenty-six feet,

---

38   Black, *The Global Interior*, 148–49 and, for the cited passage, 155.
39   Ibid., 155.
40   Menefee, "Republics of the Reefs," 87–88.
41   Ibid., 89.
42   Ibid., 94. The case was United States v. Ray, 423 F.2d 16, 18 (5th Cir. 1970).

at the top of which they posted a flag representing the Republic of Minerva.[43] These were to be the initial steps that would lay the groundwork for the creation of an expanding, artificial island upon which would then emerge a small independent country, with upwards of thirty thousand residents who would purchase settlement rights, operating as an Offshore Financial Center and earning income from the sale of Flags of Convenience.[44] With a base in Fiji, Oliver oversaw operations, including the hiring of a dredging vessel with costs estimated at $10,000 per week to create one acre of land.

Oliver had the funds. To help raise money for the venture, he had created what he called the Ocean Life Research Foundation, mobilizing the language of science to burnish the project's attractiveness. The foundation drew numerous investors, close to two thousand by 1971, according to some estimates.[45] A number of notable names appeared in support. There was, most prominently, Willard Garvey, a wheat magnate and housing entrepreneur based in Wichita, Kansas. After inheriting his father's business, he expanded into grain elevators and oil. He was also founder and president of Builders, Inc., which sought through its World Homes initiative to make homeownership affordable to the poor of Latin America and Southeast Asia. He financed World Homes in part by reaping the benefits of the policies of the Eisenhower administration, garnering some US$15 million per year in subsidies from the US government to grow (and, at times, not grow) and store grain.[46] In 1969 Garvey came across Oliver's *A New Constitution for a New Country*. He was captivated, in part because he shared Oliver's concerns and was a committed anticommunist. Garvey had once floated an idea directly to CIA director Allan Dulles. To counter Nikita Khrushchev's promise to make every man a communist, Garvey wrote, one must consider a kind of "subversion in reverse": make every man a capitalist.[47] The suggestion was born of both ideology and the opportunity for profit: For Garvey, to make every man a capitalist meant to "make every man a property owner."[48]

---

43 Lawrence A. Horn, "To Be or Not to Be: The Republic of Minerva—Nation Founding by Individuals," *Columbia Journal of Transnational Law* 12, no. 3 (1973): 520–56, as cited in Menefee, "Republics of the Reefs," 96.

44 Van Fossen, *Tax Havens and Sovereignty*, 112.

45 For sales figures, see ibid., 110

46 See Helen Gyger, *Improvised Cities: Architecture, Urbanization and Innovation in Peru* (Pittsburgh: University of Pittsburgh Press, 2019).

47 Enclosure in Willard Garvey to Allan W. Dulles, Central Intelligence Agency, September 5, 1958, accessed February 15, 2020, https://ia800803.us.archive.org/34/items/CIA-RDP80B01676R003800070016-9/CIA-RDP80B01676R003800070016-9.pdf.

48 Ibid.

In backing the Ocean Life Research Foundation, Garvey enlisted the aid of powerful friends, including Illinois industrialist and horologist Seth Atwood and famed investor John Templeton, who used his wealth to found the Templeton Foundation and promote pseudoscientific theories such as positive psychology and universal love.[49] Garvey regaled the two men with the possibilities of Oliverian exit while they gathered together in Lima, Peru, for a World Homes executive meeting.[50] Persuaded, they soon invested in Oliver's foundation, contributing $100,000 each toward the new country project. Other prominent figures, who would repeatedly appear—hazy but permanent presences—in the orbit of Oliver and his projects, soon signed on to the venture. These included Richard King, who was Australian by birth but by 1971 a naturalized US citizen living in the UK and who had already sought to create a floating city in the North Sea; and Harry Schultz, an internationally renowned investment specialist whose newsletter counted Margaret Thatcher among its readers.[51] Also investing were two men who would take the initiative to journey to the reefs and assert possession: Thurlow "Tad" Weed, a former placekicker on the undefeated 1954 Ohio State University football team and inventor of the WEED tennis racket, and ex-army pilot and businessman Robert Marks.[52]

Notably, none of the investors were from the region. The reefs had been identified as a suitable site after years of obstacles to developing on

---

49   Barbara Ehrenreich, "John Templeton's Universe," *The Nation* (October 22, 2007).

50   Maura McEnaney, *Willard Garvey: An Epic Life* (Oakland: Liberty Tree Press, 2013), 187–88.

51   See van Fossen, *Tax Havens and Sovereignty*, 112. King's relationship with Oliver would persist over the decade as he also became involved in a Vietnamese refugee resettlement scheme in the New Hebrides. See Gordon Haines, "Na-Griamel: Vietnamese Refugees Summary of Events," February 12, 1979, in Vietnamese Refugee Resettlement File, Gordon Haines Papers, National Archive of Vanuatu. King's involvement in the Minerva project is also mentioned by Edwin Noack, a planner, in File 243/1 Mr Edwin Noack, January 2, 1979, Vietnamese Refugee Resettlement Plan Folder, Gordon Haines Papers, National Archives of Vanuatu.

52   On Weed, see Griffith interview with Marvin Olsen (October 17, 1972), in Griffith, "Before the Deluge," Olsen transcript, 18; and "South Sea Reef Proclaimed a Republic by 3 Americans," *New York Times*, January 30, 1972, 11. The article is very brief and misnames Michael Oliver as "Mark Oliver." Marks was a World War II Army Air Corps pilot and, after the war, founded of a home improvement business called Build N' Save, a kind of 1960s precursor to Home Depot and Lowe's. His building skills meant he was one of the few investors in Minerva who actually participated in the construction on the reef. See the obituary for Robert Edwin Marks, *Long Beach Press Telegram*, November 14, 2009. Additional members of the Ocean Life Research Foundation may have included Charles F. and David Williams of New York and Claude Van Nerum of the New Hebrides. See James Hilton Mair, "Report on the Possible Smuggling Operations and Arms Shipment through Fiji," General Information File, Gordon Haines Archive, National Archive of Vanuatu.

land. Given the reefs' location, the new world builders may have assumed little trouble. They had investigated two possible locations in the southwest Pacific, the other being the Conway Reef which they rejected as an option when they learned that an Australian consortium was looking to develop the reef in order to build a casino.[53] The Minerva Reefs appeared more attractive. They seemed to sit within neither the territorial waters of Aotearoa New Zealand to the south nor Fiji or Tonga to the north. In addition, while recent Atlantis-style efforts near the US coasts had confronted legal or technological obstructions, projects in other parts of the globe persisted. Oliver and his backers could be cautiously optimistic, for example, given the continued occupation by the Bates family of the North Sea "fortress island" of concrete and steel they named the Principality of Sealand (and to this day one of the more famous examples—even if contested—of a micronation.)[54] Moreover, while the project of piling sand on a reef and building a small, sovereign country sounded audacious, a group of international law consultants based at the University of Auckland advised them that such an act did not appear to be illegal.[55] That they were asserting a claim to "an artificially created and uninhabited area on the high seas" as private individuals, rather than as an entity allied to a sovereign state, appeared to muddy the legal ground.[56] The UN Convention on the Law of the Sea would not address issues such as the territoriality of archipelagic states until 1982.[57] These were uncharted waters and this perceived lack of clarity in international law gave the foundation and its backers' optimism. Perhaps the dreams of a new nation, an Atlantis, need not perish, as the US courts had suggested the year prior. Perhaps. History, however, was not on their side.

In ruin over the tides

The Minerva Reefs owe their name to Captain H.M. Denham, of the H.M.S. *Herald*, who surveyed them in 1854.[58] He named them in honor of the whaler *Minerva* which had set sail from Sydney in New South Wales some twenty-five

---

53 Griffith interview with Morris Davis, in Griffith, "Before the Deluge," Davis transcript, 11.
54 See Dylan Taylor-Lehman, *Sealand: The True Story of the World's Most Stubborn Micronation* (London: Icon, 2020).
55 Davis interview with Griffith, in Griffith, "Before the Deluge," interview transcript, 11.
56 Van Fossen, *Tax Havens and Sovereignty*, 111–12. See also Lili Song, "The Curious History of the Minerva Reefs: Tracing the Origin of Tongan and Fijian Claims Over the Minerva Reefs," *Journal of Pacific History* 54, no. 3 (2019): 417–30, esp. 423.
57 United Nations Convention on the Law of the Sea, 1982, esp. Part IV, https://www.un.org/depts/los/convention_agreements/texts/unclos/unclos_e.pdf.
58 Olaf Ruhen, *Minerva Reef: A Modern Sea Epic* (Boston: Little, Brown, 1963), esp. chap. 2.

WRECK OF THE MINERVA WHALER.

Fig. 2.2: The *Minerva* on the reefs.

From Peter Bays, *A Narrative of the Wreck of the Minerva, Whaler of Port Jackson, New South Wales, on Nicholson's Shoal 24° S, 179° W.* (Cambridge: B. Bridges, 1831), frontis.

years prior, on August 16, 1829. Peter Bays, an experienced captain who had spent nine years as a prisoner of war under "the usurper Buonaparte," commanded the vessel.[59] He and his crew—twenty-two men and a dog—had their sights set on the waters south of the islands of Tonga, a prominent whaling area in the early nineteenth century. But three weeks out from Sydney, at 2:00 a.m. on September 9, the *Minerva* struck the reef that would soon bear its name. [see fig. 2.2]

The experience was harrowing. When Bays wrote his account of the shipwreck, published in England two years after, he included in the preface a lengthy quote from William Falconer's poem, "The Vessel Going to Pieces," not only to capture his own experience but to compel the reader to become a strong advocate for "the Sailor's Cause":

> Now, lash'd on by destiny severe,
> With horror fraught, the dreadful scene draws near!
> The ship hangs hovering on the verge of death,
> Hell yawns, rocks rise, and breakers roar beneath.
> Uplifted on the surge, to heaven she flies,
> Her shatter'd top half-buried in the skies,

---

59 Peter Bays, *A Narrative of the Wreck of the Minerva* (Cambridge: B. Bridges, Market Hill, 1831).

Then head-long plunging thunders on the ground,
Earth groans! air trembles! and the deeps resound!
Her giant bulk the dread concussion feels,
And, quivering with the wound, in torment reels.
Again she plunges!—hark!—a second shock
Tears her strong bottom on the marble rock.
Down on the vale of death, with dismal cries,
The fated victims shuddering, roll their eyes
In wild despair, while yet another stroke
With deep convulsion rends the solid oak.
Till, like the mine, in whose infernal cell,
The lurking demons of destruction dwell,
At length asunder torn, her frame divides.
And crashing, spreads in ruin o'er the tides.

Miraculously, none of the crew perished, and with the dawn and low tide they began to salvage what they could from the ship and subsequently set forth in the lifeboats. One boat of eight men set a northward course, never to be heard from again. The remaining fifteen men and the dog ended up crowded into a whaling boat. After one week adrift, they sighted land in the form of the small island of Vatoa. Welcomed by the island's inhabitants, they remained a week before Bays and six men set forth to find help, leaving eight men behind. Eventually all were rescued. It is unclear what happened to the dog.

The *Minerva* was not the first, nor would it be the last, ship to founder on the reefs, some of the most remote in the south Pacific. Prior to the *Minerva*, in 1807, the 375-ton Spanish brig *Rosalía*, loaded with *aguardiente*, ran aground on the reefs en route from Ilo, Peru, to Port Jackson, Australia, after being captured by the HMS *Cornwallis*. The crew of eight survived twenty-three days at sea in a lifeboat, with no instruments or maps, before washing up in an "extreme exhausted state" on Norfolk Island, some 800 miles to the southwest.[60] The island chains of Fiji were closer—380 miles northwest—but the prevailing winds, or perhaps stories of Fijian fierceness, may have prevented the charting of such a course. Ata, the southernmost island in the Tonga archipelago, was even closer, 200 miles to the northeast and inhabited by a small population whose descendants would be forced in the 1860s to flee to larger islands to escape the predations of Peruvian slave-raiders looking for

---

60 Jorge Ortíz-Sotelo and Robert King, "'A Cruize to the Coasts of Peru and Chile': HM Ship Cornwallis, 1807," *The Great Circle* 32, no. 1 (2010): 35–52, quoted passage and details on 41–42.

labor for Peru's guano islands. But that way also lay 5,000 miles of open ocean with only the occasional outpost—Pitcairn, Rapa Nui—somewhere on a broad horizon. European technologies did not include the open ocean navigational experience and embodied practice common to Fijians, Tongans, and Palauans. So the crew had headed west.

Despite increased precision in the charting of the reefs, they continued to snarl experienced captains, and the wreck of the *Minerva* would have plenty of company over subsequent decades. In 1859, only four years after the reefs were charted and named, the *Caroline* ran aground, its crew rescued and transported to Sydney. In 1866 the *Libelle* hit the reefs.[61] The schooner *Strathcona* set out from Auckland, Aotearoa New Zealand, on its maiden voyage in June 1915 only to be heaved onto the reefs seven days out of port. The crew suffered through more than a week of high seas, wind, and "low glass" before they were able to build a raft. Their isolation became obvious, and bosun and carpenter Jack Lilburn intoned in his journal day after day "no sail in sight," wryly noting that ships "must all give this reef a wider berth than what we did."[62] The crew launched a small raft on which six of the eleven men ventured out to seek aid. Lilburn remained with the schooner and documented a long week of "tremendous" seas and increased impatience on the part of the remaining men whose routine settled into tobacco and cards. They were all (including the men who set out on the launch) eventually rescued, after thirty-five days, by the crew of the *Iris*.[63]

And eventually this: in 1962 the *Tuaikaepau*, a fifty-foot-long, twenty-ton cutter bound for Aotearoa New Zealand from Tonga, struck the northwestern edge of South Minerva Reef.[64] For the Tongans and the captain, Tevita Fifita, something had clearly gone wrong. They knew all too well of the reefs. Tongan navigators had been plying the waters of the southwest Pacific for generations and still fished at the reefs.[65] Both North and South Minerva had been well charted. But rapidly rising wind, heavy seas, and "a trick of the moon" saw the *Tuaikaepau* ground onto the reefs.[66] The crew and passengers,

61 John Taylor Grider, "And I Can Live Without Going to Sea": Pacific Maritime Labor Identity, 1840–1890," PhD dissertation, University of Colorado 2006, 348; on the *Caroline* and complications of transporting its crew, see Rhoda Elizabeth Armstrong Hackler, "Our Men in the Pacific: A Chronicle of United States Consular Officers at Seven Ports in the Pacific Islands and Australasia during the 19th Century," PhD dissertation, University of Hawai'i 1978, 240–41.

62 "Jack Lilburn diary of events following the wreck of the *Strathcona* on Minerva Reef, 1915," San Francisco Maritime National Historical Park Library, HDC0120 (SAFR 14036).

63 Ibid.

64 The following paragraphs draw primarily from Ruhen's excellent *Minerva Reef*.

65 Van Fossen, *Tax Havens and Sovereignty*, 113.

66 The quote is from Fifita in "The Minerva Reef Saga—Part 1," *Fiji Times*, July 26, 2015.

all of whom survived the initial impact and night struggling with the thunderous high tide, knew they were in serious trouble. Far from shipping lanes and subject to the cold winds that blew north from Antarctica across the Tasman Sea, the Minerva Reefs infrequently saw visitors.[67] Fifita understood the chances of rescue were slim: with no radio they could not communicate their position, and no one would think to check for them here.

Fifita was correct. No one came. For three months the men struggled, holed up in the shell of a rusting Japanese fishing vessel that had foundered on the reefs two years earlier. They survived on fish, crayfish, and the small amounts of water they could either produce with a home-made still or catch from infrequent rains. Most of them suffered from various ailments, and in early October, in the span of only two days, three men died. The men buried the body of the first person to die in the reef. They wrapped his body in layers of canvass to protect it from crabs and fish. They marked the grave with a cross. Soon after, Fifita made the decision to build a raft from the remains of available wreckage. The men assembled an outrigger for the raft, rigged in such a way as to enable a crew of three to catch the prevailing southeasterly winds and head toward the archipelago of Fiji. Fifita, his teenage son Sateki, and the ship's carpenter David Uaisele eventually arrived off the coast of Kadavu, Fiji, where their vessel capsized while attempting to navigate the reefs. Fifita and Uaisele made it to shore and were able to have an SOS sent out for the men they left behind. Sateki, weakened from months of deprivation, drowned despite Fifita's efforts to save him.[68]

Tongans across the island chain celebrated the rescue and mourned the deaths. Australian writer Olaf Ruhen, who attended the proceedings and wrote an engrossing narrative of the castaways' ordeal, captured the mood: "Tongan telephone wires were running hot as people sought confirmation and news, more news. In the cinema in Nuku'alofa, the film was stopped and an announcement made. The excitement was intense for the *Tuaikaepau* had carried some of the best known Tongans."[69] The day was declared a public holiday. Schoolchildren queued for a nearly a mile to welcome the survivors home. Prince Tu'ipelehake greeted the men in front of enormous crowds as they made their way to the palace to be received by Queen Sālote (1918–1965).[70] The magnitude of the event is also reflected in the fact that Queen Sālote, a celebrated poet, memorialized the endurance of those on the

---

67 Ruhen, *Minerva Reef*, 29.
68 Ibid., passim.
69 Ibid., 280.
70 Ibid., 290–91.

Tuaikaepau and their rescue in song, a traditional form of commemoration and history-making. The first verse read:

> Behold the days of the calendar
> Fourth of the seventh, sixty-two
> Yonder voyage pulling up anchor
> At the port of Nuku'alofa
> Compass braced to give direction
> Fishing lines to be cast at Maka-o-'Oa
> The destination was charted
> Heading for Aotearoa
> Ah, but the ways of the world!
> How unknown is our journey![71]

The Minerva Reefs had become, by 1965, indelibly attached to the memory of *Tuaikaepau* and the history of its crew and passengers. A year later, Captain Fifita returned to the reefs and attached a Tongan flag to a buoy there, an act which took on the important appearance of a ceremony of annexation when conflict with Oliver's foundation erupted in 1972.[72]

Genesis

Few specifics regarding how the Republic of Minerva would function are available, but the model for its operation was Oliver's *New Constitution for a New Country*, itself modeled on the US Constitution. Indeed, much of his constitution is immediately legible to the informed reader. His new country would have executive, legislative, and judicial branches; it would have local, regional, and national administrations; it would have a military for national defense; and similar provisions. The key difference—beyond no welfare provisions and no permission for the government to print money—was the way such institutions and powers would be funded. Oliver was clear that "no level or Branch of government [would] have the power to levy taxes or compel any person or entity to supply funds for government activities of any sort" and that anyone wanting any kind of government services would have to make a voluntary payment for them.[73] Thus, resident citizens of Minerva (but not noncitizen

---

71 Queen Sālote, "Ko e Tuai-kae-pau," as translated by Melenaite Taumoefolau and reproduced in Elizabeth Wood-Ellem, *Queen Sālote of Tonga: The Story of an Era, 1900–1965* (Auckland: Auckland University Press, 1999), 280. The poem is sung, and a performance of the poem by the Afokoula Singers can be found at https://www.youtube.com/watch?v=cYodV3OunHA.

72 Van Fossen, *Tax Havens and Sovereignty*, 113; "Pacific Islanders Fight Reef Plan," *New York Times*, February 27, 1972.

73 Oliver, *A New Constitution*, 76

residents from Tonga and Fiji who would serve, in theory, as Minerva's labor force) would purchase the services they desired. Everything, including the legal and police systems, would be offered as market services for purchase.

Even then, Oliver imposed restrictions: "No person or entity shall be allowed to participate in just the particular government level(s) he (it) chooses. A person or entity desiring just local police and court protection, without wishing to pay for the National Government and National Military Forces (which serve to protect him primarily from external aggression), shall have to pay for all these services, or none at all."[74] Nonresidents (or, as Oliver termed them, non-Participants) would be denied services but in cases in which they were the beneficiaries of services nonetheless—for example, a police officer intervened to stop a Participant from assaulting a non-Participant—the non-Participant would be billed for the police officer's services.[75]

Oversight for the new country would be undertaken by what Oliver had called the Vanguard Corporation. The corporation was composed of a board of directors in charge of making most of the immediate decisions with regard to the formation of the new country. The board consisted of Oliver; Robert R. Johnson, a San Francisco–based gold coin dealer; Robert Meiers, a psychiatrist with practices in Belmont and Palo Alto and a teaching position at Stanford University; and Theodore Stokes, the former district attorney of Ormsby County, Nevada, in which Oliver's adopted hometown of Carson City sat. Also on the board was Morris "Bud" Davis, an aviation and electrical engineer based in Orange County, California, who would eventually serve as the Republic of Minerva's short-lived first and only president.[76] The corporation would work to advertise, to acquire funds to purchase, sell and improve land, and to act as a "transitional agency of government" until a sufficient number of settlers

---

74   Ibid., 76.
75   Ibid., 84. Oliver's positions here at times more closely resemble the "ultra-minimal state" outlined by Robert Nozick in his *Anarchy, State, and Utopia* than they do the "night-watchman state" of classical liberal theory. Nozick writes: "An ultra-minimal state maintains a monopoly over all use of force except that necessary in immediate self-defense, and so excludes private (or agency) retaliation for wrong and exaction of compensation; but it provides protection and enforcement services only to those who purchase its protection and enforcement policies." *Anarchy, State, and Utopia* (New York: Basic Books, 2013 [1974]), 26. Oliver's new country followed a similar line except that defense agencies such as the police would be expected to intervene to defend a victim who then would be expected to pay for that intervention. Just how much this has come to resemble the contemporary United States is captured in the satirical but painfully believable *Onion* headline: "Severely Injured Woman Heroically Fights Off Paramedics Trying to Force Her into Medical Debt," https://www.theonion.com/severely-injured-woman-heroically-fights-off-paramedics-1844671492
76   Oliver, *Capitalist Country Newsletter* 1, no. 4 (October 1968): 2; and Oliver, *Capitalist Country Newsletter* 1, no. 5 (November 1968): 1.

could establish governing structures.[77] The corporation would oversee the subdivision of land, the building of an airport, and the implementation of a zoning code for residential, commercial and industrial uses.

Funds for the country were to be raised in two ways: first, through settlers themselves who would pay a base rate for a three-acre plot of land; and second, through investors who chose not to settle in the new country but who put money into the venture and would thus share in the profits made by the corporation. The corporation's board of directors would review every application for settlement in the new country. "Capability of self-support," Oliver wrote, "or sufficient assets shall be one of the requirements for acceptance." The choice to enter the community was determined by one's ability to purchase property. Freedom may have meant, as economist Milton Friedman would title his 1981 book, "freedom to choose" but such choices were always made within constraints determined by one's purchasing power.

Yet for Oliver the market was in itself not enough of a limitation, and he introduced what was effectively an ideological litmus test. "Although neither the Corporation, nor the government which is to come after it shall in any way have authority to interfere with peoples' beliefs, the Corporation shall reserve the right to refuse entry to newcomers on the basis of collectivistic ideas held by the applicant, or for any other valid reason."[78] Oliver, in other words, had strong and clear expectations regarding "the personal philosophy of the prospective immigrant," something he clarified in his *Capitalist Country* newsletter:

> Naturally we will not knowingly accept collectivists in our new country. Nor do we want criminals, nihilists, or anarchists. While at this point, we have found that a few persons (fortunately, a very few) who wrote to me failed to understand an important point made in the book. I made a few rather strong remarks against anarchy on pages 23 and 24 of the book, and again on pages 118 and 119. I showed conclusively that anarchy has always led to tyranny. Hitler came to power when the Weimar Republic permitted his hoodlums to run wild. Before the communists came to power in Russia, it was necessary to destroy the existing Russian government. And now, the hippies, yippies and communists are joined in a foul alliance to destroy the existing government in the United States.[79]

There are two issues here worth pausing over briefly: first, the understandable confusion some had regarding libertarianism and anarchism; and second, the

---

77 Oliver, *A New Constitution*, 29–30.
78 Ibid., 33.
79 Oliver, *Capitalist Country Newsletter* 1, no. 5 (November 1968): 2.

fact that Oliver introduced regulations in a project that was intended to be determined by the market.

As Oliver learned, some of his readers required instruction in distinguishing between his libertarian ideals and those of anarchists. Oliver's friend and first president of Minerva, Bud Davis, insisted on referring to himself as an objectivist rather than a libertarian not only because of his dedication to Ayn Rand—who coined the term "objectivism" as a descriptor of her philosophical position—but also because he wished to avoid being confused with anarchists.[80] Some, perhaps many, readers in the US at the time drew little distinction between libertarian and anarchist perspectives and practices. And the fact is that in much of world, then and now, libertarian *was* synonymous with anarchist: both terms applied to those who advocated for the end of the State and the end of capitalist relations of production. In contrast, in the US, first with its strong tradition of individualist antistatism harkening back to Benjamin Tucker and Lysander Spooner, and subsequently with its anticommunist fervor and free enterprise faith, libertarian and anarchist often *appeared* synonymous but only because both were mistakenly understood to refer to the abolition or minimization of the state only. The confusion only worsened when prominent advocates for capitalism and sovereign markets freely used the term "anarchism" or "anarchy" in reference to their own work. In the late 1960s and early 1970s, economists James Buchanan and Gordon Tullock, later to be affiliated with George Mason University's Center for the Study of Public Choice, began to apply economic principles and mathematical models to the study of a society without government, leading to a 1972 volume titled *Explorations in the Theory of Anarchy*.[81] That same year the Southern Economic Association hosted a session on the "economics of anarchy" at their annual conference.[82] Over the same period philosopher Robert Nozick wrote the

---

80   Davis, as interviewed by Griffith, "Before the Deluge," 3–4.
81   For a reconsideration of the volume and the debates it sparked, see Edward Stringham, ed., *Anarchy, State and Public Choice* (Cheltenham, UK: Edward Elgar, 2005). The conflation can also be found in the way anarchist ideas could travel to neoliberal and libertarian circles with seemingly small but profound tweaks, such as when Peruvian author Hernando de Soto took the anarchist principles at work in self-aided housing— particularly those enacted in Peru by British anarchist architect John F.C. Turner—and turned them into a radical and simplified call for private property rights and titling. See Hernando de Soto, *The Mystery of Capital: Why Capitalism Triumphs in the West and Fails Everywhere Else* (New York: Basic Books, 2000) and de Soto, *The Other Path: The Invisible Revolution in the Third World* (New York: HarperCollins, 1989). On Turner and housing in Peru, see Gyger, *Improvised Cities*.
82   Laurence Moss, "Private Property Anarchism: An American Variant," in Stringham, ed., *Anarchy, State and Public Choice*, 123. Moss's paper originally appeared in a 1974 volume edited by Tullock entitled *Further Explorations in the Theory of Anarchy*.

drafts of a manuscript that would eventually become his seminal work *Anarchy, State, and Utopia* (1974), still to this day considered one of the foundational texts in US libertarian political theory. Nozick sought to offer a robust response not only to John Rawls's *A Theory of Justice* but also to the "individualist anarchism" espoused by Murray Rothbard. Nozick defended an ultraminimalist state as the best form for ensuring individual rights and freedoms. To navigate between anarchy and the state, as his book title suggested, was the closest one might come to a reasonable libertarian utopia.

But such market-libertarianism is far removed from classical and class-conscious anarchist traditions which have always been equally antagonistic toward the state *and* capitalism.[83] The primacy accorded to individual private property rights, and the dedication to capitalist social relations more broadly, is in part what distinguishes market-libertarianism from anarchism. Anarchists—regardless of the variations between, say, anarcho-communists, anarcho-syndicalists, or anarcho-primitivists—directed their wrath at the state not only because of its hierarchical and authoritarian structures but also because it functioned as a protector of exploitative systems rooted in wage labor, individual private property, and capital accumulation. In other words, they critiqued the state for producing and protecting the structures which market libertarians claimed were its primary raison d'être: private property and waged labor systems.[84] Part of the issue here was practical: that the claim made to property by the few was an abuse of the many—the laboring classes, the enslaved, the unremunerated—whose labors had in fact created property in the first place. Peter

---

83   For classic anarchist statements, see Peter Kropotkin, *Mutual Aid: A Factor of Evolution* (Boston: Porter Sargent Publishers, 1914) and Kropotkin, *The Conquest of Bread and Other Writings* (Cambridge: Cambridge University Press, 1995 [1892]). See also Michael Schmidt and Lucien van der Walt, *Black Flame: The Revolutionary Class Politics of Anarchism and Syndicalism* (Oakland: AK Press, 2013); Carl Levy, "Social Histories of Anarchism," *Journal for the Study of Radicalism* 4, no. 2 (Fall 2010): 1–44; Colin Ward, *Anarchism: A Very Short Introduction* (Oxford: Oxford University Press, 2004); and Andrej Grubačić, "The Anarchist Moment," in Jacob Blumenfield, Chiara Boticci, and Simon Critchley, eds., *The Anarchist Turn* (London: Pluto Books, 2013). In a slightly different vein, see James C. Scott's *The Art of Not Being Governed: An Anarchist History of Upland Southeast Asia* (New Haven, CT: Yale University Press, 2009) and *Two Cheers for Anarchism* (Princeton, NJ: Princeton University Press, 2012). The individualist anarchist tradition, best represented in the work of Max Stirner, did not necessarily defend market relations and contractual exchange either. See Stirner, *The Ego and His Own: The Case of the Individual against Authority* (London: Verso, 2014 [1844]).

84   In fact, one might go further and suggest they are more akin to the company-state and the joint-stock corporation—financial monopolies—than they are to Smith's vision of an invisible hand. See the brief but excellent discussion in Timothy Mitchell, "Dreamland," in Mike Davis and Daniel Bertrand Monk, eds., *Evil Paradises: Dreamworlds of Neoliberalism* (New York: New Press, 2007), 1–33.

Kropotkin's impassioned statement at the end of the nineteenth century held true decades later:

> Millions of human beings have laboured to create this civilization on which we pride ourselves today. Other millions, scattered through the globe, labour to maintain it. Without them nothing would be left in fifty years but ruins.
>
> There is not even a thought, or an invention, which is not common property, born of the past and the present. Thousands of inventors, known and unknown, who have died in poverty, have co-operated in the invention of each of these machines which embody the genius of man.
>
> Thousands of writers, of poets, of scholars, have laboured to increase knowledge, to dissipate error, and to create that atmosphere of scientific thought, without which the marvels of our century could never have appeared. And these thousands of philosophers, of poets, of scholars, of inventors, have themselves been supported by the labour of past centuries. They have been upheld and nourished through life, both physically and mentally, by legions of workers and craftsmen of all sorts. They have drawn their motive force from the environment....
>
> Science and industry, knowledge and application, discovery and practical realization leading to new discoveries, cunning of brain and hand, toil of mind and muscle—all work together. Each discovery, each advance, each increase in the sum of human riches, owes its being to the physical and mental travail of the past and the present.
>
> By what right then can anyone whatever appropriate the least morsel of this immense whole and say—This is mine, not yours?[85]

Anarchists remained no less committed to individual liberty than their libertarian brethren, but they argued that such liberty could only result from collective freedom, a phrase market libertarians might well have considered a contradiction in terms. Russian anarchist Mikhail Bakunin famously wrote that "socialism without freedom is tyranny; freedom without socialism is privilege." That is to say, freedom and equality are mutually constitutive and must exist simultaneously. Individual freedom and social solidarity were mutually reinforcing. Compare that with the sequential, rather than simultaneous, process often espoused by both libertarian and liberal thinkers: namely that equality will result from freedom in the marketplace. Murray Rothbard went further and seemed to suggest that equality was irrelevant, that egalitarianism itself

---

85   Kropotkin, *The Conquest of Bread* (London: Penguin Books, 2015 [1913]), 13–14.

was an authoritarian and antihuman ideology.[86] Competition, rather than exchange, was the basis of social reality and inequality was an acceptable norm. This was a doctrine of social inequality rooted, as Matthew Lyons argues, not in biology or God but in the theology of market competition.[87]

Theology brings us to my second point regarding Oliver's concerns. In worrying about anarchists, hippies, and communists, and in banning collectivists, Oliver revealed that freedom had its limits. Those limits were set by Oliver himself. His *New Constitution for a New Country* was a single-authored document drafted and handed down by fiat by Oliver himself, monarch of his planned community and its imagined future. Oliver's constitution was in many ways a rewrite of the contracts that created, starting in the 1950s and 1960s, what has now become a commonplace of the American property landscape: common interest developments (CIDs) or common interest homeowners' associations (CIHAs) that function as private governments with their own covenants, conditions and restrictions. A good example is Los Angeles County's 1950s Lakewood Plan, which allowed the middle-class community of Lakewood, north of Long Beach, to "incorporate" as its own legal entity but without establishing a city government or creating the necessary entities to provide basic services. Instead, the community would contract out for such things as fire and police, often, as Mike Davis observes, "at cut-rate prices determined by the county's economy of scale (i.e., indirectly subsidized by all county taxpayers.)"[88] The plan spurred numerous imitators, all eager to take advantage of such an "exit privilege."[89]

Importantly, CIDs and CIHAs privilege property ownership as being at "the heart of the social contract," a social contract architecturally expressed in the single-family home situated usually within a racially and economically homogeneous residential enclave.[90] These are, in other words, planned communities. From location and layout to rights and obligations, they are the product of the developer's designs. Writer Evan McKenzie's observations regarding planning and CIDs/CIHAs are useful here:

---

86 See the discussion in Matthew Lyons, *Insurgent Supremacists: The U.S. Far Right's Challenge to State and Empire* (Oakland: PM Press, 2018), 148–50.

87 Ibid., 55.

88 Mike Davis, *City of Quartz: Excavating the Future in Los Angeles* (New York: Vintage, 1992 [1990]), 165.

89 Ibid., 166.

90 Evan McKenzie, *Privatopia: Homeowner Associations and the Rise of Residential Private Government*, quoted in Gregory Alexander and Hanoch Dagan, eds., *Properties of Property* (New York: Wolters Kluwer Law & Business, 2012), 332; Davis, *City of Quartz*, esp. 169–70, and 153–73 more generally.

At the outset there is nothing—a state of nature devoid of people except for the developer-creator, who begets the "community" and its social order to his liking and makes it unchangeable. After that is done, the people arrive at his invitation and are permitted to live there forever according to his rules, long after he has abandoned them to their own devices. This scenario is closer to Genesis than to Locke, resembling the early days of the Garden of Eden more than the Puritans' arrival in the New World.[91]

This is in many respects a good summation of the Minerva project. The board decreed an array of codes regarding everything from housing and lot size to zoning and nuisance laws to the ideological beliefs of interested settlers. The foundation of the community's legitimacy was its dedication to the market itself. For those choosing to invest and/or settle, they would do so in an entity where the rules, rights, and restrictions had already been put in place by a self-selected board of directors. This is not a hypocrisy or conundrum specific to the Minerva founders. "The majority of the builders of utopias are determined to remain the masters in their imaginary commonwealths," wrote Marie Louise Berneri, a twentieth century anarchist activist. "While they claim to give freedom they issue a detailed code which must be strictly followed."[92]

Oliver may have been dictating human freedom, but he was still dictating. Contrary to the new country's name, what would rise on the Minerva Reefs would be not a republic but an absolutist kingdom. Unfortunately for Oliver and his backers, the reefs appeared to belong to an already-existing kingdom: Tonga.

An empire on the doorstep

In January 1972 Oliver, Davis, and Ralph McMullen, recently appointed as Minerva's secretary of state, issued a proclamation declaring the birth of the Republic of Minerva. They mailed a letter to more than one hundred governments inviting recognition of the Republic's existence and sovereignty.[93] (Only one—a sultan on the island of Timor—obliged, but any enthusiasm would have been short-lived when it was revealed that the sultan was a fiction.) To commemorate the declaration the founding fathers issued a minted coin (see

91   McKenzie, *Privatopia*, as quoted in Alexander and Dagan, eds., *Properties of Property*, 336.
92   Berneri, *Journey through Utopia: A Critical Assessment of Imagined Worlds in Western Literature* (Oakland: PM Press, 2019 [1982]), 3.
93   Lili Song, "The Curious History of the Minerva Reefs: Tracing the Origin of Tongan and Fijian Claims Over the Minerva Reefs," *Journal of Pacific History* 54, no. 3 (2019): 417–30; on the proclamation and letter see 421.

Fig. 2.3: Talisman of fear: Oliver's gold coin promoting the Republic of Minerva. Note the coordinates of longitude and latitude, along with location given as South Pacific Ocean. Of additional interest is that the coin was minted in 1973, months after it had become clear that Tonga's rights to the reefs had been secured.

Wikimedia Commons, https://commons.wikimedia.org/wiki/File:Minerva_Republic.jpg.

fig. 2.3).[94] Supporters and investors soon mobilized. Through a new entity—International Maritime Legal Research (IMLR)—they issued a call for a first wave of occupiers to go to the reefs and assist in the dredging and building of the Republic. Those who could do so would reside on one of the ships made available by two companies: T&T Enterprises and Thingwold Brothers. Those unable to make the journey could assist by investing further, pledging equipment, sponsoring a settler, or "digging through their garages for items of supplies" needed for construction.[95]

Not all involved celebrated, however. News soon emerged that one of the participants—Morris Davis—had planned with the IMLR to promote

---

94 "South Sea Reef Proclaimed a Republic by 3 Americans," *New York Times*, January 30, 1972, 11.

95 International Maritime Legal Research, "This Project Needs People Now," and "Republic of Minerva Occupation," undated mimeographs, ca. March 1972. Archives & Special Collections at the Thomas J. Dodd Research Center, University of Connecticut Library. These two documents list no authors but are produced by the IMLR, based in Toledo, Ohio, at the time and I suspect closely connected to, if not produced by, Tad Weed.

occupation of the reefs without consulting others, leading Oliver and his backers to expel Davis from the project.[96] But Oliver himself was not immune to critique. His January proclamation came as a surprise to some of his financial backers who felt it a rash and impetuous move that would only invite trouble.[97] And they were correct. Regional leaders reacted with concern and suspicion. Among those most worried? Tonga's royalty.

In 1965 Queen Sālote died. Her first-born son, Tāufaʻāhau Tupou IV, ascended to the throne. Tupou IV undertook a range of modernizing projects, dramatically increasing existing government efforts at upgrading wharf facilities, investing in shipping, and undertaking cadastral surveys. The cutting, drying, and shipping of copra (dried coconut flesh) had long been the dominant activity on the island and relatively high copra prices in the 1950s and 1960s sustained that pattern. Even so, Tupou IV sought to change the reliance on subsistence farming and copra exports. As he pushed to create industrial, nonagricultural jobs on the islands, Tupou IV developed a five-year plan with various projects, including forestry, soil, and livestock surveys; tourism development; road construction; school expansion; and the planting of some twenty-five thousand coconut trees.

Tupou IV also had broader political aspirations. In concert with the political transitions happening around the globe, Tonga began moving rapidly in the 1960s toward full political independence. Tonga had not been a colony but neither had it been fully sovereign. Self-governing in domestic matters, Tonga's defense, external affairs, and legislative matters had been controlled by the British. This relationship began to change in 1958 when the existing Treaty of Friendship underwent modification to allow Tonga more control over its judiciary and to end British control of Tongan finances. A decade later saw another reduction in British supervisory capacities and then, on June 4, 1970, Tupou IV ushered in Tonga's full independence from Great Britain by terminating the treaty that had established Tonga as a British protectorate.[98]

In the midst of this, how was one to construe the arrival of a band of settler colonists in areas long understood to be part of Tongan lifeways? For the people of Tonga, the Minerva proclamation could only have been construed as an act of imperious aggression: an affront to the memory of those who died in 1962; an infringement on the long-standing seasonal use-rights of

96   "Publisher's Notes: Minerva News," *Reason*, May 1973.

97   Maura McEnaney, *Willard Garvey: An Epic Life* (Oakland: Liberty Tree Press, 2013), 187–88.

98   Discussion of Tupou, his modernizing plans, and Tonga's political situation is indebted to I.C. Campbell, *Island Kingdom: Tonga Ancient and Modern* (Christchurch, NZ: University of Canterbury Press, 2nd rev. ed. 2001 [1992]), 207–12; see also W. David McIntyre, *Winding Up the British Empire in the Pacific Islands* (Oxford: Oxford University Press, 2014), 149–51.

Tongan fishermen; a repudiation of the practices of an oceangoing people; and an insult to a kingdom that had only two years earlier freed itself from imperial custody. Just as colonial powers retreat, libertarian exit strategists invade. Prince Tuʻipelehake made it clear: it was as if an empire had landed on Tonga's doorstep.[99]

But were the reefs part of Tonga? Or its doorstep? Or neither? Tonga's original bounds had been established by Tupou IV's namesake, King George Tupou I, in an 1887 royal proclamation. That proclamation laid claim to an area of some 395,000 square kilometers and encompassed "all, islands, rocks, reefs, foreshores and waters lying between the fifteenth and twenty-third and a half degrees of south latitude and between the one hundred and seventy-third and the one hundred and seventy-seventh degrees of west longitude from the Meridian of Greenwich."[100] While the proclamation included a substantial swath of ocean, the boundaries delineated did not extend as far south as to include the Minerva Reefs. But in the wake of the Minerva proclamation, Tupou IV began investigating. In February 1972 he sent a fact-finding mission to the reefs. The participants established a refuge station on the South Minerva Reef but Tupou IV's government made no immediate claim of possession or sovereignty. In May he himself sailed to the reefs. Shortly thereafter he ordered prisoners released from jail in order to assist in the building of a small island on each of the two reefs, each with a structure that would remain permanently above the high water mark and thus potentially allow the kingdom to claim possession.[101] And this he did: on June 15, 1972, he declared Tongan sovereignty over the reefs in a speech to Tongan legislative assembly: "I am aware Mr Speaker and Hon. Members of the House, that you are all wondering what the legal position is regarding North and South Minerva. Construction work carried out on these two reefs will, I believe, assist in erasing all uncertainty which surrounds these reefs, from this day onwards." To clarify things for the legislative body, Tupou IV explained that plans had been approved and were underway to build artificial islands on both reefs and that later that day an affirmation would be issued in the *Gazette* "declaring these two islands part of the Kingdom of Tonga." Between the time he gave the speech and issued and printed the proclamation, Tongan names had been applied to the islands: North Minerva became Teleki Tokelau (north reef) and South Minerva was renamed Teleki Tonga (south reef). Each island would have its own territorial waters, the international standard twelve miles. The government had

99   "Pacific Islanders Fight Reef Plan," *New York Times*, February 27, 1972.
100 Captain Sione Fifita, *Enhancing Tonga's Maritime Security*, Indo-Pacific Strategic Papers (Australian Defence College, Center for Defence and Strategic Studies, March 2015), 4–5.
101 See Song, "The Curious History of the Minerva Reefs," 422–24.

Fig. 2.4: Stamps of authority. Proclaiming Tongan sovereignty over the reefs. The stamp on the left reproduces Tupou IV's proclamation of sovereignty; that on the right shows the act of raising the Tongan flag over the reefs, with their respective Tongan names.
Author's personal collection.

already put aside monies to pay for the installation of a lighthouse on each reef that would serve as a physical marker of possession (see fig. 2.4).[102] The Proclamation read as follows:

> Proclamation: His Majesty King Tāufa'āhau Tupou IV in Council DOES HEREBY PROCLAIM:—WHEREAS the Reefs known as North Minerva Reef and South Minerva Reef have long served as fishing grounds for the Tongan people and have long been regarded as belonging to the Kingdom of Tonga; AND WHEREAS the Kingdom of Tonga has now created on these Reefs islands known as Teleki Tokelau and Teleki Tonga; AND WHEREAS it is expedient that we should now confirm the rights of the Kingdom of Tonga to these islands; THEREFORE we do hereby AFFIRM and PROCLAIM that the islands of Teleki Tokelau and Teleki Tonga and

---

102 "Address of His Majesty King Tāufa'āhau Tupou IV at the Opening of the Seventy-Second Session of the Legislative Assembly of Tonga at Nuku'alofa, on the 15th June, 1972," *Tonga Government Gazette* no. 11 (September 29, 1972): 1. The government issued a series of additions to its Immigration Act of 1969 clarifying the process to be followed by any visitor to Tonga and also adjusted fees and regulations of the Land Act, including fees for "Application for permit for aliens to occupy Tongan land or reside with Tongans" and fees for "Removing sand from foreshore or any Government property, for each ton or part thereof." See *Tonga Government Gazette Supplement* no. 8 (October 31, 1972), 41–45.

all islands, rocks, reefs, foreshores and waters lying within a radius of twelve miles thereof are part of our Kingdom of Tonga.[103]

A sea of islands

Oliver and his backers sought to salvage what they could. As a last-gasp effort to save their ideal republic, they tried to win over Tupou IV by offering him an array of perks, including an airline. Morris Davis traveled to Tonga to meet personally with Tupou IV, to no avail.[104] He rejected their overtures and threatened to have any colonists to Minerva arrested.[105] He also allegedly reached out to US President Richard Nixon, requesting that he intercede and ensure that Oliver and his backers did not persist with their designs. There is little to suggest that the US government acted in any way on the issue but, regardless, Tupou IV's strong response—which also included a naval show of might at the reefs—ensured that the reefs would be considered Tongan sovereign space. Controversy did not end there. British officials, for example, raised concerns as to whether the incorporation of the reefs by Tonga meant they could also lay claim to territorial waters around the reefs. Given that the structures built on Teleki Tokelau and Teleki Tonga were artificial constructions, according to the 1958 Convention on the Laws of the Sea territorial water claims could not apply.[106] But in 1974, at least, the British high commissioner was clear that the Minerva Reefs "have been incorporated in the Kingdom by proclamation, and this has received general support from the Member States of the South Pacific Forum." And, in any case, he continued, "nothing has been heard recently of the so-called Republic of Minerva."[107]

Tupou IV's assertion of sovereignty had the potential to stoke conflicts, particularly with neighboring Fiji (and in fact in the early 2000s Fiji and Tonga would clash repeatedly over the reefs and questions of sovereignty and use).

---

103 Proclamation by Tāufaʻāhau Tupou IV, *Tonga Government Gazette Extraordinary* no. 7 (June 15, 1972): 1.

104 "Minerva Update," *Reason*, October 1, 1972.

105 On threatening to arrest colonists, see Van Fossen, *Tax Havens and Sovereignty*, 114.

106 B. Hitch to Arthington-Davy, February 22, 1974, Foreign and Commonwealth Office [hereafter FCO] 76/919, National Archives of the United Kingdom [hereafter NA-Kew]; see also MJ Williams, Marine and Transport Dept., to Mr Hitch, February 19, 1974, FCO 76/919, NA-Kew,.

107 Arthington-Davy, British High Commission, Tonga, to B. Hitch, Marine and Transport Dept., FCO, January 24, 1974, FCO 76/919, NA-Kew. Even so, subsequent correspondence observed that if Tonga now claimed territorial waters around the Minerva Reefs themselves then the British ought to reserve their position. See, e.g., MJ Williams, Marine and Transport Dept., to Mr Hitch, February 19, 1974, FCO 76/919, NA-Kew; and Hitch to Arthington-Day, February 22, 1974, FCO 76/919, NA-Kew.

But at the South Pacific Forum meeting in late 1972, heads of state from Fiji, Nauru, Western Samoa and the Cook Islands agreed that Tonga had a long-standing historical association with the reefs and that any other claim to sovereignty over the reefs was unacceptable, and in particular "that of the Ocean Life Research Foundation."[108] The king could count on regional support from other heads of state in part because they too feared that the success of libertarian colonization would open up dozens of other seamounts and atolls in the southwestern Pacific to claims of ownership.[109] The question reached well beyond the bounds of one nation. As Oceanian decolonization proceeded, questions of archipelagic territorial rights to the ocean, never adequately addressed in early UN conferences on the status of the ocean, arose and led to the writing over the course of the 1970s of a series of Archipelagic Provisions that would be adopted at the 1982 Third Conference on the Law of the Sea.[110] Such provisions accentuated what continentalist paradigms had long tended to obscure: that the ocean was a human space.

Tonga, Samoa, and Fiji are oceanic archipelagos, a part of an expansive Native Sea.[111] Their inhabitants have long traversed and worked swaths of ocean as if they were a liquid prairie. Outrigger canoes, sleek and swift and outfitted with a limited number of paddlers, were most often used for shorter distances but could also travel great distances of hundreds of miles. Double-hulled canoes, often rigged with sails and with hulls measuring anywhere from sixty to one hundred feet in length, could transport multiple dozens of passengers, including settler families and their provisions, across vast expanses and turned the open ocean into a conduit rather than a barrier. Ship-building and canoe-making was a central aspect of cultural life and livelihoods throughout the insular Pacific, including in Tonga, where canoe builders achieved high social rank and whose labors the god Tangaroa ("the first builder of canoes and houses") oversaw.[112] Canoe master navigators, orienting themselves through reference to stars and horizon points and a deeply learned ability to read

---

108 Fifita, *Enhancing Tonga's Maritime Security*, 5; South Pacific Forum Suva, September 12–14, 1972, accessed June 1, 2020, https://www.forumsec.org/south-pacific-forum-suva-12-14-september-1972/.

109 Van Fossen, *Tax Havens and Sovereignty*, 113.

110 See the discussion in Mohamed Munavvar, *Ocean States: Archipelagic Regimes in the Law of the Sea* (Dordrecht: Martinus Nijhoff Publishers, 1995); *United Nations Convention on the Law of the Sea* (1982), part IV, https://www.un.org/Depts/los/convention_agreements/texts/unclos/unclos_e.pdf.

111 Damon Salesa, "Native Seas and Native Seaways: The Pacific Ocean and New Zealand," in Frances Steel, ed., *New Zealand and the Sea: Historical Perspectives* (Wellington, NZ: Bridget Williams Books, 2018).

112 Sir Peter Buck (Te Rangi Hiroa), *Vikings of the Sunrise* (Christchurch, NZ: Whitcombe and Tombs, Ltd., 1964 [1938]), 29.

the ocean and sky, traveled long distances, in the process establishing fishing and hunting grounds, settlements, and trade and communication networks. From this horizontal perspective, the ocean was less a limit or endpoint of a culture than a full-fledged part of it.[113] Nor were Oceanians immune from the opportunities that might await in work aboard the sailing vessels that plied the Pacific or from the violence of impressment, kidnapping, and enslavement that often accompanied imperial and commercial expansion.[114]

The conceptualization of the insular Pacific as composed only of its landmasses, a smattering of isolated islands in a vast ocean, is a product of territorial epistemologies other than those of Oceanians themselves. "When those who hail from continents," wrote Tongan intellectual Epeli Hauʻofa, "or islands adjacent to continents—and the vast majority of human beings live in these regions—when they see a Polynesian or Micronesian island they naturally pronounce it small or tiny. Their calculation is based entirely on the extent of the land surfaces they see."[115] Hauʻofa went on to offer a powerfully eloquent and important corrective to such ideas, one worth quoting at length:

There is a world of difference between viewing the Pacific as "islands in a far sea" and as "a sea of islands." The first emphasizes dry surfaces in a vast ocean far from the centers of power. Focusing in this way stresses the smallness and remoteness of the islands. The second is a more holistic perspective in which things are seen in the totality of their relationships. I return to this point later. Continental men, namely Europeans, on entering the Pacific after crossing huge expanses of ocean, introduced the view of "islands in a far sea." From this perspective the islands are tiny, isolated dots in a vast ocean. Later on, continental men—Europeans

113 On outrigger canoes and voyaging, see Sir Peter Buck (Te Rangi Hiroa), *Vikings of the Sunrise* (Christchurch, NZ: Whitcombe and Tombs, Ltd., 1964 [1938]); David H. Lewis, *We, the Navigators: The Ancient Art of Landfinding in the Pacific* (Honolulu: University of Hawaiʻi Press, [1972] 1974); *Sacred Vessels: Navigating Tradition and Identity in Micronesia*, dir. by Vicente Díaz (Pacific Islanders in Communication, 1997); and Paul D'Arcy, *The People of the Sea: Environment, Identity, and History in Oceania* (Honolulu: University of Hawaiʻi Press, 2006). On the revival of long-distance voyaging, see Sam Low, *Hawaiki Rising: Hōkūleʻa, Nainoa Thompson, and the Hawaiian Renaissance* (Waipahu, HI: Island Heritage, 2016) and Ben Finney, *Sailing in the Wake of the Ancestors: Reviving Polynesian Voyaging* (Honolulu: Bishop Museum Press, 2004).

114 David Chappel, *Double Ghosts: Oceanian Voyagers on Euroamerican Ships* (New York: Routledge, 2015 [1997]); David Chang, *The World and All the Things upon It: Native Hawaiian Geographies of Exploration* (Minneapolis: University of Minnesota Press, 2016); Gregory Rosenthal, *Beyond Hawaiʻi: Native Labor in the Pacific World* (Berkeley: University of California Press, 2018); and, for important cautionary comments regarding migrant agency and diaspora, DeLoughrey, *Routes and Roots*, esp. 26–27 and passim.

115 Hauʻofa, "Our Sea of Islands," *The Contemporary Pacific* 6, no. 1 (Spring 1994): 152.

and Americans—drew imaginary lines across the sea, making the colonial boundaries that confined ocean peoples to tiny spaces for the first time. These boundaries today define the island states and territories of the Pacific. I have just used the term *ocean peoples* because our ancestors, who had lived in the Pacific for over two thousand years, viewed their world as "a sea of islands" rather than as "islands in the sea." This may be seen in a common categorization of people, as exemplified in Tonga by the inhabitants of the main, capital, island, who used to refer to their compatriots from the rest of the archipelago not so much as "people from outer islands" as social scientists would say, but as *kakai mei tahi* or just *tahi* "people from the sea." This characterization reveals the underlying assumption that the sea is home to such people.[116]

This is the reality for most peoples of the sea of islands, including Tongans, who have a history of organizing expeditions that lasted for years and ranged far and wide across the southwest Pacific.[117] A long history of contact and exchange existed between and among islanders in the broader region, a history that belies assertions of isolation. This history might even suggest the existence of a kind of oceanic "geo-body" of the kind commonly now ascribed to terrestrial spaces.[118] Like the empire of the Comanche—the comanchería—reconstructed by Pekka Hämäläinen, this was a geo-body for which few maps existed until Māori intellectual and anthropologist Te Rangihiroa offered one in his 1938 *Vikings of the Sunrise* (see fig. 2.5).[119] There are risks of course in proposing a vision of this kind. The logo-map can represent a spatial imaginary that forecloses other historical relationships. For example, Te Rangihiroa's map is Polynesian, the tentacles of relation expanding from Havai'i (Raiatea) outward to Tonga and Samoa but not to Vanuatu, to Kiribati but not most of Micronesia.[120] But the map at the minimum serves

116 Ibid., 152–53. See also Albert Wendt, "Towards a New Oceania," *Mana Review* 1, no. 1 (1976): 49–60; Damon Salesa, "The Pacific in Indigenous Time," in David Armitage and Alison Bashford, *Pacific Histories: Ocean, Land, People* (London: Palgrave, 2013), 31–52; Margaret Jolly, "Imagining Oceania: Indigenous and Foreign Representations of a Sea of Islands," *Contemporary Pacific* 19, no. 2 (2007): 508–45; and David Hanlon, "The Sea of Little Lands: Examining Micronesia's Place in 'Our Sea of Islands,'" *Contemporary Pacific* 21, no. 1 (2009): 91–110.

117 D'Arcy, *The People of the Sea*, 57–58. See also Thomas, *In Oceania: Visions, Artifacts, Histories* (Durham, NC: Duke University Press, 1997), 191.

118 Thongchai Winichakul, *Siam Mapped: A History of the Geobody of a Nation* (Honolulu: University of Hawai'i Press, 1997).

119 Pekka Hämäläinen, *The Comanche Empire* (New Haven, CT: Yale University Press, 2016).

120 For a reading of the map, see DeLoughrey, *Routes and Roots*, 149–55. On Te Rangihiroa and his Pacific world, see Alice Te Punga Somerville, *Once Were Pacific: Māori Connections*

as a visual reminder of the spaces of connection and relation, of "territoriality" if not "territory," that adhere across distances and of the deep history of genealogical connection that stretches across the Native seas that compose the Pacific.[121] Regardless of the formal or legal question of sovereignty, there

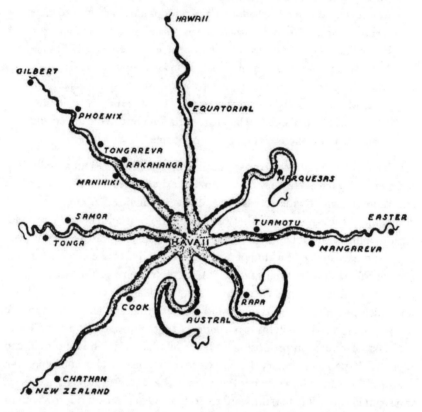

Fig. 2.5: An oceanic logo map. Sir Peter Buck (Te Rangihiroa) map illustrating the "hub of the Polynesian universe."

Buck, *Vikings of the Sunrise*, 88. Creative Commons Attribution-Share Alike 3.0 New Zealand License granted by NZ Electronic Text Centre (NZETC), Victoria University of Wellington, NZ Library Catalogue. http://nzetc.victoria.ac.nz/tm/scholarly/tei-BucViki.html.

to Oceania (Minneapolis: University of Minnesota Press, 2012), 11–20. On reproducing and avoiding settler colonial territorial and legal paradigms in indigenous cartography, see Craib, "Cartography and Decolonization," in James Akerman, ed., *Decolonizing the Map: Cartography from Colony to Nation* (Chicago: University of Chicago Press, 2017), 11–71. More broadly on decolonization, the ocean, and law, see Surabhi Ranganathan, "Decolonization and International Law: Putting the Ocean on the Map," *Journal of the History of International Law* 23 (2021): 161–83.

121　For Native seas, see Damon Salesa, "Native Seas and Native Seaways: The Pacific Ocean and New Zealand," in Frances Steel, ed., *New Zealand and the Sea: Historical Perspectives* (Wellington, NZ: Bridget Williams Books, 2018). On territoriality and territory see Liam Campling and Alejandro Colás, "Capitalism and the Sea: Sovereignty, Territory and

existed (and continues to exist) a history of relation, movement, connection, and use. In some ways, then, the establishment of Exclusive Economic Zones by the UNCLOS in 1982 and the attention it gave to archipelagic configurations and relations confirmed what Pacific islanders already knew: they were "large Ocean nations."[122]

Derelicts becalmed

Captain Tevita Fifita died in 1979. Over the course of his life he had become a well-known and highly-regarded man in Tonga. Upon his death, an island literary journal, *Faikava*, dedicated an issue to his memory in which his fellow countryman Epeli Hau'ofa, who would later author the seminal essay "Our Sea of Islands," memorialized him in a poem.

To the Last Viking of the Sunrise

Since you left, captain,
We've missed the man
Who sliced the blue-black sea
To get to Lifuka
Before the water boiled.

You've gone, Tevita
And the wet-winged tern from Minerva
Has flown to the rock
Where Sina sits waiting for the word
You will never send.

Moana's calling you
Who slipped the midway reef,
Set bow for the foamy straits,
Beating the wind, the wooden gods
Giving way to no one, north or west.

Oh tell us again
Of the day you raked the coral head

Appropriation in the Global Ocean," *Environment and Planning D: Society and Space* 36, no. 4 (2018): 776–94, who draw from David Delaney, *Territory: A Short Introduction* (Oxford: Blackwell, 2005); and Frances Steel, introduction to Frances Steel, ed., *New Zealand and the Sea: Historical Perspectives* (Wellington, NZ: Bridget Williams Books, 2018).

122 For "large Ocean nations," see Salesa, "Native Seas and Native Seaways," 101; for UNCLOS and ocean space as common heritage, see DeLoughrey, *Routes and Roots*, 30–37.

Then crashed the coast of Kandavu
Whence the mountains heard that he who dared the gods
Had tamed the sea.

You've gone, red-eyed sailor,
So have our fathers forever.
I mourn not you, not them,
But us you've left adrift,
Derelicts becalmed.[123]

It is a poem of oceanic plenitude, a celebration of a life on and with the ocean, of bellwether terns (the winds were high that day in Minerva) and the moon-goddess Sina (who could play a trick on the eye), of currents and winds that pulled and pushed Tongan vessels into the waters of the Fijian island Kadavu, and of wooden gods, of voyaging canoes, that yielded to none.[124]

For the founders of the Republic of Minerva, the reefs were a space of legal liminality, one of the few areas where establishing a new country seemed possible. The legal and political status were what mattered. As has so often been the case, however, spaces perceived by distant colonizers as open for the taking are in fact places occupied by existing populations who have given meaning to such spaces and incorporated them into a wider social and cultural horizon. For Tongans the reefs were part of a history of navigation and settlement, of rescue and loss, of meaning and mourning, and part of a geography of identity and livelihood where sea and land entwined. Teleki Tokelau and Teleki Tonga were anything but distant atolls. They were places of provision and poetry and history. No doubt, one day, maybe a thousand years hence, a hardened body will breach permanently, and a natural island will come to be in Minerva, a result of processes of the kind that had built up the reefs themselves.[125] But not until then. The only invisible hand at work here, among the atolls and seamounts of the Native Pacific, will be that of the ocean.

---

123 Hau'ofa, "To the Last Viking of the Sunrise," reproduced in Albert Wendt, ed., *Nuanua: Pacific Writing in English Since 1980* (Honolulu: University of Hawai'i Press, 1995), 382. Originally published in *Faikava: A Tongan Literary Journal* 4 (December 1979): 8. I am grateful to Hau'ofa's son for kind permission to reproduce the poem in its entirety here.
124 I am grateful to Tevita Ka'ili at BYU-Hawai'i for his insight into the references in the poem and for directing me toward the interpretations of Tongan poetry more broadly.
125 This draws on a wonderful riff in Ruhen, *Minerva Reef*, 33.

CHAPTER THREE

Libertarian Noir

Free-Market Mercenaries
of the Caribbean

THERE WERE FEW JOINTS IN WASHINGTON, DC, MORE APPEALING TO THE CITY'S powerbrokers and celebrities than Duke Zeibert's, on L Street, four blocks north of the White House. Washington Redskins football coach Vince Lombardi, and his eventual successor George Allen were both regulars along with a host of local television and radio personalities who competed for a top-ranked table in its two-toned brown and blue interior or for a seat at the counter of its dimly lit bar. The New York Yankees dined here when they were in town and, after one fine evening, teed up and tagged golf balls out along L Street. But for a political city it was the political personalities that counted, which is why journalists hovered, hopeful for a lapse in judgment and a loose tongue after one too many power lunch martinis. This was the kind of place where Harry Truman, Tip O'Neill, and Bobby Kennedy dined regularly. Duke Zeibert himself had had the honor of joining RFK's funeral train after his assassination in 1968. This was the kind of place where J. Edgar Hoover, until his death in 1972, would lunch regularly, favoring an open-faced steak tartare sandwich named the G-Man Special in his honor, even if it meant occasionally running into Jimmy Hoffa, at least until *his* death in 1971. This was the kind of place where even the staff appeared larger than life, sporting nicknames like Man O' War and carrying switchblades on gold chains. This was the kind of place, that is to say, where no one gathered for lunch on a weekday in May of 1974 would have looked twice at a motley crew of eight men in a corner table eating soft-shell crab and jellied salmon while plotting the invasion of a Caribbean island (see fig. 3.1).[1]

---

1   The details of Duke Zeibert's are from Jack Pointer, "Duke Zeibert's: How a Legendary Restaurant Brought Old DC Together," *WTOP News*, September 6, 2018, https://wtop.com/dc/2018/09/duke-zeiberts-dominion-how-an-iconic-restaurant-brought-old-dc-together/. On the G-Man Special, see Matt Schudel, "Mel Krupin, Who Ran DC Power Restaurants for Two Decades, Dies at 90," *Washington Post*, August 27, 2020. For the specifics of jellied salmon and softshell crab, see Andrew St. George, "The Amazing New Country Caper," *Esquire* (February 1975).

Fig. 3.1: Soft-shell crab and hard-boiled plots. Duke Zeibert's Restaurant, ca. 1960s.
David George "Duke" Zeibert Collection, Kiplinger Library, Historical Society of Washington, DC. Courtesy of the DC History Center.

And a motley crew they were: John Muldoon, Walter Mackem, and Ted Roussos, all former CIA operatives.[2] Muldoon had been the first director of the US government's Provincial Interrogation Center (PIC) program, a network of interrogation centers in South Vietnam and, according to one official, "a foundation stone upon which it was later possible to construct the Phoenix program," which referred to covert operations of extrajudicial assassination, torture, and sabotage established by the CIA in Vietnam in 1967.[3] Mackem too had been a CIA officer in Vietnam where he organized covert teams of ethnic Khmers to infiltrate Viet Cong territory and "snatch and snuff" the enemy. Mackem went with them. "I did it myself," he boasted. "We were

2   The CIA's chief of operations for the western hemisphere, David Atlee Phillips, informed the FBI director in June 1974 of WerBell's and Oliver's efforts to enlist Muldoon, Mackem and Roussos in their Abaco plans. See Phillips to FBI Director, undated but stamped June 27, 1974, Memorandum on Mitchell Livingston WerBell III, accessed March 13, 2018, https://www.archives.gov/files/research/jfk/releases/104-10256-10060.pdf.

3   Douglas Valentine, *The Phoenix Program* (New York: William Morrow, 1990), 108–9; on Muldoon's involvement, see ibid., 76–91. On the PIC and Phoenix more broadly, see Alfred W. McCoy, *A Question of Torture: CIA Interrogation, From the Cold War to the War on Terror* (New York: Henry Holt, 2006), 63–71.

freewheeling back then. It was a combination of *The Man Who Would Be King* and *Apocalypse Now!*"[4]

There was retired army colonel Robert Bayard, a former commander of the 82nd Airborne Division, Vietnam veteran, and a pioneer in the design and use of night-vision equipment. One year after the lunch meeting, Bayard would be murdered with a single shot to the head outside of a fashionable mall in Atlanta, Georgia at the age of fifty-six, a murder (some said political execution) that remains unsolved to this day.[5] Also at the table, observing closely and taking copious notes, was Andrew St. George, a Hungarian émigré and serious investigative but down-on-his-luck journalist who had reported from the Sierra Maestra with Fidel Castro and Che Guevara in 1958 as they advanced on Havana. Not down on his luck was Robert Anthony Carmichael Hamilton, aka the Thirteenth Baron of Belhaven and Stenton and a member of the British House of Lords. Lord Belhaven (family motto: "Ride Through") had certain personal interests in the topic of discussion.[6] All of these individuals had their eyes on the remaining two men at the table, the two men who had summoned them to this late spring lunch, two men who could hardly have been more different in style but who shared a vision for the future and a plan to bring it to fruition: a brash, brawny, and hard-drinking arms dealer named Mitchell Livingston WerBell III and Michael Oliver.

After the failure of Minerva, Oliver had regrouped. With the continued pace of decolonization, Oliver saw opportunities to find an area of land linked with a "weak colonial government, not closely tied to a 'mother' country."[7] In this he went against the tide of mainstream investors and companies looking to set up shop offshore for tax avoidance purposes. Most offshore clients

---

4   Valentine, *The Phoenix Program*, 56. Mackem was fired ("riffed") by the CIA in 1973 for a number of transgressions, including having confidential CIA documents in his safe, and subsequently investigated for his role in a potential FBI extortion case. See Raymond Reardon, "Memorandum for the Record, Subject: Walter Josef Mackem," May 21, 1976, https://archive.org/details/MitchellLivingstonWerBell/page/n68/mode/1up?q=oliver.

5   "Mystery of Ex-Colonel's Death," *San Francisco Chronicle*, July 7, 1975; "Army Colonel Is Killed, Robbed on Atlanta Street," unlabeled newspaper clipping dated July 5, 1975. Both articles are available at the 508th Parachute Infantry Regiment website, accessed May 29, 2020, https://www.508pir.org/obits/obit_text/b/bayard_rf.htm.

6   Mention of Belhaven's family motto can be found in "The Peer and the Plot to Take Over a Paradise Island," *Daily Mail* (February 11, 1975?), enclosure in Foreign and Commonwealth Office [hereafter FCO] 63/1389 (f. 12A), National Archives of the United Kingdom [hereafter NA-Kew].

7   Oliver and Harold G. Jindrich, *Capitalist Country Newsletter* 1, no. 1 (July 1968): 1. I have found very little information on Jindrich. As best as I can tell, he was born in 1929 and lived, at least in the 1970s, in California. In 1974 he had an affiliation with the Libertarian Party.

wanted security of sovereignty even as they escaped it and thus sought out dependencies and former colonies still closely tied to the mother country, for example the Cayman Islands and the Channel Islands. Not Oliver. Tax avoidance was a distant consideration. He wanted an opportune space upon which could be created an entirely new, sovereign entity. Within a year he had identified a new location for a possible libertarian country: the island and set of cays known as Abaco that belonged to the larger political archipelago of the Bahamas. The timing seemed propitious. An inchoate secessionist movement had taken root among a number of the 6,500 residents of the island. Here Oliver hoped to undertake "a moral experiment, a place where we'll try to keep individual freedom alive even if it doesn't survive in America."[8]

A moral experiment of immoral proportions. In his pursuit of individual freedom, Oliver ventured into a shadowy realm occupied by gunrunners, mercenaries, and right-wing nationalists. Oliver saw himself as a defender of freedom, struggling against a tide of corruption, malaise, and social collapse in a dark and threatening world but those with whom he allied himself were often more interested in profit than the promise of exit. Like a plot derived from classic noir, base motivations—greed, racial resentment, masculine insecurity—as much as lofty aspirations drove the effort to create the Republic of Abaco. Anticommunist counterinsurgency and militarized capitalism, white flight, and white supremacy came along for the ride. Oliver's allies in all this proved to be less Philip Marlowe, Raymond Chandler's ruminative and philosophical private detective, and more Mike Hammer, Mickey Spillane's anticommunist vigilante. These soldiers of fortune, who advertised their services in the back pages of the magazine of the same name, drew upon their connections to the government—as former CIA operatives and military veterans—in order to expand private opportunities for wealth and power in the wake of decolonization and the reconfiguration of finance and sovereignty that ensued. They could sell themselves to bidders with the implied promise that not only were they, as mercenaries, more efficient than state agents but also more readily able to plumb the dark recesses where those agents either feared or were forbidden to tread.[9] Hired guns, it would be tempting to say

---

8   As quoted in St. George, "The Amazing New-Country Caper," 154. Regarding how things would unfold following secession, Oliver was blunt: "On Abaco, I will decide."
9   For a detailed and careful study of such activity, and all the more impressive given it was written in the midst of many of the events it uncovers, see Jim Hougan, *Spooks: The Haunting of America—The Private Use of Secret Agents* (New York: William Morrow, 1978). On thinking about noir I am indebted to Robert von Hallberg, *The Maltese Falcon to Body of Lies: Spies, Noirs, and Trust* (Albuquerque: University of New Mexico Press, 2015), especially chap. 1; Carl Freedman, *Art and Ideas in the Novels of China Miéville* (London: Gylphi, 2015), esp. his chapter on *The City and the City*; and David Cochran,

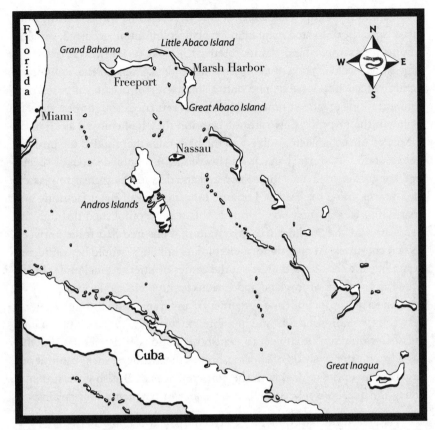

Fig. 3.2: The Bahamas.
Map by John Wyatt Greenlee.

that they thrived in spaces situated at the margins of the state and the center of free enterprise. It is a temptation to be resisted. Unregulated capitalism, the free-wheeling market, has never been the antithesis of the state in the manner that its champions proclaim. Given that the Duke Zeibert plotters intended to create a privatized state, an actual place of individual autonomy and market sovereignty, it would be more accurate to say they thrived in a space situated at the center of a free enterprise state itself: a space of libertarian noir.

Duty free

The Bahamian archipelago acquired independence from Great Britain on July 10, 1973. Independence, however, is a relative term. The economic realities

---

American Noir: Underground Writers and Filmmakers of the Postwar Era (Washington, DC: Smithsonian Books, 2000).

that helped Oliver amass his small fortune were in some ways the same ones
that shaped the mitigated manner in which decolonization occurred. Britain's
empire, for example, hardly evaporated in the wake of World War II and the
large-scale decolonization of the 1950s and the 1960s. Even as Britain's imperial
expanse receded to leave behind only a smattering of distant outposts, new
configurations of power emerged. Colonial returnees sought out ways to
maintain the favorably low rates of taxation they had enjoyed as an imperial perk rather than being subject to the high rates that funded the postwar
welfare state.[10] Powerful bankers and investors drew upon decades of special-
ized knowledge in finance in decolonized and decolonizing areas to reassert
their power, using the City of London, long a center of manufacturing and
financial power, as their pivot. In part this was accomplished through the
re-creation of the Sterling Area, a system that ensured that trade between
certain countries, frequently former colonial holdings, would be conducted
in sterling and thus keep the City at the center of international trade. In the
late 1950s the Bank of England and various commercial banks in the City of
London struck up an informal agreement: "any transaction through London
between two non-residents and in a foreign currency—at the time, mainly
dollars—would not be subject to British regulations."[11] Ronen Palan, who
has written extensively on offshoring, argues that the agreement came about
largely as an effort to deal with the consequences of British governmental
policy and questions related to British balance of payments. He explains:

> The agreement arose out of the run on the pound of 1956–7 and a subse-
> quent desire to avoid harmful effects on the British balance of payments....
> In response to the run on the pound, the Treasury raised interest rates
> from 5 to 7% and imposed a moratorium on lending to non-British
> borrowers. The two policies aimed to strengthen the pound. The mora-
> torium cut many commercial banks, which specialised in lending to
> ex-colonies or the "informal empire," off from their business. It appears
> that they reached an agreement with the Bank of England ... that they
> could continue lending as long as they interacted in dollars (or any other

10 See Vanessa Ogle, "Archipelago Capitalism: Tax Havens, Offshore Money, and the State,
    1950s–1970s," *American Historical Review* 122, no. 5 (December 2017): 1438–39.
11 Palan, "Britain's Second Empire," *New Left Project*, August 17, 2012, accessed December 2, 2016,
    http://www.newleftproject.org/index.php/site/article_comments/britains_second_
    empire. The link is no longer active, so readers should consult Palan, "The Second British
    Empire: The British Empire and the Reemergence of Global Finance," in Sandra Halperin
    and Ronen Palan, eds., *Legacies of Empire: Imperial Roots of the Contemporary Global
    Order* (Cambridge: Cambridge University Press, 2015), 46–68 and Palan, "International
    Financial Centers: The British-Empire, City-States and Commercially Oriented Politics,"
    Theoretical Inquiries in Law 11, no. 1 (January 2010): 149–76.

non-sterling currency) and intermediated between non-British clients. Such transactions—in foreign currency, between non-British clients—would not affect the British balance of payments. But the agreement seems to have yielded an unintended consequence: such transactions were "deemed" by the Bank not to be taking place in London. This liberated them from the regulatory regime not only of the UK, but also of any other country. This was the origin of "offshore."[12]

If offshoring was an "unintended consequence" of efforts to deal with decolonization and economic policy, its possibilities were soon exploited to the fullest. In particular, investors found in offshore and the transnational market for US dollars (commonly referred to as the Euromarket) a way to bypass the restrictions put into place after World War II, encapsulated in the Bretton Woods agreement, that were intended to better regulate and control investment and thus avoid the kinds of dramatic fluctuations of, and abuses in, the financial system that had helped foment world war.[13] Thus, intentionally or not, in the midst of the high era of decolonization a new form of imperial presence arose in the shape of an unregulated, parallel market running through the City of London.[14] If, as Cain and Hopkins have noted, the "City gentlemen could no longer rely on either the empire or the Sterling Area to provide them with a world role," the Euromarket could.[15]

A significant number of island states remained as part of Britain's Overseas Territories, including many in the Caribbean which became prominent tax havens. These proved attractive to investors precisely because such locations still had some attachment to British sovereignty, promising investors and tax avoiders the security that came with sovereignty.[16] Splits opened up within the British Civil Service, between the Treasury on the one hand, which opposed tax havens, and the Bank of England and British Overseas Development Ministry on the other, which saw tax havens (and the income earned from limited taxation rates or licensing fees) as a means for territories to "pay their own way" and not be a drain on Britain's economy.[17] Caribbean

---

12   Palan, "Britain's Second Empire."

13   Oliver Bullough, "Offshore Money, Bane of Democracy," *New York Times*, April 7, 2017.

14   As of 2012, somewhere around 40 percent of all international deposits and investments run through British dependencies or former colonies. Palan, "Britain's Second Empire"; Palan, "The Second British Empire"; and Palan, "International Financial Centers."

15   P.J. Cain and A.G. Hopkins, *British Imperialism, 1688–2000*, 2nd ed. (London: Longman, 2002), 641.

16   Shaxson, *Treasure Islands: Uncovering the Damage of Offshore Banking and Tax Havens* (London: Palgrave-Macmillan, 2011), 87.

17   Ibid., 91.

tax havens in particular became a haven for capital flight from the US and Latin American countries which then saved Britain's ministries thousands in foreign aid.[18] Kenneth Crook, appointed governor of the Cayman Islands in 1971, penned a letter in which he warned the banks that if they did not keep in mind that people—not just money—lived on the islands, then they "might as well buy an aircraft carrier and operate from that."[19]

White oligarchs

The ground had long since been laid for tax havens in the region, including in the Bahamas. The Caribbean had been a test site for famed mobster Meyer Lansky who dominated the casino industry in parts of the US and moved into Cuba in the 1930s, where he and his associates garnered the favor of US-backed dictator Fulgencio Batista. But as Batista's dominance appeared increasingly under threat in the late 1950s, investors began to look elsewhere. Ian Fleming, an acute observer of the postwar world, particularly as manifested in the Caribbean, repeatedly layered discussions of such practices into his James Bond stories. Just to take one example, in the short story "For Your Eyes Only," a British plantation owner in Jamaica observes the flood of money arriving on the island from investors in Cuba fearful of Batista's downfall as Fidel Castro's revolutionary movement grew: "The place [Cuba] is riddled with crooks and gangsters," the man comments. "They must want to get their money out of Cuba and into something else quick. Jamaica's as good as anywhere else now we've got this convertibility with the dollar."[20] After Castro's revolution, Lansky moved to Miami and built the first casino in the Bahamas. Soon a flood of investors and money launderers, mobsters and bankers, arrived. With casino gambling and bank secrecy laws in place, over the course of the 1960s some 350 banks and companies set up headquarters—often little more than a single room with a nameplate—on the islands.[21]

The Bahamas were still a British colony in the 1960s. "Formerly a staging post for British gun-running to the southern U.S. slave states of the Confederacy," writes Nicholas Shaxson, "and loosely governed for years by laissez-faire members of British high society, the Bahamas were effectively run by an oligarchy of corrupt white merchants."[22] That white oligarchy, known

---

18 Ibid., 101.
19 Ibid., 94–95.
20 Fleming, "For Your Eyes Only," in Fleming, *Quantum of Solace: The Complete James Bond Short Stories* (New York: Penguin, 2008), 34. Two pages later he is dead, having refused to sell his plantation to a Cuban investor.
21 Alan A. Block, introduction to *Masters of Paradise: Organised Crime and the Internal Revenue Service in the Bahamas* (New York: Routledge, 1991).
22 Shaxson, *Treasure Islands*, 89.

as the Bay Street Boys, did not look kindly on the approach of Bahamian independence, slated to take place in 1973, especially given that it would be overseen by a black prime minister, Lynden Pindling, and his all-black Progressive Liberal Party. Concerns among the white minority were colored by a fear of red internationalism (a "Communist takeover") and black nationalism (a "Pindling 'dictatorship'").[23] This convergence of racism and anticommunism was not uncommon in a British Caribbean beset by the winds of decolonization and civil rights movements. In such a context some were eager to see communist machinations behind any call for racial justice, including Fleming who wrote many of his James Bond novels while at his Goldeneye estate in Jamaica and in the 1950s alleged that the NAACP was a communist front.[24] Such fears only grew after the successful overthrow of Batista by Castro in Cuba. In the early 1970s editorialists opposed to Bahamian independence stoked rumors of a Cuban invasion rolling through the archipelago with little resistance should the British leave.[25]

On Abaco, a designation referring to the Great and Little Abaco islands and surrounding cays which lengthen out some 130 miles across the northern extremis of the archipelago, opposition to independence was strong. Many of Abaco's white residents were direct descendants of British loyalists who had fled to the islands in the wake of the American revolution. As such, they embraced an outsized, exaggerated colonial patriotism. A stroll through Marsh Harbour, Abaco's main town, would take one past the Loyalist Shoppe and the Union Jack Club and Hotel.[26] "Abaco," observed one British official, "is the only place where in my various gubernatorial progressions I have heard sung all three verses of the National Anthem generally preceded by 'Keep

---

23 Don Bohning, "Bahamas Independence Opposed in Abaco," *Miami Herald*, May 21, 1973, enclosure in FBI Acting Director to SACS New York, Miami, Atlanta, June 15, 1937 (FBI 1350966). WerBell complained to the head of the Bureau of Inter-American Affairs that "Fidel and Pindling are working together and anti-Communism is losing all over the Hemisphere." As reported in ARA to ARA–CA, "Call from Mitch WerBell," May 25, 1973 (FBI 1421912). Unless otherwise noted, all FBI document citations come from materials acquired through three FOIA requests: FOIA 1350966 (Subject: Mitchell Werbell); FOIA 1400082 (Subject: Andrew St. George); and FOIA 1421912 (Subject: Edwin Marger), hereafter referred to as FBI 1350966; FBI 1400082; and FBI 1421912.

24 Andrew Lycett, *Ian Fleming* (New York: St. Martin's Press, 2013 [1995]), 237.

25 Hartley Cecil Saunders, *The Other Bahamas* (Nassau: Bodab, 2013 [1991]), 302–11.

26 Bohning, "Bahamas Independence Opposed in Abaco." On loyalists in Abaco after the American revolution, see Christopher Curry, *Freedom and Resistance: A Social History of Black Loyalists in the Bahamas* (Gainesville: University Press of Florida, 2017) and Maya Jasanoff, *Liberty's Exiles: American Loyalists in the Revolutionary World* (New York: Alfred Knopf, 2011).

the Old Flag Flying.'"[27] Heritage functioned as code for race. The black population outnumbered whites by two to one, but the wealth sat largely in the hands of the latter.[28] Black loyalists who had fled to the Bahamas during the American revolution in the hopes of attaining their freedom found themselves still in positions of subordination. All-white settlements populated many of the cays around Abaco with black laborers often required to leave by sundown. Segregation—residential, recreational, and labor—still existed in the early 1970s in some areas, including not only in the cays and around Marsh Harbour but in the capital city of Nassau.[29] While some petitioners took pains to suggest that support on Abaco for remaining a Crown colony was widely shared by both white and black Abaconians, racial power was central to the fears of many white petitioners. Letter writers complained of a government run by black militants fomenting race hatred, but frequently the crux of their concerns seemed to be a sense of race betrayal: ardent loyalists were now being abandoned to a black government. "[I]t would appear that the present Government is prepared to hand over control of the Bahamas to the Black population," wrote Marsh Harbour's Neville Roberts, "with complete indifference to the residents who have remained loyal to the Mother Country through war and peace and whose forbearers settled these islands and developed them through the years."[30] Roberts, a wealthy resident of Abaco known for hosting parties on some floating thing he had named *Onwego*, was affectionately known as Big Daddy-O around Marsh Harbour but the Home Office official who received his letter had a different impression: "A political nut!" she or he scribbled across the letter. "No action required."[31]

A nut is not necessarily an anomaly. Numerous prominent Bahamians—some based on Nassau, others in Abaco—deployed racist arguments as they fretted over independence. The former governor-general of the Bahamas,

---

27   [John Paul], "Personality Notes: Mr Errington W I Watkins MP," FCO 63/1029, NA-Kew. The white residents of Abaco appeared afflicted by a premature form of "postcolonial melancholia:" a nostalgia for empire and a sadness at its waning, feelings amplified when expressed in a colonial outpost of a colonial outpost. Paul Gilroy, *Postcolonial Melancholia* (New York: Columbia University Press, 2005).

28   Michael Craton and Gail Saunders, *Islanders in the Stream: A History of the Bahamian People* (Athens: University of Georgia Press, 1998), 2:196.

29   Curry, *Freedom and Resistance*, 192–93; Hartely Cecil Saunders, *The Other Bahamas* (Nassau: Bodab, 2013 [1991]).

30   Neville Roberts (Union Jack Hotel, Marsh Harbour, Abaco) to Hon. Edward Heath, Prime Minister of Great Britain, 28 Jan 1971, FCO 44/492, NA-Kew. Neville Roberts is not to be confused with the Bahamas former Governor-General, Robert Neville.

31   Neville Roberts (Union Jack Hotel, Marsh Harbour, Abaco) to Hon. Edward Heath, Prime Minister of Great Britain, 28 Jan 1971, FCO 44/492, NA-Kew. For Roberts's parties and nickname, see "Neville Roberts:—Everybody's Favourite Personality," *Abaco Account* 3, no. 1 (1966): 11.

Major General Robert Neville, summarized the feelings of many white settlers whose future seemed so unsettled:

> Politically also it seems to me that this Government should welcome an opportunity to show consideration for British loyalists. It is very distressing for one who has been a Conservative all his life to hear the widespread criticism of the present British Government that, whilst they lean over backwards to placate people like Mr Amin of Uganda, every opportunity appears to be taken to kick the white people of the Commonwealth in the teeth.[32]

British officials read such missives for what they were: race-baiting by white Bahamians "who have been unable to adjust themselves to the assumption of power by the black majority."[33]

The ease with which white petitioners conflated a discourse of loyalty with a discourse of race is unsurprising. The fear of decolonization, in the end, was a fear of a loss of racial privilege. Yet the petitioners appeared to have forgotten not only that many in the black population were also descended from loyalists who had settled and developed the islands, but that a number of prominent black Abaconians affiliated themselves with the Bay Street clique's United Bahamian Party (UBP), founded in 1958, and supported Abaco remaining a Crown colony. These included Leonard Thompson, who had served as a pilot in the Canadian Air Force during World War II, was shot down on his twenty-fifth bombing mission over Hamburg, and remained a prisoner of war until being liberated by Soviet troops in 1945, and Errington Watkins, a former deputy police commissioner in Nassau. Both men sought to keep Abaco as part of the United Kingdom, drafting petitions, collecting signatures, and lobbying officials during an intense year of activity in 1971.[34] Despite those efforts, the chances for a legal process of secession by Abaco from an independent Bahamas grew dim, particularly after the 1972 general elections which revealed strong support for Pindling's Progressive Liberal Party and effectively ended the possibility of separation through the voting booth.[35]

---

32 Major General Sir Robert Neville to Lord Balneil, December 12, 1972, FCO 63/1029, NA-Kew.

33 Illegible to David Scott, West Indian Dept. FCO, July 9, 1971, FCO 63/1029, NA-Kew.

34 For controversy surrounding the process of collecting signatures and accusations of payments to black Abaconians in exchange for signing, see Meeting with Mr Ronald Bell QC, MP, on February 1 [1972?], Abaco, FCO 44/659, NA-Kew.

35 JH Fawcett to CS Roberts and DA Scott, September 28, 1972, FCO 63/1029, NA-Kew; Steve Dodge, "Independence and Separatism," in Dean Collingwood and Steve Dodge, eds., *Modern Bahamian Society* (Parkersburg, IA: Caribbean Books, 1989), 48–49.

Watkins and Chuck Hall, Nassau-born but whose mother was from Abaco, then formed the Council for a Free Abaco to continue to push their cause. They entered treacherous waters. Regardless of their loyalties to the crown, some of Abaco's businessmen grew increasingly ambivalent about secession and gave it little chance of success.[36] Moreover, many adamantly opposed armed insurrection or violent efforts at secession, including Leonard Thompson. "We wished to disassociate ourselves from the Council for a Free Abaco who are openly advocating violence," he wrote. "All desire for military glory was fulfilled for me years ago in the sky over Germany and, in the case of my brother, on the cruel seas of the North Atlantic."[37] Thompson and others had come to learn of the involvement in the movement of a perceived band of foreign adventurers looking to make a land grab.[38] In April 1973 reports circulated that an American arms dealer and his attorney had arrived in England and were looking to recruit mercenaries in support of Abaco's secession.[39] Their activities garnered the attention of British newspapers and the foreign office as well as that of ex-military personnel who sought them out to offer their services.[40] Word traveled quickly. Pindling took the floor of the Parliament in May of 1973 to denounce such predatory possibilities. A reporter present at the scene wrote that Watkins looked visible shaken by the speech.[41] Understandably so. Pindling clearly knew that Watkins had accompanied the American arms dealer on his journey through England looking for mercenaries. Even more troubling, Watkins may have been the "political leader" (whose name has been redacted in the FBI correspondence) photographed at the home of that

---

36 This according to an FBI informant. See Acting Director, FBI to Secretary of State, May 15, 1973 (FBI 1350966).

37 Leonard Thompson for Greater Abaco Council to Ronald Bell MP, April 28, 1973, FCO 63/1167 (f. 58 enc.), NA-Kew.

38 Even Abaconians had feared that separatist movements in Abaco were largely driven by efforts to grab land. The *Tribune* reported that in 1971 a group of Abaconians described the separatist movement as "the biggest land grab" ever attempted in the Bahamas. *Tribune*, June 7, 1973, 3.

39 CS Roberts, Caribbean Dept, to Mr Moss, PUSD, April 24, 1973, FCO 63/1167 (f. 17), NA-Kew; Telegram 108, Governor Bahamas to FCO, April 26, 1973, FCO 63/1167 (f. 20), NA-Kew. The attorney was Edwin Marger, at the time based in Miami Beach and who subsequently moved his offices to Georgia. Marger may have met WerBell in the Dominican Republic where Marger had business interests in the 1960s.

40 See, for example, M. Mount, letter dated April 24, 1973, enclosure in J.E.F. Codrington, Commissioner, to C.G. Mortlock, Caribbean Dept. FCO, April 26, 1973, FCO 63/1167 (f. 21), NA-Kew; and Mortlock to Codrington, April 27, 1973, FCO 63/1167 (f. 25), NA-Kew

41 American Consul Nassau to Secretary of State, Washington, DC, and American Embassy London, May 18, 1973, Wikileaks ID: 1973NASSAU00661_b. On Watkins looking shaken, see Bohning, "Bahamas Independence Opposed in Abaco."

very same arms dealer in Powder Springs, Georgia, a soldier of fortune by the name of Mitchell Livingston WerBell III.[42]

The Wizard of Whispering Death

If Mitchell Livingston WerBell's life were a novel it would be equal parts *The Dogs of War* (1974) and *The Grifters* (1963), soaked in a bottle of Islay scotch. Also known as the Wizard of Whispering Death, WerBell was a hard-drinking, chain-smoking, fast-talking figure, larger than life and his 5-feet-6-½-inch frame. Brash and brawny, even his moustache was a piece of militarized facial topiary. From the 1940s until his death in 1983 WerBell both traversed and exemplified that place where the military-industrial complex, the madcap and paranoid anticommunist underground, and the gritty violent underworld meet. An arms dealer and former OSS operative, adventurer and adman, his flamboyant self-promotion often strained the bounds of credulity. Did WerBell, as he claimed, oversee a bombing campaign of North Vietnam with live bubonic-plague-infected rats? Had he run paramilitary operations in Cuba, Nicaragua, and Guatemala? Had he led local commando teams on assassination missions behind enemy lines in China in the 1940s? Was he good friends with a king in Thailand? The recipient of a special medal of commendation from Chiang Kai-shek? A "deep cover" agent for the CIA? Was he known by everyone, as Jim Garrison claimed during his investigation of John F. Kennedy's assassination? (see fig. 3.3)[43]

---

42   Bohning, "Bahamas Independence Opposed in Abaco." On Watkins traveling with WerBell and attorney Edwin Marger, see Roberts to Sir Duncan Watson, April 30, 1973, FCO 63/1167 (f 29), NA-Kew. It seems likely but not certain that Watkins was the political leader whose name is redacted from an FBI report on American involvement in Abaconian revolutionary activities. See FBI LHM, New York, New York, "Mitchell Livingston WerBell III; Internal Security—Bahamas," June 25, 1973 (FBI 1350966). A separate FBI report included information from a redacted source claiming that Watkins was indeed at WerBell's home during the time the photographs were taken. See SAC NY to Acting Director, FBI, "UNSUBS: Revolutionary Group on Abaco Island," June 6, 1973 (FBI 1421912). The photographs were discovered at some point in May 1973. Taken by a staff photographer of the *London Daily Express*, they showed a group of men undertaking firearms training on Abaco Island and of individuals at WerBell's home posing with sub-machine guns. See Acting Director, FBI to SACs, New York/Miami/Atlanta, June 15, 1973, "Mitchell Livingston Werbell, IS-Bahamas" (FBI 1350966).

43   See Robert Eringer, "Interview with the Anti-Terrorist," *Saga Magazine*, accessed June 8, 2015, http://www.atomiclabrat.com/MAC%20Pages%20for%20Atomic%20Lab%20Rat.com/WerBell_Interview_SAGA_86%5B1%5D.pdf; Andrew St. George, "Killer at Bay," typescript in box 26, Andrew St. George collection, Yale University [hereafter ASG]; and Andrew St. George book project memo, January 10, 1976, loose leaf sheet in Folder "Mitch," box 25, ASG. New Orleans' attorney general Jim Garrison came across WerBell during his investigations of the Kennedy assassination. "He's a CIA arms contractor," Garrison noted. "Always knows what's happening in Miami.

Fig. 3.3: The Wizard of Whispering Death: Mitchell Livingston WerBell III.
Photograph by Andrew St. George. Private collection of Andrew Szentgyorgyi. By kind permission of Andrew Szentgyorgyi.

It is a testament to the inventiveness and secrecy of the national security apparatus that such claims cannot be easily dismissed. And in fact, much of the preceding paragraph would appear to be "almost always almost entirely true," as one author described the stories of CIA operative Lucien Conein, with whom WerBell served in Asia and Southeast Asia.[44] But FBI investigators and informants were dubious. Over the course of the 1960s and 1970s, they concluded that WerBell was an "opportunist," a "con-man with an unsavory reputation," a "wild man" who lived "by his wits, fast dealing and smooth talking," an "unscrupulous confidence man," and a "notorious adventurer."[45]

Furnishes most of the arms for activities in Miami. Lives 25 miles out of Atlanta. Easy to find. Everybody knows him." Collection JFKCO: John F. Kennedy Assassination Records Collection, 12/28/1992 - 9/30/1998; Series: Papers of Jim Garrison, 1965–1992; File Unit: Miscellaneous Investigative Reports and Memorandum, 3 folders, https://catalog.archives.gov/id/7564859.

44   Quoted lines from Stanley Karnow, author of *Vietnam: A History*, who interviewed Conein and is quoted in Tim Weiner, *Legacy of Ashes: The History of the CIA* (New York: Anchor Books, 2008), 695–96.

45   See SAC (Atlanta) to Director, FBI, June 17, 1965, "Subject: Mitchell Livingston Werbell III, Neutrality Matters"; Director, FBI to Attorney General, January 26, 1966, "Mitchell Livingston Werbell III, Internal Security-Cuba"; and Teletype, FBI Director to [redacted], January 22, 1970, "Mitchell Livingston Werbell III, Internal Security-Haiti." (All in FBI 1350966).

Such may have been the case, but it bears noting that con man and coun-terinsurgent are not mutually exclusive. If there be a line between grifter and mercenary, crook and spook, it is a thin one, at best. In the 1950s and 1960s some of the most effective counterinsurgency operatives who moved in and out of the CIA's orbit were men who had acquired experience in new forms of mass persuasion, including advertising, psychology, efforts at mind control, and media manipulation. US operatives who helped overthrow the democratically elected Jacobo Árbenz in Guatemala in 1954 were steeped in such techniques.[46] Edward Lansdale, whose career spanned the Cold War and took him from the Philippines to Vietnam and to Cuba, had a background in advertising. One of Lansdale's own colleagues from the OSS described him as "a Madison Avenue 'Man in the Grey Flannel Suit' con man."[47] He could just as easily have been describing WerBell, himself a former OSS man who went on in the 1950s to work as an adman and public relations consultant in Atlanta.[48]

The musings over whether he was a con man miss the point: WerBell made himself into what he needed to be to make money. WerBell's PR work had not worked out, and by the late 1950s he was financially in trouble. Cuba's revolution jumpstarted his career. From the early 1960s, WerBell insinuated himself into the center of a growing industry of paramilitary warfare and international intrigue that expanded in the wake of Castro's remarkable achievement. He had the connections to do so. WerBell's military career began in the US Army Signal Corps, but in the 1940s military intelligence recruited him to the OSS and he deployed to Kunming, China to work alongside E. Howard Hunt, Lucien Conein, and John Singlaub (see figs. 3.4 and 3.5).[49] All three men achieved some level of fame or, as the case may be, notoriety. Hunt ended up a Watergate plumber. Conein, a counterinsurgent specialist who

---

46   For such techniques as they applied to the overthrow of Jacobo Árbenz in Guatemala in 1954, see Greg Grandin, *The Last Colonial Massacre: Latin America and the Cold War* (Chicago: University of Chicago Press, 2004), esp. chap. 3; and Weiner, *Legacy of Ashes*, chap. 10.

47   As quoted in Weiner, *Legacy of Ashes*, 213.

48   FBI Communications Section, Atlanta to Acting Director, Miami office, May 2, 1973, "Mitchell Livingston Werbell III" (FBI 1350966). For a detailed study of WerBell and the secretive, paranoid world in which he operated that generated simultaneously delusions of grandeur and very real situations of power, see Hougan, *Spooks*, esp. 153–58.

49   Peter Dale Scott, *American War Machine: Deep Politics, the CIA Global Drug Connection, and the Road to Afghanistan*, rev. ed. (Lanham, MD: Rowman & Littlefield, 2014 [2010]), 52–53; 331n50; John K. Singlaub, with Malcolm McConnell, *Hazardous Duty: An American Soldier in the Twentieth-Century* (New York: Summit Books, 1991), 439; and Office of Strategic Services Personnel Files from World War II, Records Group 226, https://www.archives.gov/files/iwg/declassified-records/rg-226-oss/personnel-database.pdf. On WerBell's time in the signal corps and then "military intelligence," see FBI Report, Atlanta, GA, January 29, 1970 (FBI 1350966), 4.

Fig. 3.4: Mitchell Livingston WerBell. Undated, ca. mid-1940s. The figure on the right is unidentified but I strongly suspect it is E. Howard Hunt.

Folder "Mitch WerBell," box 2, MS1912, Andrew St. George collection, Yale University Library Manuscripts and Archives. By kind permission of Andrew Szentgyorgyi.

Fig. 3.5: Mitchell Livingston WerBell hotdogging on a motorcycle. Undated, ca. mid-1940s.

Folder "Mitch WerBell," box 2, MS1912, Andrew St. George collection, Yale University Library Manuscripts and Archives. By kind permission of Andrew Szentgyorgyi.

served in Vietnam in the 1950s and early 1960s, served as the conduit through which ran the plans to assassinate South Vietnam's president Ngo Dinh Diem in November 1963. He subsequently became head of special operations with the DEA, with lingering claims to this day that his primary task had been to establish an assassination team to murder high-level drug traffickers.[50] Singlaub became a CIA China desk officer; deputy chief of CIA mission in Korea in the early 1950s; the head of the Ranger Training Center in Fort Benning, Georgia; part of the US Military Assistance Command in Vietnam until 1968; and achieved the rank of major general in the US Army before resigning in protest over President Jimmy Carter's decision to pull ground troops from Korea in 1978.[51] Singlaub soon immersed himself with work in the protofascist World Anti-Communist League and, along with *Soldier of Fortune* magazine's founder Bob Brown, organized to bring mercenaries to Central America in the early 1980s. Although Singlaub in his autobiography

---

50   Hougan, *Spooks*, chap. 5.
51   "SOF interviews General John K. Singlaub," *Soldier of Fortune* 4, no. 1 (January 1979): 1.

sought to distance himself from WerBell, when he sat for an interview with *Soldier of Fortune* in 1978, he did so in WerBell's Georgia home.[52]

WerBell maintained at least some connections to his former OSS comrades. These connections most likely aided him in his time of need. Bankrupt in 1957, by 1962 he had gravitated to the myriad efforts to overthrow Castro and could be found offering to provide the Guatemalan Ministry of Defense weapons, ammunition, and five hundred military-trained mercenaries "to fight communism."[53] By 1966 he had linked up with various anti-Castro cabals. That year an FBI agent visited WerBell at his home in Powder Springs charged with investigating WerBell's possible role in a plot to assassinate Castro. WerBell claimed no involvement in an assassination plot but did share with the agent that one Ricardo Zaragusa had hatched a plot, but it died with him when he had a heart attack in a New York hotel room. It turned out that only Zaragusa knew the location of, and held the key to, a "family crypt in a cemetery in Cuba where arms, ammunitions and explosives are stored which were to be utilized in this assassination."[54] In all of this, however, what most caught the agent's attention was the impressive arsenal of weapons WerBell had lying around in his home, including "silencer M-3 submachine guns, Beretta silencers, explosives, brand new FALN rifles, etcetera."[55] FBI informants suspected WerBell acquired the weaponry from Manuel Ray Rivero, a former minister of public works in Cuba, who had overseen an earlier "pitiful invasion" attempt of the island.[56]

The agent and the agency left WerBell in peace. But a year later they investigated WerBell again, this time for his alleged involvement in a scheme, led by Rolando Masferrer Rojas, to invade Haiti, topple its dictator "Papa Doc" Duvalier, and establish a beachhead from which to launch an invasion of neighboring Cuba. Masferrer had been a battalion commander in the Spanish Civil War, loyal to the Republic as it fought the fascist forces of Francisco

52 Ibid., 30–31, 81–87. Singlaub later became part of a small US congressional delegation to El Salvador in the early 1980s, along with a reporter from *Soldier of Fortune* magazine. See Jim Morris, "Delegation to El Salvador," *Soldier of Fortune* 8, no. 2 (February 1983): 83–86. For more on Singlaub, particularly in the context of an "anti-communist revolution," see Kyle Burke, *Revolutionaries for the Right: Anticommunist Internationalism and Paramilitary Warfare in the Cold War* (Chapel Hill: University of North Carolina Press, 2018) and, for his links with counterinsurgency in Central America, Greg Grandin, *Empire's Workshop: Latin America, The United States, and the Rise of the New Imperialism* (New York: Henry Holt, 2006), 142–43.
53 SAC Atlanta to Director, FBI, September 26, 1967, Alleged Plan for Haitian Invasion (FBI 1350966).
54 FBI LHM, Atlanta, GA, February 11, 1966, "Mitchell Livingston Werbell III" (FBI 1350966).
55 FBI report, New York, New York, February 17, 1966 (FBI 1350966).
56 Ibid.

Franco. With the Republic's defeat in 1939, Masferrer fled to Cuba where he abandoned his republican ways. FBI agents described him as a confidant of Cuban dictator Fulgencio Batista, a gang leader, "a man with a very dark reputation," and a "legendary Caribbean pistol politician."[57] Masferrer boasted he had been responsible for the killings of more than fifteen thousand people while working for the regime. His coconspirator, Jean Baptiste Georges, was a former minister of education for the Duvalier regime.[58]

WerBell's connections to Masferrer and Georges are unclear, but it appears he was, among other things, to use his contacts in the Dominican Republic—where he had spent much of 1964 and 1965 looking to sell a consignment of weapons to the Dominican navy—to aid the invasion.[59] Things did not go as planned. The invasion imploded before it began, at least in part due to the inability of the parties involved to keep a lid on the scheme. In what must be one of the earliest instances of reality TV, CBS News collaborated with the conspirators and agreed to accompany them and film the invasion as part of a documentary.[60] The network went so far as to contribute funds to the adventure (see fig. 3.6). Unfortunately, prior to launching from Key Largo's upscale Ocean Reef resort, Masferrer and his Tigres, who numbered around 120, found themselves exposed by a local news correspondent who mistakenly reported that the invasion had already taken place.[61] Authorities arrested Masferrer and six others, indicted WerBell, and brought both him and journalist Andrew St. George before the US House of Representatives to give

---

57   The quoted passages are from Testimony of Andrew St. George to the House of Representatives, Special Subcommittee on Investigations, Committee on Interstate and Foreign Commerce, July 17, 1969, in *Network News Documentary Practices—CBS "Project Nassau"* (Washington, DC: US Government Printing Office, 1970), 32 and 158.

58   Gene Grove, "The CIA, FBI & CBS Bomb in Mission: Impossible," *Scanlan's Monthly* 1, no. 1 (March 1970): 2–4, 15–21.

59   Testimony of Andrew St. George to the House of Representatives, Special Subcommittee on Investigations, Committee on Interstate and Foreign Commerce, July 17, 1969, in *Network News Documentary Practices*, 40–41; Andrew St. George to Bob [no surname], November 1, 1969, loose page, box 20, ASG.

60   Deposition of Tom Dunkin, Network News Documentary Practices CBS "Project Nassau." Serial No. 91–55, 417–20, http://www.cuban-exile.com/doc_076-100/doc0091.html.

61   Testimony of Stanley Schacter, Assistant Customs Agent in charge of enforcement, Bureau of Customs, Miami, Fla., to the House of Representatives, Special Subcommittee on Investigations, Committee on Interstate and Foreign Commerce, July 17, 1969 in *Network News Documentary Practices*, 16–18; on the number of 120, see Testimony of Andrew St. George, to the House of Representatives, Special Subcommittee on Investigations, Committee on Interstate and Foreign Commerce, July 17, 1969, in *Network News Documentary Practices*, 56; on the CBS News correspondent's gaffe, see Testimony of Andrew St. George, 62 in ibid.

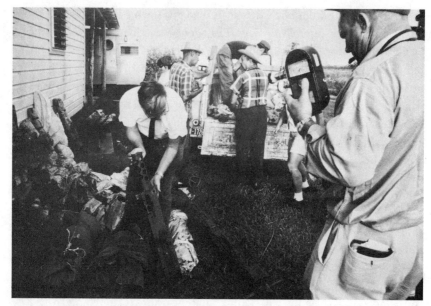

Fig. 3.6: Reality TV: "CBS & the Tigers: Filming illegal arms shipment bound for Haiti. Center—producer Jay MacMullen." The materials were unloaded from the trailer and put on the bed of the pickup, which would then be driven by a young woman, not visible in the image, to a waiting vessel.

Folder "Haiti," box 11, MS1912, Andrew St. George collection, Yale University Library Manuscripts and Archives. Photograph by Andrew St. George. By kind permission of Andrew Szentgyorgyi.

testimony on the role of CBS News, and its money, in the entire adventure.[62] A writer for *Scanlan's* reported that the plot made "the Bay of Pigs fiasco look like a set piece by Clausewitz."[63]

Bored since Vietnam

WerBell survived the disaster intact, indicted but not prosecuted. Why he was never prosecuted is unclear. Throughout his career he seemed to repeatedly avoid prosecution for his various activities, to the degree that it is at times hard to avoid lapsing into various conspiracy theories as to why that was the case, particularly given that WerBell's name popped up repeatedly on the radar of the JFK assassination investigations. In any case, WerBell returned to

---

62   Testimony of Andrew St. George, to the House of Representatives, Special Subcommittee on Investigations, Committee on Interstate and Foreign Commerce, July 17, 1969, in *Network News Documentary Practices*, 30–64.

63   Grove, "The CIA, FBI & CBS Bomb." For a more detailed overview of the venture, see Warren Hinckle and William W. Turner, *The Fish Is Red: The Story of the Secret War Against Castro* (New York: Harper & Row, 1981), 250–59.

Fig. 3.7: Home on the range: DIA and CIA men on WerBell's SIONICS compound firing range in Powder Springs, GA.

Folder "Mitch WerBell," box 2, MS1912, Andrew St. George collection, Yale University Library Manuscripts and Archives. Photograph by Andrew St. George. By kind permission of Andrew Szentgyorgyi.

his Powder Springs, Georgia, farm with its German shepherds and electronic security fences, its helipad and airstrip.[64] This was home to WerBell's SIONICS (Studies in Operational Negation of Insurgency and Counter-Subversion) training ground and Cobray School where clients paid upwards of $3,000 for a ten-day course in survival, counterinsurgency, and killing.[65] CIA and DIA (Defense Intelligence Agency) agents came to learn about new weapons and to test them on his firing range (see fig. 3.7). The CIA had an interest in WerBell's silencers, and much of WerBell's weaponry went to US Special Forces. First Lieutenant Bert Waldron, the Army's top sniper in Vietnam with

---

64 FBI Report, Atlanta, Georgia, May 5, 1970, "Mitchell Livingston Werbell III, Sionics Lab, Route 1, Powder Springs, Georgia" (FBI 1350966); St. George, "The New Country Caper," 63.

65 Paul Kirchner, *More of the Deadliest Men Who Ever Lived* (Boulder, CO: Paladin Press, 2009); Beau Cutts, "WerBell's Games Are Gung-Ho," *Atlanta Journal and Constitution*, July 27, 1980, 1A, 10A; Cutts, "Their Job: To Teach Efficiency in Killing," *Atlanta Journal and Constitution*, July 28, 1980, 1A, 6A; Cutts, "Training of a Killer," *Atlanta Journal and Constitution*, July 29, 1980, 1A, 6A; and Cutts, "WerBell Lives in a Nether, Nether Land," *Atlanta Journal and Constitution*, July 30, 1980.

122 confirmed kills, accomplished his grisly feat using a modified AR-16 rifle with a WerBell silencer attached. When he returned from Vietnam and left the service, he joined SIONICS's executive staff.[66] The school thus garnered WerBell both an income and an audience. Area newspapers took an interest in an eccentric spy figure in their midst. Neighbors were less impressed, complaining of the incessant noise of weaponry.

SIONICS was not WerBell's creation alone. Substantial financial support came from southern conservatives—"concerned segregationists"—who looked to train with and stockpile high-powered weaponry.[67] Why? Andrew St. George, a reporter who had established a close professional and personal relationship with WerBell, about whom I will say more shortly, offered an opinion worth quoting in full:

> What is the cause of these plotters, these tight-lipped enrages of traditionalism and racial "integrity"? *Whatever it is, they do not expect to further it without violence.* All of them feel, like Billy Graham, that "decay and degradation is all around us" and that just about everything that matters in the larger sense—their country's position and power, its established racial structure, its twin cornerstones of patriotism and transcendental religion, the sexual patterns which form the only knowable framework for their lives, the *patria potestas* which gives them authority over their children and homes, the very roots of cultural identity—are being undermined by what they all see as a monstrous subversive conspiracy deployed in force between New York and Washington and getting ready to send its juggernauts rolling Southward.[68]

At SIONICS, domestic terrorists, fueled by racism and reaction, would meld with libertarian paramilitaries eager to unseat Castro, overthrow communism, and earn a living killing. White supremacy and anticommunism mingled in a potent libertarian brew.[69] WerBell capitalized on this zeitgeist as the world of mercenary activity mushroomed. Soldiers, young and old, who had survived the jungles of Vietnam, Laos, and Cambodia, found returning to their old lives a near impossibility. On their return they were offered little direction or support, left relatively alone to cope with public hostility or

---

66 St. George to Bob [no surname, on *The Daily Telegraph* letterhead], November 1, 1969, box 20, ASG.
67 Ibid.
68 St. George to Bob, November 1, 1969, box 20, ASG. My emphasis.
69 For more on this mix, see Kathleen Belew, *Bring the War Home: The White Power Movement and Paramilitary America* (Cambridge, MA: Harvard University Press, 2018); and Kyle Burke, *Revolutionaries for the Right.*

indifference. John Kerry, in his Vietnam Veterans Against the War statement of April 1971, recognized the reality: the country, he wrote, "has created a monster, a monster in the form of millions of men who have been taught to deal and to trade in violence."[70] Ex-Special Forces army captain Robert Brown, who spent time at WerBell's SIONICS compound, summed up how many of his comrades felt: "I've been bored ever since Vietnam."[71] As a partial response to the boredom, Brown had founded the magazine *Soldier of Fortune: The Journal of Professional Adventurers* in 1975, which offered readers an updated version of the trifecta of war, sex, and macho heroism commonplace in 1950s and 1960s pulp magazines such as *Stag, Male, Man's Illustrated,* and *Man's Epic.*[72] The magazine also served as a clearinghouse for work in a post-Vietnam growth industry: paramilitary warfare. Disenchanted veterans turned to private opportunities, advertised in the magazine's personal pages, in places such as Angola, Rhodesia, the Congo, and El Salvador to earn money, beat back the boredom, and "get back at the Communists someplace else in the world."[73] Brown identified as a libertarian. He and many of his readers saw in the US government little more than inefficiency, betrayal, malaise, and a disturbing ambivalence toward the red tide of communism. Whether it was Kennedy's abandonment of the rebels in the Bay of Pigs, Nixon's détente, or Carter's later purging of the espionage and black ops rolls, government was the problem. The state, in their eyes, had betrayed its soldiers and its citizens. Ex-combatants put their skills to work elsewhere, fighting for money in the name of capitalism: libertarians par excellence.[74]

---

70   Kerry's testimony at NPR, accessed March 13, 2018, https://www.npr.org/templates/story/story.php?storyId=3875422.

71   Richard Woodley, "Killing Time with the War Dreamers," *Esquire* (August 1976), quoted passage on 138.

72   Gregory A. Daddis, *Pulp Vietnam: War and Gender in Cold War Men's Adventure Magazines* (Cambridge: Cambridge University Press, 2020), esp. 222–23.

73   Robert Brown as quoted in Woodley, "Killing Time," 138. The composition of mercenary forces is unclear to me, but it is worth noting that all of the military personnel who appeared in the sources I have consulted were officers, not NCOs. This is not to say that enlisted men ("grunts") did not populate the mercenary ranks, come back disenchanted from Vietnam, and the like. Rather, the point is that the officer class—with their college degrees (whether from a military academy or not), their supervisory and management roles, and their substantially higher pay—were not immune to paramilitarism and illegal war-making.

74   But when captured or killed, American mercenaries caused their government strife. Title 18 of the US Code bans working as or recruiting a mercenary. See Woodley, "Killing Time," 84. Brown and fellows travelers at *Soldier of Fortune* would soon participate as paramilitaries in counterinsurgency warfare in Central America. See Belew, *Bring the War Home,* 88–90.

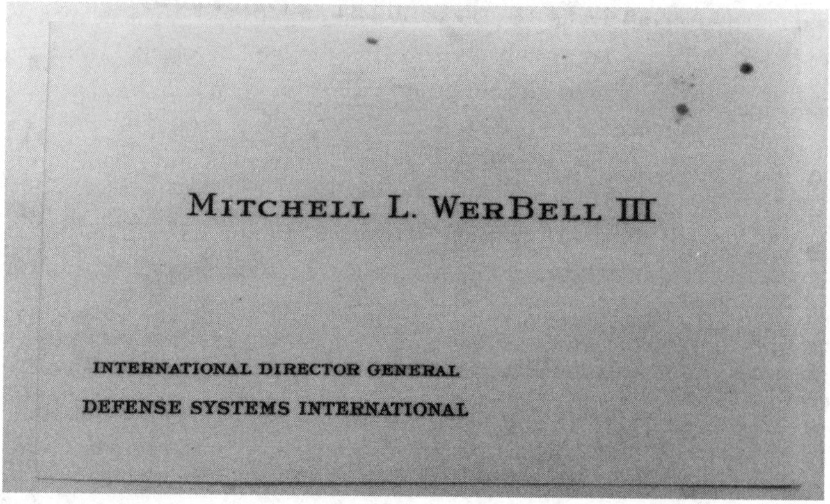

Fig. 3.8: The Business of War: WerBell's business card for Defense Systems International.

Box 25, MS1912, Andrew St. George collection, Yale University Library Manuscripts and Archives.

This growing Cold War economy founded on private security, espionage, guns for hire, and munitions sales proved ideal for men such as Mitch WerBell. Although in the 1960s he had found himself in "dire financial straights [*sic*]," the arms trade—with anti-Castro Cubans, with the US military, and with foreign militaries—brought some respite and by the early 1970s he was seeing some success as a highly regarded MM (or "munitions manipulator," a euphemism for an arms dealer).[75] His dealings took him to Vietnam, Thailand, the circum-Caribbean and elsewhere. With retired US Army colonel Robert Bayard, WerBell clandestinely smuggled weapons manufactured in socialist countries into the US where they were "fitted with expensive silencers, 'accurized' and supplied with so-called 'sanitized'—i.e. unmarked—ammunition."[76]

The silencers (or sound suppressors) were WerBell's own creations. Most famously, WerBell developed a silencer muzzle for Gordon Ingram's M-10 Lightweight Individual Special Purpose (LISP) firearm. Memorably described as "a steel kaleidoscope of Thanatos," the M-10 had a reputation as the world's deadliest handgun, firing "700 rounds per minute at an effective range of about

---

75 On WerBell's weapon acquisitions for anti-Castro groups, see SAC Miami to Director of the FBI, February 19, 1968 (FBI 1350966). Judging from the material in the FBI files, the likely group for whom WerBell was acquiring weapons was the Second National Front of Escambray. For "dire financial straights" see Memorandum, September 26, 1967, SAC Atlanta to Director of the FBI (FBI 1350966).

76 St. George, "Dept. of Assassins," typescript, unmarked folder, box 23, ASG.

250 to 300 yards" and weighing only 6.25 pounds.[77] The weapon gained substantial notoriety in the 1970s as it appeared alongside Robert Redford and Max von Sydow in Sydney Pollack's *Three Days of the Condor*, with John Wayne in the role of hardened Seattle cop *McQ*, and James Caan in *The Killer Elite*.[78] "Were the Academy Awards amended to honor its special contribution" wrote one commentator, "the M-10 would emerge as the best supporting machine gun of all time."[79] Meanwhile, far from Hollywood's red carpets and gold statues, military personnel in Israel, Uganda, Thailand, Guatemala, and the Philippines carried the weapon in their arsenal.[80] WerBell personally demonstrated the qualities of the firearm and his sound suppressor to potential customers in Thailand and Vietnam.[81]

Joan Didion, so exacting in her observations, made sure to note that it was an M-10, sans silencer, that assassins used when they killed American advisors Michael Hammer and Mark Pearlman and Salvadoran José Rodolfo Viera, head of El Salvador's Institute for Agrarian Transformation, in the lobby of the San Salvador Sheraton in 1981. (According to the US Senate Congressional Record, Hans Christ, a young Salvadoran executive at the time, was implicated as a participant in the assassination at the Sheraton, having fingered the targets for the gunmen. Christ had been a student in Marietta, Georgia, in 1974 and had "worked closely" with WerBell.)[82] Illegal possession of an M-10, *with* WerBell's silencer, landed Jesus García, a Cuban-American who smuggled weapons for the Reagan administration to the anti-Sandinista contras in Central America, in a Miami jail in 1986.[83]

What made WerBell's silencers so ubiquitous was his originality at tinkering with weapons and sound suppressors.

Before WerBell came along, silencers behaved mostly like early organ transplants. They were scientific, they filled the need, they looked great in place, but the receiving organism—the gun itself—almost invariably

77 "700 rounds" is from J. David Truby, *Silencer, Snipers & Assassins: An Overview of Whispering Death* (Boulder, CO: Paladin Press, 1972), 112; "steel kaleidoscope ..." is from St. George, "A Significant Little Gun," *Esquire* (August 1977), 69.

78 See Jack Shafer's review of Hougan's *Spooks: The Haunting of America—The Private Use of Secret Agents*, in *Libertarian Review* 8, no. 2 (March 1979): 42–44; and St. George, "A Significant Little Gun," 69.

79 St. George, "A Significant Little Gun," 69. Today the weapon features prominently in the Call of Duty video game series.

80 Ibid., 108.

81 See the photographs in Chuck Taylor, "MAC 10 SMG: The world's best submachinegun?" *Soldier of Fortune*, May 1978, 42–47, images on page 43.

82 Didion, *We Tell Ourselves Stories in Order to Live: Collected Nonfiction* (New York: Alfred Knopf, 2006), 354; *Congressional Record—Senate*, January 27, 1984, 688.

83 Didion, *We Tell Ourselves Stories in Order to Live*, 544.

rejected them. Silencers caused barrel vibration, tremendous fouling, dangerous heating, breech troubles, backblast, loss of energy. As they dissipated the gases that burst forth after every shot from the gun muzzle—for therein lies the silencer's essential function—they also dissipated the weapon's virtues, causing rounds to go wild, to fall short, to misfire or otherwise malfunction in unballistic and disagreeable ways.[84]

WerBell's silencer, with its "Pressure Relief Valve" technology, had no such defects and was impressively quiet, a fact he demonstrated to clients by firing rounds from the silenced M-10 into stacks of telephone directories in a Washington, DC, hotel room while a bellhop waited outside the door to report if he heard anything.[85] (He didn't.) His innovations in sound suppression technology—which included building a "miniaturized maze of acoustic conduits and baffles that reduce rifle fire to the sound of bouncing ping-pong balls"—led one commentator to characterize WerBell as "easily the most prolific silencer designer in the world today . . . and probably in history."[86] Prolific he was, having created suppressors for weapons ranging from a .22 caliber pistol to guns mounted on US helicopters deployed in Vietnam.

Given its performance, the M-10 and its successor the M-11 attracted substantial interest from investors. To underwrite production, promotion and distribution, WerBell and Ingram created the Military Armaments Corporation [MAC], financed largely through investments by major bankers and executives who had formed Quantum Ordnance Bankers Inc. (soon to be renamed simply Quantum) to raise money. Major investors in Quantum included a number of high-profile individuals including Charles Spofford, Stewart R. Mott, advertising executive Rosser Reeves, who gained fame for his various advertising slogans including, among others, the M&M pitch "melts in your mouth, not in your hand," and his son, Rosser Scott Reeves.[87] Investor interest seemed largely spurred by possibilities that the M-10 and M-11 were poised to replace the standard-issue .45 caliber pistols with which most US military personnel were outfitted.[88] A contract with the US government promised substantial profits, something WerBell understood as he made the pitch that rifles outfitted with his silencers "killed 1900 V.C. [Viet Cong] in six months.

84 St. George, "A Significant Little Gun," 108.
85 On the "Pressure Relief Valve" technology, see Truby, *Silencer, Snipers & Assassins*, 108–10.
86 "miniaturized maze," in Andrew St. George to Bob [no surname], 1 Nov 1969, box 20, ASG; "easily the most prolific . . . ," Truby, *Silencers, Snipers & Assassins*, 110.
87 "Confidential: Listing of Quantum's principal stockholders as of May 1st, 1973," RS Documents 1, box 23, ASG; Frank Iannamico, "Manufacturing History of Ingram-MAC Type Firearms," *Small Arms Review* 20, no. 1 (January 2016).
88 Truby, *Silencers, Snipers & Assassins*, 114.

Fig. 3.9: The world's deadliest handgun: The Ingram Mac-10, with a WerBell silencer.
https://commons.wikimedia.org/wiki/File:MAC10.jpg.

Those V.C. took only 1.3 rounds per kill. Twenty-seven cents apiece they cost Uncle Sam. That's the greatest cost effectiveness the Army's ever known."[89] Yet despite WerBell's, Ingram's, and Quantum's efforts, a contract with the US government and Department of Defense never came through. Quantum took over MAC and expelled WerBell and Ingram from the company they had founded. Perhaps WerBell's reputation preceded him, and the military brass backed away.

Times looked tough. Then in walked Michael Oliver.

Not another banana republic

As the seven other men gathered around the corner table at Duke Zeibert's finished their lunches, WerBell waited for Clifton Daniel, the Washington Bureau chief for the *New York Times* seated within earshot at a neighboring table, to finish his lunch and depart the restaurant.[90] Then, with coffee and Courvoisier served, he debriefed those gathered on the strides that had been made in organizing an invasion of Abaco: public surveys and propaganda campaigns in support of island independence; the creation of local cover organizations that hid from view who was financing the entire affair; the activities unfolding at WerBell's Powder Springs compound ("The Farm") where Bayard had been training the mercenaries who would descend on the island; and the shipments underway to the island of anti-Pindling bumper stickers, shortwave radio parts, and copies of Ayn Rand's *For the New Intellectual*. The operation had a forward headquarters in Miami, where the plotters were assisted by Vicki Jo Todd, a former Miss Nevada beauty pageant winner who a few years earlier had joined other pageant winners on a tour of military bases in Vietnam to boost troop morale.[91] Upon return she married Ralph

---

89   Ibid., 112.
90   Andrew St. George, "The Abaco Option," typescript, box 26, ASG.
91   This paragraph is based on St. George, "The Amazing New-Country Caper."

McMullen, a fellow Nevadan who had served as secretary of state in the Minerva Reef project. Todd constituted the sole female working on the Abaco project which was, like most of these undertakings, dominated by men, either as a result of their existing connections to the patriarchal war machine or because of the gravitational pull libertarianism—and capitalist adventurism—had on men in particular.

Once finished, WerBell handed things over to Oliver. Despite his demure frame and nerdy appearance—he sported a modest suit bulging with a large pocket calculator; the face of his wristwatch engulfed his forearm—Oliver was the master of ceremonies.[92] Once the invasion was over, Oliver's plans would go into effect. Backed by an influential set of unnamed investors, Oliver and his allies would privatize Abaco's public lands (Crown lands) which accounted for nearly 98 percent of the islands' landmass. Direct shares in the other 2 percent in the form of one-acre homesteads would be the key to persuading Abaconians to support the plot. Oliver was at pains to ensure the project not be misunderstood and compared with a colonial land grab or a corporate enclave or a tax haven. This was not, he emphasized, "going to be another banana republic. That's not the point; I wouldn't spend an hour's time just to make some money that way. The point is that the Republic of Abaco will be, first of all, a moral experiment, a place where we'll try to keep individual freedom alive even if it doesn't survive in America."[93] Regarding how things would unfold postsecession, Oliver was blunt: he would decide. WerBell did not speak up, but he had distinct interests in the venture. He hoped to build a new factory on the island to manufacture weapons, something he had tried to do a few years earlier when he had unsuccessfully sought to gain control of the San Cristóbal factory in the Dominican Republic.[94]

But before the machinery of secession could be put into motion, the plotters needed to determine the position of the British government. Hence the presence of Lord Belhaven. Recently married to Lady MacTaggart, whose brother-in-law lived in the Bahamian capitol Nassau, Lord Belhaven had taken a keen interest in Abaco's status and advocated for it to remain a crown colony.[95] Indeed, his advocacy had come to the attention of well-known international

---

92   On Oliver's suit and calculator, see St. George, "The Abaco Option."

93   As quoted in St. George, "The Amazing New-Country Caper," 154.

94   Van Fossen, *Tax Havens and Sovereignty*; on the San Cristóbal factory, see FBI Report, New York, New York, October 28, 1966, "Rolando Arcadio Masferrer Rojas, Internal Security-Haiti, Registration Act-Haiti-Cuba, Neutrality Matters" (FBI 1350966).

95   "The Peer and the Plot to Take Over a Paradise Island," *Daily Mail* [February 11, 1975?], enclosure in FCO 63/1389 (f. 12A), NA-Kew. On Lady McTaggart's brother-in-law see JG Doubleday to AJ Ward, Caribbean Dept., FCO, July 5, 1974, FCO 63/1268 (f. 27), NA-Kew.

investment strategist and libertarian Harry Schultz who in turn had brought the entire scenario to Oliver.[96] As the possibilities of "remain" dimmed, Lord Belhaven latched on to secession and to WerBell. After three days at WerBell's Georgia compound, he and Lady MacTaggart arrived in Washington, DC, for the lunch meeting. Belhaven was tasked with acquiring assurances from the UK government that it would not intercede if the residents of Abaco seceded. (The first man hired for the job, Colin "Mad Mitch" Mitchell, a former colonel of the Argylle & Sutherland Highlanders, had demanded too high a fee.) Lord Belhaven obliged. After his return to England, on the afternoon of June 10, he raised the issue on the floor of the House of Lords: "My Lords, I beg leave to ask the Question which stands in my name on the Order Paper. The Question was as follows: To ask Her Majesty's Government what representations they intend to make to the Government of the Bahamas urging them to cease their harassment of the people of Abaco."[97] The response? "The Abaco Islands are an integral part of the Commonwealth of the Bahamas, which became an independent sovereign State on July 10, 1973. It would not, therefore, be appropriate for Her Majesty's Government in the United Kingdom to seek to intervene in the internal affairs of the Bahamas." Those were the words of the parliamentary undersecretary of state, Lord Goronwy-Roberts. For Oliver and WerBell, they confirmed nonintervention by the UK. Plans for an invasion and eventual secession moved forward. Independence Day was scheduled for January 1, 1975.

An opaque world

No invasion took place on January 1, 1975. Abaco never seceded from the Bahamas. What happened? After the meeting in Washington, DC, Oliver seemed convinced success was imminent. "A free nation is about to be born in the Caribbean, the first nation explicitly committed to the principles of individual liberty and genuine free enterprise," he claimed in his June 1974 newsletter. "Its name is Abaco." He continued: "The Abaco Independence Movement has contacted us for political, economic and legal advice and assistance. These are being provided. In return for such aid, a mutually beneficial arrangement which will satisfy our own free enterprise goals has been agreed to."[98]

96 "Bizarre Search for a Free-Enterprise Utopia in the Sun," Daily Telegraph, October 29, 1974, enclosure in FCO 63/1389 (f.12A), NA-Kew.
97 St. George, "The Amazing New-Country Caper," 152–53.
98 M. Oliver Newsletter, June 1974, enclosure in Dept. of State to FBI, July 10, 1974 (FBI 1350966).

Fig. 3.10: Castro (left) and St. George (right) conversing, 1958.

Box 4, MS1912, Andrew St. George collection, Yale University Library Manuscripts and Archives. Photographer unknown but it may have been taken by Ernesto 'Che' Guevara who had a friendship with St. George and regularly borrowed his camera. By kind permission of Andrew Szentgyorgyi.

Fig. 3.11: In the Sierra Maestra with Che (left) and Fidel (in the hammock), 1958.

Box 4, MS 1912, Andrew St. George collection, Yale University Library Manuscripts and Archives. Photography by Andrew St. George. By kind permission of Andrew Szentgyorgyi.

That same month, Oliver hosted investigative reporter Andrew St. George in Carson City, where he "poured out his passion" for the Abaco project over the course of two days.[99] St. George had attended the lunch at Duke Ziebert's at the invitation of Mitch WerBell, with whom he had formed an unlikely professional friendship. St. George was a serious journalist with more than a decade of hardened experience. A Hungarian émigré to the US, he had arrived in New York in 1952, after six years working as an interrogator and analyst for US Army intelligence first in Budapest and then in Vienna after the war.[100] Once in the US he attended the Columbia University School of General Studies and subsequently picked up work as a writer and photographer. By the early 1960s he had garnered multiple prizes for his work. He was one of two US-based journalists (the other was Herbert Matthews) to interview Fidel Castro in the Sierra Maestra as his revolutionary forces prepared to overthrow Fulgencio Batista.[101] Castro awarded St. George and Matthews gold medals for their coverage of the Cubans' national liberation struggle.

St. George soon grew disenchanted with the revolution and, after escaping a Cuban prison with the help of a sympathetic guard, he left the island in the summer of 1959. He found work with *Life* magazine and for the next few years traveled throughout Latin America, with stints in Brazil, Uruguay, Chile, Peru, Colombia, Guatemala, and Nicaragua. He traveled some fourteen thousand miles through Latin America seeking to answer a simple question: Why do "so many Latins seem to want to live like us, but be governed like the Russians?"[102] He also began reporting on and documenting the shadowy underworld of anti-Castro movements and conspiracies, including participating in raids by the anti-Castro Alpha 66 group and one of its founders, Tony Cuesta.

In the Dominican Republic with a fellow reporter in late 1964, St. George had met WerBell and developed a lasting professional relationship.[103] It was

---

99   Andrew St. George, Loose notes, typed in unlabeled folder, box 23, ASG.
100 FBI Internal Security document NY 105-6797: Subject Andrew Szentgyorgyi, April 19, 1954, 4 (FBI 1400082). This document was part of the FBI's investigations into suspected communists.
101 St. George, "A Visit with a Revolutionary," *Coronet*, February 1958, 74–80. On St. George and his relationship with Castro and his guerrilla movement, see the essential work of Lillian Guerra, *Heroes, Martyrs, and Political Messiahs in Revolutionary Cuba, 1946–1958* (New Haven, CT: Yale University Press, 2018).
102 Andrew St. George, "The Plight of Latin America: Are the Russians Going to Finish What We Started?" typescript, August 2, 1961, box 23, ASG.
103 On St. George's life, see his short autobiographical overview, untitled, box 26, ASG. He notes that after leaving Hungary he was in Austria where "from December 1946 until my arrival in this country exactly six years later, I was employed by the Special Operations Branch of the 430th Counter-Intelligence Corps Detachment. My duties as

Fig. 3.12: Professional Freedom Fighter: Tony Cuesta's business card. "A Cuban who wants to return."

Box 22, MS1912, Andrew St. George collection, Yale University Library Manuscripts and Archives.

Fig. 3.13: International man of mystery? Mitchell WerBell poolside with a woman identified by the *Daily Telegraph* (UK) as his girlfriend.

Private collection of Andrew Szentgyorgyi. Reproduced by kind permission of Andrew Szentgyorgyi.

St. George who wrote of WerBell's skills as a silencer maker; who wrote of WerBell's central role in the world of munitions manipulations; and who nearly cost WerBell his marriage when he included a photograph of WerBell, in a robe, sitting poolside with a young woman in a bikini, identified as his girlfriend, in his article for the UK's *Daily Telegraph* (fig. 3.13).

Their relationship was a fraught one. WerBell reveled in cultivating a militarized Bond-like persona, complete with the gadgetry, the underworld allure, the hypermasculinity, and the womanizing so central to Cold War pulp fiction and popular culture.[104] St. George, tongue slightly in cheek, provided him the publicity he desired. WerBell, ever the shameless self-promoter, thrived on the attention and the fact that his stories were taking hold, emerging from the shadows. St. George, meanwhile, had struggled for more than a decade to maintain his career in journalism after being tarred as a CIA agent by the CIA itself, or so St. George firmly believed.[105] Indeed, despite having been awarded various honors for his reporting, St. George increasingly found himself isolated and going "slowly, inexorably bankrupt."[106] In the early 1970s it was his access to and writings on WerBell which helped pay the bills, something he well knew. While WerBell's "drunken rambling [was] agonizing to endure," St. George wrote to his editor, it was worth it because in his taped interviews

---

staff investigator included the debriefing of prominent Hungarian refugees, counterespionage work, assisting in the compilation of Intelligence Digests, surveys and analyses ... and lecturing to agents' training courses." Autobiographical overview, 4. See also the summary in Guy Gugliotta, "Comrades and Arms," *Smithsonian* 39, no. 1 (April 2008): 14–16.

104 Daddis, *Pulp Vietnam*, and Alexander Cockburn, "The First Fifty Years of James Bond," *Counterpunch*, October 30, 2020 (2004), https://www.counterpunch.org/2020/10/30/the-first-50-years-of-james-bond.

105 On his career difficulties as related to accusations of being CIA, see Andrew St. George to Harry Smith, esq., June 3, 1976, box 20, MS 1912, ASG. I have found no evidence that St. George was with the CIA, and he adamantly refuted such accusations throughout his life. He did share the contents of, and information from, his interviews with Fidel Castro in 1957 with the FBI's New York office, and at least one FBI officer suggested that St. George could be "used more properly as a source by the New York office in Cuban matters." Director, FBI, to SAC New York, June 20, 1958, Subject: Andrew Szentgyorgyi aka Andrew St. George. See also SAC New York to Director, FBI, June 5, 1958, Subject: Andrew Szentgyorgyi aka Andrew St. George (FBI 1400082). Those efforts were abandoned by the end of 1958 due to unspecified "derogatory information in his background," according to an FBI report. See Mr. S.J. Papich to Mr. R.R. Roach, Office Memorandum, December 31, 1958, Subject: Andrew Szentgyorgyi, Internal Security-Hungary (FBI 1400082). In a letter to his editors, St. George did mention having worked in or with the OSS. "I found myself under genuinely ominous blandishments and threats for the first time since I was an intelligence agent (for the old O.S.S. Mitch WerBell's alma mater) in World War II." St. George to Berrie and Elie [undated, ca. late 1974], box 23, ASG.

106 St. George to Berry and Ellie [no date, ca. late 1974], box 23, ASG.

with WerBell could be found journalistic gems "scattered ... like gold teeth ... in the shit of a man-eating tiger."[107]

The plot to take over Abaco was one such gem. And thus, one month after the meeting at Duke Zeibert's, St. George headed to Oliver's home in Carson City. But the enthusiasm of June soon gave way to a summer of discontent. One of the ex-CIA advisers, Roussos, had already withdrawn from the project due to concerns about Oliver's kingly pretensions.[108] Indeed, despite the claims that Abaco would be no banana republic, the venture smacked of the kinds of land-grabbing and king-making of the era of high colonialism. Oliver and WerBell could have been mistaken for Josiah Harding, a nineteenth-century British adventurer who proclaimed himself king of a northern province in Afghanistan and who achieved immortality as the protagonist of Rudyard Kipling's short story "The Man Who Would Be King." It just so happened that the film version of Kipling's story, starring Michael Caine and Sean Connery, wrapped up production even as Oliver and his associates met in DC.[109] Or perhaps the duo resembled another notorious adventurer, William Walker, the American filibusterer described, as if tailor-made for an Ayn Rand novel, as the "grey-eyed man of destiny." Aided by an array of American and European mercenaries who had served their respective militaries in campaigns in Mexico, Algeria, the Crimea, Bengal, and elsewhere, Walker had invaded Nicaragua in the mid-nineteenth century.[110]

So Roussos had abandoned ship. Meanwhile, the other two ex-CIA men at the table—Mackem and Muldoon—had reported the lunch meeting to their former employer and been advised to break all ties with WerBell.[111] Domestic agencies had been keeping tabs on both Oliver and WerBell as had the CIA, whose agents at times thought the whole undertaking sounded

---

107   Loose-leaf sheet labeled "WerBell #116—11/11," box 22, ASG.
108   St. George, "The Abaco Option."
109   Kipling, "The Man Who Would Be King"; in Kipling, *The Man Who Would Be King: Selected Short Stories* (New York: Penguin, 2011); Ben MacIntyre, *Josiah the Great: The True Story of the Man Who Would Be King* (New York: HarperCollins, 2011). See the broader discussion of private empire making in Steven Press, *Rogue Empires: Contracts and Conmen in Europe's Scramble for Africa* (Cambridge, MA: Harvard University Press, 2017).
110   For a recent revised understanding of Walker, see Michel Gobat, *Empire by Invitation: William Walker and Manifest Destiny in Central America*, esp. 109–11 for the mercenary composition of his army. See also the efforts of Walker's contemporary Orélie-Antoine de Tounens, a French attorney, who claimed the Mapuche of the Araucanía wished to make him a king in order to garner European recognition of their independence vis-à-vis Chile. See Press, *Rogue Empires*, 47, and Chatwin, *In Patagonia*.
111   FBI, January 25, 1975. SUBJECT: Mitchell Livingston WerBell III (201-259910) (FBI 1350966).

"like something right out of cheap fiction."[112] Copies of Oliver's newsletter had been circulating among FBI stations for a number of years and the FBI, the Department of State, and the Bureau of Alcohol, Tobacco and Firearms all monitored WerBell's activities, including those in Abaco.[113] More disconcerting was that, by late June when they had planned on holding a plebiscite in Abaco, Oliver and WerBell could no longer count on the support of most Abaconians, many of whom had decided in favor of remaining a part of the newly independent Bahamas. This should not have come as a surprise: the year prior Errington Watkins, one of the most prominent Bahamians who had supported remaining a Crown colony, had declared his allegiance to an independent Bahamas, walking across the floor of the House of Representatives and shaking the hand of Prime Minister Pindling.[114]

The fact is Oliver and WerBell were late to the party. The ship of secession had long since sailed, and it was largely the persistence of Lord Belhaven, rather than that of the Abaconians themselves, which kept the very idea of it on the table. In June 1974, just as the meeting at Duke Zeibert's had concluded, a briefing to Her Majesty's Government noted that the Abaco secessionist movement had splintered in two.

> One element formed the Friends of Abaco Foundation (FOA) to promote the "economic welfare of the island devoid of political overtones." With its headquarters in the USA, the FOA hopes to raise money internationally to support projects such as a study of economic conditions on Abaco, establishing Abaconian-owned businesses and encouraging tourism and investment through publicity. The Abaco Independence Movement (AIM), on the other hand, is openly political. Its aim is to achieve self-determination and home rule for Abaco through peaceful, moral, legal, and constitutional means. The movement appears to enjoy little support from either black or white Abaconians; it is being stage-managed by wealthy outsiders who see Abaco as a tax-free haven immune from Bahamas Government interference.[115]

112 CIA transcript of conversation between [redacted] and [redacted], June 1974, https://archive.org/details/MitchellLivingstonWerBell/page/n114/mode/1up?q=oliver (quoted passage at n115).
113 See FBI LHM, Las Vegas, Nevada, September 11, 1974, "M. Oliver Newsletter" (FBI 1350966), and "Activities of American Citizens in Support of Abaco Secession from the Bahamas." Acting Director, FBI to Assistant Attorney General, Criminal Division, June 21, 1973, "Mitchell Livingston Werbell III, Internal Security-Bahamas, Neutrality Issues-Bahamas" (FBI 1350966).
114 *The Tribune* (Nassau, Bahamas), June 20, 1973, 1.
115 Background briefing attached to M.P. Preston, Caribbean Department, to Mr. Larmour and Mr Woodland, June 4, 1974, FCO 63/1268 (f. 8 enclosure), NA-Kew.

Further reports that summer concurred. A small group of yachtsmen wearing AIM shirts at an Abaco regatta were seen "as a joke," and a Nassau barber, "who a year ago was a leading prophet of doom for the Government because of its policy on Abaco, and who used to [say] that secession was almost certain because of the tons of gunpowder that Abaconians had stored away," had informed the British official whose hair he regularly cut that AIM was now "virtually dead."[116]

It is not hard to imagine why the project had lost its sheen. As details became clearer of what outside forces had in mind for Abaconian secession, commitments began to wane. Few Abaconians wanted secession at the cost of armed insurrection. Nor were they eager to embrace what appeared increasingly to be a form of time-share sovereignty of the kind found in the autonomous resort of Freeport-Lucaya on neighboring Grand Bahama. In 1955 the Bay Street oligarchs and then-governor Earl of Ranfurly had signed off on a concession of some eighty square miles of land to one Wallace Groves, a Virginia financier and grifter who had served time in federal prison for mail fraud. Groves developed a free port, industrial zone, and luxury hotel on Grand Bahama on terms so generous—exemptions from all taxes, both property and personal; licensing rights; exemptions from zoning and immigration restrictions; among others—that the authors of the most detailed history of the Bahamas have argued that the government had "virtually surrendered its sovereignty over one of its largest islands."[117] Abaconians in the 1970s surely had taken note.

In the meantime, WerBell was in serious financial trouble. He had been extravagant with the arrangements when the conspirators had met in DC, with copious amounts of alcohol, fine food, and an expensive room at the Mayflower Hotel. But only weeks later, WerBell, who had promised to finance St. George's rental car for his visit to Oliver's home in Carson City, reported the rental car transaction as fraudulent, leaving St. George in a serious lurch. WerBell and Oliver had misled St. George, suggesting they had deep resources and the support of multiple millionaires for the project. Oliver reportedly at one point flashed a personal check from Minerva financier Seth Atwood.[118]

Oliver's enthusiasm thus transformed quickly into agitation and frustration. As the summer progressed, he grew increasingly concerned about what

---

116　J.G. Doubleday to A.J. Ward, Caribbean Dept. FCO, July 5, 1974, FCO 63/1268, NA-Kew.

117　Details on Freeport-Lucaya and the quoted text from Michael Craton and Gail Saunders, *Islanders in the Stream*, 2:324. See also Saunders, *The Other Bahamas*, 288, and Ogle, "Archipelago Capitalism," 1442–43.

118　St. George to WerBell, "Friday night" [ca. late May or early June 1974], Folder: Urgent Current Stuff (WerBell Car Rental), box 20, ASG.

St. George planned to write regarding the Abaco plan. One of his associates and a backer of the Abaco project, identified by St. George as Bob Johnston of Texas, dispatched a hired hand to break into the journalist's car and rifle through the contents of his briefcase. When St. George surprised the thief, a tussle ensued. St. George recovered his briefcase but at the expense of a finger, mangled by a bullet from the thief's gun.[119] Oliver paid a portion of the medical expenses and sought—unsuccessfully despite both "threats and induements [sic] on the phone"—to persuade St. George to visit him for a second time in Carson City. "I don't really want to go to Carson City," St. George wrote his editors, and "none of my remaining nine fingers wants to come along."[120]

Oliver looked to quash the article. He contacted St. George's editors at *True* magazine and managed to persuade them to pull the piece. In response, St. George warned his editors that "Oliver is not what you think, or even what he sounds like."

> He is one of the Mr. Bigs of the new right-wing revival, with close ties
> to neo-fascists in Britain and in his native Germany. He is a fairly sinister
> behind-the-scenes manipulator and paymaster, an employer of many
> dangerous types, and with his partner Bob Johnson, who is said to be even
> tougher than Oliver, he is a serious conspirator and a "real threat"—at
> least that's what two U.S. Treasury agents came to warn me about not
> long ago [Steve Csukas and Skip Lutz]. In recent years Oliver and Johnson
> have had associations with the Birchers, the Minutemen, etc., but O&J
> are to the *right* of these weak-sister organizations, and they have set up
> in business as ushers of the new dawn on their own.[121]

It is a striking set of accusations and suggests that Oliver's singlemindedness had drawn him deeper and deeper into a reactionary resistance growing in lockstep alongside an empire of special operations, one born in Central America and the Caribbean and now grown "fat and loathsome" in Southeast Asia.[122] Andrew St. George's eldest son recalls that his father was not easily frightened. He was a tough character: he had done stints in prison

---

119 St. George to Berry and Ellie, [no date, ca. fall 1974], box 23, ASG. St. George provides further details on the incident and identifies Johnston (also spelled Johnson) in "A.R. St. George. Subject: Letter from Mike Oliver's law firm, Stokes and Eck," February 14 [1975], Folder "Mitch [and] Material Related to Abaco Society," box 25, ASG.
120 St. George to Berry and Ellie, [no date, ca. fall 1974], box 23, ASG.
121 Ibid. Stephen Csukas [also Czukas] was a US special agent for thirty years, after a stint in the air force during the Korean War. A quick Google search will turn his name up in an array of documents related to the Kennedy assassination investigation as well as varied Caribbean investigations.
122 St. George to Loomis, November 17, 1970, Folder "Fund for Inv. Journ.," box 20, ASG.

in Budapest twice, first under the Nazis (he narrowly escaped execution by the Nazis when the Soviets shelled the jail, allowing him to flee) and then the Soviets. Subsequently, after falling out with Castro, he ended up in a Cuban cell from which he escaped with the help of a sympathetic guard he knew from earlier revolutionary days. But St. George feared the Abaco plotters and their entourage.[123]

The point in part is this: the world of Mitchell Livingston WerBell III—of snipers and silencers, snatch and snuff missions, counterinsurgency camps and psy-ops—may seem a world away from that of Michael Oliver, the libertarian visionary, concentration camp survivor, and real estate developer. It was not. Willingly or not, Oliver found himself in an opaque world of libertarian noir, an underworld populated by munitions dealers, mercenaries, con men, and a host of unpredictable players. Was he an unwitting or reluctant participant in this seedy universe, naively drawn in against his best intentions? Maybe. Maybe not. It is hard to tell. But in either case, there is a broader point worth making here: that the marriage of mercenaries and libertarians was not one of simple convenience or grudging collaboration. To suggest otherwise is to miss the point that capitalism and counterinsurgency, markets and mercenaries, are all too often two sides of the same coin. They are bound, in intimate and inextricable fashion, by coin itself.

A little skullduggery

After his editors at *True* pulled their support for the piece, St. George published it in the February 1975 issue of *Esquire*, with the title "The Amazing New Country Caper."[124] The essay was both hard-hitting and playfully sarcastic, although the contents and tone were mild in comparison to those of an early draft St. George penned in which he imagined a future "free Abaco" with "Chairman" Oliver as a monarch issuing profundities such as "Governmental tumescence equals individual impotence."[125] Oliver must have gotten an early look at the article as his lawyers threatened *Esquire* with legal action, claiming Oliver's reputation had been irreparably damaged with misrepresentations

123 Personal communication between the author and Andrew Szentgyorgi (August 7, 2018). On St. George's near-execution in Budapest, see the editor's introduction in *Coronet* (February 1958), 5. St. George commented at one point in a letter that his insistence on publishing the essay on Abaco had made WerBell angry and threatening for the first time in their relationship. St. George wondered if he might be on to a bigger story than just Abaco. "Goddamn it, watch your step," WerBell growled at him. St. George to Berry and Ellie [no date, ca. fall 1974], box 23, ASG.
124 St. George, "The Amazing New Country Caper," *Esquire* (February 1975).
125 St. George, "The Abaco Option," typescript, ASG.

and fabrications.[126] St. George responded that this was nothing more than "disassociated, deranged rancor, not even a rational, purposive lie." He insisted that "we have in our possession exceptionally ample documentary material to prove each and every one of our statements of fact and expressions of opinion in the Abaco article.... My initial assurance that our own handling of the evidence was fair and even tolerant in every textual and editorial aspect still stands—in truth, more than ever."[127] It did not help that St. George had not been reimbursed adequately for the expenses he incurred while interviewing Oliver or for the medical expenses associated with having been shot in the hand. To rub salt in the wound, WerBell and Oliver had coaxed St. George's wife—who had worked as a foreign affairs researcher for *Time*—into writing a report for them related to Abaco and then neglected to pay her the promised fee.[128]

The *Esquire* essay spurred additional investigations in to whether or not the plotters had violated US neutrality laws. In the Bahamas, the article's contents worried Prime Minister Pindling. Over a dinner at the home of the American Consul in Nassau, Pindling expressed his concerns to both his host and the other guest at the table, author Arthur Hailey, that WerBell and his associates constituted a real threat. The consul did not share his concerns.[129] Pindling need not have worried. WerBell and Oliver soon parted ways, acrimoniously. Oliver was frustrated by the fact that WerBell had come under investigation again, this time by the Senate Permanent Subcommittee on Investigations in 1974 on issues related to fugitive financier and con artist Robert Vesco's efforts to manufacture and sell automatic weapons in the Caribbean.[130] Vesco, on the run for securities fraud, had had a brief stint in the Bahamas and then settled in Costa Rica in 1973 with the assistance of three-time Costa Rican president José Figueres.[131] Vesco had hatched plans to build an armaments factory on lands Figueres owned and had hoped to turn a

126 "A.R. St. George. Subject: Letter from Mike Oliver's law firm, Stokes and Eck," February 14 [1975], folder "Mitch [and] Material Related to Abaco Society," box 25, ASG.

127 Ibid.

128 Ibid.

129 American Consul Bahamas Nassau to Department of State, February 24, 1975, Wikileaks ID: 1975NASSAU00302_b

130 "Bizarre Search for a Free-Enterprise Utopia in the Sun," *Daily Telegraph*, October 29, 1974, enclosure in FCO 63/1389, NA-Kew; *The Robert Vesco Investigation. Hearings before the Permanent Subcommittee on Investigations of the Committee on Government Operations* (United States Senate) (July 17, September 17, and October 7, 1974)

131 State Department to American Embassy, San José, Costa Rica, December 17, 1975, Wikileaks ID: 1975STATE296913_b; and American Embassy, San José, Costa Rica to Department of State, February 17, 1976, Wikileaks ID: 1976SANJO00813_b. On WerBell see also Stephen G. Tompkins, "Carmichael's Violent Words fed Army Fears of Urban Guerrillas," *Memphis Commercial Appeal*, enclosure in "Supplement: Wednesday, March 24, 1993," FOIA Case Number: 2016-0152-F, https://catalog.archives.gov/id/122245566.

part of Costa Rica into "a headquarters for offshore mutual funds and a world gambling, banking, and financial center."[132] All that was needed was a piece of sovereign territory ceded to him through which he could then organize such activities. The Costa Rican parliament, unlike the Bay Street Boys of Nassau who handed over Freeport, refused.

WerBell was as large in death as he was in life. In the late 1970s he linked up with right-wing conspiracy theorist Lyndon Larouche, running training sessions at his Georgia compound for members of Larouche's National Caucus of Labor Committee.[133] New lucrative opportunities arose with the fight in Afghanistan, and in 1980 WerBell hosted exiled Afghan King Hassan Durrani I at his Powder Springs, Georgia, home. Hassan appointed WerBell commander of his Royal Free Afghan Exile Army. Unfortunately for WerBell, Hassan was not an exiled king but a necktie salesman from New York.[134]

WerBell then moved to Hollywood as plans unfolded for a biopic of his life with none other than Clint Eastwood slated for the starring role.[135] The film never came to fruition. Still, Southern California was not done with WerBell. While investigating a murder, the Los Angeles police uncovered a check, from 1983, for US$1 million to WerBell from *Hustler* magazine publisher Larry Flynt, allegedly as payment for a hit on Frank Sinatra, Bob Guccione, Hugh Hefner, and Walter Annenberg. Flynt's attorney claimed the check was a dinner-party prank, and no charges were filed.[136] WerBell, who had been ill for some time, died in 1983 and allegations soon surfaced that he had been poisoned.[137]

Oliver continued to bristle about *Esquire's* publication of St. George's article, threatening legal action against both the magazine and the journalist. In a lengthy letter to the libertarian journal *Reason*, which had been following the Abaco experiment closely, Oliver accused the journalist of having written

---

132 R.T. Naylor, *Hot Money and the Politics of Debt* (New York: Linden Press/Simon and Schuster, 1987), 42–43.

133 On WerBell's work with Larouche, see Matthew N. Lyons, *Insurgent Supremacists: The U.S. Far Right's Challenge to State and Empire* (Oakland: PM Press, 2018), 84.

134 On WerBell and Afghanistan, see the brief mention in American Embassy of Peshawar to Secretary of State, Washington, DC; American Embassy Kabul; American consul Karachi; American Embassy New Delhi; and American Embassy Islamabad, December 30, 1979, Wikileaks ID: 1979PESHAW00274_e. On King Hassan's lack of royal credentials and New York employment, see Bill Bond, "Some Call Visit Royal Farce," reproduced in *Afghanistan Council Newsletter* 9, no. 1 (January 1981): 22.

135 On the biopic see Maxine Cheshire, "Hollywood Discovers the Weapons Wizard," *Washington Post*, January 18, 1980.

136 Didion, *We Tell Ourselves Stories in Order to Live*, 649.

137 Stephen G. Tompkins, "Carmichael's Violent Words Fed Army Fears of Urban Guerrillas," *Atlanta Journal/Atlanta Constitution*, Supplement, March 24, 1993, included in William J. Clinton—NSCDP, Chron File 1, no. 4, April 1993, available at https://catalog.archives.gov/id/122245566.

"distortions and outright falsehoods."[138] *"There is no such thing as a WerBell-Oliver organization,"* he stressed. The struggle, he assured readers, was political rather than military and they had engaged in no activities that libertarians would find troubling, although when pushed even Lord Belhaven (family motto: "Ride Through") had to admit that, yes, there had been "a little skullduggery" in the whole affair.[139]

138   *Reason*, May 1975, 46.
139   As quoted in "The Peer and the Plot to Take Over a Paradise Island," *Daily Mail*, February 11, 1975?, enclosure in FCO 63/1389, NA-Kew.

CHAPTER FOUR

From Farce to Tragedy

Decolonization and Adventure Capitalists in the New Hebrides

FROM THE ASHES OF ABACO, OLIVER EMERGED. IN 1975 HE AND A NUMBER OF ASSO-
ciates formed the Phoenix Foundation.[1] Among his collaborators were Harry
Schultz, at the time the "world's highest paid investment advisor" and a well-
known goldbug whose newsletter counted Margaret Thatcher as a subscriber;
Nathaniel Branden, former acolyte and paramour of Ayn Rand; and John
Hospers, a University of Southern California philosophy professor witheringly
described by one US official as "a fringe thinker of the Ayn Rand school."[2] If
the Republic of Minerva and the invasion of Abaco were farce, the Phoenix
Foundation was tragedy. Its efforts to foment and fund separatist movements
for its own financial and ideological ends would repeatedly flirt with the kind
of adventurist violence of which the Left is all too often accused.

There is some debate as to from where the Phoenix Foundation took
its name. The image of the Phoenix is common in libertarian literature as
a symbol of rebirth and renewal, of a new world of freedom rising from
the ashes of the old. But given the history I have traced thus far it is hard to
imagine that its adopters were unaware of the name's association with the US
military's program of systematic assassination of suspected communists in
Vietnam, armed no less with machine guns outfitted with Mitchell Livingston
WerBell's silencers.[3] Phoenix seemed the image of choice for anticommunists.

---

1   The articles of incorporation of Phoenix apparently were signed in 1975, with original
    signatories including Oliver, US attorney F. Thomas Eck III, and Australian Richard King,
    all of whom would be closely involved in events in the New Hebrides in the 1970s. See the
    overview provided in Gordon Haines, "Na-Griamel: Vietnamese Refugees Summary of
    Events," February 12, 1979, Gordon Haines Archive [hereafter GHA], National Archives
    of Vanuatu [hereafter NAV].
2   Mike Parsons, "Ashes to Ashes," *New Internationalist* 101 (July 1981), https://newint.
    org/features/1981/07/01/phoenix; Anthony van Fossen, *Tax Havens and Sovereignty in
    the Pacific Islands* (St. Lucia: Queensland University Press, 2012), 122. For the quote on
    Hospers see American Embassy Nassau Bahamas to U.S. Secretary of State, February
    28, 1974, Wikileaks ID: 1974NASSAU00363_b.
3   On WerBell providing the silencers for US machine guns used in the Phoenix Program,
    see R.T. Naylor, *Hot Money and the Politics of Debt* (New York: Linden Press/Simon and

The Phoenix Foundation spoke of colonized peoples yearning for freedom but fearing socialism and communism. Such peoples and their leaders "sincerely want to build their country around the individual instead of creating a monolithic government. Surprisingly, there are several such embryonic potential nations around the world. And for all their spunk, they are having a tough struggle to repel the advances of marauders, for example, neocolonialists like Russia who care not a fiddle for basic human rights. We in Phoenix are actively giving these countries the encouragement, support, physical and technical advice they require."[4]

This was not bluster. The Phoenix Foundation financially backed a right-wing separatist movement (the Frente de Libertação dos Açores, or Azores Liberation Front) that, between 1975 and 1979, sought to secede from Portugal. Phoenix funneled the movement money for weapons, flew FLA leaders to meetings across Europe in its members' private jets, and published a "slick 22-page justification of Azorean independence" that envisioned the Azores "as a potential center for international finance."[5] Phoenix showed up with regularity in embassy and consular reports on the Azorean situation, in part because Portugal's president asked US embassy officials to investigate the organization.[6] In a 1978 conversation with an American consular official, Dr. Joao Bosco Mota Amaral, then president of the Azorean Regional Government,

---

Schuster, 1987), 42. Vietnam Veteran and *Soldier of Fortune* founder Robert Brown, who had close associations with WerBell, founded Phoenix Associates in 1974 in order to recruit mercenaries to fight in Rhodesia on behalf of the white colonial state. On the recurring use of Phoenix, including later in Nicaragua, by US military and paramilitaries, see Douglas Valentine, *The Phoenix Program* (New York: William Morrow and Company, 1990), 428; on Brown's Phoenix Associates, see the pamphlet *Guns for Hire: How the C.I.A. & the U.S. Army Recruit Mercenaries for White Rhodesia* (Montreal: Kersplebedeb, 1977). Varying opinions on the origins of the name can be found in John Beasant, *The Santo Rebellion: An Imperial Reckoning* (Honolulu: University of Hawai'i Press, 1984); James Hilton Mair, "Report on the Possible Smuggling Operations and Arms Shipment through Fiji," General Information File, GHA, NAV. Haines himself, in the margins of Mair's report, argued that the name was taken from the Phoenix Islands group, which is highly unlikely. See ibid.

4   Parsons, "Ashes to Ashes."

5   American Embassy in Lisbon to Secretary of State, Washington, DC, June 20, 1979, Wikileaks ID: 1979LISBON04220_e; American Consul Ponta Delgada to Secretary of State, Washington, DC, April 4, 1979, Wikileaks ID: 1979PONTA00214_e; American Embassy in Lisbon to Secretary of State, Washington, DC, March 21, 1978, Wikileaks ID: 1978LISBON02102_d. See also *Phoenix Foundation Bulletin*, February 1978 and June 1979. Phoenix Foundation published a handbook entitled *The Azorean Fight for Freedom*, a copy of which thus far I have been unable to locate.

6   American Embassy in Lisbon to Secretary of State, Washington, DC; American Consul Amsterdam; American Consul Ponta Delgada; and American Embassy in The Hague, March 21, 1978, Wikileaks ID: 1978LISBON02102_d. See also American Embassy in Lisbon to Secretary of State, Washington, DC, June 20, 1979, Wikileaks ID: 1979LISBON04220_e.

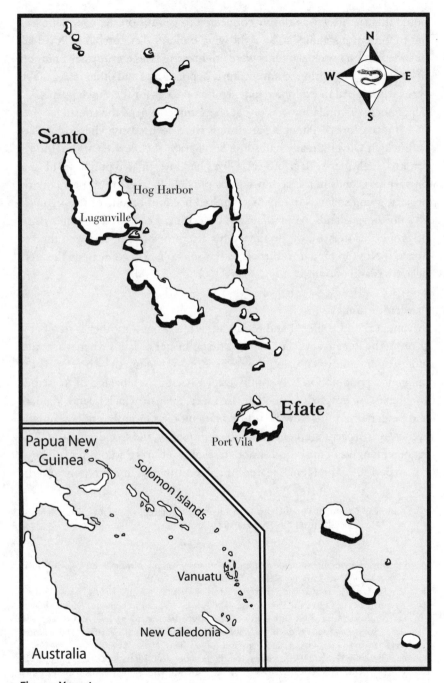

Fig. 4.1: Vanuatu.
Map by John Wyatt Greenlee.

noted that the FLA was closely connected to groups on the continent seeking to foment instability and a right-wing military dictatorship in Portugal.[7] Included among such elements were "right-wing fringe groups in a number of countries, in addition to adventurers, opportunists and other disreputable types who hoped to exploit an independent Azores for their own purposes."[8] "The Phoenix Foundation was one such example," wrote the consul.[9]

But the core of Phoenix's attentions were devoted elsewhere, to a place with which Oliver already had some familiarity: the New Hebrides. In 1970, prior to the Minerva Reef project, Oliver had investigated purchases of land on various islands in the archipelago as possible locales for his new country project, going so far as to buy five hundred hectares on one of the archipelago's northern islands.[10] But when the government outlawed the subdivision of properties in late 1971, he turned his attentions to Minerva and then to Abaco.[11] Now, in 1975, he returned with plans for a new country on the archipelago's island of Santo.

Pandemonium

In Vanuatu land is life. "Land to ni-Vanuatu is what a mother is to a baby," wrote Sethy Regenvanu, the country's first minister of lands when it acquired independence in 1980, using the local term—ni-Vanuatu—to refer to the indigenous population.[12] A southwestern Pacific archipelago of 83 islands, encompassing upwards of 5,000 square miles, 1,800 of which is land, Vanuatu had been named the New Hebrides and colonized jointly under a unique French-British arrangement formalized in 1906 as the Condominium. The arrangement was a misbegotten and misshapen effort to accommodate imperial anxieties.[13] The French feared British dominance in the region and the

---

7   American Consul at Ponta Delgada to Secretary of State, Washington, DC, March 30, 1978, Wikileaks ID: 1978PONTA00214_d.

8   Ibid.

9   Ibid.

10   On Oliver's land purchase, see *Residence de France—Synthèse Mensuelle*, NH034 (July 1970), 6–7, and *Synthèse Mensuelle*, NH034 (January 1971), in NAV.

11   Van Fossen, *Tax Havens and Sovereignty*, 110.

12   As quoted from Howard Van Trease, *The Politics of Land in Vanuatu: From Colony to Independence* (Suva, Fiji: University of the South Pacific, 1987), back cover. See also Barak Sope, *Land and Politics in the New Hebrides* (Suva, Fiji: South Pacific Social Sciences Association [1974]), chap. 1; and Margaret Jolly, *Women of the Place: Kastom, Colonialism, and Gender in Vanuatu* (Chur, Switzerland: Harwood Publishers, 1994), esp. chap. 2.

13   Worthy of note here is just how frequently such unwieldy structures were put into place in order to square the brute reality of empire with the claims to enlightened rule and citizenship. Think, for example, of US empire and its "insular territories" of Guam, American Samoa, Hawai'i, and Puerto Rico, acquired in 1898 and the residents of which were determined by a Supreme Court decision to be "foreign but in a domestic sense."

increased isolation of their colonial interests in New Caledonia. The British feared the exposure of Australia's northeastern coast to French influence and sought to support British missionaries who had made early inroads in the archipelago.[14] The result was a system of colonial occupation and rule characterized by mutual suspicion and distrust and a shared system of administration that all too frequently resulted in inertia. Ni-Vanuatu called the arrangement the Pandemonium.

Both European countries had long histories in the region, the English in Australia, Aotearoa New Zealand, the Solomons, and Fiji, and the French in New Caledonia, the Marquesas, and Tahiti. Both too had long histories of interaction with the New Hebrides. Contact and exchange had been intermittent for much of the eighteenth and early nineteenth centuries. Members of the British London Missionary Society had arrived in the 1840s. A decade later European traders of sandalwood—a large aromatic tree of the region—arrived. Sandalwood had long been a commodity for a booming market in China where it was prized for its use in the making of furniture and boxes and as incense for temples. Demand was at first satisfied by the forests of South Asia, but over time cutters moved into the Pacific, hopping across the first seventy years of the nineteenth century from Fiji to the Marquesas to Hawai'i and finally to the New Hebrides.[15] A boom emerged, lasting for some fifteen years, which brought numerous firms and traders to the islands, and in particular Santo. It is also brought a flurry of slave raiders from Australia seeking labor for sugar plantations in Queensland and labor recruiters from New Caledonia seeking workers for the mines. Simultaneously, Peruvian and Chilean slavers raided smaller islands for labor on coastal plantations and in the guano mines on the islands dotting the South American coastline.[16]

See Christina Duffy Burnett and Burke Marshall, eds., *Foreign in a Domestic Sense: Puerto Rico, American Expansion and the Constitution* (Durham, NC: Duke University Press, 2001) and Daniel Immerwahr, *How to Hide an Empire: History of the Greater United States* (New York: Farrar, Straus & Giroux, 2019).

14 The most careful and thorough history of Vanuatu is van Trease, *The Politics of Land in Vanuatu*. On the early history of the Church and British policy, see Christopher Waters, "Manuscript XXVII: Australia and the South Pacific," *Journal of Pacific History* 48, no. 2 (2013): 209–16.

15 J.R. McNeill, "Pacific Ecology and British Imperialism, 1770–1970," in Hermann J. Hiery and John M. MacKenzie, eds., *European Impact and Pacific Influence: British and German Colonial Policy in the Pacific Islands and the Indigenous Response* (London: Tauris, 1997), 123–50, esp. 129 for sandalwood; Dorothy Shineberg, *They Came for Sandalwood: A Study of the Sandalwood Trade in the Southwest Pacific, 1830–1865* (Melbourne: Melbourne University Press, 1967).

16 On slave raiding and labor recruitment there is much debate. For varied perspectives, see Peter Corris, *Passage, Port and Plantation: A History of Solomon Islands Labour Migration, 1870–1914* (Melbourne: Melbourne University Press, 1973), Kay Saunders, *Workers*

By the 1870s the sandalwood industry had caused deforestation, and on Santo French settlers and laborers turned to other activities. These included most importantly the creation of coconut plantations for copra production and increased cattle raising, activities that led settlers to expand deeper and deeper into the bush.[17] As had been the case for Aotearoa New Zealand and Hawai'i, livestock plantations expanded significantly on Santo in the early twentieth century, spurred on by growing demand and refrigerated shipping.[18] French colonizers and particularly the Societé Française des Nouvelles-Hébrides (SFNH) had laid claim to large swathes of land across the archipelago, upon which they built plantations for copra and cacao production. Conflicts soon arose between the SFNH and ni-Vanuatu as the company encroached on ni-Vanuatu gardens and village lands, leading French and British officials to create an administrative mechanism for dealing with land conflicts and overseeing the archipelago.[19] This was the birth of the Condominium arrangement in 1906, which included a joint court that, from the perspective of ni-Vanuatu, regularized and formalized land theft on behalf of colonial settlers.[20]

Despite land disputes, as well as global fluctuations in price and demand for copra, the SFNH remained prominent, and plantations persisted well into the twentieth century as copra remained the staple of the economy. With global industrialization and changing consumption patterns after World War II, cattle grazing offered opportunities to respond to new patterns of consumption and to escape the volatility of the copra market. Thus, in the 1950s settlers began moving further into the interior to clear land and graze cattle. Many bought lands subdivided by the SFNH, which by this point was largely owned by the French government. Settlers claimed they had registered title to the land, based on earlier judgments of the joint court, but islanders had long understood such lands, which they themselves occupied and worked,

---

in Bondage: The Origins and Bases of Unfree Labour in Queensland, 1824–1916 (St. Lucia: University of Queensland Press, 2015 [1982]). H.E. Maude, Slavers in Paradise: The Peruvian Slave Trade in Polynesia, 1862–1864 (Stanford: Stanford University Press, 1981) is the most detailed examination of Peruvian and Chilean raiding in the Pacific.

17 John Beasant notes the case of John Higginson, an Irish national who acquired French citizenship and in just two months in 1892 "purchased" ninety thousand hectares of land in parts of the archipelago. Beasant, The Santo Rebellion, 10. On this early history I have relied on Van Trease, The Politics of Land in Vanuatu, and Beasant, The Santo Rebellion, esp. chaps. 1 and 2.

18 McNeill, "Pacific Ecology and British Imperialism," 133.

19 Van Trease, The Politics of Land in Vanuatu, 35–41; Keith Woodward, A Political Memoir of the Anglo-French Condominium of the New Hebrides (Canberra: Australian National University Press, 2014), 24.

20 Sope, Land and Politics in the New Hebrides, 10–11.

as belonging to them by custom. Barak Sope, one of the intellectual leaders of the movement that would result in New Hebrides independence, writing in the midst of increasing land conflict in the early 1970s, summarized it thus:

> In the New Hebrides as in other Pacific islands, land rights were traditionally held by groups. Individual rights existed but only at a certain group level, so that *land was inalienable*. It is understood that one group does not hold all rights to a particular piece of land. The principle was that each piece of land was a centre of focus with groups radiating out from it with varying degrees of connection to it.
>
> Within the landholding groups the intensity of individual rights would vary at different levels. For instance, an individual may have rights to four or five pieces of land in his vicinity and elsewhere, but the intensity of his rights would differ from one piece of land to another. The person's right to use a piece of land would depend upon his position within a particular group, the location of the land, and the group's connection with that piece of land.[21]

The Condominium Joint Court was in little position to understand the varied and variegated nature of landholding and land rights, particularly given that systems of rights, use, and inheritance could vary even between islands within the archipelago.[22] Yet, operating under a substantial backlog, with a shortage of surveyors and a lack of clarity around registration and land ownership, it found itself repeatedly in the difficult situation of having to reconcile the irreconcilable: rights to land as property that could not be understood as property as such. The problem proved severe enough for the British Resident Commissioner to pursue discussions with his French counterpart in 1960 regarding ni-Vanuatu custom and land laws, resulting in the formation the following year of the Condominium Survey Department.[23]

By the early 1960s on Santo things continued to escalate. There, the SFNH had been provided title to some thirteen thousand hectares on the southern end of the island, which they named Luganville and had begun to subdivide and sell to French planters.[24] Bulldozers and fences began to appear. Santo's chiefs, as well as those from surrounding islands, responded. Led by Chief Paul Buluk, indigenous custom owners tore down fences, removed surveyors' stakes, expropriated their tools, and pulled up a cement boundary marker

---

21   Ibid., 7. Emphasis in the original.
22   Ibid., 8–9; 16–18.
23   Van Trease, *The Politics of Land in Vanuatu*, 94.
24   Ibid., 127.

from the ground.[25] The joint administration was again unsure how to respond, particularly in this instance given that the language used in the process of land registration and titling had been vague. As one French official noted, "The rights of ownership are not absolute, since very wide rights of tenure (houses, gardens, plantations ...) have been granted to the natives."[26] Phrases in the original deed—that identified rights for those "originating from the area" and those "established in the region" as well as their descendants—deepened the confusion as did a condition that ni-Vanuatu be permitted to cultivate and work the land "for as long as said area is not occupied." How did one go about defining who originated from the area? Who counted as a descendant? Was the designation specific to an area of a particular island, the island itself, or the archipelago as a whole? What were the criteria for being established in the region? And what was meant by "occupied"? Despite such questions, the authorities had to respond, particularly given that other European colonists nervously watched to see how the case would be resolved. An initial justification for the SFNH's title derived from the argument that Buluk himself was not considered to be "from the area" and that the village of Vanafo did not appear in any historical or property records.[27]

The authorities arrested Buluk and sentenced him to six months in prison. Buluk and his fellow chiefs refused to submit. They had grown increasingly concerned with European encroachment into the interior. Buluk and a number of other chiefs met and pronounced the Act of Dark Bush Land, which held that "no French planters could claimed [sic] the land beyond the cocoa and coffee plantations [sic] end."[28] For proof they referenced what was "understood from our fore Fathers and ... re-examined from the Joint Court in Vila 1963." The drafting and pronouncement of the Act of Dark Bush Land would become a major turning point in anticolonial struggle in the coming decades. As well as expressing concerns regarding encroachment, Buluk also protested that a Luganville bulldozer had dug up the bones of his ancestors and that bulldozers were destroying gardens and crops on plots of land occupied by Santo ni-Vanuatu within the bounds of the Luganville concession.[29] Buluk insisted this was the site of the village of Vanafo, but authorities argued no

25   "Report on Land Problems in the Area on the Left Bank of the Sarakata River" [English trans. of original French report], September 9, 1964, Foreign and Commonwealth Office [hereafter FCO] 141/13284, National Archives of the United Kingdom [hereafter NA-Kew].
26   Ibid. See also Van Trease, *The Politics of Land in Vanuatu*, 133–34.
27   "Report on Land Problems in the Area on the Left Bank of the Sarakata River."
28   Santo: Act of Dark Bush Land (Held April 3, 1964, at 7:30 pm), FCO 141/13284, NA-Kew.
29   R. Pujol (Avocat des Indigènes) a Monsieur le Délégué Français pour la Circonscription des Iles Nord (July 31 [19]64), FCO 141/13284, NA-Kew; Bulluck [sic] chef de la tribu Bonafo a Messieurs les Résidents Anglais et Français (Santo, July 21 1964), FCO 141/13284,

such village existed and that Buluk had mobilized his followers to squat the land. In response, colonial officials passed legislation to allow them to prosecute people they designated as squatters and trespassers more harshly (see fig. 4.2).[30]

With no satisfactory response coming from the resident commissioners, Buluk had a petition drawn up and sent to the British High Commissioner, based in the Solomon Islands, and to the United Nations.[31] In addition, he and others formed an organization—Nagriamel—to carry on the fight against developers and cattle colonists encroaching on the "dark bush." Buluk narrated the history with a particular attention to land rights and inheritance and the conflict with surveyors:

> The first distribute between the New Hebrides Natives children and the European on year 1955.
>
> First conce[rn]ing the Condominium Savyer [surveyor] are putting a new cement boundary inthrough our Natives private provate [probate] land without any permission from the chief and all the land ownership, who the right from their own home country: Thats w[h]ere the first New Hebrides Natives meeting it been started, on the *year 1955*.
>
> Second meeting conce[rn]ing the British and French Government and the Condominium Savyer: They were plan to have a New road, from village Morn[illegible] hill and right through all the Natives private provate land onto the waterfall: They have been plan out agreement to have this road to be a public. And the Natives Land owner Chief Paul Buluk, Chief Old Tom, Chief Tavue, Chief John Verikara and all the families, they didn't know anything or they didn't called to the meeting, that meeting about this new road, plan are only between the french planter and three goverment, but nothing from the Natives, Chief and all the

NA-Kew; Santo: Act of Dark Bush Land (Held April 3, 1964, at 7:30 pm), FCO 141/13284, NA-Kew.

30   This was done on May 13, 1966. See the revisions to Section 16 of the New Hebrides Summary Conviction Offences Regulation 1928, FCO 141/13284 (f. 27 and f. 32), NA-Kew.

31   For the petition, see Petition from Chief Paul Buluk Concerning New Hebrides to the UN Special Committee on the Situation with regard to the Implementation of the Declaration on the Granting of Independence to Colonial Countries and Peoples, FCO 141/13284 [Disputes Buluk-Stevens], doc. 78, NA-Kew. For letters from Buluk and Stevens to the High Commission and to the UN General Assembly and its Special Committee, see "Chief Buluk and His Witness Jim Stephen to two Resident Commissioners (March 2, 1967)," in ibid., doc. 35, and "Chief Buluk and His Witness Jim Stephen to High Commission Solomon Island [sic]," in ibid., doc. 36A. For discussion of colonial officials' response, see Memo, British District Agency, New Hebrides Buluk Affair (April 14, 1967), in ibid., doc. 39, and SAVINGRAM to The High Commissioner, Land Dispute at Santo (undated, ca. May 1, 1967), in ibid., doc. 52.

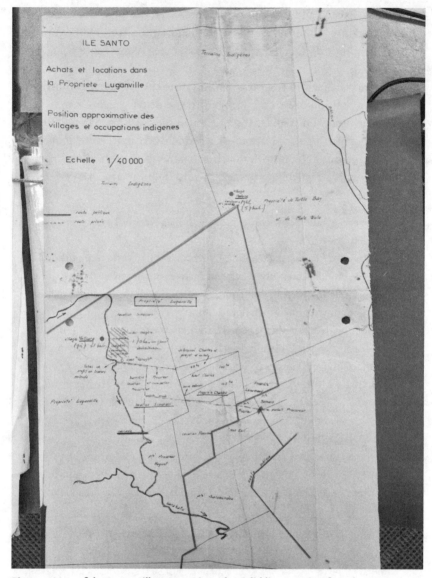

Fig. 4.2: Map of the Luganville concession (the solid line running from bottom center up to center right and then sloping downward to left) with detail of native community within its bounds (the hatched rectangle, center left, along the riverbank) and its village of Vanafo.

Courtesy of the National Archives of the United Kingdom, ref. FCO 141/13247, Attachment to R. Gauger, Delegue Francais du Condiminium des Nouvelles Hebrides pour la Circonscription des Iles du Nord a Monsieur le Delegue britannique pour la Circonscription des Iles du Nord, Santo, September 18, 1964.

landowner thats why the begining been started about this new road on year 1955, and there where all the Natives children, they not agreeable to see any more new cement boundry or Condominium Savyer to be put new cement boundry into the Natives private provate land because of this new road is not a public road, it is only a private provate road called SFNH claim.

The first time new Hebrides Natives they are wake up and think to come to be on one group to discuss all about what been happening in their country: And they called this meeting Santo New Hebrides Natives Buraoa meeting. This was the first name it been carried out from all the Santo Natives children on *year 1955 . 56 . 57 . 58 . 59 . 60 . 61 . 62* .

Second step all the islands Natives New Hebrides, they are disined to join in the meeting and they brought forward all the complaining about Savyer and the European the same problem in Santo and in the islands. This is on the *year 1962* the island have brought their matter into Santo Buraoa meeting and then, the Santo and Island Chiefs and members, they are joined for agreement to bring this matter feather [*sic*] to the court all about the Condominium Savyer and S.F.N.H. Savyer who are claim more Natives land without any permission form the Natives land owner.

Year 1962 . 63 . 64 . 65

Year 1965 all the New Hebrides Natives children Santo and Islands, they have been vorted and signed agreement for Chief President Jimmy T.P.S. Moses, and also they vorted for the Name which we called New Hebrides Na-Griamel is father and mother.

From Santo and Islands, Natives, father and mother, chiefs and members

This is on year *1965 January 15*

On the *year 1967* the agreement, they agreeable to have their own flag which they called Na-Griamel.[32]

The named witness to Buluk's testimony was Santo resident Jimmy Stevens (referred to as Jimmy T.P.S. Moses in the document). As the decade

---

32   "1955: The New Hebrides Original Families. The First Book of Chief Paul Buluk and his Witness J.T.P.S. Moses: The Book name Buraoa Movement on 55." Undated document, Stevens NaGriamel folder, GHA, NAV. I have left the grammar and spelling as it appears in the original. The reference to "private probate land" in the document is most likely intended to convey the meaning of land that is inherited and to which rights are determined ancestrally. On the formation of Nagriamel, see Van Trease, *The Politics of Land in Vanuatu*, chap. 5; Woodward, *A Political Memoir*, 25. Nagriamel is also at times spelled Na-Griamel and NaGriamel. I use Nagriamel throughout the chapter except in quotes that use an alternate spelling.

progressed, Stevens would become the central figure in the struggle over land on Santo.

Stevens (also spelled Stephens) was not "man-Santo"—that is, his lineage was not Santo lineage. Although born there, his mother was a Banks Islander, from further north in the archipelago, and his father was Tongan-Scottish. He grew up in Santo during World War II. As the Japanese expanded into the Solomon Islands, the US set up a base on Santo, on a southern plantation that would become the town of Luganville, from which to wage the war. Between 1942 and 1945 roughly a quarter of a million GIs passed through Santo to support the war effort.[33] Among them was author James Michener, at the time in the US Navy, who based his famed novel *South Pacific* on his time in the New Hebrides.[34] It would be hard to overestimate the impacts that these GIs had on their immediate surroundings. Santo's residents found new work; surplus equipment made its way into local hands; and, not least of all, Native islanders saw "other black men (American soldiers) participating in and enjoying the benefits of the white man's world."[35] The US Army hired Stevens to work first at the army hospital and subsequently as a bulldozer driver. As a result of that work and his English-language proficiency, Stevens acquired a certain stature over time and soon began mediating between varied interests—chiefs, colonial officials, and landholders—on the island. These included Paul Buluk and his followers.

Stevens was with Buluk, in 1964, when they pronounced the Act of the Dark Bush Land and had been arrested alongside Buluk in 1967. After that stint in jail, Stevens emerged with a burnished reputation as an anticolonial leader, a reputation further enhanced by his visits to the New Hebrides Joint Court ("that remote palace of injustice which for most New Hebrideans is altogether inaccessible," as one British official put it) and his vocal opposition to European land encroachment.[36] He soon acquired status as chief and accorded all the rights that came with such a designation. At the same time, he sought to have his status as a British Protected person revoked and to be designated as "native,"

33 Van Trease, *The Politics of Land in Vanuatu*, 131. More generally for the war and its impacts on Oceanians, see Tracy Banivanua Mar, *Decolonisation and the Pacific: Indigenous Globalization and the Ends of Empire* (Cambridge: Cambridge University Press, 2016), chap. 4.

34 Andrew Stuart, *Of Cargoes, Colonies, and Kings: Diplomatic and Administrative Service from Africa to the Pacific* (London: I.B. Tauris, 2001), 159.

35 Van Trease, *The Politics of Land in Vanuatu*, 132; see also Banivanua Mar, *Decolonisation and the Pacific*, 128–31; Lamont Lindstrom and Geoffrey White, *Island Encounters: Black and White Memories of the Pacific War* (Washington, DC: Smithsonian Institution, 1990), 26–30.

36 Report from British agent in Santo, no date but late May 1967, FCO 141/13247, NA-Kew.

a request officials refused on the grounds that he would have "no status at all" and thus not be "justiciable in the courts."[37] British colonial officials also resisted negotiating with Stevens as a chief but soon realized they were left with little alternative. Refusing to recognize and engage with Stevens, the British agent on Santo wrote, "is likely only to exasperate still further the sentiments which have 'created' Stephens."[38] He continued: "Whether we like it or not and whether or not his position is assailable, *for the moment*, Stephens is a chief, and should be so regarded."[39] The official's point here is important as it suggests that many in the Foreign Office seemed to think Stevens was not an authentic chief. They misunderstood how chiefly status worked. Status as chief in the New Hebrides was not comparable to that of what one would find in, say, Fiji, Tonga, or England. In these latter instances, chief is a designation closely entwined with lineage and genealogy. It is an inherited power and one legible to British officials themselves raised in an island chiefdom derived from lineage. In contrast, in the New Hebrides to be chief was a position granted vis-à-vis one's actions and the position itself existed on a kind of spectrum, with lesser and higher chiefs. Thus, there was nothing suspect or somehow inauthentic about Stevens's chiefly designation.[40] The British agent concluded with a stinging assessment for his superiors: "Stephens is a result[,] not a cause[,] and we should seek to alter the circumstances that have made his existence possible[,] not attack this "half white hope"; after all when did any judge of the Joint Court ever offer any intelligible assistance to a Melanesian?"[41]

His counsel fell on deaf ears. Over the coming decade, rather than seeing Stevens as a "result" and not a "cause," British and French officials either reduced him to caricature—a cult leader, drawing on an abundance of literature related to cargo cults—or sought to rework him into an instrument to serve their own interests.[42] Yet Stevens, as historian Howard van Trease has carefully demonstrated, was no cult leader, and Nagriamel grew to become the most important Native-led anticolonial movement on the islands.[43] Stevens

---

37 British Resident Commissioner to the Resident Commissioner for the French Republic (April 19, 1967), FCO 141/13284 [Disputes Buluk-Stevens], doc. 38, NA-Kew.
38 Report from British agent in Santo, no date but late May 1967, FCO 141/13247, NA-Kew.
39 Ibid. Emphasis in the original.
40 I am indebted to Howard van Trease for clarifying this distinction to me.
41 Report from British agent in Santo, no date but late May 1967, FCO 141/13247, NA-Kew.
42 Van Trease, *The Politics of Land in Vanuatu*, 144–47. On the uses and abuses of the term "cargo cult" and its application to various movements—political and otherwise—see Lamont Lindstrom, *Cargo Cult: Strange Stories of Desire from Melanesia and Beyond* (Honolulu: University of Hawai'i Press, 1993).
43 Van Trease, *The Politics of Land in Vanuatu*, 160; Banivanua Mar, *Decolonisation and the Pacific*, 132; Marc Kurt Tabani, "Histoire politique du Nagriamel à Santo," *Journal de la Société des Océanistes* 113 (2001–2): 151–76.

was one of the first islanders to generate a movement around the rights of indigenous peoples and to advocate for the return of alienated land. Yet neither he nor his fellow chiefs on Santo called for the expropriation, let alone the expulsion, of European landowners but rather a recognition of the rights to land of custom owners and the need to resolve conflicts over land acquired fraudulently.[44] Most land under European control had been titled fraudulently, given the process by which titles were created and formalized, but Stevens also appeared willing to recognize an idea of property in which those who had labored to plant and care for trees, particularly coconut trees, had legitimate claims to the land.[45] Stevens argued that "the real meaning of Nagriamel today [1977], and from the beginning, is not to chase out the white man, nor to drive out different islanders nor to destroy anything. No. But to find a way to break that Joint Court law which was taking away our land."[46]

Nor were Nagriamel intrinsically opposed to forms of development. Indeed, in 1969 Stevens took the lead on an arrangement between Nagriamel and André Leconte, a French industrialist based in New Caledonia with large land interests on Santo.[47] French officials encouraged the collaboration which provided Leconte with security of tenure over ten thousand hectares of land in exchange for him clearing bush land for Santo's inhabitants with his bull-dozers and trucks. An attorney for the law firm retained by Stevens expressed deep reservations about the vagueness of the language in the agreement, including the possibilities that Nagriamel were in fact not leasing but *selling* the land to Leconte outright.[48] Just as worrisome, the firm noted based on information they received from a bulldozer operator, and the general terms of the agreement, "You will be leasing or disposing of the land in return for clearing about 500 hectares."[49] Even so, the agreement apparently went forward and is a good indication of Stevens's importance and influence. But the vagueness of the contract and the dramatic disparities in familiarity with

---

44 Van Trease, *The Politics of Land in Vanuatu*, 100.
45 My thanks to Howard van Trease for his elaboration on this issue. See also Jimmy Stevens, President, "Nagriamel," in Chris Plant, ed., *New Hebrides: The Road to Independence* (Suva, Fiji: Institute of Pacific Studies, 1977), 35–40.
46 Jimmy Stevens, President, "Nagriamel," in Plant, ed., *New Hebrides*, 36. (This text is a transcript of an interview conducted with Stevens in 1977.) This perspective was under-stood by colonial officials. See, for example, JCD Lawrence, (Land Tenure Advisor, FCO, Overseas Development Administration), New Hebrides. Report on Land Matters, April 12, 1972, Item 206, Colin Allan Papers, MS 1189: Papers on the Solomon Islands and Vanuatu, 1881–1993, Pacific Manuscripts Bureau. [Hereafter CAP, PMB.]
47 Van Trease, *The Politics of Land in Vanuatu*, 145–47; Beasant, *The Santo Rebellion*, 22.
48 H. Wilshire, Webb, Son & Doyle to Jimmy Stevens, August 1, 1969, Stevens file, GHA, NAV.
49 Ibid.

the legal constructs and instruments used in land deals, not to mention the distinctive ways in which land use and ownership was understood, did not bode well for ni-Vanuatu confronting a growing wave of land speculators.

American rush

Gordon Haines sat patiently at his desk in his office in Port Vila while the man across from him, David Ford, explained himself. Ford wanted Haines to under-stand that he was not a criminal. The small blemishes on his record—fraud, for which he served a prison term of nine months in California, and a subsequent arrest in Los Angeles—were the unfortunate results of misunderstandings. And in any case, that was long ago, he had turned a new leaf and relocated to Hawai'i, and such peccadillos were certainly no reason to keep him from his business in the New Hebrides.[50] The previous year, 1970, he had made investments and dedicated substantial time to the islands and did not like the idea of being forbidden to return. Haines listened to Ford, showed him to the door of his office, and then typed up a report. Haines was probably not surprised by what he'd heard. American visitors to New Hebrides were often brought to see him, and whether or not they divulged anything as personal as a criminal record did not much matter because, as head of Britain's Special Branch in the archipelago, Haines usually already knew. With a long career in the empire's service behind him, serving in Northern Rhodesia through the end of colonial rule and then briefly in the Solomon Islands, he had arrived in the New Hebrides at the tail end of the 1960s.[51] Such a route to the southwest Pacific was commonplace in the British colonial administration. Veterans of colonial service in Africa frequently redeployed to the Pacific in the 1960s and 1970s, including a number in the New Hebrides: these included not only Haines but also David Browning, who similarly had served in Rhodesia and then made his way to Santo, and Roger du Boulay, who was in Nigeria prior to his posting as resident commissioner in Port Vila (the seat of the joint administration in the New Hebrides) in 1973.[52]

   Haines's arrival coincided with an influx of American land speculators, aspiring investors, and grifters who had been drawn by the establishment of

---

50 Gordon Haines, "Report on U.S. Land Speculation," January 14, 1971, David R. Ford file, GHA, NAV.

51 Gordon Haines, "A Short History of the Life of Gordon Richard Sydney Haines" (donated by the Editor [Bob Makin] of the *Vanuatu Independent*), National Library of Vanuatu.

52 On Browning, see reminiscences in Brian J. Bresnihan and Keith Woodward, eds., *Tufala Gavman: Reminiscences from the Anglo-French Condominium of the New Hebrides* (Suva, Fiji: Institute of Pacific Studies, 2002); on Du Boulay, see W. David McIntyre, *Winding Up the British Empire in the Pacific Islands* (Oxford: Oxford University Press, 2014), 37–38.

tax haven status in the islands in 1969, rising land values, and a push for development.[53] Ford was part of that influx, and his business was land. A real estate and travel agent based in Hawai'i (that "busy crossroads for the real estate and construction entrepreneur," as a *New York Times* article put it in 1971) Ford had been organizing multiple tours, each of thirty or so people, from Hawai'i to the New Hebrides and making a "hard sell" for them to purchase a parcel of a subdivided property.[54] He had been doing this on behalf of another Hawai'i-based land developer and speculator named Harold Eugene Peacock.[55] Peacock proved to be the real target of Haines's interest.

Peacock arrived in Santo at some point around 1967 and quickly began purchasing large lots of land and subdividing it into parcels for purchase and settlement by American and Japanese investors as well as US soldiers serving in Vietnam.[56] He claimed in early 1970 to have already sold all of the parcels.[57] He purchased a particularly large swath of land for both subdivision and resort development in and around Hog Harbor on Santo, which he renamed Lokalee after his Lokalee Ltd. Co. But Peacock soon had troubles.

---

53 Greg Rawlings, "Laws, Liquidity and Eurobonds: The Making of the Vanuatu Tax Haven," *Journal of Pacific History* 39, no. 3 (2004): 327; Van Trease, *The Politics of Land in Vanuatu*, 148. On tax havens see van Fossen, *Tax Havens and Sovereignty*; Ronen Palan, *The Offshore World: Sovereign Markets, Virtual Places, and Nomad Millionaires* (Ithaca: Cornell University Press, 2006); Vanessa Ogle, "Archipelago Capitalism: Tax Havens, Offshore Money, and the State, 1950s–1970s," *American Historical Review* 122, no. 5 (December 2017): 1431–58; Ogle, "'Funk Money': The End of Empires, the Expansion of Tax Havens, and Decolonization as an Economic and Financial Event," *Past & Present* 249, no. 1 (November 2020): 213–49; and Nicholas Shaxson, *Treasure Islands: Uncovering the Damage of Offshore Banking and Tax Havens* (London: Palgrave-Macmillan, 2011).

54 Earl A. Belle, "Islands," *New York Times*, December 26, 1971, W-1.

55 According to Barak Sope, Ford had purchased a 350-acre property on the island of Efate and a 600-acre property on Santo, with plans to subdivide both into self-contained communities. Sope, *Land and Politics in the New Hebrides*, 42.

56 On his marketing to US soldiers, see R.G. Crocombe, *The Pacific Islands and the USA* (Honolulu: East-West Center Pacific Islands Development Program, 1995), 85; Capt. James Hilton Mair, "Report on the Possible Smuggling Operations and Arms Shipment through Fiji," no date, ca. mid-1976, General Information folder, GHA, NAV. Also worth reading is the discussion about his partner Adrianus Holgen in American Embassy Suva to Secretary of State, Washington, DC, March 22, 1979, Wikileaks ID: 1979SUVA00859_e. Holgen was involved in a land scam selling Pacific islanders land in Texas that had been falsely advertised, including claiming that James Drury, star of *The Virginian* television show, lived there and would be a neighbor. Secretary of State, Washington, DC, to American Embassy Canberra, American Embassy Port Moresby, American Embassy Suva, American Embassy Suva, June 10, 1979, Wikileaks ID: 1979STATE149385_e.

57 District Monthly Intelligence Report February 20, 1970, GHA, NAV. For expressions of concern regarding land surveying on Peacock's properties, see District Monthly Intelligence Report March 17, 1970; District Monthly Intelligence Report September 28, 1970; and February 25, 1971, all in GHA, NAV.

Brash and "buccaneering," Peacock apparently drank heavily, and the resulting effects—loutishness and poor judgment—alienated both bankers and investment professionals in Port Vila. His activities also drew increasing attention from colonial officials.[58] Already wary of him due to his land purchases and mixed reputation, Condominium officials grew more suspicious when Peacock claimed to be president of Universal Export Ltd., whose most famous employee was Commander James Bond. In case Peacock had forgotten, British Resident Commissioner Colin Allan noted drily, "some of us read and enjoy Ian Fleming."[59] Allan wondered if Peacock might be a US government agent. But the crux of the matter was that Peacock's activities meant the land question could no longer be postponed.

To make matters worse, Peacock's arrival coincided with a rush of attention—sparked by the tax haven designation—from libertarian exit strategists. "Excitement is running high among Libertarians, Radical Capitalists, Individualist Anarchists and assorted freedom advocates in Hawai'i over the possibilities of developing viable retreat areas in the New Hebrides," read one notice in *Innovator*.[60] Such excitement, the writer noted, was due in part to the fact that there were "no income taxes, no business taxes, and virtually no business restrictions, no military establishment and therefore no draft."[61] And all of this unfolded as French and British officials tried to navigate the turbulent waters of anticolonial sentiment churned up by Buluk, Stevens, and Nagriamel. The growing tension around land encroachment and speculation threatened to worsen an already difficult situation on the islands and, not surprisingly, Condominium authorities closely monitored Peacock. At the same time, they grew increasingly suspicious regarding American activities in the region. It is revealing, for example, that by 1970 the Northern District Intelligence Reports from Santo sent to the British Residence Agent in Port Vila included a new, distinct subheading ("American and other property . . ."); the same would be the case for the French *Synthèse Mensuelle*.[62] Condominium authorities realized that if they did not take measures, a possible influx of American capital and settlers would alter the balance of political, economic, and social power on the islands.

58   Colin H. Allan, FCO Diplomatic Report No. 422/72, Anglo-French Condominium of the New Hebrides: Principal Developments Since August 1966, p. 11, Item 270, MS 1189, CAP, PMB.
59   Ibid.
60   William Danks, "The New Hebrides as a Libertarian Retreat Area," *Innovator*, Spring 1969, 7–44.
61   Ibid.
62   See, just for a sampling, the *Synthèse Mensuelle* for 1970 and 1971, box NH034, NAV.

The British and French administrations agreed on very little, with one exception: their distaste for Americans. Confronted with a possible American influx, in the form of both settlers and speculators, the Joint Administration decided to act. In July 1971 they issued a regulation that required landowners to obtain the approval of both British and French Resident Commissioners for any subdivisions. Furthermore the requirement applied not only to any new schemes of subdivision but also to "all existing, uncompleted sub-divisions of which, at the commencement of this Regulation, at least one quarter of the plots are not registered as having been sold."[63] And finally, to add insult to injury the regulation imposed a value-added tax on subdivisions retroactive to 1967, to be paid by the seller.[64] Resistance to the measures, by both American investors and a number of Europeans who lived in the New Hebrides, was fierce but the British and French administrations refused to reconsider. They were supported by many ni-Vanuatu who saw in the subdivisions little more than "a continuation of the land-grabbing" by foreigners that had long plagued their communities.[65]

The measures appeared to work. A French official in June 1972 reported a slowdown in the land trade and a near eradication of "pure speculation."[66] It helped that officials in Hawai'i warned would-be investors to hold off on any future land purchases.[67] That other governments in the region, such as Fiji, implemented methods to control and tax real estate transactions also helped stave off what had begun to look like a southwestern Pacific land rush. In the meantime, other speculators realized Peacock was a liability. Ford, for example, went to some pains to argue to Haines that while he had assisted Peacock in the past, he did not work for him.[68]

---

63   For a succinct explanation of the Regulation, which was provided to an irate plantation owner, and from which the quoted text comes, see A.R. Worner, Information Officer to Mrs. S.H. McMichael, June 30, 1972, Sylvia Hearn McMichael file, GHA, NAV. See also Walter Lini, "Chapter and Verse on Outside Meddling in the New Hebrides," *Pacific Islands Monthly* 51, no. 8 (August 1980): 25–26. For French officials' recognition that many of the land purchases were for the purposes of speculation rather than settlement, see *Synthèse Mensuelle*, February 1971, 1–7 and *Synthèse Mensuelle*, July 1971, 7, both in box NH034, NAV.

64   Worner, Information Officer to Mrs. S.H. McMichael, June 30, 1972, Sylvia Hearn McMichael file, GHA, NAV; Lini, "Chapter and Verse."

65   Sope, *Land and Politics in the New Hebrides*, 42.

66   *Synthèse Mensuelle*, June 1972, box NH034, NAV; van Trease, *The Politics of Land in Vanuatu*, 149–50.

67   *Synthèse Mensuelle*, November 1971, box NH034, NAV; Sope, *Land and Politics in the New Hebrides*, 44–45.

68   Gordon Haines, "Report on U.S. Land Speculation," January 14, 1971, David R. Ford file, GHA, NAV.

Peacock fought the new regulations. He stood to lose millions, a situation that only worsened for him when the purchasers of his parcels, who now could not obtain legal title to their plots, sued him. He in turn sued British Condominium officials over the retroactive legislation. The *"affaire Peacock"* became front-page headlines in the local press. Inquiries by the US State Department and Hawai'i senator Daniel Inouye ensued and Peacock's lawyer insinuated that Henry Kissinger had taken an interest in the case.[69] Such "Kissinger-rattling," as a British colonial attorney called it, had little effect.[70] Still, the suit took some five years to make its way through the courts, in part because the evidence suggested that Condominium authorities tacitly may have approved Peacock's subdivisions and then backpedaled once the scale and implications of his projects—with other foreigners and many French *colons* (settler colonialists) watching closely—became clearer. Peacock, however, did not help his case. His alleged boast that the US was emerging as a "third power" in the archipelago only furthered Condominium paranoia; any hope he may have had for French support vanished when it was revealed that he had told Senator Inouye that French behavior in the New Hebrides made "Watergate smell like Chanel No. 5!"[71] In the end he lost his suit, but by then Peacock had

---

69 See "Affaire Peacock," *Nakamal* 32 (October 25–31, 1973): 7; for the Kissinger claim, made by Peacock's attorney Anthony Curtis, see "Peacock case in London," *Nakamal* 49 (March 1–7, 1974), 1. Even with the passage of the regulation, land speculators continued to attempt to subdivide lands for sale surreptitiously. In some cases the plots were uninhabitable as buyers had subdivided land years earlier with little or no oversight, what one official termed "butcher" methods of subdivision. See Colin H. Allan, FCO Diplomatic Report No. 422/72, Anglo-French Condominium of the New Hebrides: Principal Developments Since August 1966, Item 270, MS 1189, CAP, PMB. Some parcels proved impossible to develop, being submerged at the high tide mark or little more than "vertical cliff faces that were unscaleable." See Mair, "Report on the possible Smuggling Operations and Arms Shipment through Fiji," General Information File, GHA, NAV. Such parcels were often purchased sight unseen, based on fraudulent descriptions by sales agents in Hawai'i. See British Resident Commissioner writing to The Resident Commissioner for the French Republic, January 9, 1973, Sylvia Hearn McMichael file, GHA/NAV.

70 For "Kissinger-rattling," see Paul J. Treadwell to Colin Allan, June 8, 1974 and Treadwell to Allan, February 11, 1976, both in Item 210 (Lockalee [*sic*] Ltd vs Allan, Townsend and Attorney General: correspondence and court documents re: Peacock, Michael (Minerva Reef) Oliver, Na Griamel, etc.), MS 1189, CAP, PMB. Treadwell was the British attorney general assigned to the New Hebrides as the suit progressed; Allan, along with Michael Townsend, was the named defendant in the suit, having been the British Residency Commissioner when the 1971 legislation was enacted.

71 For acknowledgment of concerns regarding foreign immigration and *colon* land expansion, see "Lokalee Proceedings Draft Defence Memorandum for Counsel," January 15, 1974; for Peacock's alleged claim of America as a "third power," see "History of Acquisition of Knowledge of Peacock's Activities up to 22.7.71"; for the Watergate quote see Treadwell to Allan, February 11, 1976, all in Item 210, MS 1189, CAP, PMB.

made other plans. Along with Oliver, he began to see in Jimmy Stevens and Nagriamel a potential means to circumvent the Condominium and recuperate what he believed was his.[72]

Black Power Pacific

Michael Oliver and Jimmy Stevens met for the first time in 1971. The meeting was not planned. They both happened to be in Suva, Fiji. Oliver was there making preparations for the Minerva Reef project. Stevens, who by this time bore the title President Chief of Nagriamel, was traveling to raise support for Nagriamel and to meet with the organization's Suva-based attorney, K.C. Ramrakha. He arrived in Suva with one of his wives, Susan Moses Rina, and a Nagriamel secretary. There, first at the offices of the Fiji Development Bank Center and subsequently at the Travelodge Hotel, Stevens met Oliver or, as the secretary referred to him, "Mr. White Oliver" (see fig. 4.3).[73] Oliver informed Stevens of friends who could assist in training in new electronic technologies and advised him to think seriously about free ports and developing land in the New Hebrides with the assistance of his "Caribbean Pacific Enterprises" company.[74] Stevens, meanwhile, began to see broader political possibilities for Nagriamel.[75]

It would be four years before the two men met again. In 1975 Oliver, accompanied by Peacock, traveled to Santo. They had plans in motion. Both were reeling from recent defeats. For Peacock the drawdown and withdrawal of American troops from Vietnam seemed to have brought his settlement plans for areas of Santo, already threatened by the acts against subdivision, to an end. Oliver, meanwhile, was recuperating from the disastrous experiment at Abaco, which had not only ended in failure but had seen him draw unwanted scrutiny from both the FBI and the public media. Stevens too was reeling.

---

72 One informant to Gordon Haines observed that Peacock funded "Mr. Jimmy Moses." Mair, Pilot notes, 8, GHA, NAV. On Peacock and his investments see American Embassy London to Secretary of State, Washington, DC, February 8, 1974, Wikileaks ID: 1974LONDON01797_b; and American Embassy, Fiji Suva to Secretary of State, American Embassy London, American Embassy Paris, United Nations New York, January 2, 1976, Wikileaks ID: 1976SUVA00006_b.

73 "The President Chief James T.P.S. Moses. Appointment Movements in Fiji." Loose sheet in GHA, NAV; *Synthèse Mensuelle*, June 1971, box NH034, NAV.

74 Ibid.

75 *Synthèse Mensuelle*, June 1971, box NH034, NAV. On Ramrakha and his efforts to assist Stevens and Nagriamel, see Ramrakha to Secretary General, United Nations, October 15, 1969, Item S-0504-0100-0008-00001, New Hebrides, K.C. Ramrakha, A/AC.109/PET.1122 - COMM.#2010, United Nations Archives. https://search.archives.un.org/uploads/r/united-nations-archives/5/0/7/50747a1a641b16e56288c53afe6fcda06cff7b87ddc2f859f 0f181e51aa2b5d7/S-0504-0100-0008-00001.PDF.

Fig. 4.3: With "Mr. White Oliver." The Travelodge in Suva, Fiji (1960s). Postcard.
Author's personal copy.

Over the course of the early 1970s he had acquired significant stature on Santo and the northern islands. Even so, he and Nagriamel were confronting the challenge of another political force: the New Hebrides National Party (NHNP).

The NHNP formed in 1971. Eventually renamed the Vanua'aku Pati [The Land that Rises Up Party] in 1977, its leadership, composed largely of Anglophone pastors, teachers and intellectuals educated by the church, advocated for full independence from colonial rule. The leading figures in the NHNP—Walter Lini, Sethy Regenvanu, Barak Sope, Grace Mera Molisa, Donald Kalpokas, among others—drew inspiration from a range of sources. As young men and women in the early 1970s, travel outside of the New Hebrides opened their eyes to the myriad political possibilities denied them at home. Travel itself was political: in order to leave the islands ni-Vanuatu had to acquire permission from colonial officials and travel with an identity card because they were effectively stateless. Kalpokas's 1974 poem captures the alienation and violence of such a system in its very title, "Who Am I?"

> Under the wings of history's two great enemies
> I was betrayed into the den of the Protocols of 1914,
> My beautiful land was alienated through fraud.
> I am ignorant of the Western shrewd culture,
> My future is uncertain,

Pandemonium is the right word
For my so-called government,
I long for a day of improvement.
I travel abroad with an identity card
For I am stateless and have no right
Of appeal in my country's high court.
Who am I, lost in the ocean of confusion?
My 'tea tare' takes very little notice of my cry.
At least I am still able to swim
But I wouldn't like to be washed ashore
On the desert of a French Pacific Republic,
Who am I?
I am that third citizen of my country,
The only condominium in the world.[76]

When permitted to travel, the founders of the NHNP were off to university or to regional church gatherings in the wider realm of the southwest Pacific.[77] Regenvanu attended the Pacific Theological College in Suva, Fiji, where he encountered other young men and women from Samoa, Tonga, Fiji, and Kiribati all studying for diplomas and degrees.[78] Others, such as Grace Mera Molisa, attended the University of the South Pacific in Fiji where, in 1977, she became the first ni-Vanuatu woman to earn a university degree. Molisa would become a leading feminist, intellectual, poet and political figure in the NHNP and worked to organize and politicize women in the archipelago.[79] Other NHNP members visited institutions in Papua New Guinea, where they were inspired by the fact that, even if Australia still exercised administrative power, it appeared that Melanesians "had a grip on the affairs of

---

76 Donald Kalpokas, "Who Am I?" as reproduced in Greg Rawlings, "Statelessness, Human Rights, and Decolonisation: Citizenship in Vanuatu, 1906–1980," *Journal of Pacific History* 47, no. 1 (March 2012): 46. Originally published in *Pacific Islands Monthly* 45, no. 9 (September 1974): 61. Reproduced here by kind permission of Jennifer Kalpokas Doan. Statelessness was shared by other Oceanians. For example, Rapa Nui, under Chilean control, were stateless until 1966.

77 On the importance of "church regionalism" and travel in the formation of ni-Vanuatu political consciousness, see Helen Gardner, "Praying for Independence: The Presbyterian Church in the Decolonisation of Vanuatu," *Journal of Pacific History* 48, no. 2 (2013): 122–43.

78 Sethy John Regenvanu, *Laef blong mi: From Village to Nation* (Port Vila: University of the South Pacific, 2004), 78–79.

79 Grace Mera Molisa, "Woman," in Walter Lini et al., *Vanuatu: Twenti wan tingting long team blong independens* (Suva, Fiji: Institute of Pacific Studies, University of the South Pacific, 1980), 256–69; "The Pacific Leader They All Knew as 'Amazing Grace,'" *Sydney Morning Herald*, April 8, 2002.

their country."[80] In the meantime, Tonga, Samoa, and Fiji had all achieved independence. "We came back (from courses overseas)," Kalpokas noted, "asking ourselves, 'Why can't the New Hebrides get such a status, or some development, to bring us on to independence?'"[81]

To further make sense of and analyze their reality, they read widely, from Marxism to liberation theology to Black Power.[82] They heard renegade Catholic philosopher Ivan Illich, who spoke in Fiji in 1972, and Paolo Freire who spoke in Papua New Guinea in 1974; they read Freire's *Pedagogy of the Oppressed* (1970) and Frantz Fanon's *The Wretched of the Earth* (1961; English translation 1963).[83] They found inspiration in Julius Nyerere's work in Tanzania and his approach to self-reliance. Ministers in the NHNP had met their Tanzanian counterparts during a World Council of Churches meeting in Port Vila in 1973.[84] The following year a number of NHNP members attended the Sixth Pan-African Congress in Tanzania and returned convinced that the party should send someone to the United Nations to speak to the UN's Committee of 24, the committee responsible for decolonization. They chose Father Walter Lini who would eventually become independent Vanuatu's first prime minister. While in the US Lini met Pauulu Kamarakafego, a Bermudan intellectual, scientist, environmentalist, and Black Power activist who had been mentored by C.L.R. James and who had worked in a number of decolonized states in West Africa.[85] Lini invited Kamarakafego to the New Hebrides. Kamarakafego visited various islands and brought his formidable skills at "doing" independence to communities: for example, teaching ni-Vanuatu how to make fuel from coconuts to use for lighting and cooking; how to refine sugar and thereby avoid relying on foreign companies; how to improve agricultural efficiency without being dependent on machinery; and the like.[86] He also spoke about global black

80   Regenvanu, *Laef blong mi*, 57, 87; Vanuatu: Political Complexion, secret report November 25, 1980, FCO 107/198, NA-Kew.

81   Kalpokas, in Brian J. Bresnihan and Keith Woodward, eds., *Tufala Gavman: Reminiscences from the Anglo-French Condominium of the New Hebrides* (Suva, Fiji: Institute of Pacific Studies, University of the South Pacific, 2002), 343.

82   Regenvanu, *Laef blong mi*, 88; 92–93; Vanuatu: Political Complexion; Banivanua Mar, *Decolonisation and the Pacific*, 193–96.

83   Gardner, "Praying for Independence," 136–37.

84   See the summary in Vanuatu: Political Complexion.

85   Walter Lini, *Beyond Pandemonium: From the New Hebrides to Vanuatu* (Suva, Fiji: Asia Pacific Books, 1980), 25–26; Banivanua Mar, *Decolonisation and the Pacific*, 190; 197–99. In official correspondence and some works, Pauulu Kamarakafego is referred to as Pauulu Brown. I have opted for Kamarakafego here, following Quito Swan's practice in his *Pauulu's Diaspora: Black Internationalism and Environmental Justice* (Gainesville: University of Florida Press, 2020).

86   Banivanua Mar, *Decolonisation and the Pacific*, 199.

solidarity, the history of blackbirding (slave-raiding), and illegal land sales.[87] That same year James Garrett, who had helped organize the Black Student Union at San Francisco State University, travelled to the New Hebrides at the invitation of Barak Sope whom he had met in Tanzania.[88] Garrett traveled in the New Hebrides with Lini and spoke to audiences about violence against African Americans in the US and the need for people of color to study technological subjects and to emancipate themselves from the perceived intellectual control of whites.[89] A number of younger ni-Vanuatu would later travel to California where they were met by Kamarakafego and Garrett and spent six months at Oba T'Shaka's Malcolm X Unity House in San Francisco.[90] Simultaneously, Grace Molisa traveled to Mexico City for the first International Women's Year conference (1975) where attendees addressed a wide range of themes, from feminism and decolonization to racism and economic marginality, and where, as historian Jocelyn Olcott argues, "First World women finally did listen closely to Third World women."[91] These travels and interactions were part of a global black liberation struggle—one that included, together, a Black Atlantic and a Black Pacific, much of Africa as well as the Americas, Melanesia, and the Caribbean—and that for members of the NHNP combined Vanuatu nationalism and black internationalism in the context of decolonization.[92]

For the members of the Phoenix Foundation, the rise of the NHNP was yet one more indication of the creeping socialism and communism they sought to flee elsewhere. They thus sought to delegitimize the NHNP by painting it as a Marxist cabal intent on establishing a communist state, making repeated allusions to "a Tanzanian type Marxist government" and "a Tanzanian Marxist regime."[93] Members of Nagriamel similarly accused the

---

87 Swan, *Pauulu's Diaspora*, 228.

88 On Garrett, see Ibram Rogers, "Remembering the Black Campus Movement: An Oral History Interview with James P. Garrett," *Journal of Pan-African Studies* 2, no. 10 (June 2009): 30–41; Swan, *Pauulu's Diaspora*, 225–27.

89 "Parti National Néo-Hébridais, Visite de Monsieur le Professeur Jimmy Gar[r]ett," loose sheet, box NH034, NAV. Garrett visited on August 11, 1974. The report here is a French translation of a document written by Gordon Haines. Continued concerns of the possible presence or return of Kamarakafego and Garrett can be found in *Synthèse Mensuelle*, December 1975, box NH034, NAV.

90 Swan, *Pauulu's Diaspora*, 226–27.

91 Olcott, *International Women's Year: The Greatest Consciousness-Raising Event in History* (New York: Oxford University Press, 2017), 5.

92 Swan, *Pauulu's Diaspora*, 227; Robbie Shilliam, *The Black Pacific: Anti-Colonial Struggles and Oceanic Connections* (London: Bloomsbury, 2015); and Banivanua Mar, *Decolonization and the Pacific*.

93 Report by Don Danvers, an architect resident in Adelaide, March 21, 1979; Richard King to Andrew Peacock, Minister of Foreign Affairs, Australia, April 2, 1979, both in

NHNP membership of being agents of "International Communism."[94] Their accusations complemented those of colonial administrators who fretted over communism and Black Power. Administrators assuaged their concerns by deporting Kamarakafego, and their counterparts in Australia preemptively banned Black Power activists from entering the country.[95] The anticommunist clamor obscured more than it revealed. Undoubtedly, Nyerere's African socialism had a lasting influence on many in the NHNP and, like Nyerere, many in the party saw resonances between socialism and indigenous understandings of how they related to the land and to each other, including an understanding that all land in the archipelago belonged to ni-Vanuatu and that previous forms of alienation by colonists, even if documented by the joint court, amounted to theft. Nor is it a surprise that efforts to address land, and proposals for land reform, met fierce resistance and were subject to caricature by opponents, with accusations of "communism" launched with abandon. Yet the NHNP, while supportive of anti-colonial and anti-imperialist struggles and governments, did not seek approval of or affiliation with the Soviet Union nor did it ally itself in any meaningful way with Mao's China. And while some in the party took more radical lines, Lini held that "we are neither 'black power' nor communists."[96] Lini's point was not to deny the political contours which shaped the NHNP. He and other leaders in the party were clearly energized and influenced by their experiences in Tanzania, by the writings and ideas of Nyerere, by the initiatives of Kamarakafego, and by a broader solidarity with a global black freedom struggle. Their anticolonial politics embraced many of the aspects that historian Quito Swan has identified as central to Black Power, including black political and economic self-determination and the overthrow of white power, capitalism, and empire.[97] Lini's demurral (which on a very practical level was part of his effort to get Kamarakafego's visa renewed) sought to push back against the one-dimensional, reactionary readings of Black Power and communism that were commonplace and that sought to delegitimize the NHNP specifically

---

Vietnamese Refugee Settlement file, GHA, NAV. See also "A message to the People of the New Hebrides from Moli Stevens," typescript, undated, ca. 1979, Vietnamese Refugee Settlement file, GHA, NAV.

94 David Browning, British District Agent, Northern District, Santo to D.G. Cudmore, Intelligence Report ND & CD2 May/June 1979, GHA, NAV.

95 Swan, *Pauulu's Diaspora*, 1. For French officials' concerns, see *Synthèse Mensuelle*, January 1971, 5, box NH034, NAV.

96 Lini, petition to the British Commissioner to extend Pauula Brown's [Kamarakafego's] visa, French translation in *Synthèse Mensuelle*, June 1975, box NH034, NAV. Original English version is unavailable so this is my translation.

97 Swan, *Pauulu's Diaspora*, 15.

and anticolonial politics more broadly. His statement was equal parts declaration of intellectual independence and anticolonial jab: as he went on to
note, neither he nor his allies seized, divided up, and sold the land of others,
a practice he termed "white power."[98] Black Power, on the other hand, was
this: "Any White man or foreigner who wants to stay there must follow what
the true New Hebrideans say. Black Power."[99]

The NHNP's blend of anticolonialism, Black Power, and socialism was
hardly a radical anomaly in a decolonizing world. Even colonial officials,
concerned as they were with "communist influences," concluded that the
NHNP was no communist outfit, which makes sense given that those very
same officials had sought to groom members of the NHNP for the eventual
transfer of power and an independent Vanuatu.[100] When anticolonial leaders,
intellectuals, and masses living under the yoke of colonial rule spoke of independence or emancipation, they often did so with a vocabulary informed as
much by socialism as by nationalism.[101] And why not? It was, after all, under
the thumb of the capitalist empires—the imperialism of free trade—which
many had lived. Thus, in the New Hebrides, members of the NHNP aspired
to what came to be called Melanesian socialism: a belief that socialism tended
to fit well the parameters of ni-Vanuatu custom. Melanesian socialism was an
understandable effort by the colonized to figure out how to reconcile generations of colonialism with a pre-colonial history that existed largely orally. It was
an effort to situate the colonized within a history not determined solely by the
colonizer and, at the same time, to chart a path to the future in an uncertain

---

98   Lini, petition to the British Commissioner to extend Pauula Brown's [Kamarakafego's]
      visa, French translation in *Synthèse Mensuelle*, June 1975, box NH034, NAV. Original
      English version is unavailable so this is my translation. The statement by Lini is inter-
      esting in the way it dovetails with Robbie Shilliam's discussion of decolonial living
      "otherwise," for example when he notes that the president of a Māori Black Power gang
      observed that the word Pākeha no longer means "European" but rather "stands for a
      type of person who . . . when it rains, will rush for shelter themselves and not care about
      others getting wet." Shilliam, *The Black Pacific*, 8.
99   As translated and quoted in Swan, *Pauulu's Diaspora*, 224.
100 Vanuatu: Political Complexion; Gordon Haines to British Resident Commissioner, June 5,
      1979, "Na Griamel Federation: Summary of Various Meetings Held by Jimmy Stephens
      following His Overseas Tour February 26–May 4, 1979," Vietnamese Refugee Settlement
      file, GHA, NAV. On cultivating a cadre for independence that would be moderate and
      not radical see J.S. Champion to Anthony Crosland, "Confidential Dispatch of 4 January
      1977: Decolonisation in the New Hebrides," in Item 270, MS 1189, CAP, PMB.
101 See Prasenjit Duara, "The Decolonization of Asia and Africa in the Twentieth Century,"
      in Duara, ed., *Decolonization: Rewriting Histories* (New York: Routledge, 2004), 8–9; Aijaz
      Ahmad, *In Theory: Classes, Nations, Literatures* (London: Verso, 1992); and Vijay Prashad,
      The Darker Nations: A People's History of the Third World (New York: New Press, 2007).

present.[102] Contrary to the claims of the Phoenix Foundation, many of those yearning for freedom did not fear socialism. They embraced it.

Adventure capitalists

By 1975 political change seemed inevitable. While the French sought to sustain their political presence in the archipelago, the British were eager to depart.[103] In the meantime, continuous pressure by the NHNP, and a broader global context of ongoing decolonization, including in many neighboring islands and lands, had led the British and French to accede to increased home rule and, that year, they scheduled elections for the creation of a Representative Assembly as well as for municipal representation.[104] Nagriamel participated in those elections and, to the surprise and consternation of Stevens, won only one seat on Santo while five seats went to the NHNP.[105] Oliver and Peacock were dismayed. Victory for the NHNP spelled trouble for their land ventures on Santo. After the election results were announced, they both visited Santo in December 1975 and met with Stevens. No record has thus far been found of what was discussed but, shortly after their departure, Stevens organized a large rally in Santo and, invoking UN Resolution 1514 of 1960 (Declaration on the Granting of Independence to Colonial Countries and Peoples), unilaterally declared the independence of the northern islands of the archipelago: an independent Nagriamel federation (see fig. 4.4). This was a remarkable declaration but one that only succeeded in generating significant turmoil—there were many communities in the northern islands who did not support Nagriamel— and in getting Oliver and Peacock banned for life from the archipelago.[106] Peacock relocated to Costa Rica while Oliver, after a short stint in Honolulu, returned to Carson City.[107] Readers of the newsletter produced by investor and goldbug Harry Schultz, who had "urged the large number of readers

---

102 Margaret Jolly, "Specters of Inauthenticity," in David Hanlon and Geoffrey White, eds., *Voyaging through the Contemporary Pacific* (Lanham, MD: Rowman & Littlefield, 2000), 274–97; Fouad Makki, "Imperial Fantasies, Colonial Realities: Contesting Power and Culture in Italian Eritrea," *South Atlantic Quarterly* 107 (Fall 2008): 735–54; Ranajit Guha, *History at the Limit of World-History* (New York: Columbia University Press, 2003).
103 Sope, *Land and Politics in the New Hebrides*, 55.
104 Van Trease, *The Politics of Land in Vanuatu*, 224–25.
105 Marian Sawer, "Jimmy Moli Stephens and the Vietnamese Refugees (Returned from a Field Trip to the New Hebrides)," typescript, March 4, 1979, Vanuatu National Library.
106 Woodward, *A Political Memoir*, 56–58; *Synthèse Mensuelle*, January 1976, box NH034, NAV.
107 On Peacock in Costa Rica, see Paul Treadwell to Colin Allan, February 11, 1976, Item 210 (Lockalee [sic] Ltd vs Allan, Townsend and Attorney General: correspondence and court documents re: Peacock, Michael (Minerva Reef) Oliver, Na Griamel, etc.), MS 1189, CAP, PMB. Peacock remained in Costa Rica at least until 1979. See Secretary of State, Washington, DC, to American Embassy San Jose, June 18, 1979, Wikileaks ID: 1979STATE157104_e.

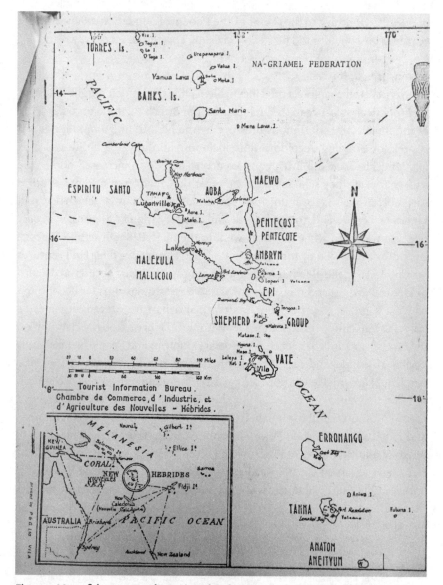

Fig. 4.4: Map of the proposed Nagriamel Federation, included with the declaration from Nagriamel and Jimmy Stevens on December 27, 1975. James Garae Bakeo, minister of foreign affairs for the Nagriamel Federation sent a copy of the map and declaration to British Prime Minister Harold Wilson in early 1976 requesting diplomatic recognition. Presumably he sent out other copies and requests as Nagriamel did receive, albeit briefly, recognition from the Sudan.

(Mahgoub Makkawi, Minister of Foreign Affairs of the Democratic Republic of the Sudan to H.E. James Garae, Minister of Foreign Affairs, Na-Griamel Federation, March 16, 1976, FCO 141/13253, NA-Kew.) Courtesy of the National Archives of the United Kingdom, ref. FCO 141/13253, "Proclamation of Independence of the Na-Griamel Federation."

of his financial newsletter to become honorary citizens of the Nagriamel Federation," had to bide their time.[108]

Over the next five years, the gravitational pull of the Phoenix Foundation drew Stevens ever closer. The stronger Lini and the NHNP grew, the more Stevens appeared willing to throw in his lot with a small but powerful band of mostly white libertarians. Why? After all, in many ways the NHNP and Nagriamel should have been natural allies as they shared much in common: land to ni-Vanuatu, the end of colonial rule, and self-determination. Up to this point they had hardly been rivals. When Barak Sope, one of the leading intellectuals in the NHNP, wrote his *Land and Politics in the New Hebrides* (1974), he thanked "the leadership and members of the Nagriamel movement" in his acknowledgments.[109]

A number of converging factors provide at least a partial explanation for Stevens's further alignment with the Phoenix Foundation. For one, the NHNP's base was in the Anglophone Protestant church, with its educated and literate leadership, which often found itself at odds with those in Nagriamel who tended to come from the bush and who embraced *kastom* (custom), what anthropologist Margaret Jolly defines as a "self-conscious perpetuation of ancestral ways and resistance to European values and practices."[110] Stevens equated custom with bush people but leaders in the NHNP, who themselves did not reject custom, understood that the equation was not so simple.[111] Custom could be mobilized for a range of purposes, including sustaining and justifying gendered inequities in communities. Stevens himself, for example, had some twenty-five wives. NHNP intellectual Grace Mera Molisa voiced her anger toward those whom she accused of:

> inadvertently
> misappropriating
> "Custom"
> misapplied
> bastardised

---

108 Van Fossen, *Tax Havens and Sovereignty*, 123.
109 Sope, *Land and Politics in the New Hebrides*, 3.
110 Margaret Jolly, *Women of the Place: Kastom, Colonialism and Gender in Vanuatu* (Chur, Switzerland: Harwood Publishers, 1994), 6 and 247–58. See also Godwin Ligo, "Kastom mo kalja/Culture et coutumes/Custom and culture," in Walter Lini et al., *Vanuatu: Twenti wan tingting long team blong independens* (Suva, Fiji: Institute of Pacific Studies, 1980), 54–65 and the essays in Siobhan McDonnell, Matthew G. Allen, and Colin Filer, eds., *Kastom, Property and Ideology: Land Transformations in Melanesia* (Canberra: ANU Press, 2017). For an overview of debates regarding custom in relation to contact, colonialism, and independence, see Jolly, "Specters of Inauthenticity."
111 Stevens, "Nagriamel," in Plant, ed., *New Hebrides*, 35.

murdered
a frankenstein corpse
conveniently
recalled
to intimidate
women
the timid
the ignorant
the weak.[112]

Others in the NHNP worried that foreign interests, such as the Phoenix Foundation, had mobilized around the idea of "custom" to further their own agendas and to cultivate a lasting political relationship with Stevens.[113]

French officials, still ambivalent regarding independence, also continued their efforts to cultivate a friendly relationship with Stevens in the hopes of protecting French property owners on Santo. The NHNP had political momentum and Nagriamel feared it would not be directing its own destiny once independence arrived, chafing against what it perceived as second-class treatment by the Anglophone dominated NHNP and its educated and politically cosmopolitan leaders. One Australian ally of Nagriamel observed that "Na-Griamel and all of the other moderate parties [who were not moderate in the adjectival sense] feel that they will be simply exchanging white colonial masters for black, who, because of tribal jealousies etc., and their interest in a foreign, non-Melanesian, ideology, are likely to prove far worse masters."[114] Such concerns marked struggles over decolonization in many places around the globe as the masses of working people, as well as ethnic and linguistic minorities, worried that a transfer of power from colonial to national rule would constitute little more than a shift from external to internal colonialism. Stevens feared as much and thus offered an alternative: drawing upon a certain cartographic logic, he emphasized that the New Hebrides was "an artificial creation, a colonial convenience," and thus aspired to create an "autonomous,

112 Grace Mera Molisa, "Custom," in *Black Stone: Poems* (Suva, Fiji: Mana Publications, 1983), 24.
113 On Lini's concerns regarding the manipulation of custom and foreign interests, see Selina Tusitala Marsh, "Black Stone Poetry: Vanuatu's Grace Mera Molisa," *Cordite Poetry Review*, February 1, 2014, accessed August 16, 2021, http://cordite.org.au/scholarly/black-stone-poetry-vanuatus-grace-mera-molisa/.
114 Report by Don Danvers, an architect resident in Adelaide, March 21, 1979, Vietnamese Refugee Settlement File, GHA, NAV.

self-governing region or province of NaGriamel as part of a New Hebrides Confederation ... based on Melanesian traditions."[115]

While some in the NHNP could countenance a form of political decentralization they could not accept outright autonomy or secession. And for good reason. Nagriamel had never been a hegemonic force on the northern islands, including Santo, as was evidenced in the party's poor showing in the 1975 elections. For all his stature, Stevens could be an ambiguous, at times polarizing, figure due to his relationships with French and foreign interests and lingering accusations of misusing Nagriamel funds.[116] Moreover, the NHNP enjoyed substantial support on Santo and elsewhere. For this reason alone, Stevens's dreams of an autonomous Nagriamel federation were unlikely to be realized, but even more so given that Santo in particular sat at the center of the archipelago's economic life with its copra plantations, beef industry and fish canning plant. In the 1970s Santo accounted for nearly 90 percent of all exports from the New Hebrides with frozen fish destined for the US, copra to France, manganese to Japan, and beef to New Caledonia.[117]

In order to pursue autonomy or secession, Stevens increasingly turned to his libertarian allies. These were the people who he imagined would help facilitate his political aspirations for the Nagriamel and bush communities on and around Santo. Increasingly, he incorporated their ideological language.

---

115 Gordon Haines to British Resident Commissioner, June 5, 1979, Vietnamese Refugee Settlement file, GHA, NAV. Stevens also recognized that prior to European contact self-governing peoples on neighboring islands interacted extensively with one another in a kind of confederal fashion. For an astute analysis of how nation-states can be both a colonial construct but also, in certain instances, an "imperfect but localized expression in nation-state form of much older exchange networks, voyaging communities, and contact zones," see David Hanlon, "A Different Historiography for 'A Handful of Chickpeas Flung over the Sea': Approaching the Federated States of Micronesia's Deeper Past," in Warwick Anderson, Miranda Johnson, and Barbara Brookes, *Pacific Futures: Past and Present* (Honolulu: University of Hawai'i Press, 2018), 81–104, quoted passage on 81. For a recent and excellent intervention on self-determination in the context of decolonization, see Adom Getachew, *Worldmaking after Empire: The Rise and Fall of Self-Determination* (Princeton: Princeton University Press, 2019).
116 By this time even Stevens's former ally, Chief Paul Buluk, had concerns with Stevens and some of the activities by some in Nagriamel. See his letter enclosed in Baker, British District Agent to Woodward, British Residency, January 8, 1975, FCO 141/13245, NA-Kew.
117 On decentralization, see Barak Sope, "Decentralization: A Future Priority," in Plant, ed., *New Hebrides*, 108–13 (excerpted from a paper Sope originally presented in 1972). On Stevens's ambiguous stature and questions of corruption, see among others *Synthèse Mensuelle*, February 1976, 4–5, box NH034, NAV; Gordon Haines, "Na-Griamel: Vietnamese Refugees Summary of Events," February 12, 1979, GHA, NAV; Jolly, *Women of the Place*, 51–52; Gary Sturgess, "Land Rights Issue behind the Bloodless Coup," *The Bulletin* 101, no. 5216 (June 17, 1980): 97–103. On Santo's economy, see *Short Survey, prepared in Aug 1975 by N.Z. External Intelligence Bureau, P.M.'s Dept. Wellington. New Hebrides*, sec. 5, p. 10, loose document, GHA, NAV.

Warnings of communist influences, of taxation, and of NHNP shenanigans appeared with regularity in Stevens' rhetoric, a sharp departure from what had been previously an agreeable, if tense, relationship between Nagriamel and the NHNP. Once nonexistent, by 1975 the slogan "Individual Rights for All" now appeared on the Nagriamel flag (see fig. 4.5). And while Stevens expressed concern about ni-Vanuatu rights to land and customary ownership, he was the contact person for an array of American investors pursuing land purchases on the northern islands. A Hawai'i attorney looking to move along a land deal on Santo wrote a counterpart in New Hebrides:

> ABOVE ALL, BE SURE to meet Jimmy Stevens and be sure he says the right things. Such as, encouraging business investment, emphasizes safety of investment, how new ideas in agriculture are needed, land titles—above all—will be honored, etc. etc. etc. Government based on *Free Enterprise* system. G.W. [the potential investor] wants to hear this. He's a great Libertarian. Don't confuse G.W. with "new policy" after independence. Don't leave anything in doubt.[118]

French colons on Santo now saw in Stevens and Nagriamel their best chance for maintaining possession, if not outright ownership, of their properties and French officials increasingly accommodated the movement, to the degree that they began to impede progress toward independence.[119] Meanwhile, the Phoenix Foundation, initially based in Oliver's hometown of Carson City, relocated to Amsterdam where it shared a telephone and

118 Memo to Claude and Roberta: Notes on August (Gus) Waegemann Purchase of John My Property, undated, Waegemann file, GHA, NAV (all caps in the original). The memo does not include the author's name but I suspect it is from Tom Niemann, an attorney and land speculator based in Hawai'i, to Claude van Nerum and his partner Roberta, sometime in late April or early May 1978. See the summary in Gordon Haines, report to the Minister of Home Affairs, Republic of Vanuatu, on A.E. Waegemann U.S. Citizen, Plantation Owner, Aore/Santo, August 26, 1980, Waegemann file, GHA, NAV and Waegemann to The Phoenix Foundation, December 20, 1978, Waegemann file, GHA, NAV. The document suggests that this was a strategy to unload some problematic property. The memo's author wrote: "Be sure to keep G.W. turned on to My Plantation ONLY. No other is for sale. Unless I cable about RT8, under no circumstances show the property.... We are really not in very good shape, but at this point it doesn't really make any difference. If we can get the Island and/or $25,000 commission, we better take it and run—maybe just run." Van Nerum was a Port Vila dentist who had become quite wealthy through his participation, with New Caledonia businessman André Leconte, in the purchase of a manganese mine in the New Hebrides. See "Manganese Leaves Forari Again," *Pacific Islands Monthly* 41, no. 8 (August 1, 1970): 126.
119 For a useful overview see Anonymous, "Na Griamel and Santo Particularism," FCO 141/13252, doc. 80, NA-Kew.

Fig. 4.5: Jimmy Stevens (center rear in white T-shirt) and others in front of Nagriamel office. The Nagriamel flag in the background includes the phrase "Individual rights for all."

VAS048919, Ogden Williams Collection, Vietnam Center and Sam Johnson Vietnam Archive, Texas Tech University. Used by permission.

telex number with Nagriamel.[120] The foundation produced a joint newsletter advertising land for investment:

> We can now provide you with 200 year leases on 10 acre (4 hectore [*sic*]) land parcels, for which we ask only US dollars 9,000—(nine thousand US dollars). For this you will not only receive the land, but also one of our Na-Griamel gold coins and four silver coins, made of one troy ounce of pure silver.... You will have your own settlements, where you will be able to live in accordance with your traditions. We already know some of you, as you came here to help us, but to have some assurance that we issue passports and provide land only to worthy persons, we will check on all applications. And only those qualified will be accepted.... Land purchasers may pay in full or may pay down only 25 per cent of the required amount, with the remainder payable over a 5 year period at 10

---

120 Phoenix Foundation's address in 1976 was Oliver's address in Carson City, NV. See K.S. Gounder, Director of Special Branch in Fiji to Gordon Haines, April 27, 1976, Ratu Osea Gavidi file, GHA/NAV. On its move to Amsterdam, see "Nagriamel and the Phoenix Foundation," Inward Telegram, Washington to BRC, Vila, August 1, 1977, FCO 141/13258, NA-Kew.

percent interest. The payments will be on a monthly or quarterly basis, as you wish. After you pay of [*sic*] the dollars 9,000—, there will be no further payments on your land for the next 200 years.[121]

By the late 1970s various foreign investors—in some form linked with or through the Phoenix Foundation—were deeply enmeshed in Santo politics and Nagriamel's plans. The array of schemes and activities are simultaneously absurd and impressive. Oliver helped finance the purchase of a plane by a Fijian chief supportive of Phoenix which was then used to deliver crates of electronic radio equipment to Nagriamel to facilitate coordination with Stevens.[122] There were suggestions he was attempting to smuggle stowaways to Hog Harbor on Santo, where Peacock's Lokalee plantation sat undeveloped.[123] As the decade progressed he funneled tens, possibly hundreds, of thousands of dollars to Nagriamel, in part by making and selling gold and silver coins adorned with the image of Stevens (see fig. 4.6). He flew island chiefs to libertarian gatherings in his home state of Nevada and accompanied Stevens on trips to the United Nations and the US Department of State.[124] When Stevens traveled it was for the purposes of meeting Oliver or his coconspirators in order to get funds and to pursue secession.[125] Meanwhile his associates, philosophy professor John Hospers and lawyer F. Thomas Eck III (both affiliated with the University of Southern California), drafted robust pronouncements on legal and political issues.[126] Financial backers included the ever-present Harry Schultz, now joined by end-of-times evangelist and libertarian investment

---

121 This is text from the "Independence Development Establishment for Na-Griamel" as quoted in "Nagriamel and the Phoenix Foundation," Inward Telegram, Washington to BRC, Vila, August 1, 1977, FCO 141/13258, NA-Kew. Another Phoenix newsletter documented not only the efforts of and support given to Nagriamel but additional attempts to create a libertarian country, such as Lonorore in the New Hebrides and Aurora, on unnamed islands in the southwest Pacific, both under the auspices of a retired US Navy officer and Hawai'i judge Luman Norton Nevels. See the July 1978 newsletter as transcribed in Gordon Haines, "Na-Griamel: Vietnamese Refugees Summary of Events," February 12, 1979, Vietnamese Refugee Settlement File, GHA, NAV.

122 K.S. Gounder, Director of Special Branch in Fiji to Gordon Haines, April 27, 1976, Ratu Osea Gavidi file, GHA, NAV; *Synthèse Mensuelle*, May 1976, 4, box NH034, NAV.

123 *Synthèse Mensuelle*, May 1976, 4, box NH034, NAV.

124 "Phoenix Connection Investigated Overseas," *Voice of the New Hebrides* 17 (March 22, 1980): 4.

125 Telegram 269, Burgess to FCO, June 15, 1977, FCO 141/13258, NA-Kew; FCO to BRC, Vila, June 15, 1977, FCO 141/13258, NA-Kew; and Browning, District Agent, Santo, District Monthly Intelligence Report up to June 22, 1977, GHA, NAV; see also *Synthèse Mensuelle*, March 1976, box NH034, NAV.

126 On the gold coins, see Van Fossen, *Tax Havens and Sovereignty*, 122; Faber and Ross H. Munro, "Spears and a Nevada Businessman Help a South Pacific Island Proclaim Itself a New Country," *People* 14, no. 3 (July 21, 1980).

Fig. 4.6: Silver coins designed by Oliver and minted at the Letcher Mint in the US. The slogan "Individual rights for all" appears above an image of Jimmy Moli Stevens; on the inverse is an image of the plant associated with the Nagriamel movement.

Voice of the New Hebrides 14 (March 1, 1980) back page.

strategist James McKeever; Ralph Fair Jr., son of a Texas oilmen and at the time involved in subdividing his parents' five-thousand-acre ranch into a libertarian homeowner's association; and Grant and Christina LaPoint, prominent Alaska Libertarian Party members.[127] French, German, English, and Australian supporters of Phoenix gathered in a house outside Melbourne, Australia, in March 1979 to discuss strategies, and household staff later reported overhearing conversations about weapons and invasions.[128] Shortly after the meeting an Australian with "fascist leanings" arrived in Vanafo, Santo, as did Robert "Bear Claws" Stutsman, a monolith of manliness at 6'6"and three hundred pounds, with a robust mustache and a .44 magnum on each hip, who took it upon himself to be Stevens's bodyguard.[129] From Oliver's hometown of Carson City, Stutsman was to be the first of around fifty American cowboys projected to come to the island to train ni-Vanuatu in cattle raising.[130]

As well as funneling money and equipment, minting coins and printing propaganda, Oliver served as Nagriamel's official representative in a Vietnamese refugee resettlement scheme. This ill-fated plan, which also involved Ogden Williams, a former CIA operative who had worked as Edward Lansdale's aide and interpreter in Vietnam in the 1950s, intended to resettle Vietnamese refugees on the Nagriamel-controlled areas of Santo and on the island of Maewo. Stevens had granted Oliver exclusive authority to act as Nagriamel's representative in the scheme.[131] Vietnamese workers had

---

127 K.S. Gounder, Director of Special Branch in Fiji to Gordon Haines, April 27, 1976, Ratu Osea Gavidi file, GHA, NAV; Edward Crane, "Libertarian Party Correspondent," *Reason*, June 1973.

128 Parsons, "Ashes to Ashes," *New Internationalist* 101 (July 1981), https://newint.org/features/1981/07/01/phoenix.

129 On Stutsman's participation, see Faber and Munro, "Spears and a Nevada Businessman"; David Browning, British District Agent, Northern District, Santo, Intelligence Report ND & CD2 May/June 1979, GHA, NAV; Gordon Haines to British Resident Commissioner, June 5, 1979, "Summary of Various Meetings Held by Jimmy Stephens Following His Overseas Tour February 26–May 4, 1979," Vietnamese Refugee Settlement file, GHA, NAV. On Stutsman, see his obituary at Memorial Solutions, accessed December 30, 2019, http://www.memorialsolutions.com/memsol.cgi?user_id=1035328.

130 Gordon Haines to British Resident Commissioner, June 5, 1979, Vietnamese Refugee Settlement file, GHA, NAV.

131 Haines to British Resident Commissioner, July 19, 1979, Vietnamese Refugee Settlement files, GHA, NAV. On Williams's biography see the oral history interviews by Harry Maurer, box 1, folder 17, item 15250117001, Ogden Williams Collection, Vietnam Center and Sam Johnson Vietnam Archive, Texas Tech University [hereafter OWC/VCSJVA]; see also Declaration by Jimmy Moli Stevens, September 1, 1979, box 3, folder 7, item # 15250307007, OWC/VCSJVA; Mike Oliver circular, Na-Griamel Federation (June 16, 1979), enclosure in Telegram Washington to Priority FCO, June 22, 1979, "New Hebrides: Vietnamese Refugees," Vietnamese Refugee Settlement file, GHA, NAV. The effort was carried out with the support of Fatima International, a Catholic lay organization, and which negotiated with Stevens and Eck to bring refugees to the northern islands. See

been brought to the islands by French planters in the 1920s to counter labor shortages, eventually being forcefully repatriated in the early 1960s.[132] The impetus for the resettlement plan this time around was debatable. In part it may have been to deal with a humanitarian crisis of the US's own making and, at the same time, to populate islands with immigrants whose anticommunist sympathies could be assured. (Former CIA director William Colby, who corresponded with Oliver and Williams, simultaneously investigated similar possibilities in New Caledonia.)[133] But others were skeptical. Officials in Washington who met with Stevens and Oliver quickly realized neither had any authority to negotiate resettlement and suggested that Stevens was largely interested in the project in order to bolster his own political position.[134] Others were even more damning. Jackie Bong Wright, a member of the National Alliance of Vietnamese Associations in the US, which had been approached by Oliver for support, warned the State Department that "any refugees who make it to the New Hebrides will be exploited as slave labour by Oliver on his development projects."[135] Her concerns were not unfounded. Refugees, according to Jimmy Stevens, were to be "allocated" to Nagriamel communities where they would work in the gardens in exchange for room and board. They would receive no wages because Nagriamel had "rescued them from the sea and given them a home."[136]

The plan soon collapsed. On the island of Maewo, the local council denounced both the plan and Nagriamel. Meanwhile, with elections approaching that could determine the fate of the archipelago's political independence, Stevens's backers were hesitant to do anything that would undercut Nagriamel's political position. It ultimately did not matter. Events

---

    Gordon Haines, "Na-Griamel: Vietnamese Refugees Summary of Events," February 12, 1979, Vietnamese Refugee Settlement file, GHA, NAV.

132 Woodward, *A Political Memoir*, 9.

133 W.E. Colby to Ogden Williams, September 20, 1979, box 3, folder 7, item # 15250307008, OWC/VCSJVA.

134 Harlan Lee (Country Officer, Pacific Island Affairs) to Lacy Wright, U.S. State Dept., May 4, 1979, box 3, folder 7, item # 15250307002, OWC/VCSJVA. Mention of Oliver accompanying Stevens appears in British Embassy, US to D. Ridgeway, South Pacific Dept. Foreign & Commonwealth Office, London, April 27, 1979, Vietnamese Refugee Resettlement file, GHA, NAV.

135 Telegram Washington to Priority FCO, June 22, 1979, "New Hebrides: Vietnamese Refugees," Vietnamese Refugee Settlement file, GHA, NAV. Evidently there were myriad schemes to exploit refugees for labor. A *Canberra Times* article from December 1, 1979, ("Graziers Hope to Use Vietnamese in Gem Scheme"), suggested that "a group of wealthy graziers with plans to market Australian gemstones world-wide hopes to establish a Pacific-island base using Vietnamese refugees as labor." Clipping in ibid.

136 Gordon Haines to British Resident Commissioner, June 5, 1979, Vietnamese Refugee Settlement file, GHA, NAV.

were overtaking Nagriamel and the Phoenix Foundation. In the November 1979 elections the NHNP—by now having changed its name to the Vanua'aku Pati (VP)—won a majority of the popular vote and two-thirds of the parliamentary seats. Condominium officials, in negotiations with the VP, acceded to a date for full independence: July 30, 1980.[137] The opportunity for secession was fading fast.

The cult of Phoenix

On May 28, 1980, only weeks prior to the scheduled date for full New Hebridean independence, eight hundred or so inhabitants of Santo, a mix of ni-Vanuatu and French *colons*, launched an insurrection. Armed mostly with clubs, spears, and bows and arrows, as well as .22-gauge rifles, they detained the local police force and captured the island's infrastructure: its airport, harbor, and radio station.[138] Over the next three months the British and French administrations, along with the VP, would attempt to resolve the crisis that was the Santo Rebellion. In the end, the archipelago achieved independence and became the new state of Vanuatu, under the leadership of democratically elected Walter Lini of the VP, only with the assistance of Papua New Guinea troops.

The rebels, led by Jimmy Stevens, fought under the name of the Vemarana Federation. Vemarana, the creation of Oliver and Stevens, reflected their respective interests, as if Nagriamel, with its aspirations for territorial secession, and Phoenix, with its newly drawn up investment and development prospectus, had merged. In the aftermath of the November 1979 elections, neither Nagriamel nor the Phoenix Foundation recognized defeat. They instead pushed harder for secession. After the elections officials reported some six hundred supporters of the VP were forced off the island of Santo.[139] Subsequently Stevens took to airwaves to speak about Santo's independence and allegedly warned "that blood would run in 1980 and that the doors of every Vanuaaku [sic] Pati supporter would have his house door marked in red."[140]

137 Lini et al., *Vanuatu*, 179–83. For the denunciations by the Maewo council, see "New Hebrides: The Phoenix Foundation, May 8, 1979. External Intelligence Bureau, Prime Minister's Department, Wellington," Vietnamese Refugee Settlement file, GHA, NAV.
138 "New Hebrides Security Situation," Memorandum by the Secretary of State for Foreign and Commonwealth Affairs, no date, ca. June 1, 1980, Records of the Prime Minister's Office [hereafter PREM] 19/316, NA-Kew; Vila to Immediate MODUK Army, Telegram 348 (June 4, 1980), PREM 19/316, NA-Kew.
139 David Browning, British District Agent, Northern District, Santo to D.G. Cudmore, British Residency, Vila, Intelligence Report N.D. December 1979 Final (December 31, 1979), GHA, NAV.
140 Ibid. The broadcast was on January 31, 1980, but included in Browning's December 1979 report which must have been submitted sometime in February 1980.

Meanwhile, the exit advocates worked from afar. Local newspapers reported that the Phoenix Foundation was only waiting for the word from Stevens to move into Santo.[141] Oliver associate attorney F. Thomas Eck III, arrived in Santo on Easter Sunday to meet with French *colons* and Nagriamel in order to draft a "confederation constitution."[142] Once drawn up, that very same month, it garnered approval "by All Na Griamel 15 islands customship, Na Griamel upper house, [and] Na Griamel Federation Chief President Moli Stevens."[143] Oliver, banned from the islands, traveled to Panama to encourage wealthy backers to invest in the new Vemarana Development Corporation, offering them copies of an investment prospectus he had coauthored with Eck and Hospers and that outlined the corporation's structure, leadership, investment opportunities, and its Vemarana Constitution. According to the authors, "Vemarana will be a genuine tax haven, offering more and far better free enterprise opportunities than any other place known to us."[144] The corporation, based in Panama, sought to attract investors by offering the opportunity to purchase shares at US$2,000 each. Each share included a ninety-nine-year lease "on one acre of land in Vemarana." With outsized optimism, they wrote:

> Assuming an initial investment of ten million dollars, total number of shares issued would be 10,000 with stated value of $2,000 per share. The investors of the ten million dollars would receive 5,000 shares plus an additional benefit of a 99-year lease on one acre of land in Vemarana for each share purchased. Persons who previously furnished seed capital in funds and services to help Vemarana would receive 5,000 shares. (Some of these persons are directors and officers of the Corporation and shall receive no other compensation for past services rendered.)[145]

This was more or less a rehash of the Nagriamel and Phoenix investment prospectus that had been produced two years earlier with the additional assurances that basic financial and communication infrastructure needs would be

---

141 "Phoenix Foundation—Waiting on the Word of Jimmy," *Voice of the New Hebrides* 13 (February 23, 1980): front page.

142 Van Fossen, *Tax Havens and Sovereignty*, 125. Eck arrived on Easter Saturday in Port Vila with Jimmy Stevens. See also Malcolm Salmon, "New Hebrides: Whether Peacock or Phoenix, a Bird of Ill Omen," *Pacific Islands Monthly* 51, no. 6 (June 1980): 18. Upon his arrival copies of the Nagriamel Constitution and one thousand Nagriamel passports were seized. Eck was given entry. *Voice of the New Hebrides* 21 (April 19, 1980): 3.

143 *An Investment in the Vemarana Federation* (Santo, New Hebrides: Vemarana Federation, 1980), 7. Copy available in the University of Hawai'i Hamilton Library Pacific Islands collection.

144 *An Investment in the Vemarana Federation*, 1.

145 Ibid., 2.

met, including "an airport in Santo capable of accommodating small and medium sized passenger jets, up to Boeing 727s ... A communication system—tied in with Intelsat.... One excellent port ... [and] Branches of the Bank of Indo-China, Barclay's Bank and the Australian-New Zealand Bank."[146] In addition, Vemarana would be one of "four similar independent but cooperation nations, which are to join together to form a Confederation."[147] To what nations the authors referred remained unstated. In the immediate wake of the insurrection, copies of the document circulated among the European residents of Port Vila.

The Phoenix Foundation with its money, its arms, its electronics, and its grandiose visions played a central role in the insurrection. Clearly this need not be exaggerated. What unfolded in May, June, and July of 1980 emerged as much from the dynamic contradictions of colonial rule, the aspirations of Nagriamel, and the machinations of French *colons* as it did from a concerted conspiracy on the part of outside interests. Peacock, Oliver, and Phoenix linked themselves to an already existing social and political movement that had long been bubbling away on Santo and a number of neighboring islands. Stevens was blunt: the movement was not a product of foreign influences but of "the thinking of man-Vemarana."[148] In many ways he was right. He and his followers had sought consistently to assume control over land in the northern islands and to retain some form of autonomy over how it was worked, distributed, and owned. That such aims were to be accomplished through alliances with foreign investors was secondary. They accepted support from wherever found. As much as the Phoenix Foundation used Stevens for its own purposes, Stevens used Phoenix for his. He was hardly the political naif that some made him out to be. Thus, one should avoid the easy—and ironically imperialist—mistake of assigning too much agency to this band of financiers and strategists.

Yet the fact is the presence of Phoenix loomed large and the continual, nagging support they provided Stevens and Nagriamel kept the embers of an imagined secession burning.[149] VP leader Walter Lini himself understood

---

146 Ibid., 1.

147 Ibid.

148 As quoted in *Voice of the New Hebrides* 8 (January 19, 1980): 4 and 5. For a blunt admission of French *colon* participation, see Philippe Delacroix's letter published as "Vanuatu: Philippe Writes Paul an Open Letter," *Pacific Islands Monthly* 52, no. 6 (June 1981): 21–22, enclosure in Item 211, MS 1189, CAP, PMB.

149 A wide variety of media took an interest in the activities of the Phoenix Foundation. See "Mystery Body Set New Target," *Papua New Guinea Post-Courier*, June 11, 1980, 8; "Nederland is brein achter Hebriden actie," *Dutch Australian Weekly*, June 27, 1980, 3; "Appeal for Help: Rebels Hold Police in New Hebrides," *Canberra Times*, May 31, 1980;

this well enough and wrote a lengthy piece to the UN, released publicly on June 2, detailing the history and activities of Oliver, Peacock, and Phoenix.[150] Nagriamel leaders did little to assuage such suspicions: Stevens visited Oliver at his home in Nevada while other members of Nagriamel flew to Freeport, in the Bahamas, to attend a three-day Monetary Seminar sponsored by Phoenix board member and high-profile investment specialist Harry Schultz.[151] Nor did Oliver or his allies hide their roles. Oliver, in an interview with *People* magazine, happily conceded that he was involved and claimed he simply wanted to help "the most disciplined people I have ever seen, not like those hippies in Berkeley."[152] Nor did Robert Doorn, secretary of the Phoenix Foundation, deny involvement, although he did seek to clarify that they were "not involved with mercenaries." He continued: "We are peaceful and remain so. We cannot of course say that there will be no violence because of political upheaval but people should be happy with us because we calm things down."[153] Thus, despite some colonial officials' initial claims that they saw little evidence of foreign involvement in the political tensions and insurrection, Phoenix's participation had now become clear to all, to the degree that the British government requested its US counterparts investigate if the organization had violated US law.[154] Their concerns stemmed in part from worries that their French counterparts wished to find a way to remain in the New Hebrides. "It would not be difficult," wrote one British official based in Port Vila, "for Santo, with its 15,000 population, to survive, even to prosper as an economic semi-dependency of New Caledonia [still a French territory], with financial and political help from the Phoenix Foundation."[155] Increasingly it appeared that France had

"Island Turmoil: US Money-Men Finance Rebel," *Papua New Guinea Post-Courier*, June 3, 1980, 8; "Farce Heads for Tragedy," *Canberra Times*, June 3, 1980, 2.

150 Lini's piece was an excerpt from a longer document he wrote, released on June 2, 1980, and had been delivered to the United Nations requesting military support to protect the people of the New Hebrides from Nagriamel and its foreign allies. The excerpt was reproduced as "Chapter and Verse on Outside Meddling in the New Hebrides," *Pacific Islands Monthly* 51, no. 8 (August 1980): 25–30.

151 Van Fossen, *Tax Havens and Sovereignty*, 126; *Voice of the New Hebrides* 28 (June 7, 1980): 3.

152 As quoted in Faber and Munro, "Spears and a Nevada Businessman."

153 "Phoenix Connection Investigated Overseas," *Voice of the New Hebrides* 17 (March 22, 1980): 4.

154 J.M.O. Snodgrass to Mr. Stratton, "Secretary of State's Meeting with M. Francois Poncet, February 2: New Hebrides," Annex B: New Hebrides Recent History, FCO 107/205, NA-Kew; "New Hebrides Security Situation," Memorandum by the Secretary of State for Foreign and Commonwealth Affairs, no date, ca. June 1, 1980, PREM 19/316, NA-Kew; Vila to Immediate FCO, Telegram 332 (June 2, 1980), PREM 19/316, NA-Kew; House of Lords, debate June 3, 1980, 1273–76 (enclosure in Tony [no surname] to Colin [Allan], July 8, 1980), in Item 211, MS 1189, CAP, PBM.

155 "New Hebrides Security Situation," Memorandum by the Secretary of State for Foreign and Commonwealth Affairs, no date, ca. June 1, 1980, PREM 19/316, NA-Kew; Telegram

intentions of maintaining the northern islands, perhaps through secession of the kind that had recently unfolded in Mayotte, in the Comoros Islands where Jean-Jacques Robert, the senior French official in the New Hebrides in 1980, had served in a similar capacity.

In any case, for all of their fears of Black Power and communists, it was a cadre of wealthy white capitalists from the United States and Australia, engaged in violent and illegal activities, with whom British and French officials found themselves confronted. For all the demeaning rhetoric that compared Jimmy Stevens to a primitive chief and sought to explain him through multiple references to cargo cults, it was in fact the Phoenix Foundation, as one island publication astutely pointed out, which most resembled "a cult" with its quasi-religious veneration of the market, its sinister underground activities, and its anticommunism.[156]

Departures

The rebellion on Santo lasted some three months. After six weeks of uneasy negotiations, a joint Condominium force was scheduled to land in Espiritu Santo on July 24, 1980.[157] French and British troops arrived in Efate, but ambivalence by the French led to yet another act of colonial inertia, with troops biding their time in the capital of Vila awaiting the word—that never came— for them to head to Santo. Ominous graffiti grew on the walls of Port Vila, threatening members of the VP and Britains and signed by a group calling themselves Organisation de l'Armée Secrète, a reference to the right-wing French terrorist group that opposed Algerian independence (see fig. 4.7).[158] VP leaders moved secretly from house to house for their own safety as the stand-off with Stevens and Vemarana lingered, even though Lini and the VP had strong island and international backing. Meanwhile, Stevens continued to operate as if Nagriamel were overseeing an independent entity. In early August he granted an oil and mineral concession to an American construction business owner with investments in the archipelago.[159]

---

21 (June 12, 1980), PREM 19/316, NA-Kew; and Vila to Immediate FCO, Telegram 332 (June 2, 1980), PREM 19/316, NA-Kew. The quoted passage comes from this final document.

156 *Voice of the New Hebrides* 11 (February 9, 1980): front page.

157 Statement to be made on the New Hebrides by Mr. Peter Blaker MP, Minister of State for Foreign and Commonwealth Affairs, in the House of Commons on Thursday, July 24, 1980, PREM 19/317, NA-Kew.

158 Included in "Vanuatu: Philippe Writes Paul an Open Letter," *Pacific Islands Monthly* 52, no. 6 (June 1981): 21, enclosure in Item 211, MS 1189, CAP, PMB.

159 Schedule A: Oil and Mineral Concession, Memorandum of Agreement, August 10, 1980, August Waegeman file, GHA, NAV. According to the finalized agreement, "The property of which is the subject of this Oil and Mineral Concession or license and/or

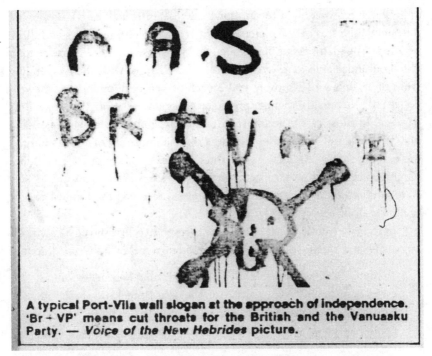

A typical Port-Vila wall slogan at the approach of independence. 'Br + VP' means cut throats for the British and the Vanuaaku Party. — *Voice of the New Hebrides* picture.

Fig. 4.7: Cutthroat politics: Graffiti from a Port Vila wall threatening execution of the British and members of the VP. OAS is reference to the French Organisation de l'Armée Secrète, a right-wing French terrorist group that opposed Algerian independence.

In "Vanuatu: Philippe Writes Paul an Open Letter," *Pacific Islands Monthly* 52, no. 6 (June 1981): 21, encl. in Item 211, MS 1189, Colin Allan Papers, Pacific Manuscripts Bureau.

In the end, the VP called in assistance from Papua New Guinea to put down the rebellion. The French and British departed the island in the same way they had governed it: haphazardly and with a debilitating uncertainty as to how to proceed vis-à-vis the other. The British had committed to the agreed-upon timetable for independence as well as territorial integrity of the archipelago, as did the UN.[160] The French hedged their bets in the final months, still wondering if the population of French landowners could stay on and make a go of it. But by August 1980, French and British officials and troops had begun to depart.

---

permit is specifically described as all Na-Griamel Custom Native Land owned or under the control of the signators to this agreement on the Island of Espiritu Santo, New Hebrides, which country is also variously known as VEMARANA and/or VANUATU."

160 On the UN, see "NEW HEBRIDES. Independence; security situation; disturbances on Santo and Tanna; Anglo/French consultations; part 1," UKMIS NY to Immediate FCO, July 17, 1980, PREM 19/316, NA-Kew.

Observers worried of retribution by the VP. British officials commented repeatedly on cases of VP police brutality against Santo residents and those believed to be members of Nagriamel.[161] Over subsequent weeks more than two thousand people were arrested. Most were charged with offenses ranging from theft, unlawful assembly, and breach of peace to joining an unlawful police force, acting in a manner prejudicial to good order, riot, and malicious damage. In most cases the courts found them guilty. They were assessed fines or jail sentences of a few months. A small number of those charged were sentenced to lengthy terms of three or more years in prison, including the three individuals most closely linked to Oliver: Stevens, Timothy Welles Nafokon, and James Garae Bakeo.[162] Stevens received the longest prison sentence—fourteen years.[163]

In the immediate aftermath of the arrests, two British officials visited Luganville and Vanafo, one of whom offered up a melancholy assessment:

> To get to Vanafo we drove some 15 miles north from Luganville without escort along the badly pitted surface of a dirt road cleared in the bush with French funding in the early 1970s. In so doing we passed through franco-phone plantations whose future title, rendered insecure by Government regulations on land tenure, lay at the very heart of the rebellion: ironically, fears of eventual dispossession have now been translated into immedi-acy.... Vanafo turned out to be a well-kept village, centrally placed on a vast tract of fertile arable land contributing substantially to Santo's 40% of the total Vanuatu copra yield. In the village centre the white

---

161 See, for example, Telegram 755, Vila to FCO, August 22, 1980, FCO 107/213, NA-Kew; Telegram 544, FCO to Vila, August 22, 1980, FCO 107/213, NA-Kew; Telegram 761, Vila to FCO, August 26, 1980, FCO 107/213, NA-Kew; British High Commission, Port Vila, Note no. 1, August 22, 1980, FCO 107/213, NA-Kew; and Y. Rodrigues, Note Verbale, 21 Août 1980, FCO 107/213, NA-Kew.

162 See District Court Register Judgment No. 678/79 to No. 812/80, Registrar Books, box SC851, NAV; Howard van Trease, ed., *Melanesian Politics: Stael Blong Vanuatu* (Suva, Fiji: University of the South Pacific, 1995), 52. In early 1976 Oliver approached the US Embassy in Suva (Fiji) to help procure visas for Garae Bakeo and Welles Nafokon. See American Embassy, Fiji Suva, to Secretary of State, American Embassy London, American Embassy Paris, United Nations New York, January 2, 1976, Wikileaks ID: 1976SUVA00006_b.

163 He attempted a prison break in 1982 with five other men but was quickly captured in the small craft they had stolen to make their getaway. For details, see Criminal Case 365.82 Vila (Public Prosecutor v. Jimmy Steven Moli), Criminal Case 366.82 Vila (Public Prosecutor v. Mr. Rolland Edmond) as well as Criminal Case 367.82 Vila (Public Prosecutor v. Mr. Bros Kaloris), Criminal Case 369.82 Vila (Public Prosecutor v. Tomaki David), Criminal Case 370.82 Vila (Public Prosecutor v. Noel Jean), and Criminal Case 371.82 Vila (Public Prosecutor v. Werry Reuben), all in box SC304, Senior Magistrate's Court, Criminal Cases, 1982, NAV.

flag which signalled the end of resistance and a peaceful takeover by the PNG forces still flew outside Jimmy Stevens' house. Nearby a mound of freshly turned earth marked the grave of his second son, killed by PNG forces two days before his father's surrender when he attempted to crash through a checkpoint outside the township. Stevens' 25 wives and 60 children huddled inside, still in a state of shock following the abrupt departure of their provider who is now, pending trial, held in Luganville prison. While detained there he need have no anxiety about the welfare of his extended family: custom will look after them from now on.[164]

In the years since the rebellion various authors have sought to make sense of Stevens's actions and, in particular, his alliance with Oliver, Peacock, and the Phoenix Foundation. Various arguments have been offered, more than a few tinged with a paternalistic prejudice and characterizing Stevens as venal, self-serving, and an opportunist.[165] Yet leaders of the VP, often at odds with Nagriamel, defended Stevens. Sethy John Regenvanu, who would become Vanuatu's first minister of lands, recalled that Stevens had "a genuine feeling for his people, that is why he had the following he did throughout the archipelago. He appealed to ordinary, simple people—the bush people of Vanuatu. He lived with them and shared their lives.... His represented an ideal model, which blended elements of the modern economy with a custom way of life, without destroying the latter."[166] Stevens had a political vision, one he believed could be brought to fruition based on his two decades of political organizing. Eager to see his aspirations for Nagriamel succeed, he allied himself with men

---

164 WS Ashford to CM Carruthers, South Pacific Dept., FCO, September 10, 1980, FCO 107/213, NA-Kew.
165 Even among the colonial bureaucracy there were agents who saw through such caricature. In 1967 a British agent on Santo had warned his superiors that the "comfortable assumption that Stevens's receipt of money can be engineered to produce his downfall is entirely erroneous." British agent in Santo, no date but late May 1967, FCO 141/13247, NA-Kew. More recently historian Howard van Trease, witness to the events in question and a longtime resident of Vanuatu, noted: "If by 'corrupt' it is meant that Jimmy Stephens made excessive personal gain out of his deals with foreign investors, there is significant lack of evidence. His life-style was by no means extravagant. Stephens lived in a thatched house, usually drove a pickup truck and dressed and ate simply. It would appear that the large grants received from abroad were spent primarily on running the organization and assisting Nagriamel members with the small development projects rather than the personal comfort of its leader." Van Trease, *The Politics of Land in Vanuatu*, 166.
166 Regenvanu, *Laef blong mi*, 99. In a reflective moment, Regenvanu offered a melancholic assessment: "I do not think we have succeeded as well as he did, although we have spoken louder than he did about it. We have had more resources at our disposal, greater political power or strength and more education." Ibid.

with money, slogans and promises. In examining Stevens's actions, perhaps the most one can say with certainty is that he, James Garae, and the supporters of Nagriamel were, as one author put it, "caught in a mesh of events" not entirely of their own making. Is that not the case for all of us? In any case, they were certainly not dupes. Was Stevens, in the end, naive? Perhaps. But certainly no more so than Michael Oliver, F. Thomas Eck III, John Hospers, Robert Doorn, and Harry Schultz.

The difference is this: Stevens spent much of the last years of his life in prison, branded a traitor, mourning the loss of a son. His friend and ally James Garae went to prison where he contracted tetanus and died. Santo had briefly become an experiment in speculation—another staging ground for adventure capitalism—and, as a result, large numbers of Santo inhabitants were forced from their homes, their futures uncertain and their communities fractured. In contrast, Oliver, Eck, Hospers, and their backers watched from a distant shore, crossed their fingers, and then, like the British and the French, went home.[167]

A Guatemalan belle epoque

There is no conclusion to this history. Michael Oliver abandoned his efforts to create a libertarian refuge. But then in 1995 he joined up with Romanian economist Stefan Mandel. Mandel had managed to game the lottery system in the 1990s by purchasing every possible combination of tickets for the Virginia lottery's $27 million jackpot. He had convinced investors to loan him money to purchase all the combinations, at the cost of some $7 million, in exchange for a share of the winnings. And he won, as he knew he would: "I knew that I would win one first prize, six second prizes, 132 third prizes and thousands of minor prizes."[168] He pulled in nearly $20 million but his investors saw little return on their investment after taxes, reimbursements, and Mandel's appropriation of nearly $2 million as a "consulting fee."[169] Meanwhile, the US lottery system, because of Mandel, no longer allows one to purchase lottery sheets and fill in one's own numbers on them. In addition, they have expanded the possible number of configurations to offset the possibility of

---

167 John Beasant, an advisor to Walter Lini in the early 1980s and author of a detailed work on the Santo Rebellion, summed up the reality: Jimmy Stevens "played the international man, and inevitably lost. The real criminals, however, go free." Beasant, *The Santo Rebellion*, 152.

168 See NPR's *Planet Money* episode entitled "The Odds of Winning the Lottery Are Not Good, but This Man Managed to Flip Them," transcript available at https://www.npr.org/2018/10/23/659988605/the-odds-of-winning-the-lottery-are-not-good-but-this-man-managed-to-flip-them.

169 Gillian Brockell, "He Won the Lottery 14 Times Using Math but His Biggest Jackpot Still Came Down to Luck," *Washington Post*, March 28, 2019.

another Mandel. On my most recent visit to Vanuatu, I looked for Mandel. He had last been reported living in Vanuatu, but I learned he had relocated to Hong Kong where he sells Vanuatu passports and citizenship to Chinese immigrants.

In the late 1990s Oliver and Mandel worked with the Israeli Mondragon group to try to create a free trade zone on Big Bay on Santo. In a subversive twist, the group took its name from the highly successful Mondragón cooperatives of the Basque region in Spain but with vastly different aims in mind: rather than creating workers' cooperatives that provide an array of economic and social services, the Israeli Mondragon group sought a ninety-nine-year lease to create an economic and cultural enclave free of taxes, customs duties and import/export regulations. The free trade zone (FTZ) would have had its own postal service, currency, and offshore financial center.[170] The effort initially moved forward, although Oliver left after a falling out with Mandel. Oliver's heart still was set on his moral experiment, creating a new country in conjunction with a few allies from his Santo days; Mandel seemed content with developing a FTZ with a complicated financing structure. In any case, it did not end well. In late 1999 and early 2000, Vanuatu's Council of Ministers and its Foreign Investment Review Board approved the project but it quickly foundered when the ombudsman, Hannington Alatoa, investigated in early 2001 and determined the deal was corrupt.[171] That same year a US court charged Vemarana board member and attorney F. Thomas Eck III with stock manipulation based on his participation in a series of "pump-and-dump schemes involving Internet stocks."[172] Found guilty, he was sentenced to seventy months in prison.

In 2006, US Ambassador to Papua New Guinea, Robert Fitts, received the following:

The Vanuatu Minister of Lands [Maxime Carlot Korman] recently signed an MOU with an obscure group of American investors to consider

170 Anthony van Fossen, "Citizenship for Sale: Passports of Convenience from Pacific Islands Tax Havens," *Commonwealth and Comparative Politics* 45, no. 2 (2007): 138–63. I use Mondragon (no accent on the final *o*) to refer to the Israeli group; references to the original Basque group carry the accented *o* (Mondragón).

171 Republic of Vanuatu, Office of the Ombudsman, Public Report on the Improper conduct by Government Officials in dealing with Mondragon's proposed free trade zone in Big Bay, Santo. The full details are available at http://www.paclii.org/cgi-bin/sinodisp/vu/other/ombudsman/2001/3.html?stem=&synonyms=&query=mondragon.

172 Henry K. Lee, "Couple Charged in Stock Scheme," *SFGate*, September 7, 2001; Henry K. Lee, "Daily Digest," *SFGate*, June 25, 2004, from which is taken the quoted passage. See also "Prosecutors, SEC Say 'Internet Incubator' Was Just an Old-Fashioned Stock Fraud," *Wall Street Journal*, September 6, 2001.

establishing a free port with an autonomous government. This closely parallels a 1980 attempt by the Phoenix Foundation which was only ended by bringing in PNG troops (ref A). The 1980 version would have had the powers to issue currency, passports, and was supposed to have featured untaxed and unregulated free flow of capital. (C) Ambassador learned Sept 6 from the Vanuatu Deputy Prime Minister that many of the same American figures are behind the current effort.[173]

At least one of those figures was Michael Oliver.[174] The MOU went nowhere.

Memories of Oliver linger. Claims circulated that he was in Santo in 2015, at the age of eighty-seven and met with fanfare. This turned out not to be true. But now, as in the 1970s, there are male chiefs and ni-Vanuatu with rights to custom land who want to see it developed, and they remember his name. Nagriamel endorsed a 2019 plan to create a free trade zone on Santo, and a Nagriamel chief, on a chance encounter on my last day in Vanuatu's National Archive, told me he wants Americans (but not Chinese) to develop land. The desires and needs are as real as the differences of opinion among custom landowners. Some counsel development while others counsel against it. Some want free trade zones and to lease land because of the promise of jobs and a potentially improved quality of life; others are concerned that FTZs constitute little more than a land grab and will bring minimal benefits to local communities. Such concerns are not new. The route to independence, as well as what it would look like, was understandably intensely debated and contested among ni-Vanuatu, and those debates were not necessarily resolved with independence.[175] Gender dynamics within ni-Vanuatu communities are often at play in such concerns. On the island of Efate, for example, land grabs have increased substantially over the past two decades, often with the complicity of male chiefs.[176] Grace Molisa, one of the leaders of the VP, excoriated both former colonizers and her fellow ni-Vanuatu who manipulated custom for patriarchal and conservative ends and reminded readers that there was a

173 American Embassy Port Moresby to Secretary of State, Washington, DC, American Embassy Canberra, United States Pacific Command, Honolulu, HI, [and] Department of Treasury, Washington, DC, September 6, 2006, Wikileaks ID: 06PORTMORESBY369_a.
174 That Michael Oliver was one of the figures is mentioned in Lora Lina, "Deported 'Phoenix' Founder Back in Vanuatu," *Vanuatu Daily Post*, December 22, 2005, reprinted in *Pacific Islands Report*, December 23, 2005.
175 For an excellent collection of essays on this theme, see Siobhan McDonnell, Matthew G. Allen, and Colin Filer, eds., *Kastom, Property and Ideology: Land Transformations in Melanesia* (Canberra: Australian National University, 2017).
176 Siobhan McDonnell, "Urban Land Grabbing by Political Elites: Exploring the Political Economy of Land and the Challenges of Regulation," in McDonnell, Allen and Filer, eds., *Kastom, Property, and Ideology*, 285–86.

continuing anticolonial struggle on the archipelago where women remained "colonized by the Free Men of Vanuatu."[177] It is worth recalling, for example, that Stevens had twenty-five wives.

Ni-Vanuatu men and women struggled for long decades for their independence, after generations of colonial rule and its self-serving vocabulary of civilization and improvement. They endured not only two dithering colonial powers; they also weathered the speculators and the opportunists who blustered about the evils of socialism and trumpeted the freedoms of capitalism. Strange freedoms, to be sure. Prior to the rebellion on Santo, a French official tried to explain why American speculators had descended on the New Hebrides in the 1970s. He concluded that they were looking to reproduce life as it was in "Guatemala in the good old days."[178] It is an unnerving indictment. As the official surely knew, the landowners' belle epoque that preceded Guatemala's democratic revolution in 1944 had been characterized by feudal lords and "their" indigenous serfs, wealthy landowners and indebted tenants, capricious rule and unquestioned submission. When presidents Juan José Arévalo and, subsequently, Jacobo Árbenz sought to finally rid the country of these last remnants of neocolonial feudalism, in part through an agrarian reform that would break up the plantations and create a class of smallholders in the countryside, Guatemala's aristocrats and United Fruit Company's shareholders reacted. They backed a CIA-sponsored military coup d'état that overthrew Árbenz and ushered in four decades of state-sponsored violence, beginning with widespread extrajudicial murders of leftist organizers and members of the Labor Party and eventually resulting in a genocide against the Maya Indians.[179]

The French official's observation was a self-serving, exculpatory barb designed to forgive his own country's colonial legacies, but it was also a sharp recognition of what lay just under the surface of the capitalist rhetoric and market idealism. Rather than a brave new world of widespread freedom, Vanuatu might have become little more than a patchwork landscape of private fiefdoms worked by a dispossessed class of ni-Vanuatu. Little more, that is, than a Melanesian banana republic.

---

177 Grace Mera Molisa, "Colonised People" in *Colonised People: Poems* (Port Vila: Black Stone, 1987).

178 Cited in Beasant, *The Santo Rebellion*, 151. For the original quote, see *Synthèse Mensuelle*, December 1975, box NH034, NAV. For similar comments, see *Synthèse Mensuelle*, March 1976, 6–7, box NH034, NAV, and *Synthèse Mensuelle*, February 1976, box NH034, NAV.

179 See Greg Grandin, *The Last Colonial Massacre: Latin America and the Cold War* (Chicago: University of Chicago Press, 2004).

PART II
Iterations of the Digirati
(1980s–present)

CHAPTER FIVE

Burning Man on the High Seas
Seasteading

BY 1990 MICHAEL OLIVER MUST HAVE APPEARED A WALKING ANACHRONISM. MUCH of what the opponents of the welfare state and the New Deal had hoped for had come to pass. Over the course of the 1980s, ideas and practices of market liberalization, privatization, and deregulation, along with expansion of the military and police, emerged as alleged common wisdom. With the triumph of the "root-and-branch radicalism of the pure free-market ideologists," as historian Eric Hobsbawm put it in his magisterial history of the modern world, even former communist states transitioned to a free-wheeling capitalism that would soon generate breathtaking levels of inequality, rather than to the forms of social democracy which had much broader appeal to their populaces.[1] Although in most instances foisted upon resistant populations, such ideas, couched as tough-love austerity, acquired status as a new orthodoxy, championed by a host of policy makers and economists in global institutions such as the World Bank, the World Trade Organization, and the International Monetary Fund. The debt crises of the 1980s curtailed the possibility of third world sovereignty and instead repurposed postcolonial nations into hunting grounds for continued extraction and unequal exchange in the form of, among other things, structural adjustment policies. "Here comes the con man, coming with his con plan," sang Bob Marley and the Wailers as the IMF descended on Jamaica in 1976.[2]

---

1   E.J. Hobsbawm, *The Age of Extremes: A History of the World, 1914–1991* (New York: Vintage, 1996), 420. Aspects of the neoliberal revolution were taken up as possible means to create a Left alternative to bureaucratic socialism, most notably by French philosopher Michel Foucault. See especially Mitchell Dean and Daniel Zamora, *The Last Man Takes LSD: Foucault and the End of Revolution* (London: Verso, 2021).

2   As quoted in Vijay Prashad, *The Darker Nations: A People's History of the Third World* (New York: New Press, 2007), 233. The song, "Crazy Baldheads," appears on Bob Marley and the Wailers, *Rastaman Vibration* (New York: Island Records, 1976). For a literary-historical evocation of Jamaica in the 1970s, see Marlon James, *A Brief History of Seven Killings* (New York: Riverhead Books, 2014).

In the US the administration of Ronald Reagan ushered in a conservative revolution that merged evangelical and social reaction with an economically liberal orthodoxy. What came to be called "neoliberalism" meant not, as already noted, a rollback of the state but instead a reallocation of its priorities. Thus, even as the administration embraced the rhetoric of the free market it simultaneously assured business owners that it was the most protectionist administration since the end of World War II.[3] Along with financial deregulation, regressive tax cuts, an assault on unions (including, most notably, the breaking of the air traffic controllers' strike), the weakening of federal government agencies, and the gradual stripping away of the social safety net, Reagan ramped up federal spending and the national deficit. He devoted huge sums to the military, accompanied by Rambo-inflected cheerleading as his administration waged numerous illegal wars in Central America that forced large numbers of Salvadorans, Guatemalans, Nicaraguans, and Hondurans to flee north for safety while simultaneously savaging the economy and social life of their countries. Federal spending skyrocketed in order to service the debt Reagan's own administration had incurred even as he touted his antigovernment credentials.[4] In the UK, Margaret Thatcher embraced similar policies with similar fervor but minus the evangelicals.[5]

The economic gloom, political uncertainties, and social anxieties that drove some libertarians' mobilizations in the 1970s seemed to be ending and with them went the various schemes to territorially exit the nation-state. The occasional island-invasion plot still appeared, such as the 1981 efforts of a Texan mercenary and a Canadian Nazi, with the support of Ku Klux Klan leader David Duke, to take over the newly independent nation of Dominica and establish a capitalist paradise. Launched from New Orleans, it ended in fiasco, ignominiously remembered as the "Bayou of Pigs."[6] But even then, there was

---

3   Kevin Doyle, "Interview with Noam Chomsky on Anarchism, Marxism and Hope for the Future," originally by Red and Black Revolution (online 1996) and reproduced in Peter Ludlow, ed., *Crypto Anarchy, Cyberstates, and Pirate Utopias* (Cambridge, MA: MIT Press, 2001), 435–49. On the administration's protectionism, see 448.

4   Kevin Kruse and Julian Zelizer, *Fault Lines: A History of the United States since 1974* (New York: Norton, 2019), 132 and passim.

5   Mark Fisher has summarized her decade in power as "the traumatic and violent defeat of the left." Fisher, "Hauntology, Nostalgia, and Lost Futures," in *K-Punk: The Collected and Unpublished Writings of Mark Fisher* (London: Repeater Books, 2018), 685. To note the absence of evangelical Christianity is not to suggest religion had no place in Thatcher's conservatism. Religious ideals were put to work in efforts to suppress abortion rights and to prosecute LGBTQ publications using blasphemy laws. See Philip Jenkins, *Decade of Nightmares: The End of the Sixties and the Making of Eighties America* (New York: Oxford University Press, 2006), 17.

6   Stewart Bell, *Bayou of Pigs: The True Story of an Audacious Plot to Turn a Tropical Island into a Criminal Paradise* (New York: HarperCollins, 2008). See also Kathleen Belew, *Bring*

no libertarian exit philosophy attached to the experiment, and generally ideas of territorial exit seemed to recede. For good reason: things were changing at home. Corporations began to incrementally encroach upon citizens' constitutional rights in various ways, to the degree that even a Reagan-appointed federal judge worried that "business has a good chance of opting out of the legal system altogether and misbehaving without reproach."[7] Evangelicals and the Moral Majority made inroads into the upper echelons of the administration, blending a decidedly narrow understanding of Christian teachings with an expansive embrace of the free market. Social conservatism and economic liberalism thrived together, in the process changing the very parameters of' what "libertarian" might mean. Such a hybrid had taken root most notably in Southern California, and especially Orange County, but it also found fertile soil in America's growing suburbs.[8] A result of what historian Kevin Kruse calls "white flight and suburban secession," suburbs such as those around Atlanta became the grounds upon which a politics of unprecedented "isolation, individualism, and privatization" came to be cultivated.[9] In such spaces, which by the 1990s accounted for more than half of the country, a form of American libertarianism—hyperpatriotic, socially conservative, racially exclusionary, rhetorically antigovernment and pro-free market—flourished, producing one of its most famous avatars in Newt Gingrich.[10] His 1994 Contract with America proved less an agreement with America than an arrangement to kill it, or at least that portion of it that did not provide the abundant subsidies his rich suburban district received.[11] His vitriolic assault on political convention helped usher in, by the early 2000s, a whole new generation of Rand-inspired libertarians (from Rand Paul and Paul Ryan to the Tea Partiers) who descended on government to strip away the remaining vestiges of anything resembling a commitment to the commonwealth even as they ensured their own government-funded well-being and embraced an increasingly exclusionary patriotism. The state itself had become fodder for further privatization, yet one more object to buy, sell, trade, and alienate. Cuts to the military were inversely

the War Home: The White Power Movement and Paramilitary America (Cambridge, MA: Harvard University Press, 2018), 85–88.

7   Nancy MacLean, Democracy in Chains: The Deep History of the Radical Right's Stealth Plan for America (New York: Penguin, 2018), 227.

8   On Southern California, see Mike Davis, City of Quartz: Excavating the Future in Los Angeles (New York: Vintage, 1992 [1990]), esp. chap. 3.

9   Kruse, White Flight: Atlanta and the Making of Modern Conservatism (Princeton, NJ: Princeton University Press, 2005). Quoted passage on 259.

10   Ibid., 259 for the statistic on suburbs; 260–61 for Gingrich.

11   Gingrich's "superrich district ... receives more federal subsidies than any other suburban region in the country." Chomsky as quoted in Doyle, "Interview with Noam Chomsky," in Ludlow, ed., Crypto Anarchy, 448.

proportional to the rise of a private security and intelligence industry that is visually apparent in the extraordinary growth of northern Virginia's DC suburbs, where government-linked private security and intelligence agencies have planted roots, and in the presence of private military contractors in Iraq and Afghanistan.

Over the course of the 1980s, across much of the globe, an unprecedented amount of public money made its ways into private coffers. In the US, tax rates for corporations and the wealthy dropped sharply, continuing a trend that began with the implementation of Reaganomics, a supply-side or trickle-down economic theory that served largely to enrich the already-rich. Armed with a team of lawyers and tax accountants they avoided paying even the pittance the gutted tax system said they owed, profiting from the fact that, in historian Vanessa Ogle's words, "some characteristics of taxation, rolled-back regulation, and carved-out economic enclaves" that began life offshore now moved onshore.[12] By the 1990s there was little need for the wealthy to abandon the ship of state, even more so given that the administration of Bill Clinton furthered the Reagan agenda with attacks on welfare, commitment to free trade, and continued deregulation.[13] Despite the commonplace rhetoric that blames the poor and welfare recipients for government deficits, it has been the wealthier (and whiter) classes and businesses who have received the lion's share of government handouts in the form of deductions, tax breaks, incentives, subsidies, and abatements, to this day doled out with little accountability in terms of the alleged trickle-down effects.[14]

The result was that the wealthy no longer needed to move abroad or territorially exit. They could stay home and secede socially, leaving most of their compatriots to bear an ever more increasing share of the tax burden and to struggle in an expanding universe of precarity.[15] They could, in other words, exit in place. Murray Rothbard, for one, would have been pleased. In 1975 he had offered a stinging critique of territorial exit projects, singling out Oliver's in particular:

---

12   Vanessa Ogle, "Archipelago Capitalism: Tax Havens, Offshore Money, and the State, 1950s–1970s," *American Historical Review* 122, no. 5 (December 2017): 1434. See also Ronen Palan, *The Offshore World: Sovereign Markets, Virtual Places, and Nomad Millionaires* (Ithaca, NY: Cornell University Press, 2003), chap. 5.

13   Kim Phillips-Fein, *Invisible Hands: The Businessmen's Crusade against the New Deal* (New York: W.W. Norton, 2010), 263–65; Kruse and Zelizer, *Fault Lines*, chap. 10.

14   See the discussion in Stephanie Coontz, *The Way We Never Were: American Families and the Nostalgia Trap*, 2nd edition (New York: Basic Books, 2016), xxvi–xxvii.

15   Van Fossen, *Tax Havens and Sovereignty in the Pacific Islands* (St. Lucia: University of Queensland Press, 2012), 130. Van Fossen cites Robert Reich with regard to the rich "seceding" from everyone else. Reich, *Work of Nations* (New York: Knopf, 1991).

For over a decade now I have heard the drums beat for the new Eden, an island, natural or man-made, that would live in either anarchistic or Randian bliss. One would think that if man can really learn from experience, then the total and abject failure of each and every one of these cockamamie stunts should have sent all of their supporters a "message"; namely, to come back to the real world and fight for liberty at home. Come to think of it, I don't see very many of the New Countryites shlepping out to Minerva, Abaco, Atlantis, an ocean platform, or a moon of Jupiter. Once again, I would love at least a year of these brethren removing themselves from the consciousness of the rest of us: either by remaining silent and returning to concerns nearer home, or, preferably, really hieing themselves posthaste to the New Atlantis and Randspeed to them.[16]

Through it all Oliver persisted. In the 1990s, as Rothbard embraced Pat Buchanan's ethno-nationalist paleo-conservatism and celebrated police violence against an array of alleged enemies, Oliver joined forces with Stefan Mandel in an ill-fated return to Santo before then collaborating with another exit aspirant to form the Atlantis Corporation and raise funds to build a new country off the coast of Panama.[17] In the meantime new libertarian exit strategies began to pop up, to the degree that, by the early 2000s, Oliver's 1970s efforts might have looked less like failures than trial runs. Of all the places where territorial exit projects seemed to resonate, it was not Washington, DC, or 'flyover' middle America, or Orange County, California. It was Silicon Valley.

Burning Man on the high seas

In 2008 Kiribati president Anote Tong spoke at a United Nations environmental forum in Aotearoa New Zealand. He left his audience with a sobering point: "To plan for the day when you no longer have a country is indeed painful but I think we have to do that."[18] It was a poignant and solemn declaration of what the future most likely held for the thousands of inhabitants of the Kiribati archipelago in the Pacific as they confronted rising sea waters and the era of the Anthropocene, the epoch of human-induced warming of the planet.

---

16 Murray Rothbard, "From the Old Curmudgeon: My New Year's Wish for the Movement," in Rothbard, *The Complete Libertarian Forum, 1969–1984* (Auburn, AL: Ludwig von Mises Institute, 2012), 1238. Originally published in *Libertarian Forum* 8, no. 12 (December 1975): 5.

17 See "Entrepreneurs Announce Project to Form New Country on Manmade Island," *Formulations: A Publication of the Free Nation Foundation* 1, no. 1, 1993: 5.

18 Tong, as quoted in "Doomed Kiribati Needs Escape Plan," *New Zealand Herald* (June 6, 2008).

That very same year, as Tong and his fellow I-Kiribati contemplated the disappearance of their Oceanian nation, entrepreneurs, engineers and investors—many linked to Silicon Valley's digital uberclass—gathered in San Francisco to hear about a new start-up that intended to make a country *appear* on the ocean.[19] This was not just any start-up, which by this time were a dime a dozen in Northern California. This one had been built on seed money provided by one of Silicon Valley's most well-known iconoclasts, entrepreneurs, and investors, Peter Thiel. It would be directed by Patri Friedman, grandson of famed free-market fundamentalist and University of Chicago economist Milton Friedman. The start-up, founded on Tax Day (April 15, 2008), called itself the Seasteading Institute (SI). Its logo: Burning Man on the high seas.

The basic premise of seasteading was simple: to build private, sovereign floating homesteads on the open ocean. Such platforms would be mobile, self-sufficient, and, most importantly for the seasteading visionaries, self-ruled. Seasteads offered various attractions, all built on the promise of allowing one to escape existing nation-states and the reigning structures of government. If established on the high seas, beyond the political and economic zones over which nation-states hold sway, one could avoid not only existing regimes and real estate demands but also be free to live as one wished (at least within the confines of living in the middle of the ocean). The laws and rules that constrained one "onshore"—whether pertaining to drug cultivation and use, gambling, prostitution, pornography, polygamy, weapons manufacturing, labor exploitation, among others—would theoretically not apply unless such activities fell under certain international prohibitions. Libertines or libertarians, many of those involved in seasteading are attracted by their deep commitment to individualist lifestyle choices that could be at odds with a state's laws or dominant forms of morality.[20] This is true not only for Patri Friedman but also

19 Chris Baker, "Live Free or Drown: Floating Utopias on the Cheap," *Wired*, January 19, 2009; Alexis Madrigal, "Peter Thiel Makes Down Payment on Libertarian Ocean Colonies," *Wired*, May 10, 2008; Philip E. Steinberg, Elizabeth Nyman, and Mauro J. Caraccioli, "Atlas Swam: Freedom, Capital, and Floating Sovereignties in the Seasteading Vision," *Antipode* 44, no. 4 (September 2012): 1532–50; Atossa Abrahamian, "Seasteading," *N+1*, June 5, 2013, https://nplusonemag.com/online-only/online-only/seasteading/. The most detailed study of the contemporary start-up societies movement, including seasteading and start-up cities, and based on interviews with many of its advocates, is Isabelle Simpson, "Cultural Political Economy of the Start-Up Societies Imaginary," PhD dissertation, Dept. of Geography, McGill University, 2021. On the digital overclass, see Anand Giridharadas, "Silicon Valley Roused by Secession Call," *New York Times*, October 28, 2013.
20 The vocabulary of some Burning Man acolytes seems to draw from the work of Hakim Bey, such as "immediatism" and "temporary autonomous zone," which itself straddles

for someone such as Bud Davis, the ill-fated first president of the Republic of Minerva, who observed in 1972 that on Minerva "people will be free to do as they damn well please. Nothing will be illegal so long it does not infringe on the rights of others. If a citizen wishes to open a tavern, set up gambling or make pornographic films, the government will not interfere."[21] This modest triad of concerns overlapped in significant ways with countercultural efforts to escape the moralizing constraints of Cold War American culture and the technocratic state that accompanied it. Simultaneous with Oliver's efforts in the 1960s and 1970s to escape state sovereignty and Davis's desires to shrug off bourgeois morality, tens of thousands of young people participated in the "largest wave of communalization" in the country's history, looking to escape the monochrome bureaucratic regimentation of one-dimensional man or the stranglehold of bourgeois mores and to find possibilities for individual freedom in world characterized by conformity, organizational hierarchy, and soul-deadening consumption.[22]

Seasteading is hardly a form of communalization, but, at some level at least, it shares similar concerns. There is a reason that Friedman, among other seasteading advocates, identifies Burning Man—the annual carnivalesque festival of art and self-expression in the Nevada desert—as an inspiration. It is the latest physical, if fleeting, manifestation of the Californian Ideology first articulated by Richard Barbrook and Andy Cameron in 1995, an ideology which is libertarian at its core and "promiscuously combines the free-wheeling spirit of the hippies and the entrepreneurial zeal of the yuppies." "This amalgamation of opposites," they continue, "has been achieved through a profound faith in the emancipatory potential of the new information technologies. In the

---

the libertarian right and anarchist left. The commitment to a radically unconstrained individual lifestyle explains why on occasion Bey (aka Peter Lamborn Wilson) shows up in more libertarian-oriented sites, including early on that of the seasteaders themselves. Bey's T.A.Z—or Temporary Autonomous Zone—is a celebration of fleeting, often underground, spaces of autonomy in which he sees more emancipatory possibilities than in a direct confrontation with the forces of the state. Bey's perspectives have been strongly critiqued as "lifestyle anarchism" by Murray Bookchin who sees in them little more than bourgeois individualism, disguised as radical politics, run amok. See Bey, *T.A.Z.: The Temporary Autonomous Zone, Ontological Anarchy, Poetic Terrorism* (Brooklyn: Autonomedia, 1991); Bey, *Immediatism* (Oakland: AK Press, 1994); and Murray Bookchin, *Social Anarchism or Lifestyle Anarchism: An Unbridgeable Chasm* (Oakland: AK Press, 1995).

21 Quoted in Mike Parsons, "Ashes to Ashes," *New Internationalist* 101 (July 1981), https://newint.org/features/1981/07/01/phoenix.

22 Fred Turner, *From Counterculture to Cyberculture: Stewart Brand, the Whole Earth Network, and the Rise of Digital Utopianism* (Chicago: University of Chicago Press, 2008), 32–33; Herbert Marcuse, *One-Dimensional Man: Studies in the Ideology of Advanced Industrial Society*, 2nd ed. (Boston: Beacon Press, 1991 [1964]); Paul Goodman, *Growing Up Absurd: Problems of Youth in the Organized Society* (New York: NYRB Classics, 2012 [1960]).

digital utopia, everybody will be both hip and rich."[23] Good thing, because seasteading, like Burning Man, is expensive.

Lifestyle emancipation is only one component of the seasteading project. There is a strong ideological orientation, one that understands freedom as a private commodity and promotes seasteading as a means to engage in libertarian experiments in governance and commitments to profit. The operating premise is that communities created out of flotillas of individual seasteads would bond based around shared ideals of how government should look and, in the process, offer a competitive alternative to that offered by traditional nation-states. Over the long term, in theory, seasteads would not only thrive but also offer various innovations in governance that would rebound back on to traditional nation-state structures, much in the way offshore financial centers and tax havens have come ashore.[24] Seasteaders, as other exit strategists, envision the emergence of a whole series of such platform configurations—a veritable seaburbia—producing their own legal and political systems and competing for citizens, much as companies compete for consumers, by reducing the "transaction costs" of opting out of the nation-state and into the libertarian marketplace of a seastead or other such platform state.[25]

---

23 Richard Barbrook and Andy Cameron, "The Californian Ideology," originally published in 1995 in *Mute 3* on the Hypermedia Research Centre website and reproduced in Peter Ludlow, ed., *Crypto Anarchy, Cyberstates, and Pirate Utopias* (Cambridge, MA: MIT Press, 2001), 363–64. See also Turner, *From Counterculture to Cyberculture*, and Richard Walker, *Pictures of a Gone City: Tech and the Dark Side of Prosperity in the San Francisco Bay Area* (Oakland: PM Press, 2018), chaps. 9 and 10.

24 For a succinct overview, see Surabhi Ranganathan, "Seasteads, Land Grabs, and International Law," *Leiden Journal of International Law* 32 (2019): 205–14; on tax havens coming ashore, see Palan, *The Offshore World*, chap. 5 and Ogle, "Archipelago Capitalism," 1434. Steinberg et al., "Atlas Swim," suggested in 2012 that seasteading may have had no real intentions of seeing projects come to fruition but rather sought to spur further the libertarian imagination. There is something to the point although the recent history and concrete efforts of SI suggest that some at least have taken the project literally.

25 Tom Bell, *Your Next Government? From Nation-States to Stateless Nations* (Cambridge: Cambridge University Press, 2017); Max Borders, "A Little Rebellion Now and Then Is a Good Thing," roundtable on Albert Hirschman's *Exit, Voice, and Loyalty* at fifty, *Cato Unbound: A Journal of Debate*, August 2020, https://www.cato-unbound.org/2020/08/21/max-borders/little-rebellion-now-then-good-thing. There is some irony in the libertarian exiters invoking Hirschman given that he made little effort to disguise his disdain for Milton Friedman's dismissive attitude toward voice and his embrace of exit. See Hirschman, *Exit, Voice, and Loyalty: Responses to Decline in Firms, Organizations, and States* (Cambridge, MA: Harvard University Press, 1970), 16–18. The broader idea of communities competing for members through the creation of governing services is developed in Robert Nozick, *Anarchy, State, and Utopia* (New York: Basic Books, 1974). The idea of governing services, at times transparently termed "protection racket," is turned into a long-term investment strategy by James Dale Davidson and William Rees-Mogg in *The Sovereign Individual: How to Survive and Thrive during the Collapse of the Welfare State* (New York: Simon & Schuster, 1997).

Seasteading is, in this iteration at least, firmly rooted in the beliefs of competitive market fundamentalism. Despite protestations in recent years by leaders in the seasteading movement who insist they have no opinions about how to design a new society, the basic starting point is private competition and the operating assumption is that on seasteads the forces of good (innovators, entrepreneurs, capitalists) will reveal to us how to live without the forces of bad (bureaucrats and politicians).

Seasteading is not as farfetched as it sounds nor is it a radically new proposal. The general term—minus the libertarian underpinnings—appeared in the 1969 intra-agency report *Our Nation and the Sea* and, in some ways, seasteading resembles a technological upgrade to the various Atlantis projects of the 1960s and 1970s. It also bears a close resemblance to the ideas of aerospace engineer Gerard O'Neill who, in the 1970s and 1980s, drew up elaborate plans and technical studies for the colonizing of earth's "orbital space with city-size habitats."[26] O'Neill envisioned such cities as "space islands" on which colonists would be able to "do their own thing" and self-select into habitats that shared their specific interests.[27] But the idea of seasteading has an even longer pedigree. Jules Verne, in a typically prescient piece of writing published in 1895, *The Self-Propelled Island*, imagined a large floating island populated only by bickering billionaires trolling around the Pacific. The story (Verne was *very* prescient) begins in San Francisco, from which four French musicians have recently departed for San Diego, where they are scheduled to perform. They soon find themselves lost en route. They begin to argue with one another. Night has fallen. Then, a moment of good fortune. A passerby discovers them and guides them to a mysterious city on the coast where they promptly indulge in a well-earned sleep. With the morning, they wake to learn that they are, in fact, aboard an artificial, mobile island. At nearly eleven square miles—roughly the size of contemporary Macau or, if you like, Cupertino—the island is a self-contained, self-governing city-state owned and operated by the Standard Island Company Incorporated. It had begun life as a planned "gigantic raft" with fashionable spas and upscale amenities to be anchored a few hundred miles offshore but soon developed instead into a mobile island that would offer the wealthy the "various advantages that the sedentary regions" of the globe did not. It has a small police force, a small army, and various regulations designed to keep the peace, including a prohibition on drinking establishments.

---

26   Daniel Deudney, *Dark Skies: Space Expansionism, Planetary Geopolitics and the Ends of Humanity* (New York: Oxford University Press, 2020), 199 and, more generally, 198–204; Peder Anker, "The Ecological Colonization of Space," *Environmental History* 10 (April 2005): 239–68, esp. 248–53.

27   Deudney, *Dark Skies*, 203.

It appears to have all one could need (except booze), including an environment free of class conflict as the poor, the laborers, the middling sorts and the struggling are nowhere to be found. Workmen are shipped in on an as-needed basis and then sent home, regulated by a class-based sundown law. They do not live on the mobile island. Residency is reserved for the very wealthy, "rich nabobs," who count their fortunes in the billions.[28] Inspired by the vision, one of the musicians offered a prediction: "by the end of the twentieth century every area of the sea would be traversed by floating cities."[29]

Not quite, but not for lack of effort. Over the past fifteen years or so the SI has continued with its efforts to create such floating facilities. The seasteaders unfortunately have found themselves bedeviled by the same issues that frustrated ocean colonizers such as Leicester Hemingway, Werner Stiefel, and Michael Oliver: most importantly questions of sovereignty and engineering. To escape state sovereignty, a seastead would have to be located on what is known as the high seas, defined in the United Nations Convention on the Law of the Sea as those areas of the ocean beyond any country's sovereignty, including its Exclusive Economic Zone, which can extend as much as two hundred miles out from the shoreline. Alternative efforts at oceanic exit will not work. Houseboats, and any floating apparatus less than twelve miles out to sea from the coastline, do not escape the reach of state political sovereignty. Nor are small, uninhabited islands far from large land masses necessarily free from state control. Mobile vehicles or cruise ships have their own constraints. L. Ron Hubbard, founder of the Church of Scientology and another Southern Californian libertarian, spent much of his existence on one of four ships at sea from 1967 to 1975, but that hardly meant he was free from the legalities and obligations to which the rest of us were bound. Taxes had to be paid, ports of call entered, a passport acquired, a formal state identity maintained. Then there is the cruise liner *The World*, the "largest private residential ship on the planet."[30] It is collectively owned by those who purchase one or more of its 165 private residences. Some of those shareholders live year-round on the yacht, but they are dependent on ports of call, flags of convenience, and state apparati for much of their livelihood. In any case, the yacht is not governed by an independent, free-market-driven coalition. Other efforts have proliferated. For example, Blueseed developed plans for floating laboratories, moored twelve miles off the coast of Half Moon Bay, where one could import foreign

---

28   Verne, *The Self-Propelled Island*, trans. Marie-Thérèse Noiset (Lincoln: University of Nebraska Press, 2015 [1895]), 29.
29   Ibid., 84.
30   The World, "Our Story," http://aboardtheworld.com/our_story.

engineers and bypass—or "hack"—US immigration laws and still link to the "Silicon Valley eco-system."[31]

But all of these have had to confront the reality of state sovereignty. The only conceivable possibility of exit on the ocean is to thus settle the "high seas." But even then it is unclear whether the high seas are free from state regulation or legal regimes. While the ocean may at times appear to be an unregulated or "lawless" space, it is not, as one scholar has noted, an "unregulated legal vacuum."[32] There is some apparent ambiguity in UNCLOS in that it asserts, on the one hand, that "no State may validly purport to subject any part of the high seas to its sovereignty" but also asserts that no "impediment to the peaceful establishment of artificial islands is placed on the high seas."[33] Yet, while the language would appear ambiguous enough to encourage continuing efforts at seasteading—what if a nonstate actor were to exercise sovereignty? can a floating platform be considered an artificial island?—that does not mean any notion of legality ceases to apply.[34] As legal scholar Surabhi Ranganathan has written in a compelling online series, "The 'freedom of the sea' is a legal institution, and private conduct is subject to national and international laws. These can be subverted, but they do not

---

31 See https://web.archive.org/web/20130423133315/http://blueseed.co/faq/. On "hacking" immigration law, see Timothy B. Lee, "Startup hopes to hack the immigration system with a floating incubator," http://arstechnica.com/tech-policy/news/2011/11/startup-hopes-to-hack-the-immigration-system-with-a-floating-incubator.ars

32 On lawlessness, see William Langewiesche, *The Outlaw Sea: A World of Freedom, Chaos and Crime* (New York: North Point Press, 2004) and Ian Urbina, *The Outlaw Ocean: Journeys Across the Last Untamed Frontier* (New York: Knopf, 2019). For "unregulated legal vacuum," see Douglas Guilfoyle, "The High Seas" in Donald Rothwell, Alex Oude Elferink, Karen Scott, and Tim Stephens, eds., *The Oxford Handbook of the Law of the Sea* (Oxford: Oxford University Press, 2015), 204. See also Liam Campling and Alejandro Colás, "Capitalism and the Sea: Sovereignty, Territory, and Appropriation in the Global Ocean," *Environment & Planning D: Society and Space* 36, no. 4 (2018): 776–94; Steinberg et al., "Atlas Swam."

33 See articles 87 and 89 of the United Nations Convention on the Law of the Sea, 1982, https://www.un.org/depts/los/convention_agreements/texts/unclos/unclos_e.pdf.

34 For arguments that take the UNCLOS ambiguity as an entry point for promoting the possibilities of seasteads, see Miguel Lamas Pardo, "Establishing Offshore Autonomous Communities: Current Choices and Their Proposed Evolution," unpublished PhD dissertation [trans. Adriana Sánchez Gómez], Escuela Politécnica Superior de Ferrol, 2011, 28; O. Shane Balloun, "The True Obstacle to the Autonomy of Seasteads: American Law Enforcement Jurisdiction over Homesteads on the High Seas," *University of San Francisco Maritime Law Journal* 24, no. 409 (2012): 410–64, esp. 452–53; and Ryan Schmidtke, "'Artificial Islands' of the Future: The Seasteading Movement and the International Legal Regimes Governing Seasteads in EEZs and on the High Seas," *Asian-Pacific Law & Policy Journal* 21, no. 1 (2019): 1–28. See also R.H. Fateh, "Is Seasteading the High Seas a Legal Possibility? Filling the Gaps in International Sovereignty Law and the Law of the Seas," *Vanderbilt Journal of Transnational Law* 46, no. 3 (2013): 899–931.

disappear merely because one moves a few miles off land."[35] Or, one might add, many miles off land. Some of the earliest proponents of seasteading clearly understood this. Wayne Gramlich, in a ruminative think piece coauthored with Patri Friedman, observed the following: "We really need to be more honest here. There is international law and it cut its teeth figuring out maritime law.... We can not wish away international law, just like we can not wish away countries claiming sovergnty [sic] over every chunk of territory on the planet."[36]

Along with sovereignty and maritime law, engineering proved to be a major hurdle. Given the water depth on the high seas, a fixed platform was untenable and thus various designs for ballasting had to be drawn up. Gramlich, whose engineering ideas in the 1990s spurred the interest of Friedman and Thiel, suggested the possibility of using hexagonal combinations of two-liter plastic bottles as floatation.[37] As interest progressed and capital was raised, architectural and engineering firms drafted various plans to deal with technical questions—rogue waves, fresh water, ballast, and so forth—but what may have sunk the dream of a high seas condominium was something more basic: labor costs. The distance from population centers meant labor costs would be substantial. As well as legal uncertainties and engineering conundrums, access to cheap labor and the need to link with metropolitan locations effectively has stalled the plan, for now, of seasteads on the high seas.

The tragedy of the commoners

It should come as no surprise that Silicon Valley, with its heady mix of technological innovation, military-intellectual complex, and countercultural and capitalist excess would generate a techno-utopian, libertarian vision of exit such as seasteading.[38] Exit societies have become a central part of techno-libertarian discourse, and engineering possible forms of exit has become a mainstay among the valley's digerati.[39] Balaji S. Srivinasan, founder of the genomics company Counsyl and self-professed "Stanford lifer," in a 2013 speech to fellow

---

35   Ranganathan, "The Law of the Sea," accessed October 26, 2020, https://www.arcgis.com/apps/MapJournal/index.html?appid=b20774fc0e4845d59797933f57a55017. See also Ranganathan, "Seasteads, Land Grabs, and International Law."

36   Wayne Gramlich, Patri Friedman, and Andrew House, "Getting Serious about SeaSteading," 2002, accessed January 6, 2021, http://www.gramlich.net/projects/oceania/seastead2/index.html.

37   Gramlich, "Seasteading—Homesteading the High Seas," accessed June 3, 2018, http://www.gramlich.net/projects/oceania/seastead1.html#Introduction.

38   On the culture and economy of San Francisco and Silicon Valley, see Walker, Pictures of a Gone City, and Turner, From Counterculture to Cyberculture.

39   Digerati was a term coined by Louis Rossetto, founder of Wired magazine. See Jedediah Purdy, "The God of the Digerati," in Ludlow, ed., Crypto Anarchy, 354; and Doherty,

start-up aficionados suggested forms of state escape such as "spending unreg-ulated digital currency, sleeping in unregulated hotels and manufacturing unregulated guns."[40] By the time Srivinasan spoke four years later at the 2017 Startup Societies Summit, Bitcoin and Ethereum, Airbnb, and 3-D printing were commonplace, and an emerging generation of exiters were predicting social singularity, a postpolitical world, exit through encryption, and off-planet colonization. They, like Srivinasan, cast such escape as a form of opting in as much as one of opting out. To exit "means [to] build an opt-in society, ulti-mately outside the United States, run by technology."[41]

Central to such projects is Peter Thiel, but he is of course building on a much longer tradition, including Stewart Brand's *Whole Earth Catalog* and call for space colonization; Marshall Savage's popular scientific guide to "colo-nizing the galaxy in eight easy steps"; and Durk Pearson's and Sandy Shaw's life extension experiments, among a host of others.[42] All of these flirted with and idealized various escapist projects, but Thiel's outsized persona, wealth, and links to Silicon Valley have helped bring more recent exit gambles into the media sunlight. Thiel has an envious resume in the world of start-up and venture capital: he cofounded PayPal, Inc.; created Clarium Capital Management; and invested very early in Facebook. By 2011, at the age of forty-four, he garnered a place on Forbes's list of the four hundred richest Americans. Thiel is a self-professed libertarian. He cites Ayn Rand as a major inspiration, and he made his name with investments of a decidedly libertarian hue, such as PayPal, which at least initially was intended to create a web-based currency that would escape or undermine tax systems associated with government, and Facebook, which promised the possibility of "supra-national communities."[43] All the same, he endorsed Donald Trump for US president in 2016, and he

---

Radicals for Capitalism: A Freewheeling History of the Modern American Libertarian Movement (New York: Public Affairs, 2007), 615.

40 Giridharadas, "Silicon Valley Roused by Secession Call," *New York Times*, October 28, 2013.

41 Giridharadas, "Silicon Valley Roused by Secession Call." For an elaboration on Srivinasan's ideas, see his "Software is Reorganizing the World," *Wired*, November 22, 2013. For a brief overview in the context of Silicon Valley and tech politics more generally, see Walker, *Pictures of a Gone City*, chap. 9.

42 Turner, *From Counterculture to Cyberculture*; Marshall T. Savage, *The Millennial Project: Colonizing the Galaxy in Eight Easy Steps* (Boston: Little Brown and Company, 1992); On Pearson and Shaw, and Extropians more generally, see Doherty, *Radicals for Capitalism*, 615–17.

43 Steinberg et al., "Atlas Swam," 6; Jacob Weisberg, "Turn On, Start Up, Drop Out," *Slate*, October 16, 2010. The quoted text comes from Weisberg. See also George Packer, *The Unwinding: An Inner History of the New America* (New York: Farrar, Straus & Giroux, 2013).

profits from a close relationship with the US security and surveillance apparatus through his company Palantir.

There is some danger in focusing too much on Thiel, as if seasteading and techno-utopias were the result largely of his initiative. They are not. But pausing at least to take stock of his role is useful in painting a condensed ideological portrait of the worlds out of which such initiatives often arise. By his own admission, Thiel's politics were birthed in the midst of Stanford's 1980s culture wars when students and administrators struggled over the meaning of a Western canon regularly taught in the campus classrooms. A student at Stanford at the time, Thiel watched as the administration and its faculty reworked the institution's core curriculum, replacing "Western Culture" with, in his words, "Multiculture—a euphemism for speech censorship, witch hunts against nonconformists, debased curricula, and anti-Western zealotry," or what he would refer to in shorthand as "intellectual anarchy."[44] Such culture wars were hardly restricted to Stanford's campus, nor were they necessarily surprising, but for Thiel the efforts to expand the core curriculum beyond the confines of a narrow band of European and Judeo-Christian writers was an attack on the "foundation of the West itself—to open inquiry, free-market capitalism, and constitutional democracy; to Christianity and Judaism; to the complex of values and judgments that help shape who we are."[45] It is a seductive but flawed confabulation. The Western Civilization curriculum at Stanford, dismantled in the wake of protests in the 1960s and then reconstituted in 1980 as Western Culture, had fifteen required texts: Genesis from the Hebrew Bible, Plato's *Republic*, selections from Homer's *Iliad* or *Odyssey*, a Greek tragedy, the *New Testament*, Augustine's *Confessions*, Dante's *Inferno*, More's *Utopia*, Machiavelli's *The Prince*, Luther's *Christian Liberty*, Galileo's *The Starry Messenger* and *The Assayer*, Marx and Engels's *The Communist Manifesto*, Voltaire's *Candide*, Freud, and Darwin.[46] Certainly here one finds representative texts of Christianity. But constitutional democracy? Not likely. Free-market capitalism? Only in the cheekiest of readings of *The Inferno*.

Thiel's experiences at Stanford deeply colored his perspectives on politics and liberty, leading him to conclude that "freedom and democracy" are not compatible. It is not an uncommon refrain in the libertarian choir. George Mason University economist Tyler Cowen observed, in reference to Asia, that

44 David O. Sacks and Peter A. Thiel, "How the West Was Lost at Stanford," Independent Institute, September 1, 1995, accessed November 20, 2021, https://www.independent.org/news/article.asp?id=5205.
45 Ibid.
46 See Justin Lai, "The Death of Stanford's Humanities Core," *Stanford Review*, accessed April 27, 2021, https://stanfordreview.org/the-death-of-stanfords-humanities-core/.

"the freest countries have not generally been democratic."[47] Why not? Because, for the purposes of Cowen's argument, freedom was defined by the freedom to engage in market transactions with little or no regulation, which would rarely have garnered popular democratic support. "In no case," he admitted, "were reforms brought on by popular demand for market-oriented ideas *per se*."[48] In other words, for advocates of the market, democracy and governmental checks and balances would not do. Such a position dovetails well with that of exit libertarians. Democracy gives too much voice—a theoretically equal voice—to the masses while checks and balances produce little more than governmental inefficiency, squabbling politicians, and inhibitors to radical change. No wonder Thiel argued that libertarians need to "find an escape from politics *in all its forms*—from the totalitarian and fundamentalist catastrophes to the unthinking demos that guides so-called 'social democracy.'"[49] That such a position is itself political Thiel surely understands. The claim that politics is inversely proportional to freedom is an ideological luxury only the wealthy can afford.

The antipolitical turn—or, more accurately, the antidemocratic turn—is not unusual, particularly among the more Promethean oriented techno-libertarians who would appear to derive as much intellectual sustenance from Max Stirner and Friedrich Nietzsche as they do from Adam Smith and Friedrich Hayek. Philosopher Nick Land, who in recent years has become an intellectual presence in tech-libertarian circles, argued that politics was "the last great sentimental indulgence of mankind" and, invoking Thiel and Patri Friedman, approvingly noted that "libertarians have ceased to care whether anyone is 'pay[ing them] attention'—they have been looking for something else entirely: an exit."[50] Land was a leading figure in the Cybernetic Cultures Research Unit in the Philosophy Department at Warwick University in the 1990s, a unit he

---

47   Cowen, "Why Does Freedom Wax and Wane? Some Research Questions in Social Change and Big Government," Mercatus Center, George Mason University, 2000, https://www.mercatus.org/system/files/Why%20Does%20Freedom%20Wax%20 and%20Wane.pdf.

48   Ibid.

49   Peter Thiel, "The Education of a Libertarian," *Cato Unbound*, April 13, 2009. My emphasis.

50   Land, "The Dark Enlightenment," accessed May 11, 2017, http://www. thedarkenlightenment.com/the-dark-enlightenment-by-nick-land/; Andy Beckett, "Accelerationism: How a Fringe Philosophy Predicted the Future We Live in," *Guardian*, May 11, 2017. For a collection of Land's writings, see Land, *Fanged Noumena: Collected Writings 1987–2007*, eds. Robin Mackay and Ray Brassier (Falmouth, UK: Urbanomic, 2018 [2011]). For a popular account of the movement and its linkages to the extreme right and figures such as Steve Bannon, see Rosie Gray, "Behind the Internet's Anti-Democracy Movement," *The Atlantic*, February 10, 2017.

helped make famous with its philosophy of accelerationism. Critic Benjamin Noys describes it this way:

> Accelerationists argue that technology, particularly computer technology, and capitalism, particularly the most aggressive, global variety, should be massively sped up and intensified—either because this is the best way forward for humanity, or because there is no alternative. Accelerationists favour automation. They favour the further merging of the digital and the human. They often favour the deregulation of business, and drastically scaled-back government. They believe that people should stop deluding themselves that economic and technological progress can be controlled. They often believe that social and political upheaval has a value in itself.[51]

Accelerationism, not coincidentally, merged cybernetics and a certain idea of the posthuman with the neoliberal assault on the state of the 1980s and 1990s.[52] (Imagine Maggie Thatcher as an amphetamine-fueled cyborg: the ultimate iron maiden.)

Accelerationism has little patience for the messy, compromising tedium of politics as we know it. But despite the posture of being on the cutting edge, there is plenty of precedent for such a position of political impatience: fifty years ago, the military juntas that violently overthrew the democratically elected representatives of their societies in places such as Chile and Argentina made similar claims about the compromised and messy nature of politics. Coup leaders intervened directly in to social and political life, asserting that politics as usual—political parties, compromise and argument, tedious stalemates, uncertainty and relativism—was the problem and that a military intervention was needed to save society or, as they termed it, Judeo-Christian civilization. The result of such antipolitical absolutism was politics of a different kind: a populace subjected to widespread torture, disappearances, and murder; an embrace of tradition through the resurrection of the Church hierarchy; the reassertion of patriarchy; the affirmation of the power of management over labor; and a radical acceleration of capitalist relations. In Chile such a regime of terror laid the groundwork for Milton Friedman and his Chicago Boys, who implemented a program of radical privatization, termed "shock therapy," that both Friedman and Pinochet knew never would have been approved through democratic means, that "sentimental indulgence"

---

51   Beckett, "Accelerationism"; Noys, *Malign Velocities: Accelerationism and Capitalism* (London: Zero Books, 2014).

52   See Noys, *Malign Velocities*, 6–8, and Michael R. Laurence, "Speed the Collapse? Using Marx to Rethink the Politics of Accelerationism," *Theory and Event* 20, no. 2 (April 2017): 412.

derided by Land and dismissed by Friedman as so many "cumbrous political channels."[53]

Land acquired in the early 2000s a following among some in Silicon Valley. After an increasingly frenetic tenure at Warwick, he hit terminal velocity and dropped out, only to return in 2013 with writings such as "The Dark Enlightenment" for the US-based movement known as neo-reaction (or NRx), most closely associated with computer programmer Mencius Moldbug (aka Curtis Yarvin).[54] Moldbug argued that the state is not going anywhere anytime soon and thus the best solution would be what he called "neocameralism": that is, convert the state into "a business which owns a country" with share-holders and customers, the ownership of which is formally transferred into the hands of the actual rulers, meaning whoever "capitalists pay for political favors."[55] Moldbug's arguments echo those found in a number of other texts one could situate within the genre of libertarian exit. These would include James Dale Davidson and William Rees-Mogg's The Sovereign Individual (1997). Davidson, a private investor and cofounder of the National Taxpayer's Union, and Rees-Mogg, a journalist and a baron, argued for the commercialization of sovereignty and the transformation of the citizen into a "Sovereign Individual" who could "optimize [their] lifetime earnings" by becoming a customer of a "government or protection service."[56] To help would-be Sovereign Individuals along in their journey to consumer independence, Davidson and Rees-Mogg, much like Phoenix Foundation member Harry Schultz, offered up an array of resources—weekly investment briefings, private consultations, offshore money management services, membership in the Oxford Club, among others—for purchase. One could also include here the writings of German-American

53   Friedman as quoted in Albert O. Hirschman, Exit, Voice, and Loyalty: Responses to Decline in Firms, Organizations, and States (Cambridge, MA: Harvard University Press, 1970), 17. On shock therapy in Chile, see Naomi Klein, The Shock Doctrine: The Rise of Disaster Capitalism (New York: Henry Holt Books, 2008); Grandin, Empire's Workshop Latin America, the United States, and the Rise of the New Imperialism (New York: Henry Holt Books, 2007); Peter Winn, ed., Victims of the Chilean Miracle: Workers and Neoliberalism in the Pinochet Era, 1973–2002 (Durham, NC: Duke University Press, 2004). Accelerationism is not limited to the right. Efforts to speed up time—Mao's Great Leap Forward or Soviet obsessions with machine men and accelerated production—unfold in authoritarian spaces built on a sense of impatience, or a desire for a clean break with the past, or a belief that catastrophic change is necessary to provide the aperture needed for resolving the tedium of reformism. For an excellent critique of catastrophic politics on both the left and the right, see Sasha Lilley et al., Catastrophism: The Apocalyptic Politics of Collapse and Rebirth (Oakland: PM Press, 2012).
54   Land, "The Dark Enlightenment."
55   See the discussion in ibid.
56   Davidson and Rees-Mogg, The Sovereign Individual, chap. 10 and, for quoted passage, 373. The new 2020 edition of the book sports a Preface by Thiel.

philosopher and anarcho-capitalist Hans-Hermann Hoppe. With a similar disdain for democratic politics to that expressed by Land, Moldbug, Davidson and Rees-Mogg, Hoppe argued that while a "private law society"—an exit state—might be the ideal, in the current context it is hard to imagine and thus the choices seemed to be between "monarchy and democracy." Hoppe advocated for monarchy, a choice that would seem to further substantiate the argument by geographer David Harvey and philosopher Alan Badiou that neoliberalism (and, I would add, libertarianism) be understood not as something new or innovative but rather as a "Restoration" of elite power akin to that of the return of the French monarchy in 1815 and all the class privileges that entailed.[57] For Hoppe, the issue is not only that democratic politics are too messy, inconvenient and inefficient for their own good but also that (theoretically at least) the monarch as an absolute sovereign has a vested interest in taking care of land and peoples because they are her or his property. In contrast, in a democracy:

> instead of a king [or queen] and a nobility who regard the country as their private property, a temporary and interchangeable caretaker is put in monopolistic charge of the country. The caretaker does not own the country, but as long as he [or she] is in office he [or she] is permitted to use it to his [or her] and his [or her] protégés' advantage. He [or she] owns its current use—*usufruct*—but not its capital stock. This does not eliminate exploitation. To the contrary, it makes exploitation less calculating and carried out with little or no regard to the capital stock.[58]

It is hard not to hear the ghost of Garrett Hardin here, with the spectres of rational choice, free-market fundamentalism, and political reaction by his side. His flawed thesis, which he marshalled as a metaphor for Malthusian concerns regarding overpopulation, held that a commons would be over-exploited because no private property rights would constrain use. Hoppe has translated Hardin into a political philosophy in which political power best operates as a private good, as a property right, limited to the few and freed from the democratic commons. Call it "The Tragedy of the Commoners."

This cloistered planet

The possible spaces of exit, of an antipolitical polity, on the planet are limited. "We've run out of frontier," explained Patri Friedman in an interview explaining

---

57   I am indebted here to the discussion in Mark Fisher, *Capitalist Realism: Is There No Alternative?* (Alresford, Hampshire, UK: Zero Books, 2009), 28–29.

58   Hoppe as cited in Land, "The Dark Enlightenment."

the founding of the Seasteading Institute.[59] Thiel too made note of this clois-
tered planet when he decided to invest in the SI. He identified three spaces to
which libertarians could look in order to escape the state: cyberspace, outer
space and the ocean. Cyberspace was and remains, paradoxically, the most
immediate in that it seems to in some sense already be with us in the form of
digital monopolies and networks and yet, at the same time, the most fantastical
and weirdly absorbing of the three possibilities. One of the most optimistic
commentators regarding cyber-exit has been techno-libertarian Timothy May
who in 1988 dismissed the earlier efforts to exit as naive about the workings
of state power. Islands and oceans would never work, he insisted. Instead, he
suggested, the promise for the future lay in a "Libertaria in Cyberspace," for a
number of reasons: virtual space is relatively expansive and coterminous with
our physical space (i.e., you only need have a computer and net access where
ever you are); the only law in operation would be private law; and significant
numbers of virtual communities can simultaneously coexist.[60] Yet a decade
later Thiel still wrote about such possibilities in the conditional: "The hope
of the Internet," he wrote in 2009, "is that these new worlds will impact and
force change on the existing social and political order. The limitation of the
Internet is that these new worlds are virtual and that any escape may be more
imaginary than real. The open question, which will not be resolved for many
years, centers on which of these accounts of the Internet proves true."[61] In the
time since Thiel wrote these words, much has changed, but the question of
possibilities and pitfalls persists. Cyberspace may have already forced change
in existing social and political orders, but of course both capitalism and the
state have themselves adapted to such changes and reconfigured their own
operations. Much as extraterritorial spaces were never the antithesis to, or
anomalies in, the nation-state territorial system, neither are digital platforms
and computational and networked structures replacements of that system.[62]

---

59   As quoted in Baker, "Live Free or Drown."
60   Timothy C. May, "Libertaria in Cyberspace," 1988, https://web.archive.org/web/
      20150912070521/http://www.notbeinggoverned.com/libertaria-cyberspace/. For a
      detailed discussion of May and his writings, see Thomas Rid, *Rise of the Machines: A
      Cybernetic History* (New York: Norton, 2016), 258–93.
61   Peter Thiel, "The Education of a Libertarian." For an early statement on cyberspace as
      a possible place of exit, see David G. Post, "Anarchy, State, and the Internet: An Essay
      on Lawmaking in Cyber-Space," originally published in the *Journal of Online Law* (1995)
      and republished in Ludlow, ed., *Crypto Anarchy, Cyberstates, and Pirate Utopias* (Cambridge,
      MA: MIT Press, 2001), 197–211; and Davidson and Rees-Mogg, *The Sovereign Individual*.
      See also Jamie Bartlett, "Forget Far-Right Populism—Crypto-Anarchists are the New
      Masters," *Guardian*, June 4, 2017.
62   Design theorist Benjamin Bratton's *The Stack* offers an analysis of the relationship
      between "planetary-scale computation and geopolitical realities." Bratton, *The Stack:*

Nor is it yet clear to what degree they are real or imaginary exits. Even with accelerating innovations, Thiel's basic point remains: cyberspace as a place of exit may be a distant proposition.[63]

Outer space proves to be similarly uncertain as an option. A range of space programs have existed over the decades, most of them limited to earth orbital space rather than "habitat space expansionism."[64] Buttressed by space enthusiasts' mobilizations of frontier mythologies, such as Mars colonization advocate Robert Zubrin's claims that frontiers produce cultures of "innovation, anti-traditionalism, optimism, individualism and freedom," libertarian exiters are pushing beyond such bounds.[65] "We must redouble the efforts to commercialize space, but we also must be realistic about the time horizons involved," Thiel wrote.[66] Again, recent activities, in particular those of Elon Musk's SpaceX, Jeff Bezos's Blue Origin, and Richard Branson's Virgin Galactic suggest that horizon may be coming into view, and a number of very rich celebrities have duly handed over six-figure down payments for a private ride into the stratosphere. But, despite the hoopla, the recent space ventures of Branson and Bezos constitute little more than billionaire vanity projects. According to the UN's 1967 Outer Space Treaty, the moon is off-limits to both nation-states and private citizens as a space to be claimed, and it is hard to believe colonization of Mars, or an elite space station a la *Elysium*, will happen anytime soon.[67] If it does, of course, it will be an option for a very limited few, despite the billions in taxpayer monies the private space enthusiasts have received, and its long-term prognosis is, according to some, not particularly good. Even Thiel, a techno-optimist at heart, sees space colonization as a long

---

On Software and Sovereignty (Cambridge, MA: MIT Press, 2015). See also Matthew Hart, *Extraterritorial: A Political Geography of Contemporary Fiction* (New York: Columbia University Press, 2020).

63 For certain the language of "singularity," "AI," "cyborg," and "crypto" has now become commonplace as the potentialities of digital life—and a different social and political order—seem to accelerate. Bestselling writers, whether utopic or dystopic, have explored these potentialities, making them appear closer to science than science fiction. Don DeLillo's *Zero K* (New York: Scribner, 2016); Annalee Newitz's *Autonomous* (New York: Tor Books, 2017); Cory Doctorow's *Walkaway* (New York: Tor Books, 2017); and Richard Morgan's *Altered Carbon* (New York: Ballantine, 2002) have picked up where William Gibson's *Neuromancer* (New York: Ace, 1984), Neil Stephanson's *Snowcrash* (New York: Bantam, 1992) and Ridley Scott's *Blade Runner* (1982) left off. Transhumanism seems poised to offer an exit that will not require territorial displacement but at the same time will be a step removed from the immediacy of our world.

64 See the excellent discussion in Deudney, *Dark Skies*.

65 Zubrin as cited in ibid., 184.

66 Peter Thiel, "The Education of a Libertarian."

67 On the UN treaty, see Bratton, *The Stack*, 456n7. For *Elysium*, see Neill Blomkamp's 2013 film of the same name. On Branson, see David Runciman, "The Stuntman," *London Review of Books* 36, no. 6 (March 2014): 21–25.

shot.[68] It remains, for now, a kind of imminent domain.[69] Reduced to the real and the terrestrial, the Extropians thus have to find nonsovereign spaces available for colonization on a planet in which there seem to be few.[70] And thus the ocean.

Climate change colonialism

Unable to solve the sovereignty and engineering dilemmas of the high seas, The Seasteading Institute moved closer to shore. Its directors set their sights on French Polynesia.

French Polynesia, and Tahiti in particular, had long been grounds for metropolitan projections of power and desire. Acquired in the mid-1800s, the Society Islands (of which Tahiti is a part), the Tuamotus, the Marquesas, and the Austral islands gave France an imperial foothold in Oceania that soon expanded out to the New Hebrides and New Caledonia. The archipelagoes served as provision points and coaling stations for France's maritime needs, but they also offered economic opportunities in terms of various resources such as copra, pearls, phosphate, and nickel. Even so, the archipelagoes that came to be incorporated as French Polynesia paled in economic importance when compared with other French holdings around the globe. What the islands did offer, however, as anthropologist Miriam Kahn writes, "was an endless source of dreams and fantasies ... a tropical looking glass for philosophical musings about the nature of mankind and for fantasy escapes from the perceived drudgery of growing industrialization in Europe." And forefront in the metropolitan imagination was Tahiti, an island favored in the writings and paintings of some of the most prominent nineteenth-century Western travelers to Oceania, including Herman Melville, Robert Louis Stevenson, and Paul Gauguin.[71]

A century later, in the 1960s, French Polynesia would acquire renown for a less idyllic image: the nuclear mushroom cloud. In the aftermath of the loss

---

68   Deudney, *Dark Skies*, passim. Of seasteading, Thiel wrote, "The technology involved is more tentative than the Internet, but much more realistic than space travel. We may have reached the stage at which it is economically feasible, or where it soon will be feasible." Peter Thiel, "The Education of a Libertarian."

69   I am indebted to Rosalind Williams's *The Triumph of Human Empire: Verne, Morris and Stevenson at the End of the World* (Chicago: University of Chicago Press, 2013) for this turn of phrase.

70   "Extropians" draw their name from Extropianism, a "doctrine of self-transformation, of extremely advanced technology, and of dedicated, immovable optimism. Most of all, it's a philosophy of freedom from limitations of any kind." See Ed Regis, "Meet the Extropians," *Wired*, October 1, 1994; and Doherty, *Radicals for Capitalism*, 616.

71   Miriam Kahn, *Tahiti beyond the Postcard: Power, Place, and Everyday Life* (Seattle: University of Washington Press, 2011), 48. For the historical overview, see Robert Aldrich, *France and the South Pacific since 1940* (Honolulu: University of Hawaii Press, 1993).

to Algeria in its war for independence, French president Charles de Gaulle pushed to fulfill his dreams that France achieve superpower status in part through the development of a nuclear weapons program. French authorities designated French Polynesia as the site for testing, and detonations began in 1966. The tests had a multitude of effects on the islands, most obviously in terms of islander health but also in transforming the local economies through the formation of a cash economy, salaried jobs, large-scale metropolitan migration, land speculation, infrastructural development, and the eventual growth of a significant tourism industry (fig. 5.1).[72]

The gravitational pull of island myth and techno-modernity proved hard to resist for the seasteaders. In late 2016 the Seasteading Institute's self-professed "seavangelist" Joe Quirk and his colleague Randy Hencken, director of the nonprofit Blue Frontiers, accompanied by a documentary film-making crew and Chapman University law professor Tom W. Bell, traveled to Tahiti to meet with officials to discuss the possibility of creating a Seazone—a special economic zone for seasteading. The visit resulted in a Memorandum of Understanding that stipulated "that French Polynesia will work with [the Seasteading Institute] to create a legal structure for seazones with a 'special governing framework' by the end of 2017; and that we [the Seasteading Institute] need to conduct site-specific environmental studies, and economic impact studies to justify the creation of seazones."[73] The future for seasteading appeared bright and the SI's website projected a seastead appearing in a Tahitian lagoon by 2020.

The claims were substantial. "Our venture," the SI board wrote, "is poised to launch a seasteading industry that will provide environmental resiliency to the millions of people threatened by rising sea levels, provide economic opportunities to people in remote and economically deprived environments, and provide humanity with new opportunities for organizing societies and governments."[74] Seasteaders mobilized to their own ends the language of

72   Kahn, *Tahiti Beyond the Postcard*, chap. 2.
73   Seasteading Institute, accessed January 3, 2017, https://www.seasteading.org/2016/12/2017-year-seasteading-begins/. The full MOU can be found at Seasteading Institute, accessed February 13, 2021, http://2oxut21weba5oivlniw6igeb-wpengine.netdna-ssl.com/wp-content/uploads/2017/01/Memorandum-of-Understanding-MOU-French-Polynesia-The-Seasteading-Institute-Jan-13-2017.pdf. See also Tom W. Bell, *Your Next Government? From the Nation State to Stateless Nations* (Cambridge: Cambridge University Press, 2018), 229–30; and Ranganathan, "Seasteads, Land-Grabs, and International Law." On the broader political context in French Polynesia at the time the MOU was created, see Lorenz Gonschor, "Polynesia in Review: Issues and Events, 1 July 2016 to 30 June 2017," *Contemporary Pacific* 30, no. 1 (2018): 156–65.
74   Seasteading Institute, accessed January 3, 2017, https://www.seasteading.org/2016/12/2017-year-seasteading-begins/.

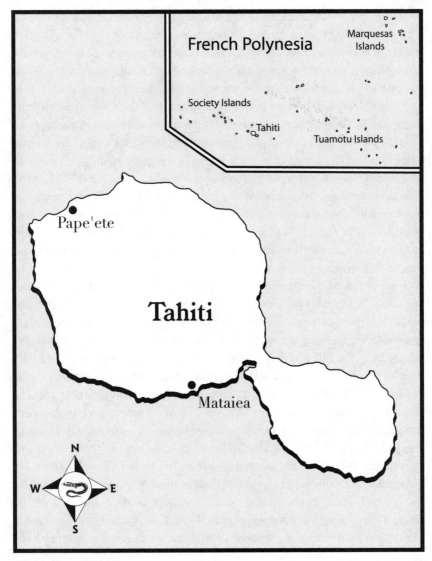

Fig. 5.1: Map of Tahiti.
Map by John Wyatt Greenlee.

resilience and climate change following the logic of neoliberal reason in which a crisis is not a threat to capitalism but one of its motors.[75] The seductive language masked a practical void. How seasteading, in its SI form, would function vis-à-vis existing states such as those in the Pacific was unclear. Take the case of environmental resiliency and seasteaders' claims that their platforms could work to prevent islanders having to flee their homelands due to rising waters. Imagine, for example, the tethering of a seastead to an undersea mount near an island that is being overcome by rising sea levels. Or imagine a multitude of anchored (fixed) platforms in a lagoon offshore. In cases in which islanders can no longer live on their homelands, then what? Would the relevant federal government or state (Tahiti? France?) lease the seastead? Pay rent? Invade? Take receipt of it as a generous gift from generous utopians? What would be the status of islanders displaced by rising waters? It is hard to imagine seasteads providing "environmental resiliency to the millions of people threatened by rising sea levels" for free or structuring themselves in such a way as to allow climate refugees to occupy seastead platforms with citizen status. Presumably the idea would be to build such structures and sell them to the Tahitian government, much in the way Japan's Shimizu Corporation is considering building a city that could house upwards of thirty thousand people atop a set of floating "lily pads" in the Pacific Ocean, an idea that drew the positive attentions of Anote Tong, then-president of Kiribati.[76] But designing and building ocean cities for purchase by existing states is a far cry from the private autonomous platforms planned for by the SI. In any case, that answers to the above questions are hard to come by—including regarding levels of community consultation—should give residents of Oceanian island communities and their representatives pause. So too should the fact that, for generations, Oceanians have modified their immediate environments of their own accord, for example through stonework and sandscaping, in order to account for environmental change and threat. That islanders have not been responsible for the dramatic scale of climate change does not mean they have

75 For a wonderful example of how such a logic can be turned on its head to point out such projects' offensiveness, see the LADBible's efforts to declare the creation of a new country out of one of the trash islands that has formed in the Pacific Ocean, accessed October 26, 2020, https://www.ladbible.com/trashisles/welcome; for a brief discussion, see Surabhi Ranganathan, "The Law of the Sea," ArcGIS Online, https://www.arcgis.com/apps/MapJournal/index.html?appid=b20774fc0e4845d59797933f57a55017.
76 Jenny Bryant-Tokalau, *Indigenous Pacific Approaches to Climate Change: Pacific Island Countries* (London: Palgrave-MacMillan, 2018), 36–38. On the absence of specifics, and the abundance of rhetoric, in seastead promotional materials, see Ranganathan, "Seasteads, Land Grabs, and International Law," esp. 206–8.

Fig. 5.2: Platform Future: A Seastead Design (Andras Gyorfi)
https://upload.wikimedia.org/wikipedia/commons/6/67/AndrasGyorfi.jpg June 13, 2009.
Creative commons.

no political agency or voice in confronting it or that their governments have
not instituted varied responses and management systems.[77]

Seasteading is yet another of the "solutions formulated elsewhere" that
advocates project onto the Pacific, that champion private-sector approaches,
and that reproduce both paternalist and colonialist forms of interaction.[78]
Clearly some involved in the project understood this. One of the participants
in the original MOU, Marc Collins, a businessman and former minister of tourism with the government of French Polynesia, sought to delink seasteading

---

77 Bryant-Tokalau, *Indigenous Pacific Approaches to Climate Change*, 39 and passim; TJ
    Demos, *Decolonizing Nature: Contemporary Art and the Politics of Ecology* (Berlin: Sternberg
    Press, 2016), esp. chap 2. Bryant-Tokalau notes that it is unclear what, if any, consul-
    tation took place between the SI and the wider Tahitian community. Bryant-Tokalau,
    Indigenous Pacific Approaches to Climate Change, 38. On sandscaping at a significant scale,
    see the case of the artificial island of Hulhumalé in the Maldives: Norman Miller, "A
    New Island of Hope Rising," September 10, 2020, https://www.bbc.com/travel/
    article/20200909-a-new-island-of-hope-rising-from-the-indian-ocean.
78 Margaret Jolly, "Conversations about Climate Change in Oceania," in Warwick Anderson,
    Miranda Johnson, and Barbara Brookes, eds., *Pacific Futures: Past and Present* (Honolulu:
    University of Hawai'i Press, 2018), 28. See also Alexander Mawyer, "Floating Islands,
    Frontiers, and Other Boundary Objects on the Edge of Oceania's Futurity," *Pacific Affairs*
    94, no. 1 (March 2021): 123–44.

from colonialism, despite the fact that seasteaders themselves used such a vocabulary. Collins suggested that seasteading was a part of a longer history of open-ocean navigation and Polynesian voyaging. "Polynesians are the original seasteaders," he wrote.[79] It was a savvy rhetorical move, linking the embodied indigenous knowledges and practices of voyaging and Pacific Island settlement—which I discussed in chapter two—with a form of high-end capitalist investment and property development. But it could also be a fraught position to assert given the importance of islander sovereignty movements, and the appearance of bending cultures and histories to the demands of a sales pitch. Calling Oceanians who settled Pacific islands "seasteaders" implicitly valorized the activities of the SI and appeared designed to mitigate the impression of seasteading as a kind of "ocean-rush," another wave of colonial expansion into the island Pacific. In any case, seasteading cannot help but evoke a settler-colonial history (even if the referent is now to the US rather than France) given its derivation from the term "homesteading," the process by which mostly white settlers in the eastern United States colonized lands to the west under the parameters of three governmental decrees: the Homestead Act of 1862, the Desert Land Act of 1877, and the Dawes Act of 1887. Privileging land grants for citizens and those petitioning for citizenship, the acts facilitated overwhelmingly white grantees' settlement of lands traditionally occupied and worked by Native peoples.[80]

History matters. Unfortunately, the most detailed work to date promoting seasteading—a book coauthored by seavangelists Joe Quirk and Patri Friedman—traffics largely in the kind of picture-book patriotism that embraces pioneer westering romances, celebrates Euro-American expansion on the frontier, and ignores the processes of conquest, expropriation, and colonization that underwrote such activities. "Every person in Western society is living in a blend of utopian experiments that largely succeeded," they write. "The sailors who took ships to the New World were utopians. They were also fed up. The new continent was a giant life raft where they could try out their utopian ideas."[81] This is a one-dimensional and self-interested use of the past. To call

---

79 Julia Carrie Wong, "Seasteading: Tech Leaders' Plans for Floating City Trouble French Polynesians," *Guardian*, January 2, 2017.

80 On land policies and homesteading I relied on Paul Frymer, *Building an American Empire: The Era of Territorial and Political Expansion* (Princeton, NJ: Princeton University Press, 2017), chap. 4; see also Alberto Milian, "Dreaming Under a Perfect Sun: Ethnic Mexicans, Leftists, and Boosters in Greater San Diego, 1900–1950," PhD dissertation, Dept. of History, Cornell University, 2018, esp. chap. 3.

81 Joe Quirk, with Patri Friedman, *Seasteading: How Floating Nations Will Restore the Environment, Enrich the Poor, Cure the Sick, and Liberate Humanity from Politicians* (New York: Free Press, 2017). I suspect Quirk and Friedman here were drawing in simplistic

it revisionist history would be kind. It is fantasy. And of course the absences in the narrative are glaring. No mention of the Africans forcibly taken and enslaved by sailors and settlers. One looks in vain for any discussion of the sheer violence that attended the march west: of Native American displacement and slaughter, of the lynching of Chileans and Mexicans and Chinese, or of the racist use of courts to dispossess Californios and Mexicanos of their livelihoods. Even less stark contestations, such as those between frontier settlers and eastern seaboard capitalists, are elided in order to make way for a saccharine and chipper tale of frontier fortitude and capitalist courage. The history of the blood and fire of primitive accumulation is replaced by the myth of the grit and pluck of entrepreneurial argonauts. The past is warped beyond recognition into a libertarian infomercial: "moral progress," the authors write, "emerges from millions of individuals competing for novel ways to profit by pleasing one another." That is not the process by which enslaved peoples emancipated themselves, by which working men and women acquired workplace rights, or by which subordinated and marginalized peoples achieved recognition. Those efforts at moral progress came about through mortal struggle, invariably pitting the vulnerable and the subjugated against the powerful collective of property owners, capitalists and exploiters who are the very heroes of liberal and libertarian theory.[82]

SI has also marketed seasteading as a venture in political ecology and not just political economy. In an anthropogenic era (often termed the Anthropocene or the Capitalocene) in which humans directly impact geologic time in accelerating and catastrophic ways, projects designed to weather an approaching planetary eco-crisis are proliferating. In an eloquent call to arms, Amitav Ghosh writes that "to imagine other forms of human existence is exactly the challenge that is posed by the climate crisis: for if there is any one thing that global warming has made perfectly clear it is that to think about the world only as it is amounts to a formula for collective suicide."[83] We may need to imagine and practice other forms of human existence, as Ghosh writes,

<hr/>

fashion from Hirschman's brief discussion of Louis Hartz's *The Liberal Tradition in America*. See Hirschman, *Exit, Voice, and Loyalty*, 106–8.

82 For a more detailed critique, see Raymond Craib, "Egotopia," *Counterpunch*, August 2018, from which this paragraph draws. The use of the myth of the western frontier, and the silencing of the violence attending westward expansion, in libertarian discourse is not exclusive to Quirk and Friedman. For a major corrective, see Greg Grandin, *The End of the Myth: From the Frontier to the Border Wall in the Mind of America* (New York: Metropolitan Books, 2019) and, for a literary rendering, Cormac McCarthy, *Blood Meridian, or the Evening Redness in the West* (New York: Vintage, 1992 [1985]).

83 Ghosh, *The Great Derangement: Climate Change and the Unthinkable* (Chicago: University of Chicago Press, 2016), 128.

but seasteading as it is promoted by the SI may not be the best place to look for inspiration. Anthropogenic climate change demands radically structural changes. Ghosh is again instructive here: "the scale of climate change is such that individual choices will make little difference unless certain collective decisions are taken and acted upon."[84] Equally passionate has been historian Dipesh Chakrabarty who sees in the crisis of global climate change a need for a new approach to history and contemporary theory.[85] Chakrabarty's suggestion in part is that the crisis impacts us all—regardless of class, for example. "There are no lifeboats here for the rich and the privileged," he claims.[86] Exit projects such as seasteading suggest otherwise, as do current private efforts to travel to, and investigate colonization of, outer space. Such undertakings are only the most prominent examples of a basic fact: there may indeed be an escape for those whom Mike Davis has aptly termed "earth's first class passengers."[87]

That escape will not be to Tahiti. The SI projected they would have the first floating platform arise from a nearby lagoon by 2020. That did not come to pass. Local representatives learned of the seasteader MOU and promptly took the wind out of its sails. Concerns about tech colonization generated substantial opposition and in early 2018 Tahiti's government allowed the MOU to die. That hundreds of residents of Mataiea still took to the streets to march against the project, a month *after* the public announcement that the MOU was null and void, demonstrates the depth of concern among island inhabitants on the front lines of such libertarian experiments.[88]

Distant archipelagos. Far-flung islands. Tonga and Minerva in 1972; Santo in 1980; Tahiti in 2017. The iterations accumulate.

---

84   Ibid., 133.
85   Chakrabarty, "The Climate of History: Four Theses," *Critical Inquiry* 35 (Winter 2009): 197–222.
86   Ibid., 221. Compare with Simon During, "Empire's Present," *New Literary History* 43, no. 2 (Spring 2012): 331–40.
87   Mike Davis, "Living on the Ice Shelf: Humanity's Meltdown," accessed September 4, 2013, http://www.tomdispatch.com/post/174949.
88   Julia Carrie Wong, "Seasteading: Tech Leaders' Plans for Floating City Trouble French Polynesians," *Guardian*, January 2, 2017; Mike Ives, "As Climate Change Accelerates, Floating Cities Look Like Less of a Pipe Dream," *New York Times*, January 27, 2017; "Hundreds March in Tahiti against Building of Floating Islands," accessed January 15, 2019, https://www.radionz.co.nz/international/pacific-news/354491/hundreds-march-in-tahiti-against-building-of-floating-islands; Melia Robinson, "An Island Nation That Told a Libertarian 'Seasteading' Group It Could Build a Floating City Has Pulled Out of the Deal," *Business Insider*, March 4, 2018.

CHAPTER SIX

Seeing Like a Country Club
Private Cities in Honduras

IN AN ERA OF SILICON VALLEY EXCESS, TECHNO-LIBERTARIAN OPTIMISM, AND MAIN-stream political malaise, exit strategies are proliferating. Seasteading is of course one. But there are others. At the 2017 Startup Societies Summit, held at the publicly funded City College of San Francisco, an array of libertarian exit strategies were on offer. Among other options one could engage in "crowd-choicing," captured best in the Free State Project which aimed to mobilize twenty thousand participants to relocate to New Hampshire by 2020 where they would, according to the FSP webpage, "create a society in which the maximum role of government is the protection of life, liberty, and property." Judging from the language on the FSP website, liberty is understood to be inversely proportional to the size of government, although it is unclear if this refers to municipal, state, or federal government or all three. As of December 2020 some five thousand people had made the move and another nineteen thousand had taken "the pledge" to do so. The FSP has its own annual Porcupine Festival (or PorcFest), a sort of backcountry Burning Man sponsored by the Koch Brothers, the free-market-oriented Foundation for Economic Education, and the libertarian Reason Foundation.[1] Others advocate nonterritorial strategies. Building on the libertarian positions of David Friedman, Hayek, and others, and steeped in the requisite vocabulary of "disruption," "innovation," "crypto-anarchy," and "decentralization," they are exploring exit strategies that embrace an encrypted existence that escapes the parameters of the state,

---

1   http://porcfest.com/about/; Livia Gershon, "A Libertarian Utopia," *Aeon*, April 28, 2014, accessed March 31, 2019, https://aeon.co/essays/what-happens-when-libertarians-try-to-build-a-new-society; Matthew Hogoltz-Hetling, *A Libertarian Walks into a Bear: The Utopian Plot to Liberate an American Town (and Some Bears)* (New York: Public Affairs, 2020); Finn Brunton, *Digital Cash: The Unknown History of the Anarchists, Utopians and Technologists Who Created Cryptocurrency* (Princeton, NJ: Princeton University Press, 2019), 190–95; David G. Post, "Anarchy, State, and the Internet: An Essay on Lawmaking in Cyber-Space," originally published in the *Journal of Online Law* (1995) and republished in Peter Ludlow, ed., *Crypto Anarchy, Cyberstates, and Pirate Utopias* (Cambridge, MA: MIT Press, 2001), 197–211.

from new digital opportunities such as cryptocurrencies to processes such as converting one's consciousness into computer code or pumping one's corpse with liquid nitrogen in order to be resuscitated once life-reviving technologies have been invented.[2] This is a world in which its residents eschew territorial escape in part because they already see a world in which the "mediating structures" of government, media, and business are collapsing. At times such collapse is helped along by natural disasters that are anything but natural, such as in Puerto Rico where in the wake of Hurricane Maria a small avant-garde of exit libertarians—quickly rechristened Puertopians—arrived with aspirations of forging a "crypto-utopia."[3] At its most optimistic, such a strategy looks toward a future of singularities—technological singularity in that computation systems and artificial intelligence will become integrated into the biological body and social singularity in that such technologies will make possible

---

2   On the influence of Friedman and Hayek in the understanding of anarchy, see, for example, Timothy C. May, "Crypto Anarchy and Virtual Communities," originally circulated in 1994 and reproduced in Peter Ludlow, ed., *Crypto Anarchy, Cyberstates, and Pirate Utopias* (Cambridge, MA: MIT Press, 2001), 65–79. For good starting points on these varied movements, see Jedediah Purdy, "The God of the Digerati," originally published in 1998 and reproduced in Ludlow, ed., *Crypto Anarchy*, 353–62; Brunton, *Digital Cash;* Paulina Borsook, *Cyberselfish: A Critical Romp Through the Terribly Libertarian Culture of High Tech* (New York: Public Affairs, 2000); George Packer, *The Unwinding: An Inner History of the New America* (New York: Farrar, Straus & Giroux, 2013), esp. 381–97; Fred Turner, *From Counterculture to Cyberculture: Stewart Brand, the Whole Earth Network, and the Rise of Digital Utopianism* (Chicago: University of Chicago Press, 2008); Mark O'Connell, *Notes from an Apocalypse: A Personal Journey to the End of the World and Back* (New York: Doubleday, 2020); and Mark O'Connell, *To Be a Machine: Adventures Among Cyborgs, Utopians, Hackers, and the Futurists Solving the Modest Problem of Death* (New York: Anchor Books, 2017); and, on San Francisco's recent history and its linkages to such activities, Richard Walker, *Pictures of a Gone City: Tech and the Dark Side of Prosperity in the San Francisco Bay Area* (Oakland: PM Press, 2018). For a careful effort to theorize the consequences of computational life and its effects on geopolitics, see Bratton, *The Stack: On Software and Sovereignty* (Cambridge, MA: MIT Press, 2016). For works of science fiction that both have shaped and built on the possible futures sprouting from the computational era, see especially Cory Doctorow, *Walkaway* (New York: Tor Books, 2017); Richard K. Morgan, *Altered Carbon* (New York: Ballantine, 2002); Don DeLillo, *Zero K* (New York: Scribner, 2016); Annalee Newitz, *Autonomous* (New York: Tor Books, 2017); William Gibson, *Neuromancer* (New York: Ace, 1984); and Neal Stephenson, *Snowcrash* (New York: Bantam, 1992).

3   Nellie Bowles, "The Dawn of a Crypto Utopia?" *New York Times*, February 3, 2018; Neil Strauss, "Brock Pierce: The Hippie King of Cryptocurrency," *Rolling Stone*, July 26, 2018. On disaster capitalism more broadly, see Naomi Klein, *The Shock Doctrine: The Rise of Disaster Capitalism* (New York: Metropolitan Books, 2007). For Puerto Rico, see Yarimar Bonilla and Marisol LeBrón, *Aftershocks of Disaster: Puerto Rico before and after the Storm* (Chicago: Haymarket Books, 2019) and Ed Morales, *Fantasy Island: Colonialism, Exploitation and the Betrayal of Puerto Rico* (New York: Bold Type Books, 2019). For how current versions of nonterritorial exit—through cryptosecession—linked to earlier ideas of pananarchism, see Trent J. Macdonald, *The Political Economy of Non-Territorial Exit: Cryptosecession* (Cheltenham: Edward Elgar, 2019).

a postpolitical world in which individuals can thrive through decentralized networks of spontaneous order with no mediating central body or institution.[4]

Although seemingly (and at times literally) outlandish, such projections are responding in some sense to very real and dramatic changes in how sovereignty is thought to work. The idea that sovereignty is rooted in bounded parcels of territory is beginning to seem almost quaintly outdated. Philosopher and design theorist Benjamin Bratton has argued that a new kind of governance, that he terms The Stack, has emerged. The Stack is an "accidental megastructure" that has come into being in a world in which "planetary-scale computation has so thoroughly and fundamentally transformed the logics of political geography in its own image that it has produced new geographies and new territories that can enforce themselves," in the process creating a "new architecture for how we divide up the world into sovereign spaces."[5] Bratton shows how the exceptions to the traditional form of nation-state sovereignty—"byzantine international and subnational bodies, a proliferation of enclaves and exclaves, noncontiguous states, diasporic nationalisms, global brand affiliations, wide-scale demographic mobilization and containment, free trade corridors and special economic zones, massive file-sharing networks both legal and illegal, material and manufacturing logistical vectors, polar and subpolar resource appropriations, panoptic satellite platforms, alternative currencies, atavistic and irredentist religious imaginaries, cloud data and social-graph identity platforms," among many others—constitute the rule.[6] In which case perhaps the territorial futures of the exit strategists are already a thing of the past?

The continued, substantial investment being made in forms of territorial exit—from plans for seasteads to efforts to colonize outer space by such tech luminaries as Elon Musk and Jeff Bezos—suggests that the materiality of territory and the concept of sovereignty continue to matter. In part this is because

4   Max Borders, presentation at the 2017 Startup Societies Summit in San Francisco (August 11–12, 2017); May, "Crypto Anarchy and Virtual Communities"; O'Connell, *To Be a Machine*, 70–76. Excellent starting points for histories of techno-libertarianism can be found in Turner, *From Counterculture to Cyberculture*, and Borsook, *Cyberselfish*; and, in relation to accelerationism, Benjamin Noys, *Malign Velocities: Accelerationism and Capitalism* (London: Zero Books, 2014).

5   Bratton, *The Stack*, xviii, 6, and 375.

6   Ibid., 375. See also Keller Easterling, *Extrastatecraft: The Power of Infrastructure Space* (London: Verso, 2016), Felicity Scott, *Outlaw Territories: Environments of Insecurity/ Architecture of Countersinsurgency* (Boston: Zone Books, 2016); Matthew Hart, *Extraterritorial: A Political Geography of Contemporary Fiction* (New York: Columbia University Press, 2020); and Matt Johnson, "Extraterritorialized! Data Havens, Red Light Districts, Radical Offshoring, and Other Extrastate Enclaves of Globalism" *Volume* 38 (2014) as reproduced at https://loganandjohnson.com/news/extraterritorialized-in-volume-38.

contemporary exit strategists are interested in more than subtraction, more than merely walking away. Rather, they envision the emergence of a whole series of microcountries that would produce their own legal and political systems and would compete for citizens, much as companies compete for consumers, by reducing the "transaction costs" of opting out of one polity and of opting into another. One could think of them as literal "market places." This is a political project which applies the language of market choice, and the assumption of competition as the natural form of social relations, to government itself, all under the guise of antipolitics and personal liberation. "Don't argue. Build," advises the Startup Societies Foundation website. And the place where ground is being broken? Honduras (fig. 6.1).

Developer politics

You can gauge the controversy surrounding Paul Romer's charter cities by the fact that their likelihood ended, in Madagascar, and began, in Honduras, with coups d'état, both in 2009. A former economist at Stanford University now employed at New York University, a Nobel Prize–winning economist and, for a brief stint in 2017 and 2018, chief economist of the World Bank, Romer is an important figure in the field of endogenous growth theory, a field in economics that he helped create in the late 1980s. The theory sought to explain why some countries grew successfully while others did not by stressing the importance of ideas, technological research and development, and "human capital" as drivers of growth.[7] Ideas, for Romer, referred particularly to the customs, institutions, and rules that predominated in a given society and that dramatically impacted the day-to-day quality of life of, and possibilities for, its population and also affected a country's economic growth. Inhibitions to growth, according to Romer, were conditioned by internal cultural and institutional limitations in the countries in question. To foment growth, it was necessary for countries to ensure they had rules and laws in place that would be enforced and attract investment. He then began to apply such arguments to the creation, rather than reformation, of places. Asserting that better rules would create places in which people would want to live, he called for the creation of new urban spaces outside of the sovereign control of a nation-state

---

7   On endogenous growth theory and, more generally, on methodological individualism and "new" orientations in economics, I am indebted to Ben Fine, "Endogenous Growth Theory: A Critical Assessment," *Cambridge Journal of Economics* 24 (2000): 245–65; and Fine, "The New Revolution in Economics," *Capital & Class* 21, no. 1 (Spring 1997): 143–48. On the idealized figure of *Homo economicus*, always lurking in the wings here, see the critiques in E.P. Thompson, "The Moral Economy of the Crowd"; Scott, *The Moral Economy of the Peasant*; and Peter Fleming, *The Death of Homoeconomicus: Work, Debt, and the Myth of Endless Accumulation* (London: Pluto Press, 2017).

Fig. 6.1: Map of Honduras, including the Bay Islands.
Map by John Wyatt Greenlee.

and into which people could freely migrate and settle. He called such spaces "charter cities."[8]

Romer envisioned such cities as a framework for improving development and quality of life around the globe. Traditional aid and development strategies had failed poorer countries. In this of course he is not alone. Commentators, officials, academics and prognosticators across the political spectrum have argued at length for changes in the structure of how aid and development operate. Just to take one example that provides a sharp contrast with Romer's attention to internal causes of underdevelopment, it was at the very height

---

8   For a good discussion of Romer's ideas, from a sympathetic but not entirely convinced author, see Sebastian Mallaby, "The Politically Incorrect Guide to Ending Poverty," *The Atlantic*, July/August 2010.

of decolonization, in the 1950s and 1960s, that Latin American and African intellectuals began to write of *neocolonialism*, critiquing traditional modes of development thinking and questioning the determinations of what constituted the end of colonial rule through the lens of international political economy. Was it purely an issue of political self-determination and formal structures of political power? Had colonial rule collapsed with the flight of the colonial powers? To what degree had national autonomy severed the unequal relationship of dependency between metropole and periphery, or north and south, or colonizer and colonized? How could, for example, the promise of self-determination be fulfilled if confronted with the strategic threat of capital flight?[9] Critics of capitalism have long stressed its deeply implicated relationship with colonialism. Thus, even as colonial empires crumbled, a variety of voices argued that the demise of colonialism might be called in to question by the persistence of capitalism. Within Latin America, intellectuals generated historical analyses and interpretations that offered trenchant explanations for a world still deeply colonized by tracing historical networks and spatial grids of capitalist dependency, in the process highlighting the structural relationship between "development" and "underdevelopment."[10] The point was that development and industrialization in western Europe and the United States was dependent upon the active underdevelopment of other countries through resource extraction and unequal terms of trade. The issues driving underdevelopment were not necessarily or solely internal—customs, corruption, or a lack of rules—but also (and at times, significantly) external in the forms of unequal trade relationships and the economic power characteristic of global capitalism.

Dependency theory, as well as the ideas generated by the nonaligned movement and the 1973 call for a New International Economic Order, offered a substantive historical critique of unequal exchange and the development of global capitalism, but by the 1980s they were drowned out by an emergent

---

9   Frantz Fanon observed, "The spectacular flight of capital is one of the most constant phenomena of decolonization." Fanon, *The Wretched of the Earth* (New York: Grove, 2004 [1961]), 103.

10   See Eduardo Galeano, *The Open Veins of Latin America: Five Centuries of the Pillage of a Continent* (New York: Monthly Review Press, 1997 [1975]); Andre Gunder Frank, *Capitalism and Underdevelopment in Latin America: Historical Studies of Chile and Brazil* (London: Penguin, 1971); Fernando Henrique Cardoso and Enzo Faletto, *Dependency and Development in Latin America* (Berkeley: University of California Press, 1979); and Walter Rodney, *How Europe Underdeveloped Africa* (London: Bogle-L'Ouverture, 1972). For a critique see Robert Brenner, "The Origins of Capitalist Development: A Critique of Neo-Smithian Marxism," *New Left Review* 104 (1977): 25–93. For an excellent overview, see Patrick Wolfe, "History and Imperialism: A Century of Theory, from Marx to Postcolonialism," *American Historical Review* 102, no. 2 (April 1997): 388–429.

neoliberalism that capitalized on the decade's debt crises.[11] If in 1964 Raúl Prebisch had argued that trade rather than aid was the way to forge a "path to equity" for countries around the globe, by 1981 Ronald Reagan had coined the same phrase for the opposite purpose: to establish a "vision of the world not as a kind of global welfare state but as a competitive arena."[12] Institutions created under the Bretton Woods agreement transformed themselves in to international creditors with substantial power over the political and economic destinies of states around the globe. State industries were dismantled, food subsidies abolished, tariffs and protectionist measures removed, currencies devalued, the public sector gutted, and long-standing efforts at agrarian reform abandoned.

One emergent popular-ideological language for this shift came in the form of Peruvian economist Hernando de Soto's work which argued that the key to reducing poverty was to encourage property titling and property formalization for those in the informal economy. De Soto's fetishization of property rights garnered widespread praise in the 1990s and dovetailed in important ways with the ideas of Romer, despite the uneven and often negative consequences of titling and formalization for the poor.[13] For many, such practices constituted a further mechanism for the wholesale privatization of the state and the nepotistic transfer of public wealth into private hands, creating a small class of new billionaires even as the middle and working classes suffered austerity, currency devaluation, and unemployment.[14] Importantly, all of this took place in the context of a new wave of accumulation and

---

11 Greg Grandin, *Empire's Workshop: Latin America, the United States, and the Rise of the New Imperialism* (New York: Holt Books, 2007), 181–85. See also Jerome Roos, *Why Not Default? The Political Economy of Sovereign Debt* (Princeton, NJ: Princeton University Press, 2019), esp. part III.

12 Grandin, *Empire's Workshop*, 186–87.

13 De Soto, *The Other Path: The Invisible Revolution in the Third World* (New York: HarperCollins, 1989) and de Soto, *The Mystery of Capital: Why Capitalism Triumphs in the West and Fails Everywhere Else* (New York: Basic Books, 2000). The critiques of Hernando de Soto's purported panacea for poverty—property titling and formalization—are numerous. For a concise critique, see John Gravois, "The de Soto Delusion," *Slate*, January 29, 2005. On the uneven consequences of property formalization see Raymond Williams, *The Country and the City* (Oxford: Oxford University Press, 1975); E.P. Thompson, *Customs in Common: Studies in Traditional Popular Culture* (New York: New Press, 1993); James C. Scott, *Seeing Like a State: How Certain Schemes to Improve the Human Condition Have Failed* (New Haven, CT: Yale University Press, 1998); James C. Scott, *The Moral Economy of the Peasant: Rebellion and Subsistence in Southeast Asia* (New Haven, CT: Yale University Press, 1976), and Raymond Craib, *Cartographic Mexico: A History of State Fixations and Fugitive Landscapes* (Durham, NC: Duke University Press, 2004).

14 In the case of Mexico, just to take one example, the country had one billionaire on the Forbes list in 1987; by 1995 it had twenty-four, even as wages and key indicators for much of the population stagnated or declined. The nouveau riche accumulated such wealth

enclosure—from the global land grab to the rise of "ecosystems services"—for which the language of "property," "security," "certification," and "title" had been duly deployed.[15] It also intersected with a resurgence in libertarian dreams of new country-making. In 1995 an unnamed group of investors (or, as they referred to themselves, "an impressive group of free-market individuals") announced the creation of the Laissez Faire City International Trust which would create and promote a new city run along principles espoused by Ayn Rand and developed on land granted to them by an unnamed "underdeveloped country." The Trust was headquartered in the former residence of the Nicaraguan ambassador to Costa Rica (see fig. 6.2).[16]

Romer's charter city idea intersected with this neoliberal apotheosis of the 1990s and early 2000s but its lineage could be traced back through decades of public choice theory and the slow conversion of the social citizen into a political consumer. Its most important early exponent was Charles Tiebout who offered, in 1956, what he called an efficiency postulate.[17] Ronen Palan explains:

> Tiebout developed, in his own words, an "extreme" theory according to which municipalities provide individuals and firms with a bundle of public services and tax regulations. Individuals and firms are likely to choose municipalities that offer desirable bundles of regulations by moving into them, and to reject those that offer less desirable bundles of regulations

---

through corrupt and crony deals in the sale of state-owned enterprises. See Grandin, *Empire's Workshop*, 188–89.

15　See Fred Pearce, *The Land Grabbers: The New Fight over Who Owns the Earth* (Boston: Beacon, 2012); the recent special issues of the *Journal of Peasant Studies*, including 38, no. 2 (2011); 39, no. 1 (2012); and 39, no. 3–4 (2012); and, for the specific case of Mexico, which is very instructive, Joel Wainwright, *Geopiracy: Oaxaca, Militant Empiricism, and Geographical Thought* (London: Palgrave, 2012); Joe Bryan and Denis Wood, *Weaponizing Maps: Indigenous Peoples and Counterinsurgency in the Americas* (New York: The Guilford Press, 2015); and Raymond Craib, "The Properties of Counterinsurgency," *Dialogues in Human Geography*, March 2014.

16　Advertisement for Laissez Faire City International Trust, *Economist*, June 10, 1995. On the LFCIT, see the report by John Kingman, "Report on a Visit to LFC, San José, Costa Rica," *Formulations*, Spring 1999, reproduced at http://freenation.org/a/f63k1.html. Shortly after the publication of this advertisement, the estate of Ayn Rand along with Penguin Books sued the LFCIT and its trustee Mikhail Largin for copyright infringement, charging that they had created bootlegged copies of the central portions of Rand's *Atlas Shrugged* and offered them to supporters. See "Peikoff vs Laissez Faire City," October 1, 1996, US District Court, Southern District of Florida. Available at https://www.courtlistener.com/docket/4238008/1/peikoff-v-laissez-faire-city/. I am grateful to Elise Burr for bringing the LFCIT advertisement to my attention and providing me a copy of the image.

17　Tiebout, "A Pure Theory of Local Expenditures," *Journal of Political Economy* 64, no. 5 (October 1956): 416–24.

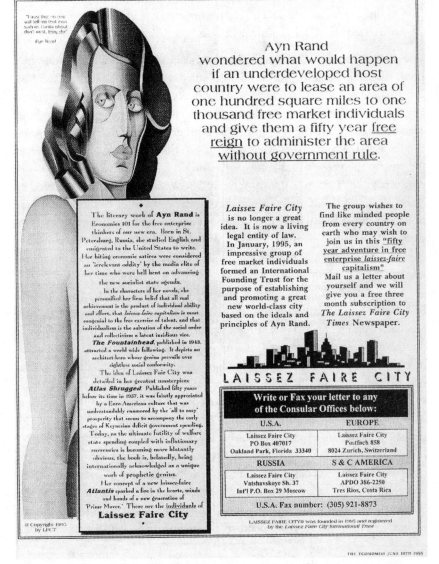

Fig. 6.2: What would Ayn Rand do? Advertisement for the Laissez Faire City, by the Laissez Faire City International Trust.

The Economist, June 10, 1995.

by moving out of them. Municipalities are therefore in competition over what Tiebout called "consumer-citizens."[18]

Tiebout's work, rooted in the methodological individualism that undergirds neoclassical economics, presumed that "consumer-citizens" are first and foremost sovereign, utility maximizing individuals (i.e., economic beings driven largely by the desire for individual gain.) In effect, as Palan goes on to note, Tiebout argued "for the superiority of market discipline over the sovereign rights of states [and] that sovereignty ... can be used as a commercial asset, for clearly the theory sees states as "selling" regulatory packages to eager consumers."[19] Tiebout's theory was, by his own estimation, an extreme or "pure" theory in that it made certain theoretical assumptions that rarely, if ever, hold true in reality: that there would exist a "perfectly elastic supply of jurisdictions," that individuals could exit from one jurisdiction and enter another cost-free and with ease, that such individuals would have full and transparent knowledge regarding all available jurisdictions, and the like.[20]

Tiebout's sorting manifesto attracted libertarians' attentions. David Friedman, son of famed economist Milton Friedman, argued in his 1973 *Machinery of Freedom* for creating a system in which governments would compete for citizens. One of Friedman's suggestions included breaking the link between political jurisdiction and geographical location entirely so that one need not physically move when opting into a political system. As one supporter of the idea wrote: "If people could switch political jurisdictions without switching location, we would have the functional equivalent of the situation Friedman envisions. Competition among jurisdictions would be higher, and the amount of state interference that people would tolerate without switching would be lower, than in a political system where jurisdiction and geographic location are linked."[21] More recent "competitive governance" advocates include tech-entrepreneur Balaji Srinivasan who sees a future of exit communities—composed of financially independent and mobile

---

18   Palan, *The Offshore World*, 69.

19   Ibid., 69.

20   David R. Johnson and David G. Post, "Law and Borders: The Rise of Law in Cyberspace," originally published in *Stanford Law Review* 48, no. 5 (May 1996): 1367–1402, and republished in Ludlow, ed., *Crypto Anarchy*, 145–95; discussion of Tiebout and quoted text on 193, n.103. Johnson and Post here draw from Robert P. Inman and Daniel L. Rubinfeld, "The Political Economy of Federalism," Working Paper 94–15, *Boalt Hall Program in Law and Economics* (1994). James Dale Davidson and William Rees-Mogg draw on Tiebout's work in their libertarian exit/investment strategy text *The Sovereign Individual: How to Survive and Thrive During the Collapse of the Welfare State* (New York: Simon & Schuster, 1997).

21   Roderick T. Long, "Virtual Cantons: A New Path to Freedom?," *Formulations* 1, no. 1 (1993), http://freenation.org/a/f11l1.html.

capitalists—who initially create a digital community and then pool their respective resources and leverage, collaborating to negotiate with states in order to coax better and better regulatory and tax packages even as they create extrageographical Network States. "Cloud first, land last" is the motto.[22] Legal scholar Tom Bell, who has been developing legal structures for various exit projects, has argued that "to make legal systems better, we must make them compete against each other."[23] With complete exit from the state proving legally, economically and politically difficult, libertarian exit projects such as these pursue "jurisdictional arbitrage"—that is, they seek to exploit differences between legal and political entities in order to create new autonomous, market-based communities that will themselves foment further competition for citizens between legal and political jurisdictions.[24]

Romer's charter city vision dovetailed with such perspectives in terms of advocating for a form of consumer choice—or opt-in—as the basis for a charter city's population. It is not unusual for those with means to choose where they wish to live. But charter cities had a catch. To create charter cities, Romer argued that countries lease or cede pieces of their sovereign territory to a foreign entity—a nation-state or group of nation-states that would essentially underwrite the project and appoint an oversight board—which would take the lead in building and governing such cities. Such cities would be built from scratch on allegedly vacant land and would be largely independent of the nation-states within which they operated, with their own institutions, oversight committees, and legal systems, among other possibilities. Residents who opted in to the city would live there under a set of terms laid out in a contract but not as citizens with a vote or a voice in how things were done. The form by which they could express their satisfaction or dissatisfaction was to stay or to

---

22 Srinivasan, to the best of my knowledge, first outlined the idea of what he termed the Network State at the 2017 Startup Societies Foundation meeting. See Ana Simina Soian and Maxime Delavallee, "The State Is Dead. Long Live the State!," https://medium.com/new-tech-revolution-sciencespo/the-state-is-dead-long-live-the-state-8afab8f9a800. For more on Srinivasan's trajectory, see Srinivasan, "Silicon Valley's Ultimate Exit," https://genius.com/Balaji-srinivasan-silicon-valleys-ultimate-exit-annotated and Srinivasan, "Technology Will Lead to a Borderless World," https://reason.com/video/balaji-srinivasan-tech-borderless-world/. For the quote and an essay in which he situates his "cloud first" model in relation to other new country projects, see Balaji S. Srinivasan, "How to Start a New Country," 1729, April 9, 2021, https://1729.com/how-to-start-a-new-country/.

23 Tom W. Bell, "What Is Polycentric Law?" The Freeman, February 24, 2014.

24 Tom Bell, Your Next Government? From Nation-States to Stateless Nations (Cambridge: Cambridge University Press, 2017); Max Borders, "A Little Rebellion Now and Then Is a Good Thing," roundtable on Albert Hirschman's Exit, Voice, and Loyalty at fifty, Cato Unbound: A Journal of Debate, August 2020, https://www.cato-unbound.org/issues/august-2020/exit-voice-loyalty-50.

leave. Romer's model was Hong Kong as established by British colonials: an enclave with no duties on imports, sales, or exports; minimal customs control; free entry to foreign capital; a prohibition on industrial regulations and closed shop labor unions; and a significant amount of political autonomy.[25]

Observers of Romer's plan pointed out that it sounded as if were advocating for colonial enclaves. It was a serious accusation. Hondurans had struggled repeatedly against transnational economic enclaves such as those created by the United Fruit Company, which controlled vast swaths of Honduran territory during the twentieth century, and, in the 1970s, against transnational corporations operating export processing zones employing cheap labor.[26] The history of US government involvement in Honduran politics and economics over the course of two centuries also did not inspire confidence. After World War II, such involvement deepened with a bilateral military agreement in 1954, the same year in which Honduran laborers staged a huge strike in the banana industry (and the US orchestrated a coup d'état in neighboring Guatemala).[27] There followed decades of military rule with US support; violent persecution of labor organizers and alleged subversives; the creation of a restrictive constitution; and the entrenchment of a two-party political system controlled by Honduras's elite families who had long-standing connections with the US. In the early 1980s the country became a staging ground for the Reagan administration's illegal wars in Central America and a venue for an array of free trade zones and export-processing locales with few labor protections and wage regulations. Privatization deepened in the 1990s and the Honduran elite implemented laws to "modernize" and "develop" the agricultural sector, effectively bringing earlier efforts at agrarian reform to an end and selling off public lands and state-owned enterprises to private buyers.[28] Uncertainties regarding property titles and ownership

---

25   Keri Vacanti Brondo, *Land Grab: Green Neoliberalism, Gender, and Garifuna Resistance in Honduras* (Tucson: University of Arizona Press, 2013), 173; Mallaby, "The Politically Incorrect Guide to Ending Poverty"; Justin Sandefur and Milan Vaishnav, "Imagine There's No Country: Three Questions about a New Charter City in Honduras," Center for Global Development: Essay June 2012, http://www.cgdev.org/content/publications/detail/1426274.

26   Dana Frank, *The Long Honduran Night: Resistance, Terror, and the United States in the Aftermath of the Coup* (Chicago: Haymarket Books, 2018), 72–73.

27   On the banana strike, see Suyapa Portillo, *Roots of Resistance: A Story of Gender, Race, and Labor on the North Coast of Honduras* (Austin: University of Texas Press, 2021); John Soluri, *Banana Cultures: Agriculture, Consumption, and Environmental Change in Honduras and the United States* (Austin: University of Texas Press, 2005), esp. chap. 5; on the coup in Guatemala, see Grandin, *The Last Colonial Massacre: Latin America in the Cold War* (Chicago: University of Chicago Press, 2004).

28   Marvin Barahona, "Auge y Decadencia de la Ideologia de la Desigualdad: Un Cuestionamiento Necesario a la Hegemonía Neoliberal," in Joaquín A. Mejía R., coord., *Estado, Despojo y Derechos Humanos* (El Progreso: ERIC-SJ, 2019), 63–102, esp. 68–70. See

claims complicated but also facilitated the process. Sugarcane and oil palm plantations expanded exponentially, often through violent expropriation and assassinations, and Honduras remains one of the most dangerous countries in the world for defenders of the environment and indigenous land rights.[29]

Romer sidestepped these structural and historical questions, instead attempting to refute accusations of colonialism by suggesting that charter cities could not be forms of colonialism because they involved choice rather than coercion. He argued that people were free to choose to live (or not live) in such cities, even if under the control and oversight of international boards and investors. They would be opt-in cities. "Charter cities," Romer claimed, "are based entirely on voluntary actions. Only a country that wants to establish a charter city will do so. Only people who want to live and work under the rules specified in the city's charter will move there. Free choice is essential for the legitimacy of the rules in a charter city. It is also what makes a charter city very different from colonial occupation."[30] It is unclear whether a city's charter could exclude people and, if so, under what criteria. Romer advocated for "extremely open immigration policies in order to attract foreign workers from all over."[31] The implication, though, is that there are in fact immigration policies with a set of criteria attached.

I will return at the end of this chapter to the question of opt-in, but for now suffice to say that, despite Romer's protestations, charter cities' resemblance to colonial enclave structures and the belief in radical market models help explain why Romer's first efforts to negotiate charter cities with a government ended poorly. In Madagascar in 2008, then president Marc Ravalomanana had sought new ways to bring investment to the country, including the potential of leasing a plot of land the size of Connecticut to South Korean Daewoo corporation and having neighboring Mauritius oversee an export processing zone. Romer visited Ravalomanana in late 2008 to float his charter cities

---

also Ana Ortega, "Las Reformas Económicas a partir de 2009 desde la Lógica Extractiva que Sostiene la Acumulación por Desposesión," in ibid., 103–27.

29   Between 1990 and 2010 the amount of Honduran land dedicated to sugarcane and African palm cultivation grew by nearly 170 percent, more than in neighboring Guatemala and more than El Salvador and Nicaragua combined. See José Luis Rocha y Equipo de Investigación del ERIC-SJ, "Experiencias de Despojo y Resistencia desde la Voz de las Comunidades: Acaparamiento, Desplazamiento Forzoso y Luchas por la Tierra en la Honduras del Siglo XXI," in Mejía R., coord., *Estado, Despojo y Derechos Humanos*, 159–91. For a careful study of collective land rights and land titling in the Hondura Moskitia, see Fernando Galeana Rodríguez, "Property and Indigenous State Formation in the Honduran Moskitia," PhD dissertation, Cornell University, 2021.

30   "Charter Cities: Q&A with Paul Romer," Center for Global Development, May 3, 2010, http://www.cgdev.org/article/charter-cities-qa-paul-romer.

31   Adam Davidson, "Who Wants to Buy Honduras?" *New York Times*, May 8, 2012.

concept, and the president was intrigued. Romer's optimism that his vision could move forward, however, was soon snuffed by a February 2009 coup d'état brought on at least in part by public protests against the various investment projects that were seen, by much of Madagascar's population, as the sale of national territory to foreigners.[32]

A coup d'état opened the possibilities for charter cities in Honduras that very same year. In the early morning hours of a Sunday in June 2009, Honduran troops escorted democratically elected president Manuel Zelaya across the tarmac of Tegucigalpa's airport and onto a plane bound, after a refueling stop at the US-run Soto Cano Air Base, for Costa Rica. When he disembarked in Costa Rica, Zelaya was still in his pajamas.[33] His arrest and expulsion came on the heels of a battle over Zelaya's efforts to hold a nonbinding referendum regarding revisions to Honduras's constitution. Despite the exculpatory contortions proffered by various political and economic interests, both within Honduras and beyond that claimed the military coup was not a military coup, it clearly was, and the UN General Assembly, the OAS, the European Union and numerous Latin American states all saw it as such. The Obama administration's own officials at the US embassy in Tegucigalpa, including then ambassador Llorens, referred to the event as a coup d'état, and in private meetings some Honduran officials admitted the overthrow "stretched the law" but defended it as a "necessary evil."[34] Despite the protestations of the OAS and much of Honduran civil society, the Obama administration refused to condemn the overthrow of a legitimate government and the leaders of the coup remained in power. Clearly more was at work here than Zelaya's legal initiative to hold a nonbinding public referendum. The broader context was one in which Zelaya alienated the ruling elite class, from which he himself came, who had long dominated the country in conjunction with US interests. Zelaya came into office as a traditional political candidate: he was from one of the two dominant parties, he supported the neoliberal model that governed the country's economy, and he generally conformed with the expectations of Honduras's powerful landowning and business elite. But nearing the end of his term in office he made two decisions that incurred the wrath of those who would soon depose him: he brought Honduras into the Bolivarian Alliance

---

32   Mallaby, "The Politically Incorrect Guide to Ending Poverty."

33   Suyapa Portillo, "Honduras: Refounding the Nation, Building a New Kind of Social Movement," in Richard Stahler-Sholk, Harry E. Vanden, and Marc Becker, eds., *Rethinking Latin American Social Movements: Radical Action from Below* (Lanham, MD: Rowman & Littlefield, 2014), 121–45. On Zelaya and the air base, see ibid., 123.

34   "PRO-COUP OPINIONS ON THE NOQH COAST AND CONGRESS," Telegram US Embassy Tegucigalpa, Honduras to Central Intelligence Agency et al., December 2, 2009, Wikileaks ID: 09TEGUCIGALPA1240_a.

for the Americas (ALBA), which had been created by Venezuela's president Hugo Chávez, and he raised the minimum wage. Importantly, as historian Suyapa Portillo points out, "Due to free trade laws, this minimum wage law would only apply to domestic producers and not the foreign *maquilas* and exporters and other free-trade sectors."[35] The practical impact of the new minimum wage and the imaginative impact of an alliance that could include Chávez was a gathering of forces against Zelaya. But on a more general level Zelaya alienated Honduran elites by daring to concern himself with the social problems confronted by most Hondurans. The men who overthrew Zelaya thus charted a markedly different course, one that included charter cities.

A charter state

Romer hailed the post-coup leadership in Honduras as committed to ending the "cycle of insecurity and instability that stokes fear and erodes trust."[36] Yet within months of the coup, Honduran security forces had illegally detained more than three thousand people and committed close to 4,500 human rights violations.[37] Interim president Roberto Micheletti suspended articles in the Honduran Constitution that dramatically curtailed Hondurans' basic freedoms of transit, assembly, and the press.[38] The military seized radio station equipment, and campaigns of disinformation regarding Zelaya proliferated, both in the Honduran and international press. Over the course of the first two years following the coup, more than thirty members of the political opposition would be disappeared or killed as would numerous journalists.[39] Documented human rights violations by the end of 2010 neared double digits *per day*. Much of the violence that came in the wake of the coup was borne inordinately by women and the LGBTQI community.[40] The coup's backers undercut the Honduran social movements—large and dynamic and inclusive, running the gamut from demands for agrarian reform to advocates for LGBTQI rights—that sought to support Hondurans' efforts to create the society in which they wanted to live. Historian Dana Frank has observed that while Honduras suffered from

---

35   Portillo, "Honduras," 125.
36   Keane Bhatt, "Reporting on Romer's Charter Cities: How the Media Sanitize Honduras's Brutal Regime," *NACLA Report on the Americas* 45 (Winter 2012): 88–90.
37   Portillo, "Honduras," 133.
38   Frank, *The Long Honduran Night*, 16; Vacanti Brondo, *Land Grab*, 168–69.
39   Dana Frank, "In Honduras, a Mess Made in the U.S.," *New York Times*, January 26, 2012, as cited by Vacanti Brondo, *Land Grab*, 169.
40   Portillo, "Honduras," 133–34. See also Regina Fonseca y Gilda Rivera, "El Impacto Diferenciado en las Mujeres del Proceso Binario de Acumulación y Despojo," in Mejía R., coord., *Estado, Despojo y Derechos Humanos*, 128–58. For monitoring and reporting of violence directed at the LGBTQI community, see cattrachas.org.

poverty and violence prior to the coup d'état, the evidence is clear that the coup "precipitated a rapid downward spiral that cast the Honduran people into a maelstrom of repression, violence, and increasing poverty. The post-coup regime destroyed the rule of law and gutted the country's welfare state—indeed, the state itself."[41] Within a few years the government had issued a Law of State Secrets, further diminishing government transparency and muzzling journalists; international organization Global Witness had declared Honduras the most dangerous country on the planet for "environmental and land defenders," the point punctuated by the continued harassment, beginning in 2013, and eventual assassination in 2016 of feminist and environmental activist Berta Cáceres.[42] This was the ground on which charter cities—sold as urban monuments to rules, prosperity, and freedom—were to rise.[43]

Opposition to the coup proved fierce and consolidated itself in the National Front of Resistance (FNRP), known generally as *la Resistencia*. Built on decades of organizing work, the FNRP brought together unions, nonprofits, indigenous groups, environmentalists, feminists, queer activists, civic organizations, and others in solidarity for months of daily protest.[44] Others felt they had little choice but to leave, migrating north to Mexico and then on to the US border, a line that they would have serious difficulty crossing and where they risked bodily violence, separation from loved ones (including children and infants), and death. They fled personal threats, the pervasive existence of violence in their communities, and worsening conditions under the coup regime that gutted the social supports that Zelaya had sought to expand. Honduras's business elite, meanwhile, assured the world that things had taken a turn for the better and promptly declared Honduras "open for business" while overseeing dubious and widely criticized elections. Held at

---

41 Frank, *The Long Honduran Night*, 4. An ex-captain in the armed forces, Santos Orellana Rodríguez, in an interview with Radio Progreso, stated that under the Hernández government the armed forces had been directly involved in assassinations and repressions around the country. See the transcription of the interview with Santos Orellana Rodríguez by Radio Progreso, trans. Adrienne Pine. Pine, Upside Down World, January 29, 2018, https://upsidedownworld.org/archives/honduras/honduras-military-intelligence-behind-assassinations-tortures-and-forced-disappearances..

42 On the 2013 Law of State Secrets and the Global Witness report, see Beth Geglia, "Honduras: Reinventing the Enclave," *NACLA Report on the Americas* 48, no. 4 (2016): 353–60, esp. 354. On the continued lack of transparency, see Edmundo Orellana, "Transparencia," *La Tribuna*, June 22, 2020. On the assassination of Cáceres, see Frank, *The Long Honduran Night*, 222–31.

43 Some charter city advocates used increased state violence as further justification for their construction. Brian Doherty, "The Blank Slate State," *Reason*, June 2013. For a libertarian critique of Doherty, see Kevin Carson, "Come See the Violence Inherent in an An-cap Utopia," Center for a Stateless Society, April 22, 2016, https://c4ss.org/content/44678.

44 Portillo, "Honduras," 128–31.

the end of 2009, those elections resulted in the presidency of Porfirio Lobo Sosa, a large landowner, member of the conservative National Party, and the former president of the Honduran National Congress who had lost the 2005 presidential election to Zelaya. His election was no surprise as opposition parties refused to participate in what was a sham. As Frank notes, "the United Nations, the Carter Center, and the OAS, with the exception of the US Republican Party and a few delegates from the Democratic Party[,] refused to observe the process."[45] Sworn in to office in January of 2010, Lobo appointed Harvard-trained economist Octavio Sánchez as his chief of staff. In the early 2000s the young Sánchez had served as an advisor to then-president Maduro and had authored a document reforming land titling and registries. The ideas of Hernando de Soto, whose Peruvian think tank argues for unleashing the credit potential of the poor through giving them title to the informal spaces they occupy and businesses they operate, loom large in such approaches, but Sánchez had also been influenced by the ideas of Romer with whom he would meet in Miami in 2010 to discuss charter cities.[46] Sánchez and Lobo were eager to leverage private solutions to Honduran problems and together they undertook a restructuring of the Honduran constitution, a restructuring that would eventually create quasi-legal bases for the creation of Employment and Economic Development Zones (ZEDEs) which would share many of the basic guiding principles encapsulated in charter cities.

In early 2011, the same year that Romer attended a conference on the "future of free cities" in the Honduran island of Roatán, the Honduran congress amended the country's constitution to allow the development of "Model Cities" under a new law for Special Development Regions.[47] The cities would be self-governing private enclaves, with their own legal systems and laws, and the Honduran Constitution, amendments to which had made the enclaves possible in the first place, would not apply.[48] A year later, however, a majority of Supreme Court Justices rejected the Model Cities Law and the constitutional amendments that had made it possible. In response, the Honduran Congress, presided over by future president Juan Orlando Hernández, removed the four justices in the majority decision and replaced them with reliable loyalists. Illegality and intimidation worked. In March 2013 the Honduran Congress

---

45 Frank, *The Long Honduran Night*, 23.

46 See OFRANEH, "'No sé si estoy observando una farsa o una tragedia': Paul Romer en referencia a las ZEDE en Honduras," November 25, 2015, accessed June 6, 2016, https://ofraneh.wordpress.com/2015/11/25/no-se-si-estoy-observando-una-farsa-o-una-tragedia-paul-romer-en-referencia-a-las-zede-en-honduras/.

47 Geglia, "Honduras: Reinventing the Enclave," 354–55.

48 Frank, *The Long Honduran Night*, 72.

approved a reworking of the constitution in order to allow for the creation in the country of special zones such as "international financial centers, international logistical centers, [and] autonomous cities" that would be exempt from nearly all local and federal laws.[49] As few as six of the Honduran constitution's 379 articles would have to apply within a ZEDE. Neither freedom of the press nor habeas corpus would have to be guaranteed and the cities could be built in areas that were populated without the prior consent of the inhabitants.[50] Anthropologist Beth Geglia notes just how autonomous ZEDEs would be:

> The zones are entitled to their own laws, police forces, currencies, tax collection procedures, social services, and, most importantly, their own common-law courts. Quite notably, the decisions of ZEDE courts are not subject to appeal to the Honduran Supreme Court. ZEDE administrations can opt to adopt legal systems from other countries and can appoint foreign judges. According to proponents of the initiative, this important concession allows investors to bypass the corruption and instability of the national system altogether, providing ultimate investment security in an otherwise unstable political environment. However, it also allows investors to bypass national laws and escape any political reforms that may be enacted through normal democratic process.[51]

Despite significant fanfare ("Who wants to buy Honduras?" asked the *New York Times*), Hondurans were troubled. "Historically, Latin America has been a place for imported economic experiments. But experiments aren't exciting for the people who live here; it's different when it's your house that's being experimented with," commented one resident of a region in which a ZEDE was slated for development.[52] Honduras's overthrown president, Manuel Zelaya, captured the reality even more succinctly: "This is nothing more than a plan to get rid of the national debt by auctioning off the country."[53]

---

49 "Honduras: CN conoce ahora otra versión de 'ciudad modelo,'" in *El Heraldo*, Tegucigalpa, March 15, 2013. My thanks to Marc Edelman for forwarding the article to me.

50 Summarized in "Shadowy Experiment," *Economist*, August 12, 2017, 32.

51 Geglia, "Honduras: Reinventing the Enclave," 355.

52 Danielle Marie Mackey, "Charter Cities: A Dangerous U.S. Economic Experiment in Honduras," *New Republic*, December 14, 2014. See also Suyapa G. Portillo Villeda, *Roots of Resistance: A Story of Gender, Race, and Labor on the North Coast of Honduras* (Austin: University of Texas Press, 2021), 244–46.

53 Mackey, "Charter Cities." In some sense, this was a move to alienate the state itself, as Marx put it; or, to be more direct, the privatization of the state. "National debts, i.e., the alienation of the state—whether despotic, constitutional or republican—marked with its stamp the capitalistic era. The only part of the so-called national wealth that actually enters into the collective possessions of modern peoples is their national debt.... The

Everyday forms of estate formation

The rush began immediately following the coup. An array of investors look-ing for opportunities arrived in Honduras. Some pushed the possibilities of the ZEDE beyond what Romer planned for his charter cities. An accounting of some of the major figures who came through—few stayed—is revealing. The Honduran *golpistas* were joined by a contingent of US-based techno-lib-ertarians and a fairly large number of US officials who had served in the Reagan administration while it waged illegal wars in Central America, using Honduras as a staging ground. From the former there was the perennial Patri Friedman who, by this point, had moved on from the Seasteading Institute to form a new venture capitalist project, Future Cities Development Inc.[54] The purpose of FCD was to create private, new cities with their own legal systems and run as kinds of free enterprise freeports.[55] Such "start-up cities" were venture capitalism disguised as adventures in freedom. Friedman made numerous appearances in neighboring Guatemala at the Francisco Marroquín University, whose campus auditoriums and lecture halls are named in honor of Milton Friedman and Ayn Rand. The university's founder, Manuel Ayau Cordón, served twice as president of the free-market Mont Pelerin Society, the membership of which included free-market luminaries such as Mises, Hayek, and Patri's grandfather Milton. He kept less distin-guished company during his time as a member of Guatemala's right-wing paramilitary Movement for National Liberation, the self-proclaimed "party of organized violence."[56]

Along with Friedman's FCD came the Free Cities Institute, founded and directed by Michael Strong and Kevin Lyons.[57] Strong directed a nonprofit called Freedom Lights Our World—with mottos such as Peace Through Commerce and Conscious Capitalism—along with John Mackey, former CEO of Whole Foods until it was sold off to Amazon's Jeff Bezos. In both cases—FCD and FCI—the rhetoric is one of entrepreneurship, innovation, and privatization, frequently coated with a patina of Silicon Valley sloganeering

---

public debt becomes one of the most powerful levers of primitive accumulation." Marx, *Capital* vol. 1, chap. 24 (1867).

54 Steinberg et al., *Atlas Swam*, 6; Vacanti Brondo, *Land Grab*, 174.

55 Greg Lindsay, "Former 'Seasteaders' Come Ashore to Start Libertarian Utopias in Honduran Jungle," *Co-Exist*, October 31, 2011, https://www.fastcompany.com/1678720/former-seasteaders-come-ashore-to-start-libertarian-utopias-in-honduran-jungle.

56 Luis Solano, "Development and/as Dispossession: Elite Networks and Extractive Industry in the Franja Transversal del Norte," in Carlota McAllister and Diane Nelson, eds., *War by Other Means: Aftermath in Post-Genocide Guatemala* (Durham, NC: Duke University Press, 2013), 126–28; on the MLN see also Joseph and Grandin, introduction to *A Century of Revolution*.

57 Vacanti Brondo, *Land Grab*, 174–75; Geglia, "Honduras: Reinventing the Enclave," 356–57.

about "making the world a better place" while making a lot of money. Strong, grumbling about Marxist professors, insisted at the 2017 Startup Societies Foundation meeting that capitalism would save the planet and, strangely, that he was a leftist.[58] Calling himself a "radical social entrepreneur," and assigning himself the title of Chief Visionary Officer, Strong has deigned himself important enough to issue his own "law": "properly structured free enterprise always results over time in higher quality, lower cost, and more customized products and services." Advocates for ZEDEs and charter cities resort repeatedly to such opinions to make their case. Here again is Michael Strong: "Prosperous nations are prosperous in large part because they make it easy to do business. Poor countries are poor largely because they make it difficult to do business."[59] Strong and FCI got on the ground early and in 2012 began plans to build a "model city" city near the Atlantic coast city of Trujillo, plans opposed by indigenous Garifuna communities who had traditionally lived and worked in the region and who clearly understood that such projects would not benefit them.[60]

FCI's and FCD's efforts collapsed as Hernández and Lobo sorted out the judicial challenges the model cities law confronted. But with the amended constitution in place by 2013, and the ZEDEs now approvingly on the books, momentum returned, and the administration created a "Committee for the Application of Best Practices" tasked with oversight of the ZEDEs. The committee was a veritable who's who of free-market fundamentalists and Reagan-era hawks. The committee had twenty-one members, named by then-president Lobo and ratified by the Honduran Congress. Of the members, only five were Honduran, including Octavio Sánchez. Foreign members included Grover Norquist who, as founder of Americans for Tax Reform, garnered fame for foisting his infamous "no new taxes" pledge on candidates for congressional office; Mark Skousen, an economic analyst and investment specialist who advertised his services on the pages of *Soldier of Fortune* magazine, and past president of the Foundation for Economic Education; and the Cato Institute's Richard Rahn who served as vice president of the

---

58 One (admittedly unlikely) possibility for this wonky statement may be that Strong carried the same idea of an entrepreneurial, enterprising Left that French philosopher Michel Foucault articulated in his later work from the 1980s. See Dean and Zamora, *The Last Man Takes LSD*.

59 For Strong's law, see Michael Strong, "An Introduction to Strong's Law," Radical Social Entrepreneurs, November 4, 2017, http://www.radicalsocialentreps.org/2017/11/an-introduction-to-strongs-law/; for his comments on prosperity see Strong, "How Zedes Can Make Honduras Popular," Austrian Economics Center, March 27, 2015, https://www.austriancenter.com/how-zedes-can-make-honduras-prosperous/.

60 Vacanti Brondo, *Land Grab*, 174–75.

US Chamber of Commerce during the Reagan administration.[61] Another committee member was Argentine Alejandro Chafuen, the author of *Faith and Liberty* on the Christian roots of free-market ideology and mentor to the conservative Students for Liberty organization that links "antipopulist" youth in Latin America with conservative think tanks in the United States (and with whom he gathered in 2015 to support impeachment of Brazilian president Dilma Rousseff).[62] Chafuen also served as the president of the Atlas Network, a "nonprofit organization connecting a global network of more than four hundred free-market organizations in over 80 countries to the ideas and resources needed to advance the cause of liberty." Founded in 1981, Atlas was the brainchild of Antony Fisher. A former British fighter pilot, Fisher found inspiration in Hayek's *The Road to Serfdom* (or, more accurately, in the *Reader's Digest* condensed version of the book that deleted Hayek's "support for a minimum standard of living for the poor, environmental and workplace safety regulations, and price controls to prevent monopolies from taking undue profits.")[63] Fisher used his wealth acquired through chicken farming to create a number of libertarian think tanks, including the Institute for Economic Affairs and the International Center for Economic Policy Studies which would be renamed the Manhattan Institute. The documents of incorporation of the ICEPS were drawn up by William Casey, soon to become Ronald Reagan's head of the Central Intelligence Agency and an aggressive advocate for confronting alleged communist subversion in Central America, in part through arming the contra forces operating out of Honduras in efforts to undermine the elected Sandinista government in neighboring Nicaragua. In 1981 Fisher moved to San Francisco—where Chafuen had also recently arrived—and created the Atlas Network. With the arrival of Reagan and Thatcher, it was propitious timing. The foundation grew rapidly with affiliate

---

61 See Carlos Dada, "Honduras y su experimento libertario en el golfo de Fonseca," *El Faro*, April 20, 2017; Mackey, "Charter Cities"; and Lizz Gabriela Mejía, "¿Quiénes deben regular los proyectos ZEDE en Honduras?" *Contracorriente*, September 28, 2020. Skousen's *Guide to Financial Privacy* was advertised in *Soldier of Fortune* 4, no. 10 (October 1979): 2. His uncle, W. Cleon Skousen, was a well-known far-right militant in Utah who had been fired as police chief of Salt Lake City for running it "like a Gestapo," cited from Rick Perlstein, *Before the Storm: Barry Goldwater and the Unmaking of the American Consensus* (New York: Nation Books, 2009 [2001]), 122. See also Matthew Lyons, *Insurgent Supremacists: The U.S. Far Right's Challenge to State and Empire* (Oakland: PM Press/Kersplebedeb, 2018), 43.

62 "The Right's New Clothes," *Brasil Wire*, September 29, 2015; on Chafuen, see Atlas Network, accessed June 6, 2016, https://www.atlasnetwork.org/.

63 Jane Mayer, *Dark Money: The Hidden History of the Billionaires Behind the Rise of the Radical Right* (New York: Doubleday, 2016), 45; on Fisher, see Brian Doherty, *Radicals for Capitalism: A Freewheeling History of the Modern American Libertarian Movement* (New York: Public Affairs, 2007), 477–80.

think tanks popping up around the globe, and Atlas pushed to have right-wing think tanks funded in Latin America just as the Reagan administration put the region in its sights. Today, Atlas-affiliated think tanks have received funding from the US State Department and the National Endowment for Democracy, and its affiliate members populate the reactionary political ranks in countries such as Venezuela, Brazil, Chile, and Honduras.[64]

Other Reaganites worked on the projects in Honduras.[65] These included Reagan's son Michael; Loren A. Smith, a federal judge and campaign advisor to Reagan in 1976 and 1980; and Faith Ryan Whittlesey, a senior staffer in the Reagan administration who sat on the board of the Ron Paul Institute for Peace and Prosperity prior to her death. Whittlesey had links previously to Central America. In 1983 she presided over the White House Outreach Working Group on Central America, which sought to generate support in the private sector for Reagan's Central America policies and created anti-Sandinista documentaries. The assistant director of the Working Group was Mark Klugmann, who also did time as a speechwriter for Reagan and George H.W. Bush and worked as a campaign volunteer for José Piñera—military dictator Augusto Pinochet's minister of labor and architect of Chile's 1981 labor code and the privatization of its pension system—when he ran for municipal office in the 1990s.[66] Klugmann too sat on the ZEDEs committee. In fact, he claimed he came up with the original idea in 2003, saying, "[I] began to share with a few leaders in the United States and Central America my concept of LEAP zones as an accelerated path to development, an outgrowth of my work doing economic reforms."[67] His connections to Honduras and the *golpistas* ran deep. On November 29, 2005, in the immediate wake of the vote that elected Zelaya to the presidency, losing presidential candidate Porfirio Lobo showed up at the US ambassador's residence in Tegucigalpa. An embassy cable (released by Wikileaks) discussing the meeting makes it clear that the results demonstrated Zelaya had won by at least 5 percent of the vote. Yet Lobo refused to concede. Lobo's visit to the residence was intended to have been one-on-one but accompanying Lobo were a party

---

64 Lee Fang, "Sphere of Influence: How American Libertarians Are Remaking Latin American Politics," *Intercept*, August 9, 2017.

65 According to a 2014 article, nine Americans, including six former Reagan administration officials, remained deeply invested in the projects. Mackey, "Charter Cities"; Geglia, "Honduras: Reinventing the Enclave," 358.

66 "Chile's Man from Harvard Campaigns in Santiago's Harlem," *Wall Street Journal*, June 19, 1992, A11.

67 Mark Klugmann, "LEAP Zones: Faster Growth with Less Conflict," *Cayman Financial Review*, July 12, 2013.

official and Mark Klugmann, described in the cable as a political consultant. The cable continues:

> The Ambassador brought up the TSE and OAS Quick Count numbers and asked Lobo if he had any other information or statistical surveys showing that he was ahead. Lobo and his team had no reply. Ambassador emphasized that the OAS had informed the Embassy that the OAS Quick Count has been accurate all 44 times it has been employed. Lobo did say that he would not concede until enough votes had been counted. *Klugman went further, handing the Ambassador a copy of the Nationalists' talking points arguing why a Nationalist Party president would supposedly be better for the USG than a Liberal Party president.* The document is similar to previous points passed to USG officials in past meeting with the National Party. (Note: The afternoon/evening of November 28 senior National Party officials and Klugman spoke with PolChief to vehemently express their concerns that no public vote count had been released, criticizing the TSE, and encouraging the Embassy not to make what they termed any premature statement about a Zelaya victory).[68]

When Lobo assumed power after the military coup against Zelaya, Klugmann met with the new president in his office in Tegucigalpa his first week in office in order to again promote his LEAP ideas.[69] Soon after, Orange County, California, congressman Dana Rohrabacher, who had strong libertarian leanings, traveled to Honduras to meet Lobo and Hernández. Klugmann was at his side. Rohrabacher called for Hondurans to "turn the page" after the coup and to reject the establishment of a truth commission and, in private meetings, encouraged the new Honduran administration to "develop its patent and copyright framework so that there will be an incentive to innovate," such as making income "derived from patents and copyrights tax-free."[70] More recently, Trump's then secretary of state Rex Tillerson and Vice President Mike Pence traveled to Honduras to meet the newly elected president (and close ally of Lobo) Juan Orlando Hernández. Klugmann was again in attendance.[71] According to Honduran veteran journalist Carlos Dada, foreign advisors such as Klugmann (and presumably others who sit on the best practices board)

---

68 Honduran Presidential Horserace Over: Someone Please Tell the Horses—Vacuum of information/leadership. US Embassy cable, Honduras, November 29, 2005, Wikileaks ID: 05TEGUCIGALPA2411_a. My emphasis.

69 Klugmann, "LEAP Zones: Faster Growth with Less Conflict."

70 US Embassy Honduras to Central Intelligence Agency et al., February 24, 2010, Wikileaks ID: 10TEGUCIGALPA169_a.

71 Dada, "Honduras y su experimento libertario."

had significant authority to negotiate transfers of "entire zones of Honduran territory to corporations that will have their own police; in which Honduran law will not apply nor will they pay taxes applied to the rest of the territory."[72]

Another island getaway

Over the course of the 2010s ZEDES and charter cities continued to be touted, like seasteads, as just over the next horizon. But construction struggled. The various figures who had arrived in Honduras with deals and ideals—whether base or noble—seemed to have limited awareness of what they were walking into. It did not help that they tripped over one another in their eagerness to be first on the ground with design proposals, building plans, and investment portfolios. A revealing moment came in 2014 when Romer withdrew entirely from the field. The fanfare, the gushing media profiles, the promises of economic salvation ... Where did it all go? Here is Romer in a 2015 interview:

> I stopped working on a project in Honduras because a group of people there is trying to create a system that establishes a type of aristocracy that will never be subject to local electoral control. They are doing this by establishing a government board that will re-appoint its own members. It will not be subject to political control by the people in the zone, nor by the citizens of Honduras, nor even voters elsewhere as was the case in Hong Kong. They are trying to create a true aristocracy in a small group of twenty or so people, who will appoint their own replacements, and who will always be in charge.
>
> There will be no flexibility, no ability to respond to future developments. And no accountability in the event that this small circle of self-appointed aristocrats misuses their powers. A core of appointees, all from the current governing party in Honduras, controls this board. As a result, the proposal there no longer passes my test: "Would I want to live there or want my children or grandchildren to live there?" So I have refused to have any further involvement in this project.[73]

Various stakeholders contested the details. In any case, that Romer was surprised by the behavior of Honduran dynasts who had orchestrated a coup with an expectation of US complicity is revealing of just how little awareness of history and politics he and many of those involved in such projects have. It is worth taking stock of the fact of that ignorance for a moment, if for

72 Ibid.
73 Paul Romer, "Interview on Urbanization, Charter Cities and Growth Theory," March 2015, accessed June 6, 2016, https://paulromer.net/interview-on-urbanization-charter-cities-and-growth-threory/.

no other reason than it is so pervasive. A *New York Times* reporter covering Romer's projects seemed to almost revel in it: "He [Romer] eventually realized something that seems obvious to any nonacademic, that poor countries are saddled with laws and, crucially, customs that prevent new ideas from taking shape."[74] Such gush over charter cities ignored the fact that it was the Zelaya administration's new ideas, not a mangle of vague customs, that spurred a coup d'état by a group of Honduran businessmen with whom charter city advocates would soon go to work. In any case, now Romer had to confront what seems obvious to any academic: that neither the problem nor the solution are ever so simple. History matters. Not only would the Honduran people *not* benefit from some form of warmed-over modernization theory, in which problems were easily blamed on dubious notions of "customs" and national character; neither would foreign investors find a blank slate upon which to apply plans devised on a distant whiteboard or the stage of TED talk.

To his credit, Romer withdrew from Honduras. Others have doubled down and, in the process, have pushed more exclusionary projects. In early 2021 the first "free private city," built along the principles enshrined in the ZEDE platform, got underway not on the Honduran mainland but, in good libertarian exit fashion, on one of the country's islands: Roatán. The project, Roatán Próspera [RP], appears to fulfill the aspirations of many who have ventured to Honduras in recent years. Partnered with the Honduran government, the investors and residents of RP, according to an "Agreement of Coexistence," will have significant autonomy with respect to regulatory powers, system of administration, and varied legal systems from which residents and companies can choose. Laws would derive from an "open-source legal system" called Ulex created by Tom Bell and his Institute for Competitive Governance. Legal conflicts would be brought to an arbitration board. In addition, the Agreement of Coexistence is not subject to change and would be immune to the popular will. While one of the negotiators of and investors in RP, German entrepreneur Titus Gebel, compared it with building Hong Kong in the Caribbean Sea, RP goes beyond the city-state and free-port models by combining significant autonomy with the provision of "government services" by private companies on an entirely contractual basis.[75] The project, deemed a

74   Davidson, "Who Wants to Buy Honduras?"

75   "Entrepreneur Gebel Launches an Independent Private City on the Honduran Island of Roatán," *Svobospol*, May 27, 2020, https://www.svobospol.cz/2020/05/27/entrepreneur-gebel-launches-an-independent-private-city-on-the-honduran-island-of-roatan/; and Jacopo Dettoni, "Will 'Prosperity Zones' Bring Wider Benefits to Honduras?" *FDI Intelligence*, December 12, 2019, accessed December 29, 2020, https://www.fdiintelligence.com/article/76384.

"prosperity hub" by its promoters, promises to enable "entrepreneurs to solve problems structurally and responsibly for the people of Honduras and the rest of the world."[76] It also boasts a number of big names, some from libertarian circles, including architect Patrik Schumacher, senior designer at Zaha Hadid Architects. Schumacher is a self-styled anarcho-capitalist who has advocated for the privatization of public spaces and an end to social housing. "Housing for everyone," he claimed, "can only be provided by freely self-regulating and self-motivating market process."[77] The advisory board—all men—includes Schumacher; Paul Critchlow, former vice chairman of Bank of America and Merrill Lynch; Joel Bomgar, a Mississippi congressman and free-market social conservative; the consul-general for the Netherlands in Honduras; two former senior executives at the Dubai International Financial Center; and trade lawyer and lobbyist Shankar Singham, whom his supporters tout as the "brains of Brexit" while his detractors have compared him to Chauncey Gardiner, the fictional gardener played by Peter Sellers in the film *Being There* whose brief banalities are misconstrued as pieces of Zen profundity by the political class.[78] Non-Hondurans dominate the executive board and three retired Arizona Supreme Court justices oversee the arbitration board.

The project has spurred resistance. For one, and unsurprisingly, the residents of Roatán did not ask wealthy entrepreneurs from distant lands to solve their "problems." But the specifics are more revealing. In 2020, in the midst of a pandemic, local residents in Roatán learned that what had been broached with them in 2017 as a "tourism project" would in fact be something quite different: a ZEDE. Roatán's village councils and associations complained that they had been misled and that their rights had been violated because little community consultation had taken place. They worried about the possibility of being governed by foreign laws, limited in their mobility on the island, and that the directors of RP, with the support of the Honduran administration, would use Article 28 of the ZEDE law, which allows for the expropriation of property for reasons of public utility or need, to dispossess islanders as the

---

76   https://prospera.hn/platform.

77   PatrikSchumacher.com, accessed November 4, 2020, http://www.patrikschumacher.com/Texts/Libertarian%20Urban%20Planning.html; Amy Frearson, "Patrik Schumacher Calls for Social Housing and Public Space to Be Scrapped," *De Zeen*, November 18, 2016; and Oliver Wainwright, "Zaha Hadid's Successor: Scrap Art Schools, Privatise Cities and Bin Social Housing," *Guardian*, November 24, 2016.

78   Prospera, accessed December 29, 2020, https://prospera.hn/about. On Singham as the brains of Brexit, see Pippa Crerar, "Shankar Singham: Is He the Brains of Brexit?" *Guardian*, September 23, 2018; and Alex Spence, "The Definitive Story of how a Washington Lobbyist Became the 'Brexiteers' Brain,'" Buzzfeed, May 22, 2018. The quote regarding Chauncey Gardiner comes from Spence.

project expands.[79] The concerns may not be unfounded. RP CEO and former investment banker Erick Brimen has assured residents of Roatán that he will not use eminent domain to expand the "prosperity hub" onto their lands but the very fact that he assumed he, rather than the Honduran government and Honduran voters, can make such an assurance is not reassuring. RP's own website is ambiguous regarding its expansion plans. It lists phase 1 as "an initial 58-acre footprint dedicated to the first homes, entrepreneurial training, and business acceleration in Roatán Próspera. This land has been transferred into the Próspera ZEDE (Zone of Economic Development and Employment) and is ready for development." The use of the word "initial" should give one pause, as should the fact that the website goes on to list two expansion phases, already mapped out, that will result in the City of Próspera.[80] It does not help circumstances that the island has experienced conflict around property rights due to longstanding ambiguities around titles and property deeds.[81] In September 2020, Brimen went to Roatán and held a town meeting in an attempt to assuage concerns, illegally it turns out because COVID restrictions were in place and Brimen ended up in a shoving match with local police.

Seeing like a country club

Advocates of the various projects discussed in this chapter embrace the language of choice and freedom and rules. In theory, choosing to enter or exit as one wishes is a prime example of competitive governance, of people voting with their feet. By way of conclusion, I want to return to this briefly. Here is why: over the previous years, the citizens of Honduras have repeatedly expressed their desire to vote with their hands, with pens and ballots, and not with their feet. They have chosen voice, not exit. They voted with their hands in 2004, electing Zelaya to the presidency only to see him overthrown by a military coup with whom, subsequently, the champions of charter cities and free private cities chose to do business. (The Seasteading Institute hosted Honduras's illegal post-coup president on June 8, 2015, for a discussion entitled "Disrupting Democracy." Hernández withdrew at the last minute,

---

79   Organización Fraternal Negra Hondurena [OFRANEH], "El retorno del dominio de caciques europeos y reyes estadounidenses a la costa norte de Honduras," September 28. 2020, accessed December 20, 2020, https://ofraneh.wordpress.com/2020/09/28/1956/; "Lizz Gabriela Mejía, "A Micronation for Sale in Roatan," *Contracorriente*, September 27, 2020.

80   Próspera, accessed April 15, 2021, https://prospera.hn/roatan/.

81   The issue arose during a 2009 visit to Roatán by then US Ambassador Llorens. See "AMBASSADOR LLORENS MAKES FIRST VISIT TO BAY ISLANDS," Telgram US Embassy Tegucigalpa, Honduras to Bureau of Western Hemisphere Affairs et al., March 24, 2009, Wikileaks ID: 09TEGUCIGALPA203_a.

and Randolph Hencken, at the time one of the directors of the SI, apologized for what he called "some confused messaging.")[82] They voted again with their hands in 2013. Huge mobilizations by supporters of the Libertad y Refundación (LIBRE) party, which had been built out of the resistance to the 2009 coup, brought voters to the polls in support of municipal, regional and national candidates, including a female socialist candidate—Xiomara Castro de Zelaya—for the presidency. Voters were denied victory, from municipal to national levels, by various forms of fraud.[83] They voted again with their hands in 2017. Opposition candidate Salvador Nasralla had campaigned in part with the promise to put a stop to what he saw as the auctioning off of Honduran territory through the ZEDE programs. Ahead in the electoral returns, Nasralla saw his approaching victory denied through electoral fraud of the baldest kind: leading by a nearly insurmountable margin in the counted returns, Nasralla watched as the electoral computing system "went down" for a full seventy-two hours. When the system came back on line, Nasralla suddenly trailed sitting president, alleged drug trafficker, and ZEDE-backer Juan Orlando Hernández by a slim and inexplicable margin. Meanwhile, the electoral returns for local and regional elections hadn't changed at all. Despite enormous popular protest—and an unprecedented moment in which the Honduran military refused to repress protestors—the electoral fraud remained. The ZEDEs continue.

Privatized exit seems to have emerged victorious over democratic and collective voice, buoyed by a regime that, by fomenting violence and stripping social safeguards, has forcibly uprooted people and put them on the move. Opting to make the dangerous journey north, they will be undocumented and exposed to further predation through a form of exile that will make their very existence an infraction.[84] How this constitutes freedom is perplexing, to say the least. As legal theorist Leslie Green explains, rights of exit are not somehow the sine qua non of freedom: "In a free and democratic society, the basic liberties are to be respected, and the right to emigrate is no compensation if they

---

82   OFRANEH, "El retorno del dominio de caciques europeos y reyes estadounidenses"; Josh Harkinson, "Honduran President Decides That Going to an Event Called 'Disrupting Democracy' Isn't Such a Good Idea," *Mother Jones*, June 10, 2015. On the coup and historical memory, see Portillo Villeda, *Roots of Resistance*, 241–66.

83   Portillo, "Honduras," 121–22.

84   They will become, as philosopher Gregoire Chamayou, argues, people exiled from humanity and against their will, not as punishment for a crime, as was the case in bygone days, but because they themselves are the crime. Their existence is the infraction. Chamayou, *Manhunts: A Philosophical History* (Princeton, NJ: Princeton University Press, 2012), 135.

are not."[85] The right to remain, under conditions determined by democratic processes, is as important as the right to leave. In a grimly ironic inversion, migrants will end up as "extraterritorials" elsewhere, in spaces where no legal status is provided them, while in their home country from which they were forced to flee a bevy of foreign investors and settlers will create an extra-territorial space granting them extensive autonomous legal status.[86]

The knot of inequity tightens if one considers that consumer-citizen exit models ignore the structural conditions which radically constrain the possibilities available to people at given points in time. Green continues: "people may be prevented from leaving without being forbidden to leave. For example, they may be unjustly deprived of the necessary resources, and this too violates their rights of exit."[87] The right to exit may be a fundamental aspect of personal autonomy—although even that claim deserves careful consideration, as scholars Lea Ypi, Sarah Fine, and Anna Stiltz, among others, have argued—but given that the ability, as much as the right, to exit can be so severely constrained, and as much by market forces as by political ones, it calls into question what the right means in the first place.[88] And here it is worth recalling that Tiebout referred to his model as a "pure" one, more akin to a thought experiment than a blueprint for future societies, because the fact is much of the world's populace is currently denied the ability to exit or move by the very forces championed by the libertarians. "Market predation and sovereign exclusion" are complementary, philosopher Gregoire Chamayou argues.[89]

If the "free private city" of Roatán will happen is uncertain. With the remarkable electoral victory of Libre candidate Xiomara Castro, in the presidential elections of November 2021, such schemes now face an uncertain future. Echoing the voice of the populace, she has made her position clear: no more ZEDEs. But the broader point is this: any "free private city" will not be free, in the sense that one can simply opt in with one's feet but not one's wallet. It comes with a real monetary cost of investment or purchase. It will not be open to all. "There is no general right to join," writes one commentator, "and therefore probably no free, unrestricted immigration. This is not only so because a governance services fee will be levied which not everybody might

---

85 Leslie Green, "Rights of Exit," *Legal Theory* 4 (1998): 165–85, as excerpted in Alexander and Dagan, eds., *Properties of Property*, 147.

86 On the illegalization and extra-territorialization of migrants, see Chamayou, *Manhunts*, esp. chap. 5.

87 Green, "Rights of Exit," 152.

88 See Sarah Fine and Lea Ypi, eds., *Migration in Political Theory: The Ethics of Movement and Membership* (New York: Oxford University Press, 2016) and Ypi, "Justice in Migration: A Closed Borders Utopia?" *Journal of Political Philosophy* 16, no. 4 (2008): 391–418.

89 Chamayou, *Manhunts*, 141.

be able to afford, but the city might be selective and impose requirements with respect to language, skills, minimum capital endowment etc."[90] Even advocates for the idea admit that such a city would resemble less a city or country and more a private "club."

A stark conclusion. Once the sales pitches and the visioning statements, the freedom squawk, and the Ayn Rand quotes have been duly digested, we are left with a barefaced truth: "free private city" is another name for an expansive, private, exclusive country club ... in someone else's country.

---

90 Jillian Godsil, "Increasing Freedom and Prosperity by Means of Private Cities," *Liberland Press* (July 25, 2020), https://liberlandpress.com/2020/07/25/increasing-freedom-and-prosperity-by-means-of-private-cities.

EPILOGUE

The World Lies Waiting . . .

HAS PRIVATIZATION AND RADICAL INDIVIDUALISM BECOME SO HEGEMONIC THAT THE most that can be mustered as a vision of freedom (let alone a vision of the social) is an exclusionary world of private floating condos on the ocean? Of private archipelagos, with their own forms of sovereignty, in which labor an entire class of dispossessed and disenfranchised workers? Of a world in which the very wealthy, supported by public monies and buoyed by the wealth created by generations of free and unfree workers, can found a private Atlantis with no obligation to the commons from which they reaped countless benefits? A world of yet more white flight? Of yet more Randian-inspired male-dominated world-building? Of patriarchal escape, or "sEXIT," as media theorist Sarah Sharma phrases it? For the vast majority of humanity who cannot afford a seastead, a sovereign and gated home in Honduras, or a flight to and cabin on Mars, the future is the present. Planned obsolescence. A more predictable exit.[1]

To some degree the previous paragraph summarizes the world in which we already live. Disparities in wealth have grown dramatically over the previous half century; the wealthy increasingly live in their own isolated and fortified archipelagos; vast sums of public resources continue to make their way into private hands; and so forth. Neoliberalism at some level appears to have commodified governance, transforming it into governing "services" and the citizen into a consumer.[2] Yet the nation-state persists, recreated and reworked

---

1   Sarah Sharma, "Exit and the Extensions of Man," *transmediale/art & digital culture*, August 5, 2017. See also Richard Walker, *Pictures of a Gone City: Tech and the Dark Side of Prosperity in the San Francisco Bay Area* (Oakland: PM Press, 2018), 143–46; Paulina Borsook, *Cyberselfish: A Critical Romp through the Terribly Libertarian Culture of High Tech* (New York: Public Affairs, 2000), 18–19, 160–64, and 243–45.

2   See Atossa Araxia Abrahamian, *The Cosmopolites: The Coming of the Global Citizen* (New York: Columbia Global Reports, 2015), on citizenship as merchandise. For an argument that the elite should bypass citizenship entirely and instead "become a customer of government or protection service," see James Dale Davidson and Lord William Rees-Mogg, *The Sovereign Individual: How to Survive and Thrive during the Collapse of the Welfare State* (New York: Simon & Schuster, 1997), quoted passage on 373. More generally on

in the context of new paradigms and new opportunities. Neoliberalism has been a state-driven project and globalization is hardly antithetical to the interests of the nation-state. New country projects and new exit strategies are not so much challenges to the nation-state as they are joint ventures intrinsically linked to it. The possibility of reshaping and transforming the state itself is a constitutive element of recent exit plans. Such projects, moreover, continue to depend on the nation-state as a source of revenue, legitimacy, and protection. Regardless of the digital hype, exit projects seem quaintly analog in their specifics. The slogan of the Start-Up Society ("Don't Argue. Build.") may sound practical and commonsensical but surely any community they form will be just as concerned with billboards, parking, industrial-use sites, infrastructure, and so forth as any other. And that means discussion, debate, and arguments. Rather than an end to politics, libertarian exit offers a form of politics in which decision-making (zoning, entry, exit, land use, taxation, and so forth) will not vanish but rather be transferred into the hands of the small population of ultrawealthy property owners. Even then, there are no guarantees that private monarchs will not bicker, fail to achieve consensus, argue rather than build, behave poorly, and politick at every opportunity. The promotional fantasies obscure these mundane realities. What may be on offer is less a brave new future-world of possibility than an amped-up version of the most dystopic aspects of our present-day reality. The visionary in this regard is not Peter Thiel or Elon Musk or Patri Friedman but J.G. Ballard. In novels such as *Cocaine Nights* and *Super-Cannes*, Ballard paints a portrait of the ultrawealthy—flesh-and-blood embodiments of compound interest—who descend on choice pieces of extraterritorial real estate that have been developed into high-tech luxury fortresses.

> An invisible infrastructure took the place of traditional civic virtues....
> The top-drawer professionals no longer needed to devote a moment's thought to each other, and had dispensed with the checks and balances of community life. There were no town councils or magistrates' courts, no citizens' advice bureau.... Representative democracy had been replaced by the surveillance camera and the private police force.[3]

Residents inhabit a world of extravagance and luxury but soon realize it is also a space of conformity and sterility. Bored and boring, they import crime for erogenous stimulation, or they leave their confines to launch brutal attacks

---

contemporary neoliberalism, see the trenchant analysis in Mark Fisher, *Capitalist Realism: Is There No Alternative?* (Winchester, UK: Zero Books, 2010).

3   J.G. Ballard, *Super-Cannes* (London: Fourth Estate, 2014 [2000]), 38.

on local populations with impunity. The specifics may sound far-fetched, but the general picture is not: when it comes to exit it is the wider populace that will absorb the costs of elite agency.[4]

To be sure, imagined alternatives should flourish and inspire, particularly as national borders harden, right-wing populists fan the flames of nationalist mythologies and racial resentment, zealots further restrict women's rights, and monopoly capitalism exaggerates an already-grotesque disparity in wealth and power. No wonder many are compelled now, as they have been in the past, to engage in social and political experimentation. But in many instances—from the Zapatista communities of southern Mexico to the "territories in resistance" in parts of South America—these are "exile" efforts to live beyond capitalism, not just the state, and as open and autonomous communities rather than self-professed new countries. Such communities cannot dispose of or ignore the world of states and capital, nor are they free from conflict and difference. They are not intended to be. But they are built on solidarity rather than charity, cooperation rather than competition, and a striving for communal luxury rather than individual extravagance.[5] Even advocates of "exitocracy"—of a

---

4   Ballard writes fiction, but it's fiction that is all the more powerful for how closely it rubs against reality. In some existing planned communities, geographer Andy Merrifield reports, "Shopping and living spaces are so utterly flat and sterile that planners and owners ludicrously have to 'program' them for animation. Spontaneous expression is thought so unlikely in these contexts that consultants are employed to hire street musicians to perform!" Andy Merrifield, *Metromarxism*, 181. For a discussion of Ballard in relation to ideas of extraterritoriality, see Matthew Hart, *Extraterritorial: A Political Geography of Contemporary Fiction* (New York: Columbia University Press, 2020), esp. chap. 5.

5   See, among others, Andrej Grubačić and Denis O'Hearn, *Living at the Edges of Capitalism: Adventures in Exile and Mutual Aid* (Berkeley: University of California Press, 2016); Raúl Zibechi, *Territories in Resistance: A Cartography of Latin American Social Movements*, trans. Ramor Ryan (Oakland: AK Press, 2012), esp. chap. 6; Kristin Ross, *Communal Luxury: The Political Imaginary of the Paris Commune* (New York: Verso, 2015). On the new enclosures and the commons see: "New Enclosures," Midnight Notes Collective, eds., *Midnight Notes* 10 (1990); Peter Linebaugh, *Stop, Thief! The Commons, Enclosures, and Resistance* (Oakland: PM Press, 2014); and Silvia Federici, *Caliban and the Witch*. More broadly, Henri Lefebvre, *State, Space, World: Selected Essays*, eds. Neil Brenner and Stuart Elden (Minneapolis: University of Minnesota Press, 2009); Lefebvre, *Critique of Everyday Life*, 3 vols., trans. Gregory Elliott (London: Verso, 2008 [1947; 1961; 1981]); Guy Debord, *Society of the Spectacle*, trans. Donald Nicholson-Smith (New York: Zone Books, 1995 [1967]); and, more recently, scott crow, *Black Flags and Windmills: Hope, Anarchy, and the Common Ground Collective* (Oakland: PM Press, 2014). There is substantial irony in the fact that the "exile" communities at times more faithfully reflect the alleged spirit of Burning Man (even if they understandably and thankfully may know little or nothing about it) than do the libertarian exiters who cannot stop talking about it. For example, decommodification is one of the central tenets of Burning Man, yet the libertarian exiters are commodification on steroids, insisting that nothing be immune from the market, including "governing services."

government forged through individual exit and that provides an alternative to state-directed technocracy by privileging "indirect maneuvering in the private sphere, primarily but not solely by means of the exit mechanism"—are clear that before any such movement can take place there would need to be a dramatic redistribution of wealth to ensure that the choice of exit is equally available to all.[6]

There are, of course, many aspects of libertarian concern that resonate. The nation-state has been a murderous construct. But one could say the same for big business. In either case, it is hard to take the high ground in this respect if you are doing business with, say, the illegal regime that controls Honduras. It should come as no surprise that, for all their antigovernment rhetoric, contemporary exit libertarians' conceptual vocabulary often mirrors that of US officials and empire-builders who, in a 2002 National Security Strategy document, declared "freedom, democracy and free enterprise" to be the foundations of liberty.[7] Or take contemporary drug laws and penalties in the US which have been a disaster and one of a multitude of impositions on a person's liberty. Libertarians have joined others in vociferously protesting inane laws and draconian penalties. But the cold irony is that the people subjected most harshly and inequitably to US drug laws—young black men—are also those who rarely find themselves in a position to exit. The coldest irony of all is that in many cases the state has in fact abandoned them entirely *except* when it comes to persecution. Gil Scott-Heron's 1970 poem "Whitey on the Moon" is as relevant now as it was over fifty years ago, with its potent opening refrain: "A rat done bit my sister Nell/ (With Whitey on the Moon)/ Her face and arms began to swell/ (And Whitey's on the Moon)/ I can't pay no doctor bill/ (But Whitey's on the Moon)/ Ten years from now I'll be paying still/ (While Whitey's on the Moon)."[8] The only federal and state monies available

---

6   See especially Jeffrey Friedman, *Power without Knowledge: A Critique of Technocracy* (New York: Oxford University Press, 2020), esp. chap. 7. See also Leslie Green, "Rights of Exit," in Gregory Alexander and Hanoch Dagan, eds., *Properties of Property* (New York: Wolters Kluwer Law & Business, 2012), which deftly articulates the problem with flat arguments for exit or for "voting with one's feet" that do not consider the structural constraints most people face.

7   Grandin, *The Last Colonial Massacre*, xiii.

8   Gil Scott-Heron, "Whitey on the Moon." For an excellent discussion, see Andrew Russell and Lee Vinsel, "Whitey on Mars: Elon Musk and the Rise of Silicon Valley's Strange Trickle-Down Science," *Aeon*, February 1, 2017. Fifty years later medical costs skyrocket, bills still need to be paid, and an even wealthier Whitey is shooting for the moon and Mars, eager to create a new Atlantis. The latest in the Atlantis genealogy is Atlantis Sea Colony ("colonizing the ocean by providing underwater hotels, houses and habitats"), the directors of which are investigating possible colonization sites off the coast of Florida and the Caribbean. See Atlantis Sea Colony, accessed August 6, 2021, http:// atlantisseacolony.com/. As has been evident across the breadth of this book, Atlantis

seem to be not for schools, libraries, parks, homes, and the like but prisons and police. Contrary to the divinations of market theologians, the increased privatization of both of those industries has served to ratchet up rather than reduce repression. Meanwhile, "persecuted" libertarians and Silicon Valley's über-class indulge away in the Nevada desert or revel in Acapulco at what is billed as the world's "largest anarcho-capitalist conference."[9]

The promotional literature that extols free-market states, private cities, and crypto-utopias often reads less like innovation in governance and more like euphemistic cover for fairly rudimentary and age-old practices—land- and water-grabbing and real-estate speculation—albeit wrapped in the trendy language of disruption and decentralization.[10] Libertarian exit is less a rejection of the state than it is a form of arbitrage, as exiters freely admit. It is less an argument for "no state" than it is an argument for the privatization of the state; it is less a rational experiment in governance than it is an indulgent theology of the self. The sales pitch offers readers an inverted understanding of world history: what has long been identified as the central threat to working peoples' well-being (i.e., capitalist exploitation) is proffered as the solution; what has long been a fundamental cause of instability (i.e., imperialist adventurism) is now allegedly an effect; what has long constrained human freedom (i.e., private possession) is celebrated as its foundation.[11] The result of new forms

---

has been largely a space of the white colonial imaginary. For a contrasting anticolonial Atlantis, attentive to race and history, see the discussions of the work of 1990s Detroit techno-duo Drexciya who imagined a black Atlantis on the ocean floor populated by the unborn children of enslaved women who died in the Middle Passage. See Katherine McKittrick, *Dear Science and Other Stories* (Durham, NC: Duke University Press, 2021), esp. 52–57; Kodwo Eshun, "Drexciya: Fear of a Wet Planet," *Wire* 167 (January 1998): 19–20; Asad Haider, "Black Atlantis," *Viewpoint Magazine*, March 5, 2018; Nettrice R. Gaskins, "Deep Sea Dwellers: Drexciya and the Sonic Third Space," *Shima* 10, no. 2 (2016): 68–80; and Benjamin Noys, *Malign Velocities*, 53–54. More broadly, see Robin D.G. Kelley, *Freedom Dreams: The Black Radical Imagination* (Boston: Beacon Press, 2002).

9   Anarchapulco.com, accessed February 23, 2021, https://anarchapulco.com/untitled-yet/.

10 They are part of an ongoing process of what geographer David Harvey has called accumulation by dispossession: that is, processes of primitive accumulation but now unfolding in a later phase of capitalist accumulation. Harvey, "The 'New' Imperialism: Accumulation by Dispossession," *Socialist Register* 40 (2004): 74. The fact that crypto-currency utopians landed in Puerto Rico after Hurricane Maria, filled with promises of Bitcoin magic and shared prosperity, similarly points toward a historical pattern in which, in this instance, primitive accumulation is achieved through debt, and libertarian utopians can attempt to assume control of the state, a process Marx referred to as the "alienation of the state" by private interests. Jerome Roos, "The New Debt Colonies," *Viewpoint Magazine* no. 6 (February 1, 2018), https://viewpointmag.com/2018/02/01/new-debt-colonies.

11 On this last point, see Henri Lefebvre: "The important thing is not that I should become the owner of a little plot of land in the mountains, but that the mountains be open to me—for climbing or for winter sports. The same applies for the sea and the air, regions

of territorial exit will not be an opt-in borderless world of entrepreneurial abundance but a world of hardened borders, privileged excess, and collective scarcity; a world pockmarked, as novelist and political theorist China Miéville observes, with private territories "as ferociously exclusive as those of any other state, and more than most."[12] Or, just as frightening, a world composed largely of private (e)states interspersed with a smattering of crowded public enclaves.

Arguments in support of libertarian exit abound of course. Should not individuals be free to exit if they wish to do so? Self-professed seavangelists Joe Quirk and Patri Friedman make their plea: "People should be allowed to opt out of governments they didn't choose.... Seastead pioneers don't need you to vote for them. They only need you to not petition your politicians to stop them."[13] A strange plea. There are currently no laws prohibiting them from opting out, of exiting, of renouncing their citizenship.[14] They have that choice. They have chosen not to make it. They might argue that such a choice is not a choice at all, given that it would leave them vulnerable and unprotected unless they had a state within which to opt *in*. Welcome to the reality for most of the world's population which is subject to the unequal laws and coercive forces of both the state *and* the market and lacks even the most minimal of the financial and political resources necessary for exit and entrance. The coin is as tyrannical as the crown.

Exit is expensive. It has a cost not only for those who buy in but for most of the planet's population who cannot and do not. The new country projects spearheaded by Michael Oliver, John Hospers, Harry Schultz, and their allies created economic and political turmoil in the Caribbean and Oceania where colonized peoples sought to achieve the promise of independence and

---

of the world where the notion of 'private' possession becomes more or less meaningless, but whose appeal and attraction to the 'free' individual is all the more powerful because of that. In this way and in this way alone the world becomes mine, my estate, because I am a [hu]man. In this way and this way alone is the world the future of (social) man. Only in this way can the 'private' individual, the individualistic model of man, be superseded, and concrete and truly free individuality attained." Lefebvre, *Critique of Everyday Life* (vol. 1), 158.

12   China Miéville, "Floating Utopias: Freedom and Unfreedom of the Seas," in Mike Davis and Daniel Bertrand Monk, eds., *Evil Paradises: Dreamworlds of Neoliberalism* (New York: New Press, 2007).

13   Joe Quirk with Patri Friedman, *Seasteading: How Floating Nations Will Restore the Environment, Enrich the Poor, Cure the Sick, and Liberate Humanity from Politicians* (New York: Free Press, 2017), 301.

14   United Nations Universal Declaration of Human Rights (UNDHR), Article 13.2 states that "everyone has the right to leave any country, including his own," and Article 15.2 states that "no one shall be arbitrarily ... denied the right to change his nationality." As cited in Lea Ypi, "Justice in Migration: A Closed Borders Utopia?" *Journal of Political Philosophy* 16, no. 4 (2008): 391–418 (quoted text on 401).

self-determination. In our own era, the technologies used to build seasteads, power Space-X rockets, and the like are dependent on forms of human labor, extractivism and extrusionism—already radically unequally distributed in terms of health and economic impacts—which further damage the planet on which the rest of us and those who come after us need to live. Private exit outsources its expenses onto the public. The ecological and political costs of exit technologies are not externalities to the vast majority of humanity who remain. Instead, they add to the cumulative debris of the social Anthropocene that has negatively and unequally impacted working people and the poor for centuries.[15] At the same time, exit promoters benefit from taxpayer subsidies, corporate welfare, and international free trade agreements that restrict efforts at climate change mitigation.[16] Exit, in other words, is not a neutral act. Urban theorist and historian Mike Davis argues that the only realistic scenario in which climate change, for example, is addressed equitably, such that the worst consequences are not born by the poor and future generations to come, is one in which the wealthy do not have a "preferential exit option." To be clear, this is not an argument for the further hardening of national borders or the political containment of the populace or the general restriction of movement. Nor is it an argument against exit per se. The crux of the argument is not to be found in the term "exit" but in the term "preferential," which highlights the dramatic inequities in the possibilities for and the consequences of exit.[17]

---

15   Kathryn Yusoff, *A Billion Black Anthropocenes or None* (Minneapolis: University of Minnesota Press, 2018); Rob Nixon, *Slow Violence and the Environmentalism of the Poor* (Cambridge, MA: Harvard University Press, 2011); Katerina Martina Teaiwa, *Consuming Ocean Island: Stories of People and Phosphate from Banaba* (Bloomington: Indiana University Press, 2015); and Michael J. Watts, *Silent Violence: Food, Famine, and Peasantry in Northern Nigeria* (Berkeley: University of California Press, 1983).

16   On trade agreements and climate mitigation, see Naomi Klein, *This Changes Everything: Capitalism vs. the Climate* (New York: Simon & Schuster, 2014), esp. chap. 2.

17   Davis, *Old Gods, New Enigmas: Marx's Lost Theory* (London: Verso, 2018), 211. From one perspective, the idea of denying anyone an exit option may sound extreme, but the logical and moral issues involved have been carefully and powerfully argued by political philosopher Lea Ypi in her "Justice in Migration: A Closed Borders Utopia?" *Journal of Political Philosophy* 16, no. 4 (2008): 391–418. See also Anna Stiltz, "Is There an Unqualified Right to Leave?" in Sarah Fine and Lea Ypi, eds., *Migration in Political Theory: The Ethics of Movement and Membership* (New York: Oxford University Press, 2016), 57–79. And of course, as noted, much of the world's populace is already denied an exit option and not by repressive governments solely but also by the "workings" of the market. For another perspective on exit—monetary or capital exit—see Nicholas Shaxson's *Treasure Islands*, in which he poses the following question: if a country is misruled, he asks, then "why should it only be the wealthy elites who get to protect their money by going offshore? If a country has unjust laws, then providing an offshore escape route for its wealthiest and most powerful citizens is the best way to take the pressure off the only constituency with real influence for reform." Shaxson, *Treasure Islands: Uncovering the Damage of Offshore Banking and Tax Havens* (London: Palgrave Macmillan, 2011), 157.

Preferential exit, under radically unequal conditions, is not benign withdrawal in the pursuit of autonomy and self-government but a continuation of class warfare by other means.

Postscript

I wrote a good portion of this book during a pandemic. As the weeks of closures, social distancing, and death stretched into months and then into years, a flurry of articles on seasteading and ocean colonization appeared almost daily in various media outlets.[18] Were seasteads an attractive proposition in the age of pandemic, whether because islands were somehow less susceptible or because tech workers could now work remotely from any site as they wished? Was the life aquatic an answer to pandemic, as well as climate catastrophe? Would technology at last come to our rescue? It was an opportune moment for exit advocates to find a silver lining in dark times and double down on promoting disaster capitalism as libertarian salvation.[19] Hardly mentioned was that people in the US were also living in the midst of a hopeful revolt against white supremacy, police violence and brutality, and the racialized structural violence of capitalism. On this score, libertarian exit had relatively little to say. A politics of sublime indifference, as Donna Haraway puts it.[20]

---

18   For a sampling see David Ingram, "A Good Time to Live on the Ocean? 'Seasteaders' Double Down during the Pandemic," *NBC News*—Tech News, June 17, 2020; Oliver Wainwright, "Seasteading: A Vanity Project for the Rich or the Future of Humanity?" *Guardian*, June 24, 2020; Adriana Hamacher, "This Libertarian Bitcoin Trader Wants to Build a City on the Sea," *Decrypt*, June 25, 2020; Katie Canales, "Silicon Valley's Elite Wants Yet Again to Abandon Land and Live on Floating Cities in the Middle of the Ocean That Operate outside of Existing Governments," *Business Insider*, June 18, 2020; Margi Murphy, "Silicon Valley Elites Plan to Quit Terra Firma for Seasteading Communities," *Telegraph*, June 12, 2020.

19   For a critique of libertarian individualism and anti-governmentality philosophies, such as those associated with the negative biopolitics of Giorgio Agamben, with respect to the pandemic, see Benjamin Bratton, *The Revenge of the Real: Politics for a Post-pandemic World* (London: Verso, 2021).

20   Nor would one find mention of the social uprising against neoliberalism in Chile that gathered momentous force in October 2019 and led to a national vote supporting the rewriting of the 1980 constitution that had enshrined free-market dogma. Nor mention of the (eventually successful) efforts of Bolivians to vote out of office an illegal, reactionary, and racist coup regime, backed by the US. The list could go on. The point is not that libertarian exiters should have to be attentive to every social movement around the globe; rather, the point is that they are resoundingly silent when it comes to the politics of voice—and the demands of freedom and equality—in precisely the places where libertarian and neoliberal advocates have had their way for far too long. The full quote from Haraway reads: "There is a fine line between acknowledging the extent and seriousness of the troubles and succumbing to abstract futurism and its affects of sublime despair and its politics of sublime indifference." Donna Haraway, *Staying with the Trouble: Making Kin in the Chthulucene* (Durham, NC: Duke University Press, 2016), 4.

Over the course of researching and writing this book, various exit schemes have come and gone. Some died a quiet death; others imploded in spectacular fashion. Still others linger, hoping to stay viable and biding their time offering various incentives (a digital currency, a fundraising gala, competitions to find a state willing to take them, and so forth) until firmer footing can be established. The most extravagant plans have been reigned in, chastened by the world. But they will return. In the meantime, more modest, but no less unsettling, proposals arise. For example, the governor of the US state of Nevada proposed legislation that would allow tech firms to form "separate local governments" in so-called Innovation Zones. Designated an option solely for firms specializing in "blockchain, autonomous technology, the Internet of Things, robotics, artificial intelligence, wireless, biometrics and renewable resource technology," Innovation Zones would require that companies own at least seventy-eight square miles of undeveloped and uninhabited land, away from an urban center or taxed area. Companies would be permitted "to form governments carrying the same authority as counties, including the ability to impose taxes, form school districts and courts and provide government services."[21] The plans suggest something more like a company town than a libertarian country but this may be an early instance of the boomerang effect for which exiters advocated, in which global experiments such as Honduran ZEDEs, charter cities, and seasteads rebound on to domestic US political and economic ground. If these Innovation Zones do come to pass, one of the first zones is slated for construction just east of Carson City. Fifty years after Michael Oliver sought out distant archipelagos to create a new country, some preliminary and limited iteration may take root a short drive from his home.

History catches up with us. Still, the more ambitious forms of libertarian exit—new countries, seasteads, and space colonies—remain a hypothesis. Despite the expenditures of verbiage and cash, their future is uncertain, their reality still a wish. One thing, however, is certain: as the histories recounted in this book can attest, "between the wish and the thing the world lies waiting."[22]

---

21 "Nevada Bill Would Allow Tech Companies to Create Governments," *AP News* (February 4, 2021) https://apnews.com/article/legislature-legislation-local-governments-nevada-economy-2fa79128a7bf41073c1e9102e8a0e5f0.

22 Cormac McCarthy, *All the Pretty Horses* (New York: Alfred A. Knopf, 1992), 238.

Acknowledgments

ALL BOOKS ARE A STRUGGLE TO WRITE. THIS ONE WAS NO DIFFERENT AND I STRUGGLED to strike a balance between critique and comprehension. One strives to be objective as determined by the epistemological standards of one's discipline, but that is not the same as neutrality nor is it a call for one to withhold judgment. E.P. Thompson, in his vigorous and invigorating critique of philosopher Louis Althusser and his equally vigorous and invigorating defense of empiricism and humanism, argued that "while we may not attribute value to process, the same objections do not arise with the same force when we are considering the choices of individuals, whose acts and intentions may certainly be judged (as they were judged by contemporaries) within the due and relevant historical context."

> Only we, who are now living, can give a "meaning" to the past. But that past has always been, among other things, the result of an argument about values. In recovering that process, in showing how causation actually eventuated, we must, insofar as the discipline can enforce, hold our own values in abeyance. But once this history has been recovered, we are at liberty to offer our judgment upon it.[1]

We are at liberty to offer our judgment, of acts and intentions, in their context. To put it in a libertarian idiom, we are free to offer our judgment of the choices our subjects make. When confronted with a range of possible choices, what choices does one make? And why? The effect on others of such choices is in part (in large part?) the basis of how they might be judged. When philosopher Jean-Paul Sartre argued that "man is condemned to be free," this is what I take him to have meant: free to make choices (as determined by the constraints into which we are born) but choices that will invariably impact others and thus their

---

1   E.P. Thompson, *The Poverty of Theory & Other Essays* (London: Merlin Press, 1978), 234.

freedom and well-being.[2] In which case the choices you make, your practice of freedom, is never yours alone. And it is on that basis—that of cause and effect, not solely intentionality—that one evaluates, critiques and, yes, offers judgment. Freedom is not a place, or the result of technology, or an individual achievement, or something defined via private contract and exchange. It is a social condition inextricably linked to the material and imaginative lives and needs and desires and hopes and dreams of others. We are social beings. We are condemned to be free. From that obligation, there is no exit.

I am indebted to many archivists and librarians: Augustine Tevimule and Anne Naupa (National Archive of Vanuatu); Margaret Kailo (National Library of Vanuatu); Heather Furnas, Tony del Plato, Virginia Cole, and the Interlibrary Loan staff at Cornell University's Olin Library; Bill Landis and James Kessenides (Yale's Sterling Memorial Library Manuscripts and Archives); the staff at the Harry Ransom Humanities Center at the University of Texas at Austin; Kathy Lafferty (University of Kansas Spencer Research Library); and Stuart Dawrs and Eleanor Kleiber (University of Hawai'i Pacific Islands Collection). My thanks to Don Paterson and Robert Early at University of South Pacific Emalus Campus, Port Vila, Vanuatu, for reading suggestions (and kava), and to Tēvita O. Ka'ili at Brigham Young University–Hawai'i for sharing insights into the poetry of Hau'ofa and Queen Sālote. I am particularly grateful to Jennifer Kalpokas Doan, Epeli Hau'ofa, and Viran Molisa Trief, who each provided me kind permission to reproduce poems by their family members, and to Greg Rawlings, Jenny Bryant-Tokalau, Howard van Trease, and Seona Smiles for putting me in touch with Jennifer, Epeli, and Viran.

Several people closely linked to the protagonists in this book were very generous with their time, their memories, and their archives. I am particularly grateful to Andrew Szentgyorgyi who shared his documents, photographs, and memories and also read and commented on chapter three and then, subsequently, read the entire manuscript. Lily Guerra put me in touch with Andrew, for which I am very grateful. My thanks to Howard van Trease who helped get me access to the papers of Gordon Haines in Vanuatu, read and commented on chapter four, and shared his own memories of Vanuatu and the Santo rebellion. And I thank Michael Oliver for speaking with me. In the course of researching this book, I took a chance and called a number I had found and left a message on the machine that answered. I did not expect to hear

---

2   I am indebted to the astute reading of Sartre's *No Exit* by Matt Hanson, "The Staying Power of Sartre's *No Exit*," *American Interest*, October 19, 2019, https://www.the-american-interest.com/2019/10/19/the-staying-power-of-sartres-no-exit.

back. Yet twenty minutes later, Oliver returned my call. He understood pretty quickly that we did not share similar perspectives on many things (something confirmed for him after our call when he looked up my profile), yet he spoke with me then, and in a subsequent phone call, for some time and on a range of topics. I have not included material from those conversations in this book—they were conversations, not interviews—but they did help me understand Oliver and his projects better. I am grateful to him for returning my initial call.

The financial support for my research came from various departments, programs, and offices at Cornell University, including the Institute for the Social Sciences Contested Global Landscapes theme project (led by my colleagues Wendy Wolford and Chuck Geisler) and the ISS small grant program; the Society for the Humanities; the College of Arts & Sciences Dean's Fund; the Department of History; and the Latin American Studies Program. Many thanks to audiences and fellow panelists at the various places where parts of this work have been presented: the European Social Science History Conference in Belfast; the World Society, Planetary Natures: Crisis and Sustainability in the Capitalocene and Beyond conference at Binghamton University; the Exile and Enclosure conference at Cornell University; the 2017 International Conference of Anarchist Geographies and Geographers held at the Cucino del Popolo in Massenzatico Italy; the Cornell University Summer Institute on Land; and the Cornell History Department colloquium. I am grateful to kind invitations to present on my research from K. Sivaramakrishnan and Jim Scott at Yale's Program in Agrarian Studies; Matt Evangelista at Cornell University's Judith Reppy Institute for Peace and Conflict Studies; Marcella Hayes at the Harvard Graduate Student Association; Jadwiga Pieper and Celeste Bustamante for the Border Crossings: Gender, Sexuality, and Rights conference at the University of Arizona; Alejandra Bronfman and Alexander Dawson at the University of Albany; Steve Hirsch at Washington University St. Louis; Amie Campos and Kevan Aguilar for the Geography Working Group at the University of California–San Diego; Kari Soriano Salkjelsvik at the University of Bergen and Oda Sortland at the University of Bergen Student Society; Miriam Bodian at the Institute for Historical Research at the University of Texas at Austin; Denis O'Hearn at the Fernand Braudel Center at Binghamton University; and Daniel Marshall at the Cornell Telluride Association House. Preliminary excursions into this material appeared in the exhibition "Contingency Plans: Or, Living with Unstable Grounds," curated by Adam Bobbette and Daan Roggeveen at the University of Hong Kong Shanghai Study Center and, with the support of Jeffrey St. Clair, in *Counterpunch* (August 2018).

Many thanks to colleagues and friends who have shared comments, critiques, and suggestions. Given how far afield most of this material is from my own training as a Latin Americanist, I am even more grateful for their patience and indulgence. Huge thanks to Kyle Harvey, Susana Romero Sánchez, Geoffroy de LaForcade, Daviken Studnicki-Gizbert, Cynthia Brock, Ronen Palan, and J. Kēhaulani Kauanui who read the entire manuscript and offered important critiques and ideas. Penultimate chapter drafts benefitted from close readings by Larry Glickman, Julilly Kohler-Hausmann, Ernesto Bassi, María Cristina García, Howard van Trease, Ken Roberts, Suyapa Portillo, Russell Rickford, Robert Travers, Josh Savala, Daniela Samur, Ryan Edwards, Andrew Szentgyorgyi, Raymond Craib (the elder), and Julie Craib. I have benefitted from comments, suggestions, and critiques from Denis O'Hearn, Andrej Grubačić, Tamara Loos, Eric Tagliacozzo, Durba Ghosh, Judi Byfield, Suman Seth, Jenny Mann, Amie Campos, Spencer Beswick, Manuel Berduc, Nick Myers, Sebastian Díaz Angel, Nate Norris, Kevan Aguilar, Jim Scott, Claudia Verhoeven, Jomarie Alano, David Hanlon, Paul Nadasdy, Ana Maria Candela, Wendy Wolford, Penny Von Eschen, Kevin Gaines, Derek Chang, Steven Wolf, Fernando Galeana, Esra Akcan, Aaron Sachs, Alberto Harambour, Ed Baptist, Olga Litvak, Pablo Abufom, Nick Mulder, Barry Strauss, Paulo Drinot, Rachel Weil, Ian Merkel, Gil Joseph, Barbara Weinstein, Finn Brunton, Stefan Huebner, Kirsten Weld, Jeff Gould, Adina Berk, Neema Kudva, Sara Pritchard, Willie Lee Hiatt, Marc Edelman, Debjani Battachayrra, Lilly Irani, Wendy Matsamura, my colleagues in the New Enclosures working group (in particular Fouad Makki, Barry Maxwell, Chuck Geisler, Kasia Paprocki, Phil McMichael, and Onur Ulas Ince) and my Society for the Humanities Manuscript group (Simone Pinet, Saida Hodžić, Marina Welker and Jessica Cooper). And last but not least, my thanks to Suman Seth for reading this, with always a sharp eye and a generous soul, when I really needed it.

It has been a joy working with PM Press (thanks to John Yates, Brian Layng, Cara Hoffman, Stephanie Pasvankias, Steven Stothard, Joey Paxman, Gregory Nipper, Dan Fedorenko, and Jonathan Rowland), and I am honored that the book is a part of the Spectre series. Ramsey Kanaan and Sasha Lilley have been supportive of this project from the very beginning and have worked hard to ensure my vision of it came to fruition. I am especially indebted to Sasha, who read the manuscript multiple times and whose detailed comments, generous ruminations, and gentle nudgings have made it a much, much better book. My gratitude to Stiller Zusman, whose archipelagic artwork (*Traveler Sweeps*) graces the cover. The excellent maps were made on short notice by John Wyatt Greenlee, a historian whose superb, *longue durée* history of eels hopefully will be published soon. Big thanks to Andy Schultze and Vicky Victoria for the quiet writing space and nightly decompression at the Fox & Hounds in DC that got me over the hump in my writing; and to Suman

Seth, Amber Lia-Kloppel, Leonardo Vargas-Méndez, Lourdes Cabrera, Tamara Loos, Neema Kudva, Eric Tagliacozzo, Robert Travers, and Durba Ghosh for friendship and camaraderie and conversation through the years. Politics is as much labor as it is imagination, and I have been inspired now for more than decade by the relentless commitment and work of my partner Cynthia Brock, and by our three children who inhabit the world with immense generosity of spirit. This book is for my sister Linda and for my two dear friends—Andrew "Big Andy" Schultze and Gary "Twisted" Sisto—for decades of sisterly and brotherly love.

Bibliography

Archives
National Archives of the United Kingdom
    Foreign Colonial Office records
National Archives of Vanuatu
    Gordon Haines papers
    Supreme Court records
    Land records
    General collection
National Library of Vanuatu
    Newspaper collection
University of Hawai'i at Manoa
    Pacific Islands Collections
University of Texas at Austin H. Ransom Center
    Leicester Hemingway Collection
Yale University Manuscripts and Archives
    Andrew St. George papers

Archives accessed digitally
Australian National University (Pacific Manuscripts Bureau)
    Colin Allan Collection, Papers on the Solomon Islands and Vanuatu
Office of Strategic Services Personnel Files
    World War II, Records Group 226
San Francisco Maritime National Historical Park Library
Texas Tech University Vietnam Center and the Sam Johnson Vietnam Archive
    Ogden Williams Collection
United Nations Archives
United States Holocaust Memorial Museum
    Arlosen Archives
University of Connecticut Library
    Archives & Special Collections, Thomas J. Dodd Research Center

Government documents
Commission on Marine Science, Engineering and Resources. *Our Nation and the Sea: A Plan for National Action*. Washington, DC: United States Government Printing Office, 1969.
Tonga Government Gazette Extraordinary no. 7 (June 15, 1972).
Tonga Government Gazette no. 11 (September 29, 1972).
Tonga Government Gazette Supplement no. 8 (October 31, 1972).
United Nations Convention on the Law of the Sea (1982). https://www.un.org/depts/los/convention_agreements/texts/unclos/unclos_e.pdf.

US Congress. House of Representatives, Special Subcommittee on Investigations, Committee on Interstate and Foreign Commerce, July 17, 1969. *Network News Documentary Practices—CBS "Project Nassau."* Washington, DC: US Government Printing Office, 1970.

US Congress. The Robert Vesco Investigation. Hearings before the Permanent Subcommittee on Investigations of the Committee on Government Operations (United States Senate) (July 17, September 17, and October 7, 1974).

US Department of State, Bureau of Intelligence and Research, Office of the Geographer, "National Claims to Maritime Jurisdiction," Limits in the Seas, no. 36, 5th Revision. Washington, DC, 1985.

US Federal Bureau of Investigation files provided through Freedom of Information Act requests
FOIA 1350966 (Subject: Mitchell Werbell)
FOIA 1400082 (Subject: Andrew St. George)
FOIA 1421912 (Subject: Edwin Marger)

Periodicals and Newspapers

Abaco Account
Afghanistan Council Newsletter
Atlanta Journal and Constitution
Atlantis News
Brasil Wire
The Bulletin (Sydney, Australia)
Canberra Times
Capitalist Country Newsletter
Contracorriente (Honduras)
Daily Mail
Daily Telegraph
Dutch Australian Weekly
The Economist
El Faro (Honduras)
El Heraldo (Tegucigalpa, Honduras)
Esquire: The Magazine for Men
Fiji Times
Formulations: A Publication of the Free Nation Foundation
The Freeman
The Guardian
Huffington Post
Innovator
Libertarian Forum
Libertarian Review
M. Oliver Newsletter
Miami Herald
Nabanga (Vanuatu)
Nakamal (Vanuatu)
The Nation
New York Times
New Zealand Herald
Pacific Islands Monthly
Papua New Guinea Post-Courier
People
Phoenix Foundation Bulletin
Playboy
Reason

San Francisco Chronicle
Scanlan's
SF Gate
Small Arms Review
Smithsonian
Soldier of Fortune
Sydney Morning Herald
Tribune (Nassau, The Bahamas)
True Magazine
Vanuatu Daily Post
Voice of the New Hebrides
Wall Street Journal
Washington Post

Secondary Sources

Abrahamian, Atossa Araxia. *The Cosmopolites: The Coming of the Global Citizen.* New York: Columbia Global Reports, 2015.

Abrahamian, Atossa. "Seasteading." *N+1.* June 5, 2013. https://nplusonemag.com/online-only/online-only/seasteading/.

Agnew, Jean-Cristophe. *Worlds Apart: The Market and the Theater in Anglo-American Thought.* Cambridge: Cambridge University Press, 1988.

Ahmad, Aijaz. *In Theory: Classes, Nations, Literatures.* London: Verso, 1992.

Aldrich, Robert. *France and the South Pacific since 1940.* Honolulu: University of Hawaii Press, 1993.

Alexander, Gregory, and Hanoch Dagan, eds. *Properties of Property.* New York: Wolters Kluwer Law & Business, 2012.

Andersson, Anthony. "Green Guerrillas and Counterinsurgent Environmentalists in the Petén, Guatemala." *Global Environment: A Journal of Transdisciplinary History* 14, no. 1 (2021): 15–57.

Angle, Sharron. Angle, *Right Angle: One Woman's Journey to Reclaim the Constitution.* Bloomington, IN: AuthorHouse, 2011.

Anker, Peder. "The Ecological Colonization of Space." *Environmental History* 10 (April 2005): 239–68.

Anonymous. *Guns for Hire: How the C.I.A. & the U.S. Army Recruit Mercenaries for White Rhodesia.* Montreal: Kersplebedeb, 1977.

Armstrong Hackler, Rhoda Elizabeth. "Our Men in the Pacific: A Chronicle of United States Consular Officers at Seven Ports in the Pacific Islands and Australasia during the 19th Century." PhD dissertation, University of Hawai'i, 1978.

Baker, Chris. "Live Free or Drown: Floating Utopias on the Cheap." *Wired,* January 19, 2009.

Ballard, J.G. *Cocaine Nights.* Berkeley: Counterpoint, 1998 [1996].

———. *Super-Cannes.* London: Fourth Estate, 2014 [2000].

Balloun, O. Shane. "The True Obstacle to the Autonomy of Seasteads: American Law Enforcement Jurisdiction over Homesteads on the High Seas." *University of San Francisco Maritime Law Journal* 24, no. 409 (2012): 410–64.

Banivanua Mar, Tracey. *Decolonisation and the Pacific: Indigenous Globalisation and the Ends of Empire.* Cambridge: Cambridge University Press, 2016.

Baptist, Edward. *The Half Has Never Been Told: Slavery and the Making of American Capitalism.* New York: Basic Books, 2014.

Barahona, Marvin. "Auge y Decadencia de la Ideologia de la Desigualdad: Un Cuestionamiento Necesario a la Hegemonía Neoliberal." In Joaquín A. Mejía R., coord., *Estado, Despojo y Derechos Humanos.* El Progreso: ERIC-SJ, 2019.

Barley, Nigel. *White Rajah: A Biography of Sir James Brooke.* Boston: Little Brown, 2002.

Bassi, Ernesto. *An Aqueous Territory: Sailor Geographies and New Granada's Transimperial Greater Caribbean World.* Durham, NC: Duke University Press, 2017.

————. "Small Islands in a Geopolitically Unstable Caribbean World." *Oxford Research Encyclopedia: Latin American History*, March 2019.

Bayer, Osvaldo. *La Patagonia Rebelde*. Buenos Aires: Planeta, 1980. Published in English as *Rebellion in Patagonia*. Translated by Paul Sharkey and Joshua Neuhouser. Chico, CA: AK Press, 2016.

Bays, Peter. *A Narrative of the Wreck of the Minerva*. Cambridge: B. Bridges, 1831.

Beasant, John. *The Santo Rebellion: An Imperial Reckoning*. Honolulu: University of Hawai'i Press, 1984.

Belew, Kathleen. *Bring the War Home: The White Power Movement and Paramilitary America*. Cambridge, MA: Harvard University Press, 2018.

Bell, Stewart. *Bayou of Pigs: The True Story of an Audacious Plot to Turn a Tropical Island into a Criminal Paradise*. New York: HarperCollins, 2008.

Bell, Tom W. "What Is Polycentric Law?" *Freeman*, February 24, 2014. http://fee.org/freeman/detail/what-is-polycentric-law.

————. *Your Next Government? From Nation-States to Stateless Nations*. Cambridge: Cambridge University Press, 2017.

Benton, Lauren. *The Search for Sovereignty: Law and Geography in European Empires, 1400–1900*. Cambridge: Cambridge University Press, 2010.

Berneri, Marie Louise. *Journey through Utopia: A Critical Examination of Imagined Worlds in Western Literature*. Oakland: PM Press, 2019 [1950].

Bey, Hakim. *Immediatism*. Oakland: AK Press, 1994.

————. *T.A.Z.: The Temporary Autonomous Zone, Ontological Anarchy, Poetic Terrorism*. Brooklyn: Autonomedia, 1991.

Bhatt, Keane. "Reporting on Romer's Charter Cities: How the Media Sanitize Honduras's Brutal Regime." *NACLA Report on the Americas* 45 (Winter 2012): 88–90.

Birchall, Matthew. "History, Sovereignty, Capital: Company Colonization in South Australia and New Zealand." *Journal of Global History* 16, no. 1 (March 2021): 141–57.

Black, Megan. *The Global Interior: Mineral Frontiers and American Power*. Cambridge, MA: Harvard University Press, 2018.

Block, Alan A. *Masters of Paradise: Organised Crime and the Internal Revenue Service in the Bahamas*. New York: Routledge, 1991.

Boaz, David. *The Libertarian Reader: Classic & Contemporary Writings from Lao-Tzu to Milton Friedman*. New York: Simon & Schuster, 2015.

Bonilla, Yarimar. *Non-Sovereign Futures: French Caribbean Politics in the Wake of Disenchantment*. Chicago: University of Chicago Press, 2015.

Bonilla, Yarimar, and Marisol LeBrón. *Aftershocks of Disaster: Puerto Rico Before and After the Storm*. Chicago: Haymarket Books, 2019.

Bookchin, Murray. *Post-Scarcity Anarchism*. Berkeley, CA: Ramparts Press, 1971.

————. *Social Anarchism or Lifestyle Anarchism: An Unbridgeable Chasm*. Oakland: AK Press, 1995.

Borders, Max. "A Little Rebellion Now and Then Is a Good Thing." *Cato Unbound: A Journal of Debate*, August 2020. https://www.cato-unbound.org/2020/08/21/max-borders/little-rebellion-now-then-good-thing.

Borsook, Paulina. *Cyberselfish: A Critical Romp through the Terribly Libertarian Culture of High Tech*. New York: Public Affairs, 2000.

Bradbury, Ray. *The Martian Chronicles*. New York: Simon & Schuster, 2012 [1945].

Bratton, Benjamin. *The Revenge of the Real: Politics for a Post-Pandemic World*. London: Verso, 2021.

————. *The Stack: On Software and Sovereignty*. Cambridge: MIT Press, 2015.

Brenner, Robert. "The Origins of Capitalist Development: A Critique of Neo-Smithian Marxism." *New Left Review* 104 (July–August 1977): 25–92.

Bresnihan, Brian J., and Keith Woodward, eds., *Tufala Gavman: Reminiscences from the Anglo-French Condominium of the New Hebrides*. Suva, Fiji: Institute of Pacific Studies, 2002.

Brondo, Keri Vacanti. *Land Grab: Green Neoliberalism, Gender, and Garifuna Resistance in Honduras*. Tucson: University of Arizona Press, 2013.

Brown, Matthew. "Inca, Sailor, Soldier, King: Gregor MacGregor and the Early Nineteenth-Century Caribbean." *Bulletin of Latin American Research* 24, no. 1 (2005): 44–70.

Brown, Wendy. *Undoing the Demos: Neoliberalism's Stealth Revolution*. Boston: Zone Books, 2016.

Browne, Harry. *How I Found Freedom in an Unfree World: A Handbook of Personal Liberty*. n.p., 1973.

Brunton, Finn. *Digital Cash: The Unknown History of the Anarchists, Utopians, and Technologists Who Create Cryptocurrency*. Princeton, NJ: Princeton University Press, 2019.

Bryan, Joe, and Denis Wood. *Weaponizing Maps: Indigenous Peoples and Counterinsurgency in the Americas*. New York: The Guilford Press, 2015.

Bryant-Tokalau, Jenny. *Indigenous Pacific Approaches to Climate Change: Pacific Island Countries*. London: Palgrave Macmillan, 2018.

Buck, Sir Peter (Te Rangi Hiroa). *Vikings of the Sunrise*. Christchurch, NZ: Whitcombe and Tombs, 1964 [1938].

Burgin, Angus. *The Great Persuasion: Reinventing Free Markets since the Great Depression*. Cambridge, MA: Harvard University Press, 2012.

Burke, Kyle. *Revolutionaries for the Right: Anticommunist Internationalism and Paramilitary Warfare in the Cold War*. Chapel Hill: University of North Carolina Press, 2018.

Burns, Jennifer. *Goddess of the Market: Ayn Rand and the American Right*. New York: Oxford University Press, 2009.

Cain, P.J., and A.G. Hopkins. *British Imperialism, 1688–2000*. 2nd ed. London: Longman, 2002.

Campbell, I.C. *Island Kingdom: Tonga Ancient and Modern*. 2nd rev. ed. Christchurch, NZ: University of Canterbury Press, 2001 [1992].

Campling, Liam, and Alejandro Colás. "Capitalism and the Sea: Sovereignty, Territory and Appropriation in the Global Ocean." *Environment and Planning D: Society and Space* 36, no. 4 (2018): 776–94.

———. *Capitalism and the Sea: The Maritime Factor in the Making of the Modern World*. London: Verso, 2021.

Cardoso, Fernando Henrique, and Enzo Faletto. *Dependency and Development in Latin America*. Berkeley: University of California Press, 1979.

Chakrabarty, Dipesh. "The Climate of History: Four Theses." *Critical Inquiry* 35 (Winter 2009): 197–222.

Chamayou, Grégoire. *Manhunts: A Philosophical History*. Princeton, NJ: Princeton University Press, 2012.

———. *La Société Ingouvernable: Une Généalogie du Libéralisme Autoritaire*. Paris: La Fabrique Editions, 2018.

Chang, David. *The World and All the Things upon It: Native Hawaiian Geographies of Exploration*. Minneapolis: University of Minnesota Press, 2016.

Chappell, David. *Double Ghosts: Oceanian Voyagers on Euroamerican Ships*. New York: Routledge, 2015 [1997].

"Charter Cities: Q&A with Paul Romer." Center for Global Development, May 3, 2010, http://www.cgdev.org//article/charter-cities-qa-paul-romer.

Chatwin, Bruce. *In Patagonia*. London: Penguin Classics, 2003 [1977].

Clastres, Pierre. *Society Against the State: Essays in Political Anthropology*, trans. Robert Hurley. New York: Zone Books, 1989.

Clavel, Damian. "What's in a Fraud? The Many Worlds of Gregor MacGregor, 1817–1824." *Enterprise & Society: First View* (2020): 1–40.

Coates, Ta-Nehisi. "The Case for Reparations." *The Atlantic* (June 2014).

Cochran, David. *American Noir: Underground Writers and Filmmakers of the Postwar Era*. Washington, DC: Smithsonian Books, 2000.

Cockburn, Alexander. "The First Fifty Years of James Bond." *Counterpunch*, October 30, 2020 (2004). https://www.counterpunch.org/2020/10/30/the-first-50-years-of-james-bond/.

Coontz, Stephanie. *The Way We Never Were: American Families and the Nostalgia Trap.* 2nd ed. New York: Basic Books, 2016.

Cooper, Melinda. "Neoliberalism's Family Values: Welfare, Human Capital, and Kinship." In Dieter Plehwe, Quinn Slobodian, and Philip Mirowski, eds., *Nine Lives of Neoliberalism.* London: Verso, 2020.

Corris, Peter. *Passage, Port and Plantation: A History of Solomon Islands Labour Migration, 1870–1914.* Melbourne: Melbourne University Press, 1973.

Cowen, Tyler. "Why Does Freedom Wax and Wane? Some Research Questions in Social Change and Big Government." Mercatus Center, George Mason University, 2000. https://www.mercatus.org/system/files/Why%20Does%20Freedom%20Wax%20and%20Wane.pdf.

Craib, Raymond. *Cartographic Mexico: A History of State Fixations and Fugitive Landscapes.* Durham, NC: Duke University Press, 2004.

———. "Cartography and Decolonization." In James Akerman, ed., *Decolonizing the Map: Cartography from Colony to Nation* (Chicago: University of Chicago Press, 2017), 11–71.

———. "The Properties of Counterinsurgency." *Dialogues in Human Geography* 4, no. 1 (March 2014): 86–91.

Crane, Ralph, and Lisa Fletcher, *Island Genres, Genre Islands: Conceptualisation and Representation in Popular Fiction.* London: Rowman & Littlefield, 2017.

Craton, Michael, and Gail Saunders, *Islanders in the Stream: A History of the Bahamian People.* Athens, GA: University of Georgia Press, 1998.

Crocombe, R.G. *The Pacific Islands and the USA.* Honolulu: East-West Center Pacific Islands Development Program, 1995.

crow, scott. *Black Flags and Windmills: Hope, Anarchy, and the Common Ground Collective.* 2nd ed. Oakland: PM Press, 2014.

Curry, Christopher. *Freedom and Resistance: A Social History of Black Loyalists in the Bahamas.* Gainesville: University Press of Florida, 2017.

Curtis, Adam. "The Use and Abuse of Vegetational Concepts." *All Watched Over by Machines of Loving Grace,* Episode 2. May 2011. BBC Two.

Daddis, Gregory A. *Pulp Vietnam: War and Gender in Cold War Men's Adventure Magazines.* Cambridge, MA: Cambridge University Press, 2020.

D'Arcy, Paul. *The People of the Sea: Environment, Identity, and History in Oceania.* Honolulu: University of Hawai'i Press, 2006.

Davidson, James Dale, and Lord William Rees-Mogg, *The Sovereign Individual: How to Survive and Thrive During the Collapse of the Welfare State.* New York: Simon & Schuster, 1997.

Davis, Mike. *City of Quartz: Excavating the Future in Los Angeles.* New York: Vintage, 1992 [1990].

———. "Living on the Ice Shelf: Humanity's Meltdown," 2008. http://www.tomdispatch.com/post/174949.

———. *Old Gods, New Enigmas: Marx's Lost Theory.* London: Verso, 2018.

Dean, Mitchell, and Daniel Zamora, *The Last Man Takes LSD: Foucault and the End of Revolution.* London: Verso, 2021.

Debord, Guy. *Society of the Spectacle.* Translated by Donald Nicholson-Smith. New York: Zone Books, 1995 [1967].

Deese, R.S. *Climate Change and the Future of Democracy.* Cham, Switzerland: Springer, 2019.

Delaney, David. *Territory: A Short Introduction.* Oxford: Blackwell, 2005.

DeLillo, Don. *Zero K.* New York: Scribner, 2016.

DeLoughrey, Elizabeth. *Routes and Roots: Navigating Caribbean and Pacific Island Literatures.* Honolulu: University of Hawai'i Press, 2007.

Demos, T.J. *Decolonizing Nature: Contemporary Art and the Politics of Ecology.* Berlin: Sternberg Press, 2016.

de Soto, Hernando. *The Mystery of Capital: Why Capitalism Triumphs in the West and Fails Everywhere Else.* New York: Basic Books, 2000.

————. *The Other Path: The Invisible Revolution in the Third World.* New York: HarperCollins, 1989.

Deudney, Daniel. *Dark Skies: Space Expansion, Planetary Geopolitics, and the Ends of Humanity.* New York: Oxford University Press, 2020.

Diamond, Jared. *Collapse: How Societies Choose to Fail or Succeed.* New York: Penguin, 2005.

Didion, Joan. *We Tell Ourselves Stories in Order to Live: Collected Nonfiction.* New York: Alfred Knopf, 2006.

Doctorow, Cory. *Walkaway.* New York: Tor Books, 2017.

Dodge, Steve. "Independence and Separatism." In Dean Collingwood and Steve Dodge, eds., *Modern Bahamian Society.* Parkersburg, IA: Caribbean Books, 1989.

Doherty, Brian. *Radicals for Capitalism: A Freewheeling History of the Modern American Libertarian Movement.* New York: Public Affairs, 2007.

Duara, Prasenjit. "The Decolonization of Asia and Africa in the Twentieth Century." In Prasenjit Duara, ed., *Decolonization: Rewriting Histories.* New York: Routledge, 2004.

Duffy Burnett, Christina. "The Edges of Empire and the Limits of Sovereignty: American Guano Islands." *American Quarterly* 57: 3 (September 2005): 779–803.

Duffy Burnett, Christina, and Burke Marshall, eds., *Foreign in a Domestic Sense: Puerto Rico, American Expansion, and the Constitution.* Durham, NC: Duke University Press, 2001.

Duggan, Lisa. *Mean Girl: Ayn Rand and the Culture of Greed.* Berkeley: University of California Press, 2019.

Dunkerley, James. *Crusoe and His Consequences.* New York: OR Books, 2019.

During, Simon. "Empire's Present." *New Literary History* 43, no. 2 (Spring 2012): 331–40.

Easterling, Keller. *Extrastatecraft: The Power of Infrastructure Space.* London: Verso, 2016.

Ehrlich, Paul, and Anne Ehrlich, *The Population Bomb.* New York: Ballantine Books, 1968.

Ellroy, James. *Underworld U.S.A. Trilogy,* vol. 1: *American Tabloid* and *The Cold Six Thousand;* vol. 2: *Blood's a Rover.* New York: Everyman's Library Contemporary Classics, 2019.

Eringer, Robert. "Interview with the Anti-Terrorist." *Saga Magazine.* http://www. atomiclabrat.com/MAC%20Pages%20for%20Atomic%20Lab%20Rat.com/WerBell_ Interview_SAGA_86%5B1%5D.pdf.

Escobar, Arturo. *Encountering Development: The Making and Unmaking of the Third World.* Princeton, NJ: Princeton University Press, 2011.

Eshun, Kodwo. "Drexciya: Fear of a Wet Planet." *Wire* 167 (January 1998): 19–20. https://web. archive.org/web/20130121213605/https://www.thewire.co.uk/in-writing/essays/ drexciya_fear-ofa-wet-planet.

Faber, Nancy, and Ross H. Munro, "Spears and a Nevada Businessman Help a South Pacific Island Proclaim Itself a New Country." *People* 14, no. 3, July 21, 1980.

Fang, Lee. "Sphere of Influence: How American Libertarians are Remaking Latin American Politics." *Intercept,* August 9, 2017.

Fanon, Frantz. *The Wretched of the Earth.* New York: Grove, 2004 [1961].

Farrant, Andrew, Edward McPhail, and Sebastian Berger, "Preventing the 'Abuses' of Democracy: Hayek, the "Military Usurper" and Transitional Dictatorship in Chile?" *American Journal of Economics and Sociology* 71, no. 3 (July 2012): 513–38.

Fateh, RH. "Is Seasteading the High Seas a Legal Possibility? Filling the Gaps in International Sovereignty Law and the Law of the Seas." *Vanderbilt Journal of Transnational Law* 46, no. 3 (2013): 899–931.

Federici, Silvia. *Caliban and the Witch: Women, the Body and Primitive Accumulation.* Brooklyn: Autonomedia, 2004.

Fifita, Sione. *Enhancing Tonga's Maritime Security,* Indo-Pacific Strategic Papers. Australian Defence College, Center for Defence and Strategic Studies, March 2015.

Fine, Ben. "Endogenous Growth Theory: A Critical Assessment." *Cambridge Journal of Economics* 24 (2000): 245–65.

————. "The New Revolution in Economics," *Capital & Class* 21, no. 1 (Spring 1997): 143–48.

Finney, Ben. *Sailing in the Wake of the Ancestors: Reviving Polynesian Voyaging*. Honolulu: Bishop Museum Press, 2004.

Firth, Rhiannon. "Utopianism and Intentional Communities." In Carl Levy and Matthew S. Adams, eds., *The Palgrave Handbook of Anarchism*. London: Palgrave Macmillan, 2019.

Firth, Stewart. "Sovereignty and Independence in the Contemporary Pacific." *Contemporary Pacific* 1, no. 1–2 (1989): 75–96.

Fisher, Mark. *Capitalist Realism: Is There No Alternative?* Winchester, UK: Zero Books, 2010.

———. *K-Punk: The Collected and Unpublished Writings of Mark Fisher*. London: Repeater Books, 2018.

Fleming, Ian. "For Your Eyes Only." In Fleming, *Quantum of Solace: The Complete James Bond Short Stories*. New York: Penguin, 2008.

———. *Goldfinger*. London: Penguin, 2008 [1959].

Fleming, Peter. *The Death of Homoeconomicus: Work, Debt, and the Myth of Endless Accumulation*. London: Pluto Press, 2017.

Fonseca, Regina, and Gilda Rivera, "El Impacto Diferenciado en las Mujeres del Proceso Binario de Acumulación y Despojo." In Joaquín A. Mejía R., coord., *Estado, Despojo y Derechos Humanos*. El Progreso: ERIC-SJ, 2019.

Frank, Dana. *The Long Honduran Night: Resistance, Terror, and the United States in the Aftermath of the Coup*. Chicago: Haymarket Books, 2018.

Freedman, Carl. *Art and Ideas in the Novels of China Miéville*. London: Gylphi, 2015.

Friedan, Betty. *The Feminine Mystique*. New York: W.W. Norton, 1963.

Friedman, David. *The Machinery of Freedom: Guide to a Radical Capitalism*. 2nd ed. Chicago: Open Court, 1989 [1973].

Friedman, Jeffrey. *Power without Knowledge: A Critique of Technocracy*. New York: Oxford University Press, 2020.

Friedman, Milton. *Capitalism and Freedom*. Chicago: University of Chicago Press, 2002 [1962].

Fromm, Erich. *Escape from Freedom*. 2nd ed. New York: Holt, 1969 [1941].

Frymer, Paul. *Building an American Empire: The Era of Territorial and Political Expansion*. Princeton, NJ: Princeton University Press, 2017.

Fuller, Buckminster. *Operating Manual for Spaceship Earth*. Carbondale: Southern Illinois University Press, 1969.

Funnell, Lisa and Klaus Dodds. *Geographies, Genders and Geopolitics of James Bond*. London: Palgrave Macmillan, 2017.

Galeana Rodríguez, Fernando. "Indigenizing Development: State Formation and Indigenous Self-Determination in the Honduran Moskitia." PhD dissertation, Dept. of Development Sociology, Cornell University, 2021.

Galeano, Eduardo. *The Open Veins of Latin America: Five Centuries of the Pillage of a Continent*. New York: Monthly Review Press, 1997 [1975]

Ganor, Solly. *Light One Candle: A Survivor's Tale from Lithuania to Jerusalem*. New York: Kodansha International, 1995.

Gardner, Helen. "Praying for Independence: The Presbyterian Church in the Decolonisation of Vanuatu." *Journal of Pacific History* 48, no. 2 (2013): 122–43.

Gaskins, Nettrice R. "Deep Sea Dwellers: Drexciya and the Sonic Third Space." *Shima* 10, no. 2 (2016): 68–80.

Geglia, Beth. "Honduras: Reinventing the Enclave." *NACLA Report on the Americas* 48, no. 4 (2016): 353–60.

Gershon, Livia. "A Libertarian Utopia." *Aeon*, April 28, 2014. https://aeon.co/essays/what-happens-when-libertarians-try-to-build-a-new-society.

Getachew, Adom. *Worldmaking after Empire: The Rise and Fall of Self-Determination*. Princeton: Princeton University Press, 2019.

Ghosh, Amitav. *The Great Derangement: Climate Change and the Unthinkable*. Chicago: University of Chicago Press, 2016.

Gibson, William. *Neuromancer*. New York: Ace, 1984.

Gilroy, Paul. *Postcolonial Melancholia*. New York: Columbia University Press, 2005.

Gladwin, Thomas. *East Is a Big Bird: Navigation and Logic on Puluwat Atoll*. Cambridge, MA: Harvard University Press, 1995.

Glickman, Lawrence. *Free Enterprise: An American History*. New Haven, CT: Yale University Press, 2020.

Gobat, Michel. *Empire by Invitation: William Walker and Manifest Destiny in Central America*. Cambridge, MA: Harvard University Press, 2018.

Gonschor, Lorenz. "Polynesia in Review: Issues and Events, 1 July 2016 to 30 June 2017." *Contemporary Pacific* 30, no. 1 (2018): 156–65.

Goodman, Paul. *Growing Up Absurd: Problems of Youth in the Organized Society*. New York: NYRB Classics, 2012 [1960].

Graeber, David. *Possibilities: Essays on Hierarchy, Rebellion and Desire*. Oakland: AK Press, 2007.

Gramlich, Wayne. "Seasteading—Homesteading the High Seas" http://www.gramlich.net/projects/oceania/seastead1.html#Introduction.

Gramlich, Wayne, Patri Friedman, and Andrew House. "Getting Serious about SeaSteading," 2002. http://www.gramlich.net/projects/oceania/seastead2/index.html.

Grandin, Greg. *Empire's Workshop: Latin America, The United States, and the Rise of the New Imperialism*. New York: Henry Holt, 2006.

———. *The End of the Myth: From the Frontier to the Border Wall in the Mind of America*. New York: Metropolitan Books, 2019.

———. *The Last Colonial Massacre: Latin America and the Cold War*. Chicago: University of Chicago Press, 2004.

Gravois, John. "The de Soto Delusion." *Slate*, January 29, 2005. http://www.slate.com/articles/news_and_politics/hey_wait_a_minute/2005/01/the_de_soto_delusion.html.

Gray, Rosie. "Behind the Internet's Anti-Democracy Movement," *The Atlantic*, February 10, 2017.

Green, Leslie. "Rights of Exit." *Legal Theory* 4 (1998): 165–85. Excerpted in Gregory Alexander and Hanoch Dagan, eds., *Properties of Property*. New York: Wolters Kluwer Law & Business, 2012.

Green, Martin. *Dreams of Adventure, Deeds of Empire*. New York: Basic Books, 1979.

Grider, John Taylor. "'And I Can Live Without Going to Sea': Pacific Maritime Labor Identity, 1840–1890," PhD dissertation, University of Colorado, 2006.

Griffith, Duff Whitman. "Before the Deluge: An Oral History Examination of Pre-Watergate Conservative Thought in Orange County, California," MA thesis, California State University at Fullerton, 1976.

Grove, Gene. "The CIA, FBI & CBS Bomb in Mission: Impossible." *Scanlan's Monthly* 1, no. 1 (March 1970): 2–4, 15–21.

Grubačić, Andrej. "The Anarchist Moment." In Jacob Blumenfield, Chiara Boticci, and Simon Critchley, eds., *The Anarchist Turn*. London: Pluto Books, 2013.

Grubačić, Andrej, and Denis O'Hearn. *Living at the Edges of Capitalism: Adventures in Exile and Mutual Aid*. Berkeley: University of California Press, 2016.

Guerra, Lillian. *Heroes, Martyrs, and Political Messiahs in Revolutionary Cuba, 1946–1958*. New Haven, CT: Yale University Press, 2018.

Gugliotta, Guy. "Comrades and Arms." *Smithsonian* 39, no. 1 (April 2008): 14–16.

Guha, Ranajit. *History at the Limit of World History*. New York: Columbia University Press, 2003.

Gunder Frank, Andre. *Capitalism and Underdevelopment in Latin America: Historical Studies of Chile and Brazil*. London: Penguin, 1971

Gyger, Helen. *Improvised Cities: Architecture, Urbanization and Innovation in Peru*. Pittsburgh: University of Pittsburgh Press, 2019.

Haider, Asad. "Black Atlantis." *Viewpoint Magazine*, March 5, 2018. https://www.viewpointmag.com/2018/03/05/black-atlantis/.

Halliday, Roy. "Operation Atlantis and the Radical Libertarian Alliance: Observations of a Fly on the Wall." *Formulations* 30 (Summer 2002): 24–31.

Hämäläinen, Pekka. *The Comanche Empire*. New Haven, CT: Yale University Press, 2016.

Hanlon, David. "A Different Historiography for 'A Handful of Chickpeas Flung over the Sea': Approaching the Federated States of Micronesia's Deeper Past." In Warwick Anderson, Miranda Johnson, and Barbara Brookes, *Pacific Futures: Past and Present*. Honolulu: University of Hawai'i Press, 2018.

———. "The Sea of Little Lands: Examining Micronesia's Place in 'Our Sea of Islands,'" *Contemporary Pacific* 21, no. 1 (2009): 91–110.

Haraway, Donna. *Staying with the Trouble: Making Kin in the Chthulucene*. Durham, NC: Duke University Press, 2016.

Hardin, Garrett. "Lifeboat Ethics: The Case against Helping the Poor." *Psychology Today* 8 (September 1974): 38–43.

Harkinson, Josh. "Honduran President Decides That Going to an Event Called 'Disrupting Democracy' Isn't Such a Good Idea." *Mother Jones*, June 10, 2015.

Hart, Matthew. *Extraterritorial: A Political Geography of Contemporary Fiction*. New York: Columbia University Press, 2020.

Harvey, David. *A Brief History of Neoliberalism*. New York: Oxford, 2005.

———. "The 'New' Imperialism: Accumulation by Dispossession." *Socialist Register* 40 (2004): 63–87.

Hau'ofa, Epeli. "Our Sea of Islands." *Contemporary Pacific* 6, no. 1 (Spring 1994): 148–61.

———. "To the Last Viking of the Sunrise." *Faikava: A Tongan Literary Journal* 4, December 1979.

———. "To the Last Viking of the Sunrise." In Albert Wendt, ed., *Nuanua: Pacific Writing in English Since 1980*. Honolulu: University of Hawai'i Press, 1995.

———. *We Are the Ocean: Selected Writings*. Honolulu: University of Hawai'i Press

Hayek, Friedrich. *The Road to Serfdom*. Chicago: University of Chicago Press, 1944.

Hinckle, Warren and William W. Turner. *The Fish Is Red: The Story of the Secret War Against Castro*. New York: Harper & Row, 1981.

Hirsch, Steven, and Lucien van der Walt, eds. *Anarchism and Syndicalism in the Colonial and Postcolonial World: The Praxis of National Liberation, Internationalism, and Social Revolution*. Leiden, NL: Brill, 2010.

Hirschman, Albert. *Exit, Voice, and Loyalty: Responses to Decline in Firms, Organizations and States*. Cambridge, MA: Harvard University Press, 1970.

Hobsbawm, E.J. *The Age of Extremes: A History of the World, 1914–1991*. New York: Vintage, 1996.

Hogoltz-Hetling, Matthew. *A Libertarian Walks into a Bear: The Utopian Plot to Liberate an American Town (and Some Bears)*. New York: Public Affairs, 2020.

Hougan, Jim. *Spooks: The Haunting of America—The Private Use of Secret Agents*. New York: William Morrow, 1978.

Hudson, Peter James. "On the History and Historiography of Banking in the Caribbean." *Small Axe* 18, no. 1 (March 2014): 21–37.

Huntington, Samuel. "The United States." In Michael Crozier, Samuel Huntington, and Jojo Watanuki, *The Crisis of Democracy: Report on the Governability of Democracies to the Trilateral Commission*. New York: Columbia University Press, 1975.

Hyde, Lewis. *Common as Air: Revolution, Art, and Ownership*. New York: Farrar, Straus & Giroux, 2010.

Hymer, Stephen. "Robinson Crusoe and the Secret of Primitive Accumulation." *Monthly Review* 63, no. 4 (September 2011).

Immerwahr, Daniel. "Heresies of Dune." *LA Review of Books*, November 19, 2020.

———. *How to Hide an Empire: A History of the Greater United States*. New York: Farrar, Straus & Giroux, 2019.

Ince, Onur Ulas. *Colonial Capitalism and the Dilemmas of Liberalism*. New York: Oxford University Press, 2018.

James, Marlon. *A Brief History of Seven Killings*. New York: Riverhead Books, 2014.

Jansen, Jan, and Jürgen Osterhammel, *Decolonization: A Short History*, trans. Jeremiah Riemer. Princeton, NJ: Princeton University Press, 2019.

Jasanoff, Maya. *Liberty's Exiles: American Loyalists in the Revolutionary World*. New York: Alfred Knopf, 2011.

Jenkins, Philip. *Decade of Nightmares: The End of the Sixties and the Making of Eighties America*. New York: Oxford University Press, 2006.

Johnson, Matt. "Extraterritorialized!" *Volume* 38 (2014). http://loganandjohnson.com/news/extraterritorialized-in-volume-38.

Jolly, Margaret. "Conversations about Climate Change in Oceania." In Warwick Anderson, Miranda Johnson, and Barbara Brookes, eds., *Pacific Futures: Past and Present*. Honolulu: University of Hawai'i Press, 2018.

———. "Imagining Oceania: Indigenous and Foreign Representations of a Sea of Islands." *Contemporary Pacific* 19, no. 2 (2007): 508–45.

———. "Specters of Inauthenticity." In David Hanlon and Geoffrey White, eds., *Voyaging through the Contemporary Pacific*. Lanham, MD: Rowman & Littlefield, 2000.

———. *Women of the Place: Kastom, Colonialism, and Gender in Vanuatu*. Chur, Switzerland: Harwood Publishers, 1994.

Kahn, Miriam. *Tahiti Beyond the Postcard: Power, Place, and Everyday Life*. Seattle: University of Washington Press, 2011.

Kalpokas, Donald. "Who Am I?" *Pacific Islands Monthly* 45, no. 9 (September 1974): 61.

Kelley, Robin D.G. *Freedom Dreams: The Black Radical Imagination*. Boston: Beacon Press, 2002.

Kilgore, De Witt Douglas. *Astrofuturism: Science, Race, and Visions of Utopia in Space*. Philadelphia: University of Pennsylvania Press, 2003.

Kinane, Ian. *Theorising Literary Islands: The Island Trope in Contemporary Robinsonade Narratives*. London: Rowman & Littlefield, 2017.

Kipling, Rudyard. "The Man Who Would Be King." In Kipling, *The Man Who Would Be King: Selected Stories*. London: Penguin, 2011.

Kirchner, Paul. *More of the Deadliest Men Who Ever Lived*. Boulder, CO: Paladin Press, 2009.

Klein, Naomi. *The Shock Doctrine: The Rise of Disaster Capitalism*. New York: Metropolitan Books, 2007.

———. *This Changes Everything: Capitalism vs. The Climate*. New York: Simon & Schuster, 2014.

Kropotkin, Peter. *The Conquest of Bread*. London: Penguin Books, 2015 [1892].

———. *The Conquest of Bread and Other Writings*. Cambridge: Cambridge University Press, 1995 [1892].

———. *Mutual Aid: A Factor of Evolution*. Boston: Porter Sargent Publishers, 1914 [1902].

———. *Mutual Aid: A Factor in Evolution*. Mineola, NY: Dover Books, 2006 [1902].

Kruse, Kevin. *White Flight: Atlanta and the Making of Modern Conservatism*. Princeton, NJ: Princeton University Press, 2005.

Kruse, Kevin, and Julian Zelizer, *Fault Lines: A History of the United States since 1974*. New York: Norton, 2019.

Lai, Justin. "The Death of Stanford's Humanities Core." *Stanford Review*, March 14, 2015. https://stanfordreview.org/the-death-of-stanfords-humanities-core/.

Lamas Pardo, Miguel. "Establishing Offshore Autonomous Communities: Current Choices and Their Proposed Evolution." PhD dissertation. Translated by Adriana Sánchez Gómez, Escuela Politécnica Superior de Ferrol, 2011.

Land, Nick. "The Dark Enlightenment." http://www.thedarkenlightenment.com/the-dark-enlightenment-by-nick-land/.

———. *Fanged Noumena: Collected Writings 1987–2007*. Edited by Robin Mackay and Ray Brassier. Falmouth, UK: Urbanomic, 2018 [2011].

Langewiesche, William. *The Outlaw Sea: A World of Freedom, Chaos, and Crime*. North Point Press, 2005.

Laurence, Michael R. "Speed the collapse? Using Marx to Rethink the Politics of Accelerationism." *Theory & Event* 20, no. 2 (April 2017).

Lefebvre, Henri. *Critique of Everyday Life*. 3 vols. Translated by Gregory Elliott. London: Verso, 2008 [1947; 1961; 1981].

————. *State, Space, World: Selected Essays*. Edited by Neil Brenner and Stuart Elden. Minneapolis: University of Minnesota Press, 2009.

Levy, Carl. "Social Histories of Anarchism." *Journal for the Study of Radicalism* 4, no. 2 (Fall 2010), 1–44.

Lewis, David H. *We, the Navigators: The Ancient Art of Landfinding in the Pacific*. Honolulu: University of Hawai'i Press, 1974 [1972].

Ligo, Godwin. "Kastom mo kalja/Culture et coutumes/Custom and culture." In Walter Lini et al., *Vanuatu: Twenti wan tingting long team blong indepdens*. Suva, Fiji: Institute of Pacific Studies, 1980.

Lilley, Sasha, David McNally, Eddie Yuen, and James Davis. *Catastrophism: The Apocalyptic Politics of Collapse and Rebirth*. Oakland: PM Press, 2012.

Lindsay, Greg. "Former 'Seasteaders' Come Ashore To Start Libertarian Utopias In Honduran Jungle." *Co-Exist*, October 31, 2011. https://www.fastcompany.com/1678720/former-seasteaders-come-ashore-to-start-libertarian-utopias-in-honduran-jungle.

Lindstrom, Lamont. *Cargo Cult: Strange Stories of Desire from Melanesia and Beyond*. Honolulu: University of Hawai'i Press, 1993.

Lindstrom, Lamont, and Geoffrey White, *Island Encounters: Black and White Memories of the Pacific War*. Washington, DC: Smithsonian Institution, 1990.

Linebaugh, Peter. *Stop, Thief! The Commons, Enclosures, and Resistance*. Oakland: PM Press, 2014.

Linebaugh, Peter, and Marcus Rediker, *The Many-Headed Hydra: Sailors, Slaves, Commoners, and the Hidden History of the Revolutionary Atlantic*. Boston: Beacon, 2013.

Lini, Walter. *Beyond Pandemonium: From the New Hebrides to Vanuatu*. Suva, Fiji: Asia Pacific Books, 1980.

Liu, Lydia H. "Robinson Crusoe's Earthenware Pot," *Critical Inquiry* 25, no. 4 (Summer 1999), 728–57.

Locher, Fabian. "Neo-Malthusianism, Environmentalism, World Fisheries Crisis, and the Global Commons, 1950s-1970s." *The Historical Journal* 63, no. 1 (2020): 187–207.

Long Roderick T. and Tibor R. Machan, eds., *Anarchism/Minarchism: Is a Government Part of a Free Country?* Aldershot: Ashgate, 2008.

Losordo, Dominic. *Liberalism: A Counter History*. London: Verso, 2011.

Low, Sam. *Hawaiki Rising: Hōkūle'a, Nainoa Thompson, and the Hawaiian Renaissance*. Waipahu, HI: Island Heritage, 2016.

Ludlow, Peter, ed., *Crypto Anarchy, Cyberstates, and Pirate Utopias*. Cambridge, MA: MIT Press, 2001.

Lycett, Andrew. *Ian Fleming*. New York: St. Martin's, 2013.

Lyons, Matthew N. *Insurgent Supremacists: The U.S. Far Right's Challenge to State and Empire*. Oakland: PM Press, 2018.

Macdonald, Trent J. *The Political Economy of Non-Territorial Exit: Cryptosecession*. Cheltenham: Edward Elgar, 2019.

Macintyre, Ben. *Josiah the Great: The True Story of the Man Who Would Be King*. New York: HarperCollins, 2004.

Mackey, Danielle Marie. "Charter Cities: A Dangerous U.S. Economic Experiment in Honduras." *New Republic*, December 14, 2014.

MacLean, Nancy. *Democracy in Chains: The Deep History of the Radical Right's Stealth Plan for America*. New York: Penguin 2018.

Madrigal, Alexis. "Peter Thiel Makes Down Payment on Libertarian Ocean Colonies." *Wired*, May 10, 2008.

Maier, Charles. *Once Within Borders: Territories of Power, Wealth and Belonging Since 1500*. Cambridge, MA: Harvard University Press, 2016.

Makki, Fouad. "Imperial Fantasies, Colonial Realities: Contesting Power and Culture in Italian Eritrea." *South Atlantic Quarterly* 107 (Fall 2008): 735–54.

Mallaby, Sebastian. "The Politically Incorrect Guide to Ending Poverty." *The Atlantic*, July/August 2010.

Mann Borgese, Elisabeth. *The Oceanic Circle: Governing the Seas as a Global Resource*. Tokyo: United Nations University Press, 1998.

Marcuse, Herbert. *One-Dimensional Man: Studies in the Ideology of Advanced Industrial Society*, 2nd ed. Boston: Beacon Press, 1991 [1964].

Margolies, Dan. "Jurisdiction in Offshore Submerged Lands and the Significance of the Truman Proclamation in Postwar U.S. Foreign Policy." *Diplomatic History* 44, no. 3 (June 2020): 447–65.

Marshall, Peter. *Demanding the Impossible: A History of Anarchism*. Oakland: PM Press, 2010.

Marx, Karl. *Capital: A Critique of Political Economy*, vol. 1. New York: Penguin Books, 1990 [1867].

Maude, H.E. *Slavers in Paradise: The Peruvian Slave Trade in Polynesia, 1861–1864*. Stanford: Stanford University Press, 1981.

Mawyer, Alexander. "Floating Islands, Frontiers, and Other Boundary Objects on the Edge of Oceania's Futurity." *Pacific Affairs* 94, no. 1 (March 2021): 123–44.

Maximoff, G.P. *The Political Philosophy of Bakunin*. New York: Free Press, 1953.

Maxwell, Barry, and Raymond Craib, eds., *No Gods No Masters No Peripheries: Global Anarchisms*. Oakland: PM Press, 2015.

Mayer, Jane. *Dark Money: The Hidden History of the Billionaires Behind the Rise of the Radical Right*. New York: Doubleday, 2016.

McAnany, Patricia, and Norman Yoffee, eds., *Questioning Collapse: Human Resilience, Ecological Vulnerability, and the Aftermath of Empire*. New York: Cambridge University Press, 2010.

McCarthy, Cormac. *All the Pretty Horses*. New York: Alfred Knopf, 1992.

———. *Blood Meridian, or the Evening Redness in the West*. New York: Vintage, 1992 [1985].

McCoy, Alfred W. *A Question of Torture: CIA Interrogation, From the Cold War to the War on Terror*. New York: Henry Holt, 2006.

McCray, W. Patrick. *The Visioneers: How a Group of Elite Scientists Pursued Space Colonies, Nanotechnologies, and a Limitless Future*. Princeton, NJ: Princeton University Press, 2012.

McDonnell, Siobhan, Matthew G. Allen, and Colin Filer, eds., *Kastom, Property and Ideology: Land Transformations in Melanesia*. Canberra: ANU Press, 2017.

McEnaney, Maura. *Willard Garvey: An Epic Life*. Oakland: Liberty Tree Press, 2013.

McGirr, Lisa. *Suburban Warriors: The Origins of the New American Right*. Princeton, NJ: Princeton University Press, 2001.

McIntyre, W. David. *Winding Up the British Empire in the Pacific Islands*. Oxford: Oxford University Press, 2014.

McKenzie, Evan. *Privatopia: Homeowner Associations and the Rise of Residential Private Government*. New Haven, CT: Yale University Press, 1994.

McNally, David. *Monsters of the Market: Zombies, Vampires, and Global Capitalism*. Chicago: Haymarket Books, 2011.

McNeill, J.R. "Pacific Ecology and British Imperialism, 1770–1970." In Hermann J. Hiery and John M. MacKenzie, eds., *European Impact and Pacific Influence: British and German Colonial Policy in the Pacific Islands and the Indigenous Response*. London: Tauris, 1997.

Menand, Louis. *The Free World: Art and Thought in the Cold War*. New York: Farrar, Straus & Giroux, 2021.

Menefee, Samuel Pyeatt. "Republics of the Reefs: Nation-Building on the Continental Shelf and in the World's Oceans." *California Western International Law Journal* 25 (1994): 81–111.

Merrifield, Andy. *Metromarxism: A Marxist Tale of the City*. New York: Routledge, 2009.

Micronations: The Lonely Planet Guide to Home-Made Nations. London: Lonely Planet Publications, 2006.

Miéville, China. *Between Equal Rights: A Marxist Theory of International Law*. Chicago: Haymarket, 2006.

————. "Floating Utopias: Freedom and Unfreedom of the Seas." In Mike Davis and Daniel Bertrand Monk, eds., *Evil Paradises: Dreamworlds of Neoliberalism*. New York: New Press, 2007.

Milian, Alberto. "Dreaming under a Perfect Sun: Ethnic Mexicans, Leftists, and Boosters in Greater San Diego, 1900–1950." PhD dissertation, Dept. of History, Cornell University, 2018.

Mirowski, Philip, and Dieter Plehwe, eds., *The Road to Mont Pelerin: The Making of the Neoliberal Thought Collective*. Cambridge, MA: Harvard University Press, 2015.

Mitchell, Timothy. "Dreamland." In Mike Davis and Daniel Bertrand Monk, eds., *Evil Paradises: Dreamworlds of Neoliberalism*. New York: New Press, 2007.

Molisa, Grace Mera. *Black Stone: Poems*. Suva, Fiji: Mana Publications, 1983.

————. "Colonised People." In *Colonised People: Poems*. Port Vila: Black Stone, 1987.

————. "Woman." In Walter Lini et al., *Vanuatu: Twenti wan tingting long team blong independens*. Suva, Fiji: Institute of Pacific Studies, University of the South Pacific, 1980.

Mongey, Vanessa. *Rogue Revolutionaries: The Fight for Legitimacy in the Greater Caribbean*. Philadelphia: University of Pennsylvania Press, 2020.

Monroe, Frederick Fales. "Coastal State Control and Global Ocean Harvest." PhD dissertation, School of International Service, American University, 1990.

Morales, Ed. *Fantasy Island: Colonialism, Exploitation and the Betrayal of Puerto Rico*. New York: Bold Type Books, 2019.

Morgan, Richard. *Altered Carbon*. New York: Ballantine, 2002.

Moss, Laurence. "Private Property Anarchism: An American Variant." In Stringham, ed., *Anarchy, State and Public Choice*.

Munavvar, Mohamed. *Ocean States: Archipelagic Regimes in the Law of the Sea*. Dordrecht: Martinus Nijhoff Publishers, 1995.

Najafi, Sina, and Christina Duffy Burnett, "Islands and the Law: An Interview with Christina Duffy Burnett." *Cabinet* 38 (Summer 2010): 60–66.

Naylor, R.T. *Hot Money and the Politics of Debt*. New York: Linden Press / Simon and Schuster, 1987.

Nette, Andrew, and Iain McIntyre, eds. *Dangerous Visions and New Worlds: Radical Science Fiction, 1950–1985*. Oakland: PM Press, 2021.

Newitz, Annalee. *Autonomous*. New York: Tor Books, 2017.

Nichols, Robert. *Theft Is Property: Dispossession and Critical Theory*. Durham, NC: Duke University Press, 2020.

Nickerson, Michelle. *Mothers of Conservatism: Women and the Postwar Right*. Princeton, NJ: Princeton University Press, 2012.

Nixon, Rob. *Slow Violence and the Environmentalism of the Poor*. Cambridge, MA: Harvard University Press, 2011.

Noys, Benjamin. *Malign Velocities: Accelerationism and Capitalism*. London: Zero Books, 2014.

Nozick, Robert. *Anarchy, State, and Utopia*. New York: Basic Books, 1974.

O'Connell, Mark. *Notes from an Apocalypse: A Personal Journey to the End of the World and Back*. New York: Doubleday, 2020.

————. *To Be a Machine: Adventures Among Cyborgs, Utopians, Hackers, and the Futurists Solving the Modest Problem of Death*. New York: Anchor Books, 2017.

Ogle, Vanessa. "Archipelago Capitalism: Tax Havens, Offshore Money, and the State, 1950s—1970s." *American Historical Review* 122, no. 5 (December 2017): 1431–58.

————. "'Funk Money': The End of Empires, The Expansion of Tax Havens, and Decolonization as an Economic and Financial Event." *Past & Present* 249, no. 1 (November 2020): 213–49.

Olcott, Jocelyn. *International Women's Year: The Greatest Consciousness-Raising Event in History*. New York: Oxford University Press, 2017.

Oliver, Michael. *A New Constitution for a New Country*. Reno: Fine Arts Press, 1968.

Organización Fraternal Negra Hondureña [OFRANEH], "El retorno del dominio de caciques europeos y reyes estadounidenses a la costa norte de Honduras." September 28, 2020. https://ofraneh.wordpress.com/2020/09/28/1956/.

———. "'No sé si estoy observando una farsa o una tragedia': Paul Romer en referencia a las ZEDE en Honduras." November 25, 2015. https://ofraneh.wordpress.com/2015/11/25/no-se-si-estoy-observando-una-farsa-o-una-tragedia-paul-romer-en-referencia-a-las-zede-en-honduras/.

Ortega, Ana. "Las Reformas Económicas a partir de 2009 desde la Lógica Extractiva que Sostiene la Acumulación por Desposesión." In Joaquín A. Mejía R., coord., *Estado, Despojo y Derechos Humanos.* El Progreso: ERIC-SJ, 2019.

Ortíz-Sotelo, Jorge, and Robert King, "'A Cruize to the Coasts of Peru and Chile': HM Ship Cornwallis, 1807." *Great Circle* 32, no. 1 (2010): 35–52.

Ostrom, Elinor. *Governing the Commons: The Evolution of Institutions for Collective Action.* New York: Cambridge University Press, 1990.

Packer, George. *The Unwinding: An Inner History of the New America.* New York: Farrar, Straus & Giroux, 2013.

Palan, Ronen. "Britain's Second Empire." *New Left Project.* August 17, 2012.

———. "International Financial Centers: The British-Empire, City-States and Commercially Oriented Politics." *Theoretical Inquiries in Law* 11, no. 1 (January 2010): 149–76.

———. *The Offshore World: Sovereign Markets, Virtual Places, and Nomad Millionaires.* Ithaca: Cornell University Press, 2006.

———. "The Second British Empire: The British Empire and the Reemergence of Global Finance." In Sandra Halperin and Ronen Palan, eds., *Legacies of Empire: Imperial Roots of the Contemporary Global Order.* Cambridge: Cambridge University Press, 2015.

Panitch, Leo, and Sam Gindin. *The Making of Global Capitalism: The Political Economy of Empire.* New York: Verso, 2013.

Parsons, Mike. "Ashes to Ashes." *New Internationalist* 101 (July 1981). https://newint.org/features/1981/07/01/phoenix.

Pearce, Fred. *The Land Grabbers: The New Fight over Who Owns the Earth.* Boston: Beacon, 2012.

Pendle, George. "New Foundlands." *Cabinet* 18 (Summer 2005): 65–68.

Perlstein, Rick. *Before the Storm: Barry Goldwater and the Unmaking of the American Consensus.* New York: Nation Books, 2009 [2001].

Phillips-Fein, Kimberly. *Invisible Hands: The Businessmen's Crusade Against the New Deal.* New York: W.W. Norton, 2010.

Plant, Chris. *New Hebrides: The Road to Independence.* Suva, Fiji: Institute of Pacific Studies, 1977.

Polanyi, Karl. *The Great Transformation: The Political and Economic Origins of Our Time.* 2nd ed. Boston: Beacon Press, 2001 [1944].

Popkin, Samuel. *The Rational Peasant: The Political Economy of Rural Society in Vietnam.* Berkeley: University of California Press, 1979.

Portillo, Suyapa. "Honduras: Refounding the Nation, Building a New Kind of Social Movement." In Richard Stahler-Sholk, Harry E. Vanden, and Marc Becker, eds., *Rethinking Latin American Social Movements: Radical Action from Below.* Lanham, MD: Rowman & Littlefield, 2014.

———. *Roots of Resistance: A Story of Gender, Race, and Labor on the North Coast of Honduras.* Austin: University of Texas Press, 2021.

Prashad, Vijay. *The Darker Nations: A People's History of the Third World.* New York: New Press, 2007.

Prashad, Vijay, and Alejandro Bejarano, "We Will Coup Whoever We Want: Elon Musk and the Overthrow of Democracy in Bolivia." *Monthly Review On-line* (July 28, 2020). https://mronline.org/2020/07/28/we-will-coup-whoever-we-want-elon-musk-and-the-overthrow-of-democracy-in-bolivia/.

Press, Steven. *Rogue Empires: Contracts and Conmen in Europe's Scramble for Africa.* Cambridge, MA: Harvard University Press, 2017.

Proudhon, *What Is Property? Or an Inquiry into the Principle of Right and of Government* (1840).

Quirk, Joe, with Patri Friedman. *Seasteading: How Floating Nations Will Restore the Environment, Enrich the Poor, Cure the Sick, and Liberate Humanity from Politicians.* New York: Free Press, 2017.

Rameau, Max. *Take Back the Land: Land, Gentrification and the Umoja Village Shantytown.* Oakland: AK Press, 2012 [2008].

Ranganathan, Surabhi. "Decolonization and International Law: Putting the Ocean on the Map." *Journal of the History of International Law* 23 (2021): 161–83

———. "Seasteads, Land Grabs, and International Law." *Leiden Journal of International Law* 32, no. 2 (June 2019), 205–14.

Rawlings, Greg. "Laws, Liquidity and Eurobonds: The Making of the Vanuatu Tax Haven." *Journal of Pacific History* 39, no. 3 (2004): 325–41.

———. "Statelessness, Human Rights, and Decolonisation: Citizenship in Vanuatu, 1906–1980." *Journal of Pacific History* 47, no. 1 (March 2012).

Rawls, John. *A Theory of Justice.* Cambridge, MA: The Belknap Press, 1971.

Regenvanu, Sethy John. *Laef blong mi: From Village to Nation.* Port Vila: University of the South Pacific, 2004.

Regis, Ed. "Meet the Extropians." *Wired*, October 1, 1994.

Rid, Thomas. *Rise of the Machines: A Cybernetic History.* New York: W.W. Norton, 2016.

Robertson, Thomas. *The Malthusian Moment: Global Population Growth and the Birth of American Environmentalism.* New Brunswick, NJ: Rutgers University Press, 2012.

Robin, Corey. *The Reactionary Mind: Conservatism from Edmund Burke to Sarah Palin.* New York: Oxford University Press, 2011.

———. "When Hayek Met Pinochet." https://coreyrobin.com/2012/07/18/when-hayek-met-pinochet/.

Robinson, Kim Stanley. "The Gold Coast." In *Three Californias: The Wild Shore, The Gold Coast, and Pacific Edge.* New York: Tor Books, 2020.

Rocha, José Luis y Equipo de Investigación del ERIC-SJ, "Experiencias de Despojo y Resistencia desde la Voz de las Comunidades: Acaparamiento, Desplazamiento Forzoso y Luchas por la Tierra en la Honduras del Siglo XXI." In Joaquín A. Mejía R., coord., *Estado, Despojo y Derechos Humanos.* El Progreso: ERIC-SJ, 2019.

Rodney, Walter. *How Europe Underdeveloped Africa.* London: Bogle-L'Ouverture, 1972.

Rogers, Ibram. "Remembering the Black Campus Movement: An Oral History Interview with James P. Garrett." *Journal of Pan-African Studies* 2, no. 10 (June 2009): 30–41.

Roos, Jerome. "The New Debt Colonies." *Viewpoint Magazine* no. 6 (February 1, 2018), https://viewpointmag.com/2018/02/01/new-debt-colonies.

———. *Why Not Default? The Political Economy of Sovereign Debt.* Princeton, NJ: Princeton University Press, 2019.

Rose, Carol. *Property and Persuasion: Essays on the History, Theory and Rhetoric of Ownership.* London: Routledge, 1995.

Rosenthal, Gregory. *Beyond Hawai'i: Native Labor in the Pacific World.* Berkeley: University of California Press, 2018.

Ross, Kristin. *Communal Luxury: The Political Imaginary of the Paris Commune.* London: Verso, 2015.

———. *Fast Cars, Clean Bodies: Decolonization and the Reordering of French Culture.* Cambridge, MA: MIT Press, 1996.

Rothbard, Murray. *The Complete Libertarian Forum, 1969–1984.* Auburn, AL: Ludwig von Mises Institute, 2012.

———. *For a New Liberty.* New York: Macmillan, 1973.

Rothwell, Donald, Alex Oude Elferink, Karen Scott, and Tim Stephens, eds., *The Oxford Handbook of the Law of the Sea.* New York: Oxford University Press, 2015.

Rozwadowski, Helen. *Fathoming the Ocean: The Discovery and Exploration of the Deep Sea.* Cambridge, MA: Belknap Press, 2005.

Ruhen, Olaf. *Minerva Reef: A Modern Sea Epic*. Boston: Little, Brown, 1963.

Runciman, David. "The Stuntman," *London Review of Books* 36, no. 6 (March 2014): 21–25.

Russell, Andrew, and Lee Vinsel, "Whitey on Mars: Elon Musk and the rise of Silicon Valley's strange trickle-down science." *Aeon*, February 1, 2017. https://aeon.co/essays/is-a-mission-to-mars-morally-defensible-given-todays-real-needs?

Sacks David O., and Peter A. Thiel, "How the West Was Lost at Stanford." *Independent Institute*, September 1, 1995. http://www.independent.org/newsroom/article.asp?id=5205

Sacred Vessels: Navigating Tradition and Identity in Micronesia. Directed by Vicente Díaz. Pacific Islanders in Communication, 1997.

Salesa, Damon. "Native Seas and Native Seaways: The Pacific Ocean and New Zealand." In Frances Steel, ed., *New Zealand and the Sea: Historical Perspectives*. Wellington, NZ: Bridget Williams Books, 2018.

———. "The Pacific in Indigenous Time." In David Armitage and Alison Bashford, eds., *Pacific Histories: Ocean, Land, People*, 31–52. London: Palgrave, 2013.

Sandefur, Justin, and Milan Vaishnav, "Imagine There's No Country: Three Questions about a New Charter City in Honduras." Center for Global Development: Essay (June 2012). http://www.cgdev.org/content/publications/detail/1426274.

Saunders, Hartley Cecil. *The Other Bahamas*. Nassau: Bodab, 2013 [1991].

Saunders, Kay. *Workers in Bondage: The Origins and Bases of Unfree Labour in Queensland, 1824–1916*. St. Lucia: University of Queensland Press, 2015 [1982].

Savage, Marshall T. *The Millennial Project: Colonizing the Galaxy in Eight Easy Steps*. Boston: Little, Brown, 1992.

Schep, Dennis. "Freeing Space: Building Worlds Outside of State and Capital." *ROAR*, December 23, 2020. https://roarmag.org/essays/freeing-space-building-worlds-outside-of-state-and-capital/

Schmidt, Michael, and Lucien van der Walt, *Black Flame: The Revolutionary Class Politics of Anarchism and Syndicalism*. Oakland: AK Press, 2013.

Schmidtke, Ryan. "'Artificial islands' of the Future: The Seasteading Movement and the International Legal Regimes Governing Seasteads in EEZs and on the High Seas." *Asian-Pacific Law & Policy Journal* 21, no. 1 (2019): 1–28.

Scott, Felicity. *Outlaw Territories: Environments of Insecurity/Architecture of Counterinsurgency*. Boston: Zone Books, 2016.

Scott, James C. *The Art of Not Being Governed: An Anarchist History of Upland Southeast Asia*. New Haven, CT: Yale University Press, 2009.

———. *The Moral Economy of the Peasant: Rebellion and Subsistence in Southeast Asia*. New Haven, CT: Yale University Press, 1976.

———. *Seeing like a State: How Certain Schemes to Improve the Human Condition Have Failed*. New Haven, CT: Yale University Press, 1998.

Scott, Peter Dale. *American War Machine: Deep Politics, the CIA Global Drug Connection, and the Road to Afghanistan*. Revised edition. Lanham, MD: Rowman & Littlefield, 2014 [2010].

Serge, Victor. *Unforgiving Years*, trans. Richard Greeman. New York: New York Review Books, 2008.

Sharma, Sarah. "Exit and the Extensions of Man." *transmediale/art & digital culture*, August 5, 2017. https://transmediale.de/content/exit-and-the-extensions-of-man.

Shaxson, Nicholas. *Treasure Islands: Uncovering the Damage of Offshore Banking and Tax Havens*. London: Palgrave Macmillan, 2011.

Shears, Richard. *The Coconut War: The Crisis on Espiritu Santu*. North Ryde, NSW: Cassell Australia, 1980.

Shilliam, Robbie. *The Black Pacific: Anti-Colonial Struggles and Oceanic Connections*. London: Bloomsbury, 2015.

Shineberg, Dorothy. *They Came for Sandalwood: A Study of the Sandalwood Trade in the Southwest Pacific, 1830–1865*. Melbourne: Melbourne University Press, 1967.

Simmons, A. John. "Historical Rights and Fair Shares." *Law and Philosophy* 14, no. 2 (May 1995): 149–84.

Simpson, Isabelle. "Cultural Political Economy of the Start-Up Societies Imaginary." PhD dissertation, McGill University, 2021.

———. "Operation Atlantis: A Case Study in Libertarian Island Micronationality." *Shima: The International Journal of Research into Island Cultures* 10, no. 2 (2016): 18–35.

Singlaub, John K. with Malcolm McConnell. *Hazardous Duty: An American Soldier in the Twentieth-Century.* New York: Summit Books, 1991.

Slobodian, Quinn. *Globalists: The End of Empire and the Birth of Neoliberalism.* Cambridge, MA: Harvard University Press, 2018.

Soian, Ana Simina, and Maxime Delavallee, "The State Is Dead. Long Live the State!" https://medium.com/new-tech-revolution-sciencespo/the-state-is-dead-long-live-the-state-8afab8f9a800.

Solano, Luis. "Development and/as Dispossession: Elite Networks and Extractive Industry in the Franja Transversal del Norte." In Carlota McAllister and Diane Nelson, eds., *War by Other Means: Aftermath in Post-Genocide Guatemala.* Durham, NC: Duke University Press, 2013.

Soluri, John. *Banana Cultures: Agriculture, Consumption, and Environmental Change in Honduras and the United States.* Austin: University of Texas Press, 2005.

Song, Lili. "The Curious History of the Minerva Reefs: Tracing the Origin of Tongan and Fijian Claims Over the Minerva Reefs." *Journal of Pacific History* 54, no. 3 (2019): 417–30.

Sope, Barak. *Land and Politics in the New Hebrides.* Suva, Fiji: South Pacific Social Sciences Association [1974].

Squire, Rachel. "Seabeds. Sub-marine Territory: Living and Working on the Seafloor During the Sealab II Experiment." In Kimberley Peters, Philip Steinberg, and Elaine Stratford, eds., *Territory Beyond Terra.* London: Rowman & Littlefield, 2018.

St. George, Andrew. "The Amazing New-Country Caper." *Esquire,* February 1975.

———. "A Significant Little Gun." *Esquire,* August 1977.

———. "A Visit with a Revolutionary." *Coronet,* February 1958, 74–80.

Stedman Jones, Daniel. *Masters of the Universe: Hayek, Friedman, and the Birth of Neoliberal Politics.* Princeton, NJ: Princeton University Press, 2012.

Steinberg, Philip E. *The Social Construction of the Ocean.* Cambridge: Cambridge University Press, 2001.

Steinberg, Philip E., Elizabeth Nyman, and Mauro J. Caraccioli, "Atlas Swam: Freedom, Capital, and Floating Sovereignties in the Seasteading Vision." *Antipode* 44, no. 4 (September 2012): 1532–50.

Stephenson, Neal. *Snowcrash.* New York: Bantam, 1992.

Stevens, Warren K. *The Story of Operation Atlantis.* Saugerties, NY: Atlantis Publishing Co., 1968.

Stiltz, Anna. "Is There an Unqualified Right to Leave?" in Sarah Fine and Lea Ypi, eds., *Migration in Political Theory: The Ethics of Movement and Membership.* New York: Oxford University Press, 2016. Stirner, Max. *The Ego and His Own: The Case of the Individual Against Authority.* London: Verso, 2014 [1844].

Strauss, Erwin. *How to Start Your Own Country.* Boulder, CO: Paladin Press, 1999 [1984].

Strauss, Neil. "Brock Pierce: The Hippie King of Cryptocurrency." *Rolling Stone,* July 26, 2018. https://www.rollingstone.com/culture/culture-features/brock-pierce-hippie-king-of-cryptocurrency-700213/.

Stringham, Edward, ed., *Anarchy, State and Public Choice.* Cheltenham, UK: Edward Elgar, 2005.

Stuart, Andrew. *Of Cargoes, Colonies, and Kings: Diplomatic and Administrative Service from Africa to the Pacific.* London: I.B. Tauris, 2001.

Swan, Quito. *Pauulu's Diaspora: Black Internationalism and Environmental Justice.* Gainesville: University of Florida Press, 2020.

Tabani, Marc Kurt. "Histoire politique du Nagriamel à Santo." *Journal de la Société des Océanistes* 113 (2001–02): 151–76.

Taylor-Lehman, Dylan. *Sealand: The True Story of the World's Most Stubborn Micronation.* London: Icon, 2020.

Teaiwa, Katerina Martina. *Consuming Ocean Island: Stories of People and Phosphate from Banaba.* Bloomington: Indiana University Press, 2015.

Te Punga Somerville, Alice. *Once Were Pacific: Māori Connections to Oceania.* Minneapolis: University of Minnesota Press, 2012.

Thiel, Peter. "The Education of a Libertarian." *Cato Unbound*, April 13, 2009. http://www.cato-unbound.org/2009/04/13/peter-thiel/education-libertarian.

Thomas, Nicholas. *In Oceania: Visions, Artifacts, Histories.* Durham, NC: Duke University Press, 1997.

Thompson, E.P. *Customs in Common: Studies in Traditional Popular Culture.* New York: New Press, 1993.

———. *The Poverty of Theory & Other Essays.* London: Merlin Press, 1978.

Thongchai Winichakul, *Siam Mapped: A History of the Geobody of a Nation.* Honolulu: University of Hawai'i Press, 1997.

Tiebout, Charles M. "A Pure Theory of Local Expenditures." *Journal of Political Economy* 64, no. 5 (1956): 416–24.

Todes, Daniel. *Darwin Without Malthus: The Struggle for Existence in Russian Evolutionary Thought.* New York: Oxford University Press, 1989.

Toffler, Alvin. *Future Shock.* New York: Random House, 1970.

Truby, J. David. *Silencer, Snipers & Assassins: An Overview of Whispering Death.* Boulder, CO: Paladin Press, 1972.

Tullock, Gordon. *Further Explorations in the Theory of Anarchy.* Blacksburg, VA: University Publications, 1974.

Turner, Fred. *From Counterculture to Cyberculture: Stewart Brand, the Whole Earth Network, and the Rise of Digital Utopianism.* Chicago: University of Chicago Press, 2008.

Tusitala Marsh, Selina. "Black Stone Poetry: Vanuatu's Grace Mera Molisa," *Cordite Poetry Review*, February 1, 2014. http://cordite.org.au/scholarly/black-stone-poetry-vanuatus-grace-mera-molisa/.

Underkuffler, Laura S. *The Idea of Property.* New York: Oxford University Press, 2003.

Urbina, Ian. *The Outlaw Ocean: Journeys Across the Last Untamed Frontier.* New York: Knopf, 2019.

Valentine, Douglas. *The Phoenix Program.* New York: William Morrow, 1990.

van der Walt, Lucien, and Michael Schmidt. *Black Flame: The Revolutionary Class Politics of Anarchism and Syndicalism.* Oakland: AK Press, 2009.

van Fossen, Anthony. "Citizenship for Sale: Passports of Convenience from Pacific Islands Tax Havens." *Commonwealth and Comparative Politics* 45, no. 2 (2007): 138–63.

———. "Secessionist Tax Haven Movements in the Pacific Islands." *Canadian Review of Studies in Nationalism* 28 (2001): 77–92.

———. *Tax Havens and Sovereignty in the Pacific Islands.* St. Lucia, Queensland: University of Queensland Press, 2012.

van Trease, Howard, ed., *Melanesian Politics: Stael Blong Vanuatu.* Suva, Fiji: University of the South Pacific, 1995.

———. *The Politics of Land in Vanuatu: From Colony to Independence.* Suva, Fiji: University of the South Pacific, 1987.

Vemarana Development Corporation. *An Investment in the Vemarana Federation*, mimeograph. Santo, New Hebrides: Vemarana Federation, 1980.

Verne, Jules. *The Self-Propelled Island*, trans. Marie-Thérèse Noiset. Lincoln: University of Nebraska Press, 2015 [1895].

Viotti da Costa, Emilia. *The Brazilian Empire: Myths and Histories*, revised edition. Durham, NC: University of North Carolina Press, 2000.

von Hallberg, Robert. *The Maltese Falcon to Body of Lies: Spies, Noirs, and Trust.* Albuquerque: University of New Mexico Press, 2015.

Wainwright, Joel. *Geopiracy: Oaxaca, Militant Empiricism, and Geographical Thought.* London: Palgrave, 2012.

Walker, Richard. *Pictures of a Gone City: Tech and the Dark Side of Prosperity in the San Francisco Bay Area.* Oakland: PM Press, 2018.

Ward, Colin. *Anarchism: A Very Short Introduction.* Oxford: Oxford University Press, 2004.

Warner, Andy, and Sofia Louise Dam, *This Land Is My Land: A Graphic History of Big Dreams, Micronations, and Other Self-Made States.* San Francisco: Chronicle Books, 2019.

Waters, Christopher. "Manuscript XXVII: Australia and the South Pacific." *Journal of Pacific History* 48, no. 2 (2013): 209–16.

Watts, Michael J. *Silent Violence: Food, Famine, and Peasantry in Northern Nigeria.* Berkeley: University of California Press, 1983.

Wei, Xiaoping. "From Principle to Context: Marx versus Nozick and Rawls on Distributive Justice." *Rethinking Marxism* 20, no. 3 (July 2008): 472–86.

Weiner, Tim. *Legacy of Ashes: The History of the CIA.* New York: Anchor Books, 2008.

Weisberg, Jacob. "Turn On, Start Up, Drop Out." *Slate*, October 16, 2010.

Weisberger, Mindy. "U.S. Navy's 'Aquanauts' Tested the Boundaries of Deep Diving. It Ended in Tragedy." *Live Science*, February 12, 2019.

Wendt, Albert. "Towards a New Oceania." *Mana Review* 1, no. 1 (1976): 49–60.

Williams, Eric. *Capitalism and Slavery.* Durham: University of North Carolina Press, 1994 [1944].

Williams, Raymond. *The Country and the City.* Oxford: Oxford University Press, 1973 [1975].

Williams, Rosalind. *The Triumph of Human Empire: Verne, Morris and Stevenson at the End of the World.* Chicago: University of Chicago Press, 2013.

Winn, Peter, ed., *Victims of the Chilean Miracle: Workers and Neoliberalism in the Pinochet Era, 1973–2002.* Durham, NC: Duke University Press, 2004.

Wolfe, Patrick. "History and Imperialism: A Century of Theory, from Marx to Postcolonialism" *American Historical Review* 102, no. 2 (April 1997): 388–429.

Wood, Ellen Meiksins. *The Origin of Capitalism: A Longer View.* London: Verso Press, 2002.

Wood-Ellem, Elizabeth. *Queen Sālote of Tonga: The Story of an Era, 1900–1965.* Auckland: Auckland University Press, 1999.

Woodley, Richard. "Killing Time with the War Dreamers." *Esquire*, August 1976.

Woodward, Keith. *A Political Memoir of the Anglo-French Condominium of the New Hebrides.* Canberra: Australian National University Press, 2014.

Ypi, Lea. "Justice in Migration: A Closed Borders Utopia?" *Journal of Political Philosophy* 16, no. 4 (2008): 391–418

Yusoff, Kathryn. *A Billion Black Anthropocenes or None.* Minneapolis: University of Minnesota Press, 2018.

Zerzan, John. *Elements of Refusal.* Columbia, MO: Paleo Editions, 1999 [1988].

Zibechi, Raúl. *Territories in Resistance: A Cartography of Latin American Social Movements.* Translated by Raymor Ryan. Oakland: AK Press, 2012.

Index

Page numbers in *italic* refer to illustrations. "Passim" (literally "scattered") indicates intermittent discussion of a topic over a cluster of pages.

About the Author

Raymond Craib is the Marie Underhill Noll Professor of History at Cornell University and the author of *The Cry of the Renegade: Politics and Poetry in Interwar Chile, Cartographic Mexico: A History of State Fixations and Fugitive Landscapes*, and with Barry Maxwell, co-editor of *No Gods No Masters No Peripheries: Global Anarchisms*.

ABOUT PM PRESS

PM Press is an independent, radical publisher of books and
media to educate, entertain, and inspire. Founded in 2007
by a small group of people with decades of publishing,
media, and organizing experience, PM Press amplifies the
voices of radical authors, artists, and activists. Our aim is to
deliver bold political ideas and vital stories to all walks of life and arm the dreamers
to demand the impossible. We have sold millions of copies of our books, most
often one at a time, face to face. We're old enough to know what we're doing and
young enough to know what's at stake. Join us to create a better world.

PM Press
PO Box 23912
Oakland, CA 94623
www.pmpress.org

PM Press in Europe
europe@pmpress.org
www.pmpress.org.uk

FRIENDS OF PM PRESS

These are indisputably momentous times—the financial system is melting down globally and the Empire is stumbling. Now more than ever there is a vital need for radical ideas.

In the many years since its founding—and on a mere shoestring—PM Press has risen to the formidable challenge of publishing and distributing knowledge and entertainment for the struggles ahead. With hundreds of releases to date, we have published an impressive and stimulating array of literature, art, music, politics, and culture. Using every available medium, we've succeeded in connecting those hungry for ideas and information to those putting them into practice.

Friends of PM allows you to directly help impact, amplify, and revitalize the discourse and actions of radical writers, filmmakers, and artists. It provides us with a stable foundation from which we can build upon our early successes and provides a much-needed subsidy for the materials that can't necessarily pay their own way. You can help make that happen—and receive every new title automatically delivered to your door once a month—by joining as a Friend of PM Press. And, we'll throw in a free T-shirt when you sign up.

Here are your options:

- **$30 a month** Get all books and pamphlets plus 50% discount on all webstore purchases

- **$40 a month** Get all PM Press releases (including CDs and DVDs) plus 50% discount on all webstore purchases

- **$100 a month** Superstar—Everything plus PM merchandise, free downloads, and 50% discount on all webstore purchases

For those who can't afford $30 or more a month, we have **Sustainer Rates** at $15, $10, and $5. Sustainers get a free PM Press T-shirt and a 50% discount on all purchases from our website.

Your Visa or Mastercard will be billed once a month, until you tell us to stop. Or until our efforts succeed in bringing the revolution around. Or the financial meltdown of Capital makes plastic redundant. Whichever comes first.

No Gods, No Masters, No Peripheries: Global Anarchisms

Edited by Raymond Craib and
Barry Maxwell

ISBN: 978-1-62963-098-4
$27.95   408 pages

**NO GODS
NO MASTERS
NO PERIPHERIES**
★
Global Anarchisms

Edited by
Barry Maxwell and Raymond Craib

Was anarchism in areas outside of Europe an import and a script to be mimicked? Was it perpetually at odds with other currents of the Left? The authors in this collection take up these questions of geographical and political peripheries. Building on recent research that has emphasized the plural origins of anarchist thought and practice, they reflect on the histories and cultures of the antistatist mutual aid movements of the last century beyond the boundaries of an artificially coherent Europe. At the same time, they reexamine the historical relationships between anarchism and communism without starting from the position of sectarian difference (Marxism versus anarchism). Rather, they look at how anarchism and communism intersected; how the insurgent Left could appear—and in fact was—much more ecumenical, capacious, and eclectic than frequently portrayed; and reveal that such capaciousness is a hallmark of anarchist practice, which is prefigurative in its politics and antihierarchical and antidogmatic in its ethics.

Copublished the with Institute for Comparative Modernities, this collection includes contributions by Gavin Arnall, Mohammed Bamyeh, Bruno Bosteels, Raymond Craib, Silvia Rivera Cusicanqui, Geoffroy de Laforcade, Silvia Federici, Steven J. Hirsch, Adrienne Carey Hurley, Hilary Klein, Peter Linebaugh, Barry Maxwell, David Porter, Maia Ramnath, Penelope Rosemont, and Bahia Shehab.

"Broad in scope, generously ecumenical in outlook, bold in its attempt to tease apart the many threads and tensions of anarchism, this collection defies borders and category. These illuminating explorations in pan-anarchism provide a much-needed antidote to the myopic characterizations that bedevil the red and black."
—Sasha Lilley, author of Capital and Its Discontents

"This wonderful collection challenges the privileging of Europe as the original and natural laboratory in which anti-statist ideas developed as well as the belief that anarchism and Communism could not intersect in fruitful ways. Drawing on non-Western locations (from Latin America, the Middle East, North Africa, and South Asia) its authors demonstrate how antiauthoritarian movements engaged with both local and global currents to construct a new emancipatory politics—proving that anarchy and anarchism have always been global."
—Barry Carr, La Trobe University

Pictures of a Gone City: Tech and the Dark Side of Prosperity in the San Francisco Bay Area

Richard A. Walker

ISBN: 978-1-62963-510-1
$26.95   480 pages

The San Francisco Bay Area is currently the jewel in the crown of capitalism—the tech capital of the world and a gusher of wealth from the Silicon Gold Rush. It has been generating jobs, spawning new innovation, and spreading ideas that are changing lives everywhere. It boasts of being the Left Coast, the Greenest City, and the best place for workers in the USA. So what could be wrong? It may seem that the Bay Area has the best of it in Trump's America, but there is a dark side of success: overheated bubbles and spectacular crashes; exploding inequality and millions of underpaid workers; a boiling housing crisis, mass displacement, and severe environmental damage; a delusional tech elite and complicity with the worst in American politics.

This sweeping account of the Bay Area in the age of the tech boom covers many bases. It begins with the phenomenal concentration of IT in Greater Silicon Valley, the fabulous economic growth of the bay region and the unbelievable wealth piling up for the 1% and high incomes of Upper Classes—in contrast to the fate of the working class and people of color earning poverty wages and struggling to keep their heads above water. The middle chapters survey the urban scene, including the greatest housing bubble in the United States, a metropolis exploding in every direction, and a geography turned inside out. Lastly, it hits the environmental impact of the boom, the fantastical ideology of Tech World, and the political implications of the tech-led transformation of the bay region.

"With Pictures of a Gone City, *California's greatest geographer tells us how the Bay Area has become the global center of hi-tech capitalism. Drawing on a lifetime of research, Richard Walker dismantles the mythology of the New Economy, placing its creativity in a long history of power, work, and struggles for justice.*"
—Jason W. Moore, author of *Capitalism in the Web of Life*

"*San Francisco has battened from its birth on instant wealth, high-tech weaponry, and global commerce, and the present age is little different. Gold, silver, and sleek iPhones—they all glitter in the California sun and are at least as magnetic as the city's spectacular setting, benign climate, and laissez-faire lifestyles. The cast of characters changes, but the hustlers and thought-shapers eternally reign over the city and its hinterland, while in their wake they leave a ruined landscape of exorbitant housing, suburban sprawl, traffic paralysis, and delusional ideas about a market free enough to rob the majority of their freedom. Read all about it here, and weep.*"
—Gray Brechin, author of *Imperial San Francisco: Urban Power, Earthly Ruin*

From ■SPECTRE▶ from PM Press

Catastrophism: The Apocalyptic Politics of Collapse and Rebirth

Sasha Lilley, David McNally, Eddie Yuen, and James Davis with a foreword by Doug Henwood

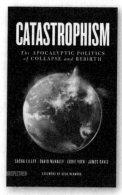

ISBN: 978-1-60486-589-9
$16.00   192 pages

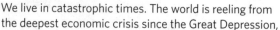

We live in catastrophic times. The world is reeling from the deepest economic crisis since the Great Depression, with the threat of further meltdowns ever-looming. Global warming and myriad dire ecological disasters worsen—with little if any action to halt them—their effects rippling across the planet in the shape of almost biblical floods, fires, droughts, and hurricanes. Governments warn that no alternative exists than to take the bitter medicine they prescribe—or risk devastating financial or social collapse. The right, whether religious or secular, views the present as catastrophic and wants to turn the clock back. The left fears for the worst, but hopes some good will emerge from the rubble. Visions of the apocalypse and predictions of impending doom abound. Across the political spectrum, a culture of fear reigns.

Catastrophism explores the politics of apocalypse—on the left and right, in the environmental movement, and from capital and the state—and examines why the lens of catastrophe can distort our understanding of the dynamics at the heart of these numerous disasters—and fatally impede our ability to transform the world. Lilley, McNally, Yuen, and Davis probe the reasons why catastrophic thinking is so prevalent, and challenge the belief that it is only out of the ashes that a better society may be born. The authors argue that those who care about social justice and the environment should eschew the Pandora's box of fear—even as it relates to indisputably apocalyptic climate change. Far from calling people to arms, they suggest, catastrophic fear often results in passivity and paralysis—and, at worst, reactionary politics.

"This groundbreaking book examines a deep current—on both the left and right—of apocalyptical thought and action. The authors explore the origins, uses, and consequences of the idea that collapse might usher in a better world. Catastrophism *is a crucial guide to understanding our tumultuous times, while steering us away from the pitfalls of the past."*
—Barbara Epstein, author of *Political Protest and Cultural Revolution: Nonviolent Direct Action in the 1970s and 1980s*

From ■SPECTRE▶ from PM Press

Stop, Thief!
The Commons, Enclosures,
and Resistance

Peter Linebaugh

ISBN: 978-1-60486-747-3
$21.95   304 pages

In this majestic tour de force, celebrated historian Peter Linebaugh takes aim at the thieves of land, the polluters of the seas, the ravagers of the forests, the despoilers of rivers, and the removers of mountaintops. Scarcely a society has existed on the face of the earth that has not had commoning at its heart. "Neither the state nor the market," say the planetary commoners. These essays kindle the embers of memory to ignite our future commons.

From Thomas Paine to the Luddites, from Karl Marx—who concluded his great study of capitalism with the enclosure of commons—to the practical dreamer William Morris—who made communism into a verb and advocated communizing industry and agriculture—to the 20th-century communist historian E.P. Thompson, Linebaugh brings to life the vital commonist tradition. He traces the red thread from the great revolt of commoners in 1381 to the enclosures of Ireland, and the American commons, where European immigrants who had been expelled from their commons met the immense commons of the native peoples and the underground African-American urban commons. Illuminating these struggles in this indispensable collection, Linebaugh reignites the ancient cry, "STOP, THIEF!"

"There is not a more important historian living today. Period."
—Robin D.G. Kelley, author of *Freedom Dreams: The Black Radical Imagination*

"E.P. Thompson, you may rest now. Linebaugh restores the dignity of the despised luddites with a poetic grace worthy of the master . . . [A] commonist manifesto for the 21st century."
—Mike Davis, author of *Planet of Slums*

"Peter Linebaugh's great act of historical imagination . . . takes the cliché of 'globalization' and makes it live. The local and the global are once again shown to be inseparable—as they are, at present, for the machine-breakers of the new world crisis."
—T.J. Clark, author of *Farewell to an Idea*

Capital and Its Discontents: Conversations with Radical Thinkers in a Time of Tumult

Sasha Lilley

ISBN: 978-1-60486-334-5
$20.00   320 pages

Capitalism is stumbling, empire is faltering, and the planet is thawing. Yet many people are still grasping to understand these multiple crises and to find a way forward to a just future. Into the breach come the essential insights of *Capital and Its Discontents*, which cut through the gristle to get to the heart of the matter about the nature of capitalism and imperialism, capitalism's vulnerabilities at this conjuncture—and what can we do to hasten its demise. Through a series of incisive conversations with some of the most eminent thinkers and political economists on the Left—including David Harvey, Ellen Meiksins Wood, Mike Davis, Leo Panitch, Tariq Ali, and Noam Chomsky—*Capital and Its Discontents* illuminates the dynamic contradictions undergirding capitalism and the potential for its dethroning. At a moment when capitalism as a system is more reviled than ever, here is an indispensable toolbox of ideas for action by some of the most brilliant thinkers of our times.

"*These conversations illuminate the current world situation in ways that are very useful for those hoping to orient themselves and find a way forward to effective individual and collective action. Highly recommended.*"
—Kim Stanley Robinson, *New York Times* bestselling author of the *Mars Trilogy* and *The Years of Rice and Salt*

"*In this fine set of interviews, an A-list of radical political economists demonstrate why their skills are indispensable to understanding today's multiple economic and ecological crises.*"
—Raj Patel, author of *Stuffed and Starved* and *The Value of Nothing*

"*This is an extremely important book. It is the most detailed, comprehensive, and best study yet published on the most recent capitalist crisis and its discontents. Sasha Lilley sets each interview in its context, writing with style, scholarship, and wit about ideas and philosophies.*"
—Andrej Grubačić, radical sociologist and social critic, co-author of *Wobblies and Zapatistas*

From ▮SPECTRE▶ from PM Press

Patriarchy of the Wage: Notes on Marx, Gender, and Feminism

Silvia Federici

ISBN: 978-1-62963-799-0
$15.00   152 pages

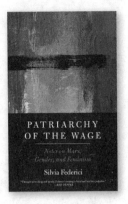

At a time when socialism is entering a historic crisis and we are witnessing a worldwide expansion of capitalist relations, a feminist rethinking of Marx's work is vitally important. In *Patriarchy of the Wage*, Silvia Federici, best-selling author and the most important Marxist feminist of our time, asks why Marx and the Marxist tradition were so crucial in their denunciation of capitalism's exploitation of human labor and blind to women's work and struggle on the terrain of social reproduction. Why was Marx unable to anticipate the profound transformations in the proletarian family that took place at the turn of the nineteenth century creating a new patriarchal regime?

In this fiery collection of penetrating essays published here for the first time, Federici carefully examines these questions and in the process has provided an expansive redefinition of work, class, and class-gender relations. Seeking to delineate the specific character of capitalist "patriarchalism," this magnificently original approach also highlights Marx's and the Marxist tradition's problematic view of industrial production and the State in the struggle for human liberation. Federici's lucid argument that most reproductive work is irreducible to automation is a powerful reminder of the poverty of the revolutionary imagination that consigns to the world of machines the creation of the material conditions for a communist society.

Patriarchy of the Wage does more than just redefine classical Marxism; it is an explosive call for a new kind of communism. Read this book and realize the power and importance of reproductive labor!

"Silvia Federici's work embodies an energy that urges us to rejuvenate struggles against all types of exploitation and, precisely for that reason, her work produces a common: a common sense of the dissidence that creates a community in struggle."
—Maria Mies, coauthor of *Ecofeminism*

"Federici has become a crucial figure for young Marxists, political theorists, and a new generation of feminists."
—Rachel Kushner author of *The Flamethrowers*

"Federici's attempt to draw together the work of feminists and activist from different parts of the world and place them in historical context is brave, thought-provoking and timely. Federici's writing is lucid and her fury palpable."
—Red Pepper

From ■SPECTRE▶ from PM Press

Critique of the Gotha Program

Karl Marx
with an Introduction by Peter Hudis and
a Foreword by Peter Linebaugh

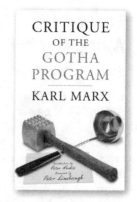

ISBN: 978-1-62963-916-1
$15.95   156 pages

Marx's *Critique of the Gotha Program* is a revelation. It
offers the fullest elaboration of his vision for a communist
future, free from the shackles of capital, but also the state.
Neglected by the statist versions of socialism, whether
Social Democratic or Stalinist that left a wreckage of coercion and disillusionment
in their wake, this new annotated translation of Marx's Critique makes clear for
the first time the full emancipatory scope of Marx's notion of life after capitalism.
An erudite new introduction by Peter Hudis plumbs the depth of Marx's argument,
elucidating how his vision of communism, and the transition to it, was thoroughly
democratic. At a time when the rule of capital is being questioned and challenged,
this volume makes an essential contribution to a real alternative to capitalism,
rather than piecemeal reforms. In the twenty-first century, when it has never been
more needed, here is Marx at his most liberatory.

"*This is a compelling moment for a return to Marx's most visionary writings. Among
those is his often neglected,* Critique of the Gotha Program. *In this exciting new
translation, we can hear Marx urging socialists of his day to remain committed to a
truly radical break with capitalism. And in Peter Hudis's illuminating introductory essay
we are reminded that Marx's vision of a society beyond capitalism was democratic
and emancipatory to its very core. This book is a major addition to the anti-capitalist
library.*"
—David McNally, Distinguished Professor of History, University of Houston and
author of *Monsters of the Market*

"*In their penetrating account of Marx's famous hatchet job on the 19th-century left,
Hudis and Anderson go to the heart of issues haunting the left in the 21st century:
what would a society look like without work, wages, GDP growth, and human self-
oppression.*"
—Paul Mason, writer for *New Statesman* and author of *Postcapitalism: A Guide to
Our Future*

"Critique of the Gotha Program *is a key text for understanding Marx's vision of an
emancipated society beyond capitalism. With an excellent introduction by Peter Hudis,
this new translation is both timely and important. Returning to Marx's pathbreaking
essay can give new direction to the political struggles of our time.*"
—Martin Hägglund, Yale University, author of *This Life*